Improving
College Teaching

Improving

College

Teaching

EDITED BY *Calvin B. T. Lee*

AMERICAN COUNCIL ON EDUCATION · *Washington, D.C.*

Contributing Authors

JAMES I. ARMSTRONG, President, Middlebury College

WILLIAM ARROWSMITH, Chairman, Department of Classics, University of Texas

ALEXANDER W. ASTIN, Director, Office of Research, American Council on Education

JOHN W. ATHERTON, President, Pitzer College, The Claremont Colleges

M. MARGARET BALL, Dean of the Woman's College and Associate Dean of Arts and Sciences, Duke University

DONALD BARR, Headmaster, The Dalton Schools

SAMUEL BASKIN, President, Union for Research and Experimentation in Higher Education; Director, Program Development and Research in Education, Antioch College

DANIEL BELL, Professor of Sociology, Columbia University

BERNARD BERELSON, Vice-President, The Population Council

CARL W. BORGMANN, Director, Program in Science and Engineering, The Ford Foundation

CLARK BYSE, Professor of Law, Law School of Harvard University; President of the American Association of University Professors

JOHN TYLER CALDWELL, Chancellor, North Carolina State University at Raleigh

ALLAN M. CARTTER, Chancellor, New York University; formerly Vice-President, American Council on Education

CHARLES COGEN, President, American Federation of Teachers

A. W. DENT, President, Dillard University

MICHAEL DROSNIN, Former Student, Columbia College

N. L. GAGE, Codirector, Stanford Center for Research and Development in Teaching, Stanford University

JOHN W. GUSTAD, Associate Dean, College of Arts and Sciences, The Ohio State University

R. J. HENLE, S.J., Academic Vice-President, Saint Louis University

ROGER W. HEYNS, Chancellor, University of California, Berkeley

HAROLD HOWE II, United States Commissioner of Education

JAMES A. JOHNSON, Student, Woodrow Wilson School of Public and International Affairs, Princeton University; formerly National Affairs Vice-President, United States National Student Association

LAURA KENT, Staff Assistant, American Council on Education

JOHN E. KING, President, University of Wyoming

CALVIN B. T. LEE, Staff Associate, American Council on Education

ARTHUR A. LUMSDAINE, Professor and Chairman, Department of Psychology, University of Washington

ROBERT F. McDERMOTT, Brigadier General, United States Air Force; Dean of the Faculty, United States Air Force Academy

WILBERT J. McKEACHIE, Chairman, Department of Psychology, University of Michigan

NEILL MEGAW, Professor of English, Williams College; Chairman, Committee C on College and University Teaching, Research and Publication, American Association of University Professors

CHARLES MUSCATINE, Professor of English, University of California, Berkeley

ROBERT A. NISBET, Professor of Sociology, University of California, Riverside

DONALD D. O'DOWD, Provost, Oakland University

DEXTER PERKINS, Professor Emeritus of History, University of Rochester and Cornell University

BILL J. PRIEST, President, Dallas County Junior College

ESTHER RAUSHENBUSH, President, Sarah Lawrence College

EDWARD JOSEPH SHOBEN, Jr., Director, Commission on Academic Affairs, American Council on Education

RICHARD H. SULLIVAN, President, Association of American Colleges; formerly President, Reed College

PAULINE TOMPKINS, General Director, American Association of University Women

MARTIN TROW, Professor of Sociology, University of California, Berkeley

NILS Y. WESSELL, President, Institute for Educational Development, New York

LOGAN WILSON, President American Council on Education

O. MEREDITH WILSON, President, University of Minnesota

W. MAX WISE, Associate Director, The Danforth Foundation

Foreword

ALTHOUGH TEACHING may not be the oldest profession, it is undoubtedly the most venerable art. It is still presumed generally to be the most important function of colleges and universities. Of late, however, teaching is said to have fallen into a state of neglect. The stepped-up emphasis on research and public service, it is charged, has meant that less attention is paid to teaching. The graduate school's stress on scholarly productivity, the spreading use of inexperienced teaching assistants, inflexibilities of the curriculum, academic recognition and reward systems, expanding student enrollments—these and other factors are felt to be deterrents to better performance in many classrooms and laboratories.

In view of the manifestly improved preparation of most high school graduates today, it can no longer be claimed that entering students simply are not ready for college-level work. Moreover, since Berkeley and subsequent developments on other campuses, it can no longer be said that the undergraduate is "the forgotten man" in higher education. He has indeed become the subject of considerable journalistic as well as academic solicitude.

The American Council on Education has been in the vanguard of those showing a special interest in the student and his problems, as evidenced in its 1965 Annual Meeting, which focused on one concern, "The Student in Higher Education." In 1966 the Council chose as the theme of its Forty-ninth Annual Meeting the topic, "Improving College Teaching: Aids and Impediments," and this volume of essays is an outgrowth of that meeting. The topical shift does not mean that we are no longer concerned about the student; rather, it constitutes a recognition that more and better learning is causally related to improved teaching.

This book is not intended primarily for subject-matter specialists and classroom teachers, though many could profit from reading it, but for academic administrators having an indirect, yet no less real responsibility for teaching as a basic institutional endeavor. From these discussions, educational leaders and others may get insight into a wide range of current issues and problems; we hope they will be carefully read by those who believe in the importance of maintaining and improving the quality of teaching on the nation's campuses.

LOGAN WILSON, *President*
American Council on Education

November 1966

Preface

THE AMERICAN ACADEMIC COMMUNITY in general, and this volume in particular, are concerned with questions about college teaching. The essays published here include data-gathering articles, reviews of practices, critical essays, commentaries of opinion, analyses of the academic community, and probings about the present nature of the teaching profession.

In preparation for the Annual Meeting of the American Council on Education in New Orleans on October 12–14, 1966, eight background papers were commissioned and given limited circulation to members of the Council prior to the conference. These essays are by: Dexter Perkins, Robert A. Nisbet, Wilbert J. McKeachie, Samuel Baskin, Daniel Bell, W. Max Wise, Allan M. Cartter, and John W. Gustad. A number of faculty members, students, and administrators were selected to comment on the positions and analyses of these authors. The commentaries presented here are not simply a set of proceedings, but rather are critical essays that focus on particular areas of concern and controversial opinions.

Supplementing the background papers, the *Educational Record* devoted its Summer issue to the theme of the Annual Meeting, "Improving College Teaching: Aids and Impediments." The following articles from that issue are reprinted here: "University Teaching and Excellence" by Allan M. Cartter; "Undergraduate Teaching at Large State Universities" by Martin Trow; "College Teachers and Teaching: A Student's View" by Michael Drosnin; "Current Practices in the Evaluation and Training of College Teachers" by Alexander Astin and Calvin Lee; "Student Evaluation of Teaching" by Laura Kent; "The Colleges' Crisis of Integrity: A Headmaster's View" by Donald Barr; "Collegiate Education for Modern Culture" by R. J. Henle, S.J.; "Knowledge Structure and Curriculum Development" by Calvin Lee. Laura Kent, assistant editor of the *Educational Record*, was responsible for editing the essays which are reprinted here.

O. Meredith Wilson's "Teach Me, and I Will Hold My Tongue"

and William Arrowsmith's "The Future of Teaching" were the keynote addresses of the Annual Meeting. "Less Teaching and More Conversation" by U.S. Commissioner of Education Harold Howe II was the closing address of the conference.

The papers have been edited and revised for the purposes of this book. Personally and for the American Council on Education I should like to express my appreciation to all the authors whose essays appear in this volume. I want to thank the members of the American Council on Education's Board of Directors and the executive staff for their assistance in planning the conference from which *Improving College Teaching* took its shape. Special thanks are owed to E. J. Shoben, Jr., John F. Morse, William Reidy, and Stephen Strickland, on whose notes from the floor discussions in New Orleans I relied heavily in the preparation of the sections of "Dissenting Views" and "Additional Views." I especially want to thank Olive Mills of the Council staff for her editorial services in reviewing and preparing all of the manuscripts for publication.

CALVIN B. T. LEE

Contents

Improving College Teaching: Inquiry and Quest

CALVIN B. T. LEE

IMPROVING TEACHING is a continuing concern, an on-going, never-ending enterprise on every college campus. Yet discussions of the subject too often lapse into lamentations about the deterioration of under-graduate teaching, or about the poor preparation of scholars for teaching. That this is futile is bad enough, but it is also unprofessional for a profession devoted to inquiry.

If there are impediments to good college teaching, they should be openly and specifically identified and examined critically. In addition, it is imperative that ways to improve college teaching be devised, explored, and appraised. Although solutions to such problems are elusive and consensus is difficult to achieve, a painstaking search obviously is demanded.

Each of us comes to this inquiry with a different background and with different biases and commitments. But all of us are engaged in this enterprise as a rigorous intellectual activity, for such an inquiry requires not only organized reflection but also empirical study, disciplined probing with the tools of scholarly research, and thoroughgoing consideration of data, positions, and opinions.

In this book, by focusing attention on faculty, we attempt to explore impediments to classroom teaching as well as aids that would enhance it. The student is not treated here as a separate subject for study because it is implicit in this endeavor that the learning process depends in large measure on the faculty. The student is in the forefront of our concern when we probe into the conditions of teaching and learning. And we attempt to penetrate to the heart of the problems of college teaching when we inquire into matters of training and of the quantity and quality of the academic men.

Yet the problems of the academic community are not isolated from

1

those of the larger society, for the problems, particularly those arising out of the drain of faculty away from the campus, are the result of new and expanded demands, commitments, temptations, and challenges that originate outside the institution. The university world responds to stimuli from Federal and state aid as well as from business and industry. Higher education has in recent years assumed many new responsibilities, responsibilities which make it the largest single supplier of educated manpower to society, a research and development arm of the government, a consultant to industry, and the administrator of community programs.

Today, the conflicts among academic loyalties appear to be more numerous and more severe than ever before. A college teacher's interest in bettering teaching and learning can now be diverted by other demands. A centrifugal force pulls faculty members to heavy involvements with their professional societies, consultations, and publications. It is said that the chances of advancement in the teaching profession seem to depend increasingly upon the scholar's visibility off the campus, his knack for bringing large grants to the university, and his ability to bargain on the basis of competing offers. There is some truth in all of these charges, but how much? How general are these maladies in an academic community of over two thousand institutions? To what extent are the smaller colleges affected, and how much should they take as warning? Any inquiry into the profession and performance of teaching must seek to identify those points where reconciliation or adjustment can be made so that better teaching conditions in the academic community are fostered.

Partly because of his outside activities, the college teacher today has achieved the highest status in American society that he has ever had. And those teachers desiring simply to teach and to teach well are also drawn into outside activities—like it or not—to a great extent because methods have not been devised for evaluating college teaching. If the university does not reward faculty members for their devotion to teaching and to students, one can only infer that such dedication is not considered important.

While vital, creative faculty members and students are using their energies off campus, too many of the problems the institutions face because of larger enrollments and expanding knowledge are left, by and large, unattended. Innovations in classroom techniques and new media for teaching college students are too frequently ignored or condemned before any effort is made to explore their practicality and effectiveness. Although most faculty members dedicate themselves to exploring new ideas in their disciplines, too few are interested in research on learning and innovation in teaching. A gap exists between the theory of learning and the practice of teaching; new developments in the class-room are too generally met with hostility. In this regard, faculty members are particularly guilty.

In the next few years most colleges and universities in this country should re-examine their instructional programs with a view to instituting reforms. They must, for the changes in the expectations of our society, the vast accumulation of new knowledge, the increasing numbers of students, and the changing roles of both educational institutions and faculty necessitate assessment.

This volume attempts to prepare educators for the task ahead. In probing the problems of improving college teaching, we must seek to re-examine closely the academic community today, the academic man, the process of teaching and learning, the process of evaluating teaching, and the possibilities of curriculum reform. Our inquiry into these complex areas should be taken as an attempt to seek evidence and to suggest possible solutions. The answers will not emerge as formulae or simple dichotomies of either-or and cause-effect. They can be only suggestive, tentative, and approximate.

We have sought to identify the areas of concern and have brought together commentaries on these problems. In a sense this volume is a stock-taking at this period of higher education. Its purpose is to indicate ways in which we can meet the challenge of the future in higher education. The problems are difficult and the solutions, elusive. But a profession that is dedicated to seeking truth must attempt such an inquiry.

PART ONE

The Academic Community

Teach Me,
And I Will Hold My Tongue

O. MEREDITH WILSON

For all of us who are formally and professionally involved in education, it is well that we be reminded, periodically, of two apparently contradictory propositions that lie at the heart of our enterprise:

1. Each new generation of men begins with a long headstart over any of its predecessors. Today's man takes for granted, as he uses them, a host of very sophisticated tools and institutions, and he accepts casually the boon of a rich artistic inheritance laid up in store for him by several millenia of painters, composers, authors, historians, and philosophers. The late twentieth-century world into which modern man is born is compounded from the labor and creativeness of Egypt, Babylon, Greece, Judea, Rome, China, India, Japan, Renaissance Europe, to name but a few. Sometimes the effects are seen as an overlay or lamination, sometimes as an inlay. Sometimes they appear as new streams that create reinforcing layers of culture and conviction; sometimes they have come together as two streams in confluence, the composite culture remaining imperfectly joined, the elements of the mix never disappearing. But weak or strong, beautiful or appalling, the late twentieth-century civilization is compounded from corporate structures, technical skills, scientific knowledge, and artistic treasures so rich as to make unquestioned the long headstart with which tomorrow's college students can begin.

2. However rich the cultural heritage may be, each new child must start from the beginning—an exciting, lovable, vulnerable, innocent and uniformed, helpless bundle of biochemistry. And each must make the full journey from complete ignorance to knowledge. For him as an individual, the richness of our culture may mean that it is more promising, more exciting, more worthwhile to make the journey from ignorance to knowledge. But it also means that he has farther to travel. This late twentieth-century society has done wonders in matters of travel. We

7

can go places men only dreamed of going, at speeds unmatched before, and in comfort and security that, in the language of my own college senior, "boggles the imagination." We have improved the speed, the comfort, and the security on almost every other road. But for the road from ignorance to knowledge, we have little more help to offer than was available after man first mastered the art of writing. We have extended the length of the educational road, increased the time available for the journey, perhaps enriched the scenery along the way. But each new child of the twentieth century sets out to make the trip psychologically as alone and technically as ill-equipped as was Alexander, son of Philip; and we provide him, as guides, teachers no better equipped with technical mastery of the art of teaching than was Aristotle. I wish we could be sure that in thoughtfulness and dedication they would be as good.

As a capsule essay on the conditions of education in our time, and as introduction to my remaining remarks, I offer the following: Never has a civilization had so rich a heritage to transmit to the young; never has the survival of a culture been so dependent on the successful transfer of highly technical and complex formulae; never have so many had so much desire to learn or so much that they had to be taught; and never has teaching occupied so low a priority among the chores academic practitioners must do, though only a generation ago these practitioners were automatically thought of as "the teaching officers of the university."

The first university had one task: to preserve the intellectual heritage of the race by implanting the valued traditions of the past in the breasts of the young men who were about to commence leadership, and to prepare some of them with a mastery of the arts and crafts of medicine and law, and of the philosophy and theology required for church service. Discovery was then scarcely a factor in a professor's life. He was obsessively concerned with preservation of the heritage, and his means to that end was to teach it to the young. Times have changed. Academic folklore is now drenched with tales of disenchantment with teaching. The cynic says: Universities would be wonderful places for professors, if only there were no students; they would be fine places for students to learn, if only there were no professors. Recently it has seemed that teachers and students had little in common except for one conviction: the campus, whether a good place or a bad one, would be better if it weren't for the administration.

Whatever the asperities that are current, the problem of college teaching is significant *now*, and its ramifications are manifold. It is clear that the teaching process is complex; that it can be served by a variety of new inventions not formerly available; and that teaching is less obsessively the objective of the institution than heretofore.

Nevertheless, it remains true that the role of teaching is critical to the survival of our society. It is also true that, whether our support comes from private donors or from state legislators, the typical university would not be supported and could not exist unless its benefactors believed that it was teaching—and teaching well. Our problem is not that teaching is not needed or, when we think about it, respected. It is rather that the obligation to advance knowledge is a fundamental one. Research has, in many areas, overtaken the teaching enterprise as the first interest of our teaching officers, and the products of research are more easily measured and their quality more quickly rewarded than is teaching. If, as a result of the drama, the glamour, and the importance of research, teaching is overshadowed, and if we wish to restore teaching to a place of honor in the university, it may be useful to recall Plato's wise observation: "What is honored in a country will be cultivated there." If teaching is honored on our campuses, it will be cultivated there and will finally be done well there. If it does not find honor, expressed in the respect and prestige granted the teacher by his colleagues and by the dollars paid him by the comptroller, it is not likely to be cultivated nor to improve.

To have begun as I did seems to pit research and teaching against each other. That is not my intention. My purpose may be served if I first suggest a working definition. What is teaching? Is it merely the communication of known truths? If so, how does the accumulation of past information escape the sterile characteristics of dogma? Or how does the dogmatic curriculum of the university gain acceptance while the dogmas of organized religion are challenged as unexamined and therefore unworthy? Perhaps rather than simply the transmission of known truths, the function of teaching at the university level is helping students to learn. Thorstein Veblen, in his *The Higher Learning in America*, was perhaps the most strident of all our commentators in his insistence that a university is not a place of teaching, but of learning. Taking advantage of this assumption may be one of the ways to make our universities more efficient, because by so doing we harness the greatest energy available to us on the campus.

There are, by anyone's count, at least ten times as many students as teachers in American universities. If we conceive of them as supplicants gathering to be taught, we place the emphasis on a relatively small part of our population as being the active agents. On the other hand, if we think of them as learners, they become the essential engines of the educational process, and we unleash ten times as much intellectual power as is assumed in the alternate view. Moreover, we place emphasis upon the exercise of inquiring mental muscles rather than upon the storage capacity of the subject-student. We place the emphasis upon the process of discovery and creation rather than upon preservation and retention. Preservation and retention are appropriate ideals for a society that has known a golden age and is satisfied with its own times or content with the hope of recovering the glories of a departed era. But I doubt that it would be of much satisfaction to the present generation of either leaders or students. When we underline the role of discovery and creation and conceive of the teacher as one helping the learner understand the processes of discovery and creation, the roles of research and teaching take on new relationships, and the discordant conflict disappears.

I should not like to be interpreted as arguing that research as we now know it is an unmixed good. I am not prepared to defend the researcher as being *ipso facto* the best teacher, nor am I prepared to defend the present criteria of productivity as the means by which we should judge teachers. I am, however, eager to encourage reconsideration of the question of research in the process of instruction. If it is recognized that our world is confronted with a web of problems, whose resolution has escaped us, and if our chore in education is to deliver a better world to a new generation, then cultivating the ability in others to discover solutions to problems which we have been unable to solve should be one of the first objectives in the educational process. If, then, the researcher conceives of his research as a teaching exemplar rather than allowing it to become his end objective and his obsessive interest, his role as researcher may be more important than his role as a conductor through which may flow the almost inexhaustible fund of detailed knowledge stored in our libraries. If a teacher's self-judgment or self-evaluation is affected by his observation of the progress of his apprentice learners, then the teacher's value is appropriately affected by his research productivity. If his research productivity is motivated by his own selfish interests and if he judges the value of his research by its contribution to his own advancement, then the example of research that he sets is unfortunate and his research as a teaching asset is at best accidental, and probably nil.

Whether the role of the instructor is transmitting codified knowledge or teaching the techniques for independent learning and research, one thing is absolutely essential. There must be an institutional concern for the faculty's effect on students. This is the first requirement. If teaching is honored by the institution, it will be cultivated and its quality will in some way be assessed. And whatever hypothesis men may have concerning the appropriate criteria for judging teachers, the question we should always be exploring is: How were the student learners affected?

It would be hard to exaggerate the stake man has in the maintenance of our pace in discovery. But it also remains imperative that we successfully transmit the wisdom of the past. Perhaps no one has dealt with greater originality or insight with man's intellectual capital and his stake in its maintenance than Waddington in his little volume *The Ethical Animal*.[1] At the risk of oversimplification, I would describe his thesis as being this: that man's evolution through intellectual growth has transformed man's life more in a few thousand years than all the physical mutations of a million years were able to do. He has not sprouted wings, but he flies. He has not redeveloped gills and fins, but he survives and moves at great speed under water. He has not grown a heavy fur coat or modified his control on body temperature, but he prospers in every climatic zone. All these he has done as a consequence of stored intellectual capital.

These achievements are based on the power of a cultivated and informed mind. The inventors, the discoverers, and the sponsors of change inhabit our campuses. One of the things they have to convey is the conviction that change may be induced through reason, reflection, and choice. Research thereby becomes part of the tradition this generation must communicate to the next. There is little wonder that, in a universe marked by such great change, where by intellect man has achieved so much in adaptability and in mastery of his environment, the younger denizens of a campus—the students—are restive. They have been taught so much about change, have seen so much change themselves, that now almost anything seems possible. Yet the world they inherit is or seems to be only a web of undesirable improbabilities; considering what their mind teaches them about man's ability to force his environment to respond to his will, they consider a good world to be possible. Little wonder, then, that they find their real world intolerable. Like Job, the young intellectual sees himself as life's finest product assailed by life's greatest and most unreasoned ills. And, like Job, he would like to escape his sorrows; he wants even more to understand his world than to escape from it. If the campus were really listening, it could hear the student crying, as Job did: "Teach me and I will hold my tongue." And, if we heard that cry, the act of teaching would be honored on the campus, and it would be cultivated there.

[1] New York: Atheneum, 1961.

Conflicting
Academic Loyalties

ROBERT A. NISBET

I$_T$ $_{IS}$ $_{TEMPTING}$ to begin such a paper as this in the manner of the late Rachel Carson in her memorable *Silent Spring*. Few who have read that book will have forgotten her haunting first chapter, a few sentences from which will serve to recall theme and mood.

There was once a town in the heart of America where all life seemed to live in harmony with its surroundings. The town lay in the midst of a checkerboard of prosperous farms, with fields of grain and hillsides of orchards where, in spring, white clouds of bloom drifted above the green fields. . . . Then a strange blight crept over the area and everything began to change. Some evil spell had settled on the community. . . . Everywhere there was a shadow of death. . . . There was a strange stillness. The birds, for example, where had they gone? Many people spoke of them, puzzled and disturbed. . . . The roadsides, once so attractive, were now lined with browned and withered vegetation as though swept by fire. These too were silent. . . . No witchcraft, no enemy action had silenced the rebirth of new life in this stricken world. The people had done it themselves.[1]

And so, under the spell of cognate nostalgia, could one write on the academic community. It might begin somewhat as follows:

There was once a university in the heart of America where all life seemed to be in harmony with its surroundings. The university lay in a verdant grove of academe; autonomous, self-perpetuating, and buoyant. In the spring black and white clouds of commencement robes signaled the end of another prosperous year of learning; a year in which professors had taught and students had listened. Then a strange blight crept over the university, and everything began to change. Some evil spell had settled on the academy. Everywhere there was the shadow of death. There was a strange stillness in the classroom. Teachers no longer taught; students no longer listened. The professors, for example, where had they gone? Many people spoke of them, puzzled and disturbed. Classrooms once vi-

[1] Boston: Houghton Mifflin Co., 1962.

12

brant with dialogue were now dull with apathy. The campus, once green, was now arid with alienation or else afire with revolt. No witchcraft, no enemy action had silenced the rebirth of new life in this stricken world. The professors had done it themselves!

Whether in fact Miss Carson's town, or one like it, ever existed in America is no doubt as open to question as whether such a university ever existed. The selective filter of memory is a wondrous device. I have talked with older persons who swear they did indeed live in such a town. If they have forgotten blight and plague and soil depletion that kept even small populations on the edge of hunger, they have not forgotten that it was once possible to pick fruit from trees and vegetables from plants that did not contain the threat of death or lingering illness, the result of Malathion and other pesticides.

Academics who are over fifty years of age do not have to ask whether such a university ever existed. We remember it vividly. And we do not let our younger colleagues forget that we remember it! If the selective filter in our minds dims the memory of research that failed for want of financial support, of academic leave that could not be granted, of professional meetings missed for want of travel money, of teaching that was superficial or rote like because of heavy teaching loads, of classes that were cut by students because of athletic instead of political demonstrations, we assuredly do not forget that there was time in the American university when teaching and scholarship were not merely the primary but the exclusive functions of the university.

I would be the last, in short, to deride either Miss Carson's picture of the town where "all life seemed to live in harmony with its surroundings" or the picture I have drawn of the university. There is reality in each, as there is reality also in the account of the intervening changes brought about by contaminants. For toxic chemicals, substitute governmental or industrial research grants. For vast chemical companies, substitute Federal agencies and the great foundations. For chemical interference with the ecological harmonies of nature, substitute professionalization or computerization of academic counseling, of teaching, and research.

But as there is reality in each picture so is there also fantasy; and, with it, possible deception. For just as modern American agriculture could not possibly meet the challenge of the population revolution in our century nor the fantastic rise in consumer affluence, nor the ceaseless spread of city and suburb except through utilization of chemicals that indubitably present hazards to health and to the balance of nature, neither could the university today fulfill its ancient responsibility to society and state save by new functions, new roles, new liaisons with the environing society that also present hazards: to teaching, learning, and creative scholarship.

SOURCES OF CREATIVITY

If there is a single transcending challenge before university presidents today—the successful meeting of which will alone place them in the heavenly choir now occupied by the William Rainey Harpers, the Charles Eliots, and the Daniel Coit Gilmans—it is that of somehow keeping the university in a vital relationship to a political and industrial society that, by reason of its infinite complexity, is insatiable in appetite for professional information, advice, and operational knowledge, and, at the same time, protecting and nourishing those fragile, life-giving activities within the university that are not primarily concerned with giving professional advice to society and that require relative autonomy from the demands of society as the condition of intellectual creativeness.

I say *relative* autonomy. There are those—of whom Robert Hutchins is perhaps foremost—who see the answer to academic complexity and to conflicts of academic loyalty in a monastic retreat to organizations of a type so opulently exemplified by his Center for the Study of Democratic Institutions in Santa Barbara. Mr. Hutchins seems to think that such an organization is related more closely than is the present university in America to the great university tradition of Western Europe that began in the twelfth century. Mr. Hutchins is wrong. He is thinking of the monastic tradition; one which—whatever its pietistic graces, its value as a haven for the tender-minded, its role in the ritual perpetuation of texts and ideas—has been generally sterile in furthering intellectual advancement. The odium under which the words "monk" and "monkish" lay for many hundreds of years in the minds of intellectuals in Western society had almost nothing to do with the fact of religious identification and almost everything to do with the monastery's sequestration from the powerful currents which were altering European thought and life. The university, in contrast to the monastery, beginning with the great Bologna in law and Padua in medicine and Paris in theology, has ever been in the thick of things; ever related to the professional needs of society, be these legal, medical, and theological, as they were in the beginning, or scientific, administrative, and industrial as they have come also to be in our age.

I cannot agree that the answer to the contemporary university's problems, to its academic conflicts, lies in making it more like a monastic center aimed at contemplation and criticism of the world. I cannot agree, first, because for the university to retreat from active engagement in society's professional needs would be to fly in the face of a tradition of professional service that began almost a thousand years ago at Bologna and Paris and, second, because I cannot help believing that such disregard would result in the kind of social irresponsibility that breeds, not creativeness and leadership, but inanition and irrelevance. The great minds in the history of Western thought have been minds concerned first and foremost with intellectual problems *drawn from* the practical needs of society, with their own individual relation to these problems and needs frequently that of professional consultant. This was as true of a Plato and Aristotle, who never disdained to draw philosophical problems and principles from their practical consultantships in the service of kings, as it was fifteen hundred years later of the powerful Roman law teachers in the medieval university who, in their own consultantships with struggling monarchs, helped to found the national state and create, incidentally, the basic problems of modern European moral and political philosophy.

Immaculate conception and fastidious separation from the hurly-burly of society have never been elements in the historic university, not, at least, during its great and creative periods, of which the present is surely one. There have been, alas, ages of inanition and stupefying ritualism in the history of the university, and these have been (such as in the eighteenth century in Europe, extending through most of the nineteenth in England) ages when the university was indeed an autonomous center for meditation, reading, and dialogue, when it was sheltered from political, economic, professional, and technological currents in the surrounding society. Then the torch of intellectual leadership in society passed from the university to the hands of those like Diderot, Gibbon, Voltaire, and Bentham for whom the university stank of dry rot. The makers of the great *Encyclopédie* in eighteenth-century France had very professional objectives indeed and their work was specifically described in its title as being an encyclopedia of *sciences, arts,* and *crafts.*

It is, I believe, a point worth emphasizing that the really outstanding academic centers in twentieth-century United States—those centers where, by common assent, the foremost creative minds in the humanities as well as the sciences have existed, centers such as Harvard, Chicago, Columbia, and Berkeley—have been set within contexts of vigorous professionalism. The American university may indeed be, as Mr. Hutchins has, for a third of a century, been charging it with being, shot through with professionalism—a term that in his usage seems to include everything not reducible to instant dialogue. But it would not be hard, I think, to show that within this third of a century more creativeness—in the arts and letters as well as in the sciences and the professional schools—has come forth from the university campus than during any period preceding. It might also be emphasized that it is within this same third of a century that the university in America has reached a type and level of distinction that has made it the object of respect and even emulation in Europe (where the professional nature of the university has always been understood).

I shall indicate below some grounds for apprehension regarding the long-range effects on the university of some of the massive research and training projects now entered into so often and so uncritically by universities at the behest of government and industry. But this is a reflection of lack of discriminating judgment and of magnitude of the projects, not of professionalism as such. On the evidence of history, it would appear to be insulation of the university from the evocative forces of polity, economy, and profession that periodically plunges it into irrelevance and inanition or pushes it to a level of abstraction that reaches pure sound.

THE ALTERED NATURE OF SERVICE TO THE NATION

All of this does not mean, of course, that the problem of conflicting loyalties is not a real one at the present time. Even if the university in America is today closer to its historic type than some of its critics believe, we still cannot be blind to some extremely difficult problems, the result of major changes that have taken place in the relation of the university to society.

Change in any institution is, at bottom, change in the social roles that are held by individuals. We often speak of political, economic, or social change as though it were a matter of supra-individual processes in large institutions and social structures. But genuine social change is never present until the roles, habits, attitudes, and life styles of *individuals* are irreversibly affected. This is as true of the university as it is of family, church, or state. Social change thus inevitably precipitates conflict among allegiances, meanings, and roles.

Equally true and vital, however, is the fact that the *source* of major change is almost never to be found in forces within the institution but rather in the tensions that develop *between* the institution and the surrounding social order; tensions which are caused by significant alterations in the organization's functional relation to the social order. The family is an obvious example of this. It was only when, as a consequence of the impact of the industrial and democratic revolutions in the last century, the social function of kinship was sharply modified that conflicts of role and allegiance within the family became a cardinal aspect of the American social scene. This is not to say that role conflicts had never before existed; only that under the external impetus of major economic and legal changes they assumed unprecedented intensity.

It is not different with the university. Behind the present intensity of role conflicts in the academic world lie two structural changes of profound importance, both aspects of the history of the university in America since the second World War. The first is manifest in the increasing *directness* of the university's relation to government and industry; the second is the spreading *professionalization* of academic disciplines. Although both have been widely commented upon, it is useful here to describe each briefly before taking up some of the conflicts which arise from the changes.

Down until approximately a generation ago, the university's contribution to society was essentially *indirect*: expressed almost exclusively through the time-honored functions of teaching and scholarship. It is difficult to recall, even as recently as the 1930's, more than the barest number of instances in which the university contributed directly to the working machinery of society—to government, industry, agriculture, and the professions. There were, to be sure, the agricultural experiment stations and, here and there, fact-finding bureaus for the assistance of state and municipal governments. But these were rare, confined to some of the public universities and, it is amusing now to recall, kept rather carefully segregated from the main academic community. Seldom did even professional schools of law, medicine, and engineering offer direct service to government or industry. And in the area of the liberal arts and sciences such service was unheard of except, starting with the first World War, from a few chemists. Governmental agencies and industries supplied their own research. That fields such as mathematics and physics, much less economics and political science, had anything of importance to give directly to government and industry would have been as appalling a thought to professors as it would have been hilarious to politicians and business tycoons of the day. Professors should be seen in the classroom, not heard in the marketplace; so might the homely maxim have been paraphrased. All of this is not to imply that universities were either ghettoes or feudal enclaves of privilege. Their concern with the problems of society was deep, as is evidenced by the textbooks written, by the kinds of courses taught (often more "vocational" than today), and by the prime importance on university campuses of professional schools and colleges.

Far from being fastnesses of monastic contemplation, they were, as I have already suggested, thoroughly in the thick of things: things religious, political, and economic. Conflicts of power and ideology within them could be titanic, as the Second Battle of Princeton, with President Wilson and Dean West as opposing generals, made splendidly evident. But such conflicts were personal, not of role or function. By everyone it was understood (and by no one more clearly than Woodrow Wilson) that the "university in the nation's service" was emphatically not a service station, not a department store, but a setting within which teaching and scholarship would seek to *inspire* to service, not provide it—at piece rates!

Very different, of course, is the contemporary university; the institution that Clark Kerr has so well called the "multiversity." Nothing in the recent social history of the United States is more remarkable than the bridging of the gulf that once lay between the university and the practical machinery of society. There is no university today that is not involved in a wide variety of direct services to government at all levels, to industry, to the professions and arts, and to the mass media. If such involvement were strictly institutional—that is, *sponsored* by the academic institution but kept separate from academic activities as the agricultural experiment station was once kept separate —the change would be perhaps minor in its impact upon academic life and loyalty. But, as is only too evident, involvement reaches down to the very heart of the university: to the professor, to the nature of research done, and inevitably to the character of the teaching done.

"Service station" and "department store" as terms to describe categorically and undiscriminatingly the contemporary American university are unfair. As I indicated above, it is difficult to see how a society as large and complex as ours could possibly maintain itself except by a use of university resources that is bound to be more direct than it was in other ages. The problem, however—and it is, I believe, the major problem of academic policy in our society—is that of making sure that government and industry, in the process of *using* university resources, do not also *shape* university resources. For neither society nor the university will have been well served if the relationship between them proves in the long run to have diverted the university from furnishing society that type of knowledge for which it is uniquely fitted. It is a dangerous misconception to suppose that the university is the proper scene of *all* types of knowledge, research, and teaching. For the university to establish—even worse, take over—research that can be as well, if not better, done in governmental or industrial laboratories must inevitably, through a kind of Gresham's Law, harm the kind of work that it can uniquely do.

There is a conflict today that may seem now no larger than a man's hand but that is bound to become major. It is the conflict between the scientist's role of autonomous and free-ranging investigative mind, obeying the ancient maxim that he goes farthest who knows not where he is going, and his very different role which, however carefully its "independence" is guaranteed in the fine print, is nevertheless *not* autonomous (not in the crucial psychological sense) if only because in application for funds a title had to be seized upon, and in seizing upon a title a mission constructed and because, with each passing month, one's commitment to this mission becomes ever greater. The difference, in purely creative terms, between "basic" and "applied" science seems to me of less moment than the difference between "open" and "mission-oriented" science.

PROFESSIONALIZATION OF THE DISCIPLINES

The second major structural change in the contemporary university is a consequence of the increasing professionalization of scholarly disciplines. This is most notable, of course, in the natural sciences, but it is becoming ever more characteristic of the social sciences and even the humanities. Whereas, as recently as a generation ago, physics, biology, mathematics, economics, psychology, or sociology had disciplinary identity only insofar as each drew it from the larger and encompassing profession of university teaching, today each has its own professional identity. Once, to be a physicist or sociologist meant, beyond any possible question, that one held academic rank in a college or university. Today each is more like engineer or physician. To be a sociologist at the present time means that one is *probably* in a university (more probably, on the statistical evidence, than if one is a chemist) but he may easily be in government, private industry, or even, with shingle out, in practice. From being primarily and essentially a university member whose field was, more or less incidentally, sociology, one is today a sociologist whose job is, more or less incidentally, in a university. More and more academic fields now conceive of themselves as professions, with university connections incidental, more a matter of housing than umbilical tie. In fields like law, medicine, and engineering, the tension between academy and profession has, on the whole, worked itself out. There is at least a working arrangement. The role issues are clearer. After all, the overwhelming majority of lawyers and physicians are nonacademic, and few organizations in modern society are more potent and more prestige-conferring than the American Bar Association and the American Medical Association. But in many other academic fields the tensions are great because of the relative recency of the change.

These are the structural changes that, above any others I can easily think of, lie behind present conflicts of academic role and loyalty.

Two preliminary points should be made about the contexts of these conflicts before we turn to their detail. First, for individuals, such conflicts are likely to be difficult only in proportion to one's eminence as scholar or scientist. The greater a man's value to the university as the master of a learned discipline, the greater his value as a professional man to government, industry, foundation, or profession. That these conflicts of role and loyalty are not merely abstract or potential is attested to by the frequent decisions, often perplexing, sometimes agonizing, that the individual must make through the period of his greatest creativity; decisions concerning alternative careers or, within the single career of academic man, decisions of allocation of time toward the varied demands which his own eminence brings upon him from profession, government, and research institute as well as academic department.

Second, just as the intensity of role conflicts varies among individuals in the measure of their personal distinction (and also, to be sure, in the "hotness" of the special fields they have chosen), so does intensity vary with the type and distinction of academic institution. A recent year spent in one of the great Ivy League universities, supplemented since by some random questioning of others, suggests clearly to me that the intensity of academic-professional conflict is less—both for the man and for the university—in a Harvard or Princeton than it is in even such justly renowned public universities as Berkeley and Ann Arbor. However distinguished the public university may be in eminence of its faculty and wealth of capital resources, it has not yet reached the point where it seems to provide the same anchoring sense of identity and to promote the same overriding loyalty to academy, that we find in some of the greater private universities. I am not, needless to emphasize, suggesting that the factors "public" and "private" are the crucial ones. European experience alone would cast doubt upon such a conclusion over the long run. And the spectacle of Berkeley makes plain that aggregations of scholars and amassments of financial resources as imposing as any to be found in the greatest private universities are perfectly compatible with public status.[2]

But aggregation does not a community make nor capital riches an aristocracy. The line between even Berkeley and a Harvard or Princeton is a clear one when we turn from human and financial resources to the subtle but potent matters of internal academic structure, hier-

---

[2] It is a point worth emphasizing, however, that Berkeley, partly through heavy endowments but chiefly through the unique constitutional position held by the University of California, has come the closest of all the public universities to being "private."

archy, and professorial role. In older universities, as in older aristocracies, internal processes of dislocation, of status anxiety, and of role conflict are, on the whole, more moderate, under the impact of external change than they are in the newer social strata or universities. When we move down the scale of institutional eminence from a Berkeley or Ann Arbor to those public universities (and a few of the newer private ones as well) which, through recent effort to catapult themselves upward, must bear some of the storied marks of the *nouveau riche*, internal strains of structural dislocation, status mobility, and role confusion can be deadly.

Obviously, in this differentiation among universities, we are dealing for the most part with factors over which neither faculties nor administrations have present control: sheer historical length of university eminence, number of academic luminaries reaching back for many decades, number of distinguished alumni, the social prestige that even for academic man attaches to private and endowed—in contrast to tax-supported—wealth, and a cultural style that only centuries can form. To pretend that the internal life of universities, any more than that of aristocracies, is not affected by such matters would be to pretend nonsense. But I am convinced that this differentiation of universities, and the difference in incidence and intensity of role conflicts and strains, is also the result of factors over which faculties and administrations *do* have some control. Among these are type, magnitude, and sway of university involvement in extramural ventures, and, second, the degree to which the purely *professional* attainments of faculty members outweigh, as values, internal contribution to the residual functions of the university.

But whatever the causes of this differentiation—historical and social, academic and administrative—it is a real one, to be seen in the varying intensity of the conflicts within the contemporary university.

TEACHING-RESEARCH: NATURE OF THE CONFLICT

Unquestionably the major conflict of loyalties on today's campus is that between teaching and research. Such conflict would appear inevitable, given the scope and nature of much of the research done. We are still prone to say, as did our academic forebears, that there cannot be, at bottom, conflict, for good teaching requires the insemination of ongoing research, and good research requires the stimulus of ongoing teaching. But these words have, increasingly, the ring of incantation. For plainly, much that passes under the name of research —including most of the consultative activities that today spring from the university's altered role in society and from the professionalization of academic discipline—does *not* require teaching, in fact, finds teaching to be avocational at best, distractive at worst. The reason lies in the massiveness and character of more and more of the research that is today done in universities.

The university, in taking over research activities that once existed (to the degree that they existed at all) in the U.S. Department of Agriculture, Bureau of Mines, Ordnance or Quartermaster Service, or in General Motors or General Electric laboratories, has increasingly taken over projects that do not at all require the ambience of teaching or the physical presence of graduate students for their successful prosecution. And we do little service to teaching or the nature of the university when we pretend that students are required for such projects. Assistants, yes, but not students. This is, I believe, the single most impressive difference between research today in the universities and the research of a generation ago.

No doubt there were conflicts of a sort between teaching and research before the multiversity entered the scene. But these, if they existed, were relatively few and small. They had to be. For, quite apart from the fact that teaching was, even in the major universities, incontestably academic man's first moral obligation, if not love, the invariable and unyielding pivot of one's contractual relation to the university and membership in the academic community was the teaching role. Teaching was as much the essence of one's academic image of himself as it was of society's stereotype of the academic profession.

But the major reason for the relative lack of conflict before the present generation was the character of research done in the universities and colleges. It was small in scope, personal in character, finite in aspiration, and, on the whole, optional. It was not, as it so often is today, immense, heavily bureaucratized, infinite, and compulsive. Let me use one example—admittedly extreme but far from unrepresentative: the multibillion dollar industrial-military research enterprise that is the University of California's atomic energy research project—spread out in three gigantic locations in Berkeley, Livermore, and Los Alamos. It is useful and sobering to recall that this vast project began in the late 1920's in the hands of one man, the late Ernest O. Lawrence, at Berkeley, without technical assistance beyond what was given by graduate students, without so much as a secretary, much less administrative assistant, and the whole of it housed—I recall vividly—in a room that would be too small today to take care of a departmental typing pool. Apart from teaching—that is, of graduate students—it is difficult to imagine Professor Lawrence's Nobel-prize-winning achievement ever having got off the ground. And apart from his own research genius, directly impressed upon students, not diffused through layer upon layer of technical-administrative staff, it is equally difficult to imagine the teaching impact that he made upon a generation of physicists.

The point is, the principal criterion of university-level research, down until a couple of decades ago, was its adaptability to the function of teaching. Such was the small, personal, and interactive character of research (in science as well as in the humanities) that it could properly be regarded, for graduate students at least, as but another mode of teaching. And in an age when research budgets were minuscule, when they rarely allowed the employment of research technicians, graduate students were as indispensable to the research function as professorial research was to their own education.

I am not suggesting, of course, that the *only* function of university or college research was instructive. Far from it. Beginning in the late nineteenth century with Eliot at Harvard, Gilman at Johns Hopkins, Jordan at Stanford, Benjamin Ide Wheeler at Berkeley, Harper at Chicago, and Wilson at Princeton, research came in for its own due. The difference between the university, properly called, and the more typical American *academy*, however it was called, lay in the increasing emergence of research as a legitimate activity of the university. But the truth remains: research then was given primary justification by what it did for teaching, for a level of teaching that had not previously existed on the American campus. And such research, in any event, depended for its audience on, was indeed exclusively addressed to, fellow scholars and scientists—*not* the men of affairs in government and industry whose primary interest in its operational or practical character has become increasingly directive in the academic community.

The major cause of present difficulties—of conflicts in academic role and loyalty that sometimes threaten to drive the university's historic and still essential functions underground—is not, therefore, the mere fact of the university's taking on the operational problems of society. It lies in the widening, undiscriminating, often frenzied, tendency to take on *any and all types* of research problems. The really serious and responsible criticism to be leveled at many universities today is that in the understandable and laudable act of making their resources available to a society desperately in need of knowledge, they have taken on not only the kinds of research project for which the university alone is adequately fitted *but also types of research project and development that could more easily and appropriately be placed in nonuniversity settings.* In some universities it is, alas, the second type that shows signs of proliferating the fastest and most widely. And, I would argue, it is in these universities that academic conflicts—between teaching and research, between university and professional affiliation—are most vivid and, often, wasteful of intellectual resources.

Professor Harrison Brown of Caltech has recently estimated that at the present time 1.3 billions of Federal dollars are invested in ongoing research in American universities and colleges and that this sum is two-thirds of all the university research funding in existence. In an age of cold war it would be folly, of course, to pretend that much of this does not serve military objectives, and, in passing, it might be observed that if occasionally some of it is embarrassedly discovered to be going into CIA activities, this means merely that it is serving the needs of *invisible* rather than *visible* war, a difference that would not, in all probability, have seemed of much moral consequence to earlier generations of university scientists and scholars.

The essential problem is not, however, that of the source and application of research funds; and it will not be met by recommendations which as seriously misunderstand the nature of the university as they flout the needs of a complex society. The university, to re-echo Woodrow Wilson's words, must certainly be in the nation's service. But it must serve *as it is uniquely fitted to serve:* through research that is compatible with university ends and structure, research small enough in scope to permit not only the utilization of students *as students*—rather than as technicians—but professors *as professors* rather than as project supervisors, first, second, and third grade.

How would we rank universities in the United States at the present time according to their ability to recognize projects that are, and are not, congenial to the distinctive character of the university? This single criterion could have far-reaching relevance to the future of universities and may well be more closely connected with future greatness than a measure of present number of distinguished faculty might suggest.

My impression is that the private universities, especially those of the Ivy League, have shown generally greater judgment in this respect than have the public universities, even the most distinguished of them. To say that such must inevitably be the case since public universities, by virtue of their "public" character, are bound to accept research projects that private universities may avoid misses the point. In the first place, public universities are state or municipal, not Federal, in this country, and no more bound to accept vast Federal projects than are the private universities. Second, few persons will have missed the frenetic search for and efforts to capture large projects in the public universities, leading to their employment of full-time representatives in Washington, experts in the art of catching the scent of dollars over the horizon. Admittedly, private universities have also played the game, justifying it by the number of new faculty positions made possible or by internal funds left free for use by, say, the classics instead of going to the sciences. But I believe that private universities have more often been saved from the full consequences of this game by putting limits to it—the result of a more nearly finite, rather than infinite, image of themselves. Moreover, as I have already suggested, private universities seem somehow to have retained greater strength in *internal* prestige systems: those founded upon primacy of the academic role. In certain universities today there is, alas, a tendency for a man's reputation—his promotion indeed—to rest upon the dollar size of the Federal grants he administers. A kind of inverse prestige scale develops at these universities. The closer a faculty member is to the *historic* functions of the university—regular teaching, research small enough in scope to use as a teaching medium, and curricular committee work—the lower he is on a prestige scale that has at its top faculty members whom students (and even colleagues) rarely see, so surrounded as they are by research administrative staff, so frequent their absence from campus on consultative work, so preoccupied are they by matters remote from local academic concern.

THE BLURRING OF ACADEMIC VALUES

There is today a blurring of the academic image, one that is the direct result of the kind of forces we have been describing. If this blurring is less obvious at a Princeton or Harvard than it is at a Berkeley or Ann Arbor—let alone at universities long content with mediocrity but now striving with every possible million dollars to achieve instant greatness—it cannot be missed even in the Ivy League. The difference between academic and nonacademic on the campus becomes ever more tenuous under the spur of professionalization of field and of a Faustian conception of the university. It used to be said that there was more difference between two professors one of whom was an administrator than between two administrators one of whom was a professor. This may still be true in a few areas of the university, the sciences included, but in more and more instances it is not. How could it be? For the physical or social scientist engaged more and more typically in large-scale research, more and more visible as *professional* physicist, biologist, or sociologist, working on an around-the-calendar schedule, housed in special institute or laboratory quarters (sometimes with Do Not Enter, not merely on his door but on the fence around his building), equipped with staffs of secretaries and technicians formidable enough to frighten away all but foundation executives or Federal supervisors, with budgets to prepare, applications to make out for further funds, and payroll sheets to sign—given all of this, it is hard for the individuals involved not to look like civil servants or businessmen. Add to this the man's constantly rising number of consultantships, incessant "site visits," and almost ceaseless travel to meetings and conferences, and the traditional image of academic man often seems less real than that of business executive or bureau chief.

Elsewhere [3] I have suggested that it becomes steadily more difficult, given this momentous change in academic role, to justify to non-academic intellectuals the iron protection, the differential privilege, that is enjoyed by academic intellectuals in the form of tenure. In a day when academic man lacked the occupational mobility that his present professional identity gives him—with ready entry into government, profession, and even business—when he was the victim, so to speak, of a specialization that was as fragile as it was narrow, with life made precarious by hostile winds that all too often blew across the academic landscape, when, in short, he was literally and exclusively academic man rather than professional man, there was much to justify tenure even when its costs could be measured, as they still can be in mummification. But that day is departed. Other grounds have to be found today on which to justify the differential privilege of tenure, academic freedom being the commonest and certainly the most respectable. But to plead necessitous or fragile circumstance for today's affluent man of science or letters is to plead a case that is at best naïve, at worst cynical.

Professionalization and the vast increase in research activities have inevitably led to a change in the criteria of achievement within the university. It is almost impossible today for a faculty member to win prestige in an academic environment on the basis of the largely moral or "human" qualities that in decades past gave certain individuals influence on the campus even when their scholarly or professional fame was slight. The sociologist Max Weber, in his treatment of a typology of educational systems, pointed to two opposite types of teachers: the one primarily able at "awakening charisma," the other at "imparting specialized expert training." It is reasonably clear that the second has become overwhelmingly dominant, though I would not wish to suggest that the two types are as irrevocably separated as Weber seems to imply.

The change in criteria of achievement and promotion can make for minor tragedies today, especially in some of the smaller colleges that have traditionally emphasized qualities in a professor that might be expected to "awaken charisma." Consider the plight of the professors in a certain celebrated liberal arts college that I have been told of. Tradition requires that the faculty member's office door be open to students all hours of the day except when he is at class. Students, I am told, are relentless in their insistence upon this open-door policy. But with inconsistency verging on downright betrayal, the same students will ridicule their professors because they lack the research reputations held by faculty members at a neighboring university.

Administrations might take warning. The same criteria of success that have become operative in faculty minds become, within a few years, and in different intensity, the criteria that students themselves apply to faculty. There is a rising tendency on the part of even undergraduates to rate their teachers less upon qualities that traditionally have counted and that undergraduates might be presumed competent to judge, and more and more on what filters down to them about a faculty member's professional eminence or national visibility as creative mind. Is the day too far off when one can expect to overhear an undergraduate saying, "Take Jones's course; he just got half a million from NIH" instead of the more familiar type of recommendation? Fortunately, probably a long way off. But students are nonetheless alive to the research reputations of their teachers, and nothing is more pathetic on campus today than the plight of the man who, after the bulk of his career has been spent at teaching alone, and with little if anything accrued in the way of professional reputation, suddenly awakens to the fact that in today's academic setting the man who has *only* his teaching to offer to students does not even have that.

The once familiar characterization of a faculty member as a good teacher but a poor research man is very likely to be fatal in the university today. Awareness of this has led many a naturally good young teacher to hide his light under a bushel lest he thereby run the risk of this currently invidious tag being applied to him. As one very candid assistant professor once put it to me in a letter: "I hope I never get labeled in any student or faculty evaluation as a good man with undergraduates. Until my research record is unchallengeable, I can get farther by dull teaching of undergraduates. This will at least leave open the *possibility* that my research promise may therefore be high." Students— and, of course, notably graduate students—are quick to absorb shifts in values, and one detects a certain suspicion among the more sophisticated students of that faculty member whose teaching scintillates through possession of older graces.

If the changed role of the university professor—that is, his increased professionalization and prominence as expert in national service—were accompanied by a decline in attractiveness of the university to undergraduate students, the conflict between research and teaching, between professional and academic roles, would be less intense; would certainly be less obvious. But, plainly, the university becomes ever more attractive to high school graduates and to their parents. Hordes of undergraduates, seemingly unfrightened by rumors of grim impersonality and bureaucratization at State U, pour through its gates each year. Once there, they adapt themselves astonishingly well despite the reports of alienation, of political activism supposedly founded upon curricular discontent, of defiant sexual experimentation, and escapist use of narcotics [4] that the public has come to read with all the delighted horror that, in a more innocent age of our history, went into the reading of missionary reports on the outrageous customs of the heathen. Moralistic tractarianism, it may be accepted as a principle, does not vary in amount from generation to generation; only in content and medium. Undergraduates, for the American reading public, have succeeded Polynesians and Nigerians, just as *Look* and *Life* have succeeded the good old *Missionary Review*.

Why undergraduates like large university settings (and my own view is that for the rest of this century such settings will become more, not less, attractive) is not altogether clear, but it may have something to do with Cardinal Newman's pregnant observation in his *The Idea of a University* that what students do by way of educating each other— through mere rubbing of shoulders together for four years—within an *exciting atmosphere*—is of more importance, both morally and intellectually, than what is done *for* them by a faculty. (This can be paraphrased by saying that students, in the long run, like to be where the action is, not where new umbilical cords are provided.) In any event, it might be noted that the fall-off in applications for undergraduate admission at Berkeley the past two years has been infinitesimal by comparison with what it could have been, given the rather horrifying yellow journalism (written by academic as well as nonacademic) in newspapers and magazines about Berkeley.

But while the university's popularity with undergraduates seems to be undiminished, the kinds of conflict we have noted between academic man's role as teacher and scholar, on the one hand, and his role as a corporate executive in research project, as industrial adviser, as government consultant, or even as independent intellectual in arts and letters remain nonetheless obvious; and galling to academic man himself.

Academic prestige today, on and off the campus, depends, to a degree never known heretofore, upon intellectual qualities that are not merely distinguishable but actually separable from older academic functions. This may be vivid only in the physical and social sciences (humanists are fond of saying it is) but I think it is scarcely less real in arts and letters. The university's prestige in the literary and artistic marketplace is today quite as great as in the industrial or governmental marketplace. Witness the increasing efforts of nonacademic literary editors and other

---

[4] A large percentage of the public seems to think that the same students are involved in all of these modes of reactive behavior. Quite apart from simple observation, mere common sense would suggest, however, that this, if true, would be what the *New Yorker* used to call the neatest trick of the week.

impresarios to "capture" professors in the humanities. The enlargement of the humanist's national image—reflected in his widening appearance in magazines and at White House parties—has come to mean as much to him as the enlargement of the scientist's national image, and with similar results upon the more prosaic and routine duties on the campus. This reality is often overlooked by the humanist, convinced as he is that he alone today keeps the vestal flame aglow. In the same way that the substantive difference between academic and nonacademic science has become less significant—the result of nonacademic centers allowing more individual research autonomy and "mission-oriented" contracts within the university allowing, in fact, less—so has the line between academic and nonacademic humanism grown less distinct. Thus, the national visibility that was once enjoyed only by the nonacademic humanist—by a T. S. Eliot or an Edmund Wilson—is now, increasingly, enjoyed by the academic, whose contributions to nonacademic prestige journals often seem to matter more to him than those he submits to strictly academic journals. Both in the humanities and the sciences academic minds today enjoy a national visibility that is distinct from their academic habitats.

It is this extraordinary professional visibility and renown in the republic of letters, arts, and sciences coupled with the diminishing appeal of such traditional university functions as teaching and academic fellowship with students that creates the notable conflict on all campuses between the Locals and the Cosmopolitans. Except for transient periods of moralistic fervor on the part of the Cosmopolitans, attention to matters of curriculum and academic policy is left to the Locals. The Cosmopolitans—too deeply engaged in more profitable or prestigious work at the professional or national level—care little for such duties; that situation can sometimes result in the chairman, the dean, and the president getting their advice on curriculum, educational policy, and other vital matters from those whose chief qualification is availability rather than insight or wisdom. Worse than this, however, is that indifference of the influential and notable toward time-honored curriculum and policy committees has something of a downgrading effect on these committees, on their intrinsic function and their attractiveness to the less notable of the faculty. There is inevitably a perceived stratification of academic-administrative functions on a campus, and it requires little vision or shrewdness today by a faculty member on his way up to sense that those committees most directly concerned with teaching, especially undergraduate, are less desirable than those concerned with, say, research and external relations.

Here, as in other spheres, however, it is possible, I believe, to differentiate between private and public universities. While the attraction of service on curriculum and internal policy committees has declined at a Yale or Princeton, it has not declined as much. Just as the image of the undergraduate teacher still glows more brightly, so does the appeal of activities directly concerned with teaching. We come back to the point made earlier: such is the continuing prestige of a Harvard or Princeton as an autonomous community that external research and consultative work at even highest professional levels can oftentimes seem less gratifying to ego, less important somehow, than the unsung, relatively invisible, and wholly unpaid duties of intramural character.

No doubt to many a veteran professor of the Ivy League, remembering how it used to be, the differentiation I am drawing will seem tenuous. I am far from claiming that even at Princeton teaching holds undiminished luster. But there is no question that the status of the student, undergraduate as well as graduate, and the general esteem in which teaching is held, are higher in the Ivy League universities and in private universities generally than in the public universities. And among the public universities there is, I am convinced, a scale of faculty regard for the student that is roughly in proportion to the scale of institutional excellence. That is, there is more interest in, more effectiveness and distinction of teaching at, say, Berkeley or Ann Arbor than at certain other institutions where, in recent frenetic attempts to achieve quality overnight, contracts have been made with eminent individuals which in their heavy and public emphasis upon research have had the predictable effect of downgrading the status of teaching. When, however, as not infrequently happens, one of these eminent individuals shows that he is keenly interested in students and in teaching, and that isolation from curriculum is the last thing he is interested in, the consequences can be extraordinarily fruitful.

There is also, apparently, a reasonably high, positive correlation between an academic man's excellence as scholar or creative mind and his respect for teaching. Not every form of teaching, to be sure. But when, after all, did *every* form of teaching ever interest all members of a faculty? Teaching is many things. It is research conducted with students (in contrast to hired technicians). Teaching is the excitement that can be generated in a student's mind by mere presence on the same campus with faculty minds known to be creative and to be esteemed by the profession. Teaching is the random suggestion, however inarticulate, conveyed perhaps osmotically, that a certain problem is important to investigate. Teaching is casual conversation. Teaching is lecturing to large audiences. (In how many academics is there not something of the actor *manqué*, something that is stimulated and gratified by the mere existence of an audience?) Teaching, above all, is something that is important to say. It may be safely assumed that in ancient Athens or in medieval Paris large numbers came to hear Aristotle or Abelard not primarily because either was reputed to be a "good teacher" but because he was known to have something to say worth listening to. Teaching is many things. And the only possible prescription for it at university or college level is to see that somehow, in some way, active junior minds are in some kind of contact with active senior minds. We are told that Enrico Fermi took as much pleasure in his freshman class in introductory physics at the University of Chicago after the war as he ever had in any of his signal contributions to theoretical physics. We do not know *how* he taught; only that, like Mt. Everest, he was *there*, to be, so to speak, scaled by students.

For either administration or faculty to take method or organization of teaching too seriously is, of course, fatal. Several years ago I saw a list prepared by someone in the U.S. Office of Education of what purported to be the "twenty-three indispensable qualities of the good teacher." It was computer-based. Good grooming and pleasing manner were placed just behind "clear organization of subject matter" in importance. Let us, however, overlook that particular juxtaposition of the computer mind, and fix attention only on "clear organization of subject matter." I think irresistibly of three or four great teachers of this century I have been privileged to know: Gilbert Lewis in chemistry, Edward Tolman in psychology, Carl Sauer in geography, A. L. Kroeber in anthropology. Not one of them would have passed muster on this item any more than on most of the other items so solemnly listed. Seminal minds are almost never very clear in their organization of subject matter. How could they be and at the same time leave generations of students—undergraduate and graduate—with the feeling that in knowledge as in a woman's beauty there is something wonderful and beckoning that eludes precise classification?

Today, in too many quarters, we are bedeviled by the image of Old Chips—a good fellow, kind to students, interested in their personal lives, a "character," and "who may not have been a scholar but was a real guy" in the bleary memories of older alumni. But the first step in any rational view of the present situation is to forget Chips. Modern students—the better ones, at least—have little interest in his resurrection and would have little time for him were he to suddenly appear. He would simply embarrass them.

There is a widespread belief today in higher education that a foremost task is that of somehow making large universities seem like small colleges. But this is dangerous business, for there is tyranny implicit in all efforts to make large organizations—be they nations, corporations, or universities—seem like small communities. My own unabashed view is that a more important task, given the complexity, the quality, the

style, of twentieth-century American culture, is that of making many
small colleges seem more like universities. And this means—in addition
to the first requirement, which is that of *greater intellectual creativeness*
from the faculty, with time allowed from classroom routine for its expression—the formation of a scene in which some of the cosmopolitan-
ism, the excitement of diverse numbers, and the social freedom of the
large university are somehow made present. Many of us would echo
Dean DeVane's belief that a large college of liberal arts set within a
university has, on balance, advantages over the small independent
college, and most of these advantages flow from exposure of liberal arts
students to a scene that is more diverse professionally, richer in variety
of opportunities offered, and, generally, more stimulating and maturing
than that to be found in the small college.

It would be unfortunate for the university to deny itself its natural
advantages or to blur these through techniques and curricula more
appropriate to the small college. The problem of conflicting academic
loyalties can be a perplexing one, and nowhere is its incidence so great as
in the university, in contrast to the college. But the primacy of research
in the contemporary university is here to stay, as is the professionalization of the academic disciplines, so recently gained in the fields of the
liberal arts and sciences. To seek suddenly, through either administrative fiat or faculty-committee policy, a setting in a particular university, college, or school in which "teaching, not research" is declared to
be primary, will only have unanticipated consequences of a deleterious
nature. Some recent experiences in medical schools along this line are
perhaps instructive, a warning to the naïve and unwary in all spheres.
The Harvard Medical School is, on the clear record, a place of distinguished teaching, as well as research. But if of a sudden that great
school were to be advertised as a place *primarily* concerned with teaching, with training physicians, the results would be as costly to its teaching effectiveness in the long run as to its research eminence.

THE ACADEMIC MAN AND THE INSTITUTION
OF HIGHER EDUCATION

The present intensity of conflicts of academic loyalty would appear
almost certain to lessen in the years immediately ahead. There are
several reasons for this. In the first place the university is an institution,
and institutions (in contrast, say, to sects) have their own mechanisms
for the assimilation of change and of the role conflicts induced by
change. An institution is, after all, multipurpose, and it is not therefore
as vulnerable to sudden modifications of environment as are social
entities whose specialization of function renders them less adaptable.

This evolutionary principle is, I believe, as likely to be applicable to centers for research or dialogue as to biological organisms.

Second, change of an internal, academic-administrative nature may be expected. Administrations (and faculty members), profiting from some recent embarrassing experiences in contract research, will almost certainly begin to make sharper and more critical distinction between types of research congenial to the nature of a university and types that are not congenial. The essence of today's problem is not, I repeat, the prestige of research but the sway of certain types of research that are difficult to harmonize with teaching at any level. It seems likely that in the better universities more and more of these latter types of research will be left by choice to the nonacademic research centers that are proliferating in the United States.

Third, while the heady wine of professionalization is now indeed a major influence on the academic scene, nothing can withstand the long-run appeal of the university itself as the primary loyalty of those fortunate enough to be its members. I use "fortunate" advisedly. Even in the great, long-established professions of law and medicine, one cannot but be struck by the continuing magnetism of the university law and medical schools and by the sacrifice in income that will be gladly endured for the assured intellectual stimulation (also, not to be missed, the social prestige) that come from faculty status. The university is, and is likely to remain for a long time, the bearer of more intellectual influence and of more social status in the United States than any other single institution. It holds much of the position once held by the church and clergy. It is as easy, we should not forget, for an aristocracy to be founded upon academic merit (reinforced by tenure, to be sure) as upon land or military prowess. The professoriat in the United States today comes closer than either the business or governmental class to resembling a feudal nobility. It has its barons and lords (Nobel prize winners, National Academy members, Guggenheim fellows, *et al.*), its immense influence on nation, its unique *esprit*, its honor, its *noblesse oblige*, its unrivaled sense of mutual aid and corporate protectiveness, and is even, apparently, becoming more and more endogamous. Nothing in the world mattered so much to the late President Kennedy, or would mean more to President Johnson, than support of the professoriat.

Finally, there is the sheer, unquenchable love of teaching (in whatever form) that lies in the heart of not merely academic man but of man in general. The impulse to inform, to instruct, to mold, to indoctrinate, is a powerful one in the human race. Whether teaching is a variant primarily of gossip or of the sermon is not clear, but the same impulse that leads to each of these leads equally to teaching.

There is evidence, as I said above, that a positive correlation exists between excellence (institutional and individual) and faculty interest in students. This correlation is not likely to diminish, and it may be taken for granted, I believe, that its implication will become more, not less, vivid in the academic world at large.

Commentaries on
Conflicting Academic Loyalties

JOHN T. CALDWELL, PAULINE TOMPKINS,
CLARK BYSE, CHARLES COGEN

Educational Leadership Is Where You Find It

JOHN T. CALDWELL

PROFESSOR NISBET's is an entirely useful analysis and commentary on "conflicting academic loyalties" in contemporary American higher education, but it is more analytical and diagnostic than prescriptive. Professor Nisbet is quite perceptive in his observation on "the social prestige that even for the academic man attaches to private and endowed . . . wealth, and a cultural style that only centuries can form." He observes that the older universities, and especially the older private universities, enjoy a more composed and poised view of themselves and their place in the scheme of things, hence elicit greater institutional loyalty from faculty. Although this point has some validity, he wisely adds that "public" and "private" are not the crucial factors. He includes Michigan and California as examples of the "public" universities. His point would have been strengthened by reference to the University of Virginia and the University of North Carolina at Chapel Hill. Both have been public and aristocratic and poised and have enjoyed social prestige for a century and a half in one case and a century and three-quarters in the other. Probably the differences reside in academic prestige, longer average faculty tenure, more stability of core faculty, and more controlled growth—which do affect institutional loyalties.

It is at least implicit in Professor Nisbet's observations that the academic role of teacher-scholar, in contrast to big-money research and public service, has a better chance to exist and be rewarded in the older, more prestigious institutions. Is there evidence to support this view, or is this surmise? Is the point based on quite personal experience and subjective observation? Could it be that those in only second place "work harder," even at teaching? And could it be that an unmentioned factor, the difference in selectivity of students, really creates more difference in academic role-playing on several campuses than do other factors discussed by the author? I don't know. But his generalization does not leave me entirely convinced nor is it entirely helpful, for we cannot all become, at will, private or endowed or hallowed.

In dealing with the question of *kinds of research* undertakings and size of research enterprises that he feels are more appropriate and those kinds less appropriate to the campus enterprise, the point seems to me either overdone or faulty on several counts: (1) Assuming that there is some valid criterion on which to exclude certain types of research from the university, do violations of the criterion of any consequence actually characterize our university campuses? (2) Although Professor Nisbet does not attempt a definitive distinction between the two kinds, the factor of size of project is posed as one and in my judgment is of dubious validity. At least there is no criterion of size that I know of on which agreement could be found. Probably, acceptability rests more on skillful and adequate management, adequacy of financing and division of labor than it does on size. (3) The suggestion that a criterion of kind of research is or could be well enough defined to be used in ranking universities is indeed questionable. (4) Finally, on the point of the appropriateness of various kinds of research, one has the feeling that Professor Nisbet is thinking of, but not articulating, the hierarchical superiority of pure over applied research. (5) Research will be done. It is arguable that universities must make certain that the ablest scholars are not siphoned away from the campuses to do it elsewhere.

An isolated question: Does a private *or* a public university, by capturing "large projects" (presumably in the sciences) free "internal funds . . . for use by, say, the classics . . ."? I have not found it so.

As useful as some of these provocative observations and suggestions of Professor Nisbet's are, my own feeling is that we must beware of the generalization. A particular example, which displays my own bias, challenges the generalization: I cannot think of an educational enterprise in which there is a more magnificent and inspiring commitment to superb teaching, pure research, applied research, small and large research undertakings, and public service than in the School of Agriculture and Life Sciences at North Carolina State University. The land-grant universities are, in the scheme of things, not our oldest universities nor are they aristocratic. Nor are they all alike. I make only this point: educational leadership is where you find it, commitment to teaching is where you find it, in any class or category of institution.

But these comments should not be allowed to obscure a very real admiration for Professor Nisbet's extraordinarily helpful paper, both felicitous and candid in expression, and optimistic. He has acquired some ivy in his mental garden, but ivy is after all graceful, and he could be right!

National Needs
and Legitimate Institutional Aspirations

PAULINE TOMPKINS

IN AN ARTICLE in the April 16–30 issue of *School and Society*, John W. Shirley, of the University of Delaware, suggested that "possibly the basic underlying cause of the government-education conflict is the unresolved question of the purpose of education in a democratic society." He noted that "educators have been inclined to stress the historical and the traditional [goals and values], and government has been more concerned with the relevant." [1] Professor Nisbet bridges this gap with an incisive definition of the fundamental issue confronting higher education. Instead of an either/or dichotomy, here is a concept of a fine, dynamic balance, a journey rather than a destination.

Some such premise regarding the underlying purposes of higher education is a precondition for significant discourse about the improvement of college teaching and conflicting academic loyalties. It provides the milieu for our discussion. In addition, it is important to recall characteristics of the environment in which higher education functions: the growing commitment to education beyond the high school; the burgeoning of enrollments and the sprouting of hundreds of new institutions serving multiple purposes; the expanded demands upon higher education in the interests of the individual student, of the nation's manpower and research and development needs, and of the country's mounting involvement in international education. These and other features suggest the enormous energy pulsing throughout the educational world today. Its momentum provides the zest and the opportunity for engineering bold, imaginative plans to strengthen college teaching.

The above statements of premise and promise supply the backdrop for my comments on Professor Nisbet's paper.

The two major "structural changes" which he believes aggravate the problem of conflicting academic loyalties are: increased university relationships and involvement with government and industry, and the grow-

[1] Shirley, "Problems Involved in Cooperation between Universities and Government Agencies," p. 222.

ing professionalization of academic disciplines. Both seem destined to continue. The conflicts growing out of them are real and serious, and have aroused the concern of government as well as education. House Report No. 1158, issued October 13, 1965, entitled *Conflicts between the Federal Research Programs and the Nation's Goals for Higher Education*, is one of the most carefully considered documents on the problem. It is the result of a subcommittee study under the chairmanship of Congressman Reuss of Wisconsin, a study which elicited testimony from over two hundred educators, administrators, and citizens. Noting that government and education share the goals of extending scholarship and developing intellectual resources, the report points out that "the immediate interests of one are not necessarily those of the other." Three specific conflicts are identified, all related to manpower needs of government and education, both now and in the future. The committee found that the primary emphasis of government on manpower in the natural sciences has diverted too many scientists and engineers into research, and that "too few are available for teaching." It recommended that the Bureau of the Budget obtain more reliable data on scientific manpower, that it weigh priorities between teaching and research, that all holders of Federal fellowships and research assistantships be required to do some undergraduate teaching, that science teaching fellowships be instituted, and that there be an annual Presidential award for outstanding undergraduate teachers.

The alarums registered by the House committee have been echoed within the past year by faculty committee reports from Yale, Cornell, and Berkeley. Each considered the effect on undergraduate education of faculty concentration on research. Each concluded that undergraduate teaching had suffered at its institution and that teaching ability was given insufficient weight in determining promotions and tenure.

Professor Nisbet predicts that higher education will generate its own corrective forces to cope with conflicting academic loyalties. The American Council on Education's exploration at this time of the problem in its larger setting is perhaps the most recent evidence of this point. In this exploration several observations may serve to sharpen the issues.

First, it would be prudent to remind ourselves that "all generalizations are false, including this one." One cannot talk about improving college teaching as though higher education were a monolith. Professor Nisbet speaks primarily to the situation in the large university, but makes some important distinctions between public and private institutions. The problem differs in size and intensity among universities and is massively different from the spin-off or fallout problems precipitated in smaller colleges. And, in turn, they cannot be lumped together in any meaningful way. Our lauded diversity in higher education becomes the nemesis of analyses which slide around it. Professor Nisbet's excellent paper loses conviction at precisely those rare points where he lards his concern with generalizations.

Second, the danger of generalizing is compounded by the absence of adequate data. The House Report testifies to this lack. "How many professional people have the Federal programs actually taken from the manpower pool which also supplies colleges and universities?" the committee asked, and stated in reply that the question "cannot be answered with confidence because . . . Federal agencies have not made systematic continuing estimates of basic employment data." There is a dearth of hard descriptive information about the impact of conflicting academic loyalties within different kinds of institutions, about the attitudes of students, teachers, and administrators, and about numerous related matters. We are lavishing heat and energy over a crisis of indeterminate magnitude. (Perhaps the lack of scientific precision in many discussions of the problem is in itself mock proof that the scientists and statisticians have fled the campus!)

Finally, there are a number of constructive steps which colleges can take. Professor Nisbet suggests several, including the need to make smaller institutions seem like universities in order to capture the cosmopolitan flavor and intellectual aura of a more diversified community. Where this is geographically feasible the idea has merit. Interinstitutional cooperative arrangements, originating forty years ago in the United States with the Claremont Plan, substantiate the soundness of the concept. Professor Nisbet also advances the thesis of a positive correlation between institutional and individual excellence and faculty interest in students, and suggests that appreciation of this will help to reduce tensions.

There is some reason to question how much value is placed on teaching by many colleges and universities. It would be interesting to know, for example, how many develop plans for long-term faculty recruitment based on projected needs; how many seek conscientiously to interest undergraduates in teaching as a profession; how many envisage their faculty needs in the context of the particular types of institutions they are, the kinds of students they attract, the underlying philosophy they espouse, and the nature of their curricula.

The kind of institutional appraisal implicit in these comments requires objective study by individuals or groups brought to the campus for this purpose. To be maximally useful, such studies must go beyond the institution's self-image to the wider perspective of the nation's needs in higher education. Stated another way, self-restraint in the institution's exercise of diversity, practiced in the interest of educational requirements more broadly conceived, should bring into sharper focus the legitimate aspirations of the college and its corresponding requirements for faculty. Out of such an exercise one might see the emergence of a healthy upgrading of teaching to provide an effective match for the too-often uncontested status symbols attendant on professionalism, research, and extracampus involvement in government and industry. This suggests one avenue leading to an improvement in college teaching and to a lessening of conflicting academic loyalties.

Identifying and Correcting Specific Evils: The Role of the Faculty

CLARK BYSE

THE TERRAIN depicted by Professor Nisbet is only part of the total academic landscape. His comments, devoted almost exclusively to the university, exclude the large and important segment of American higher education represented by the colleges of the nation. According to a relatively recent study of the National Science Foundation,[1] the increase in research and development supported by funds from outside grants or contracts—primarily those of the Federal Government—has occurred principally in the 306 institutions granting graduate degrees in science and engineering in the United States. Of the total 175,600 scientists and engineers employed by the more than 2,000 colleges and universities in this country, the 306 graduate institutions accounted for 144,600, or 82 percent, of the total. Among the 306 graduate institutions, the first 20 accounted for 50 percent of the total full-time equivalents of professional manpower resources engaged in research and development. The first 50 schools accounted for 75 percent, and the first 100 schools for 93 percent, of the time devoted to research and development. This is not to say that the problem is not quantitatively significant. But it is to say that it is primarily a university phenomenon and that the number of universities involved is not large.

Professor Nisbet has painted with a broad brush. His picture lacks the detail of Brueghel's "Spielende Kinder." It is, rather, more a Cezanne. Of course, an artist must paint as he feels, and he should be commended, not criticized, if the result is a work of art, as Professor Nisbet's paper surely is. Still, the beholder may suggest that in this case the opus in some respects does not conform to the expectations or specifications of the patron who commissioned it—or at least not to the published "Purpose and Plan" of the Forty-ninth Annual Meeting,

[1] "Science and Engineering Professional Resources in Colleges and Universities, 1961," *Reviews of Data on Research and Development*, No. 37 (Washington: National Science Foundation, 1963).

which states that impediments to teaching should be *"specifically* identified and examined,"* that "merely lamenting . . ., deploring . . ., or
regretting is futile and that the meeting should *"focus* on ways of improving college teaching and of reducing the obstructions." (Emphasis
added.)

With all respect and despite its many delightful and valuable features, Professor Nisbet's paper does, it seems to me, suffer from a lack
of detail. What *specifically* are the practices that create what problems,
on what campuses, in what disciplines or departments, at what times?
What *specifically* have been the adverse effects on teaching—again, on
what campuses, in which disciplines or departments, at what times?
What *specific* countermeasures have been prepared or adopted by some
of our 2,000 colleges or universities? How have these remedies worked
when put into practice—for example, have they created other problems?
And, could they be utilized by other institutions?

To the extent the teaching function has been harmed by "the increasing *directness* of the university's relation to government and industry" or by "the spreading professionalization of academic disciplines,"
the remedy will not be found in any monolithic or a priori reform measure imposed by administrative or general faculty ukase. My conception
of how reform measures should evolve is as follows: Generalizations and
abstract principles are suspect; allegations of deficiencies and evils are
to be thoroughly investigated institution by institution, discipline by
discipline, department by department; if, as appears likely, investigation
discloses weaknesses, specific reform measures carefully tailored to correct
particular defects are to be proposed; affected individuals and other
segments of the university community are to be given an opportunity to
appraise, comment on, and seek modifications of, the proposed remedy
before it becomes operative. This method—patiently pursuing fact, preparing remedial measures in light of the specific evil disclosed, and giving
those affected a role in the process—is costly, slow, and unspectacular.
But it is clear to me that only through such rational processes will meaningful and lasting reforms be achieved.

Fortunately, the task of identifying specific evils and proposing remedial measures has been undertaken by some institutions and by governmental and private organizations. The job is difficult but by no means
impossible. The time for lamenting, deploring, and regretting is well
past. Now is the time for concrete, specific, scholarly action by interested faculty and administrative groups.

Information can be acquired and standards of conduct can be proposed by national associations. It may be, therefore, that as in the case
of a somewhat related problem—that of coping with conflicts of interest
in government-sponsored research—the American Council on Education

and the American Association of University Professors should join together in an effort to develop general guidelines or standards.

If such a joint endeavor is undertaken, I hope that individual institutions will not relax their individual efforts, for the draftsmen of a joint statement will need concrete data from the various institutions, and, also, whatever joint statement might be evolved would have to be implemented on individual campuses.

In either event—whether developing a joint statement or adopting individual reforms—administrators and faculties have a responsibility to work cooperatively in achieving solutions for at least two reasons.

First, at some institutions it is said that administrators emphasize their desire that faculty members take steps to obtain sponsored research projects to help support the institution and to provide jobs for graduate students. To the extent that administrative desires influence faculty action, it is apparent that in such institutions administrative cooperation is necessary. Similar problems and a similar need for faculty cooperation may well exist in those institutions whose individual faculty members independently seek sponsored research projects.

Second, in my opinion, administration and faculty must share responsibility for establishing institutional policies and rules. Policies or rules unilaterally imposed by governing boards or administrators but developed without faculty participation will often be defective because their effect on the faculty's discharge of their teaching and research functions has not been ascertained. Problems of conflicting loyalties in our colleges and universities will, I believe, be aggravated—not ameliorated—unless faculty members are consulted in the development of remedial measures. If, however, faculty members share in the responsibility for working out solutions, if they participate meaningfully in the decisional process, there is every likelihood that they will accept the solutions and that their feelings of loyalty to the institution will be intensified.

Representatives of the American Council on Education, the Association of Governing Boards of Universities and Colleges, and the American Association of University Professors have been working on a joint "Statement on Government of Colleges and Universities." It is my earnest hope that trustees, administrators, and faculty members will take steps to see that the statement is approved by their institutions. Such approval will not solve every problem but it would go far toward providing a mechanism and milieu for joint solution of such problems as conflicting academic loyalties and other difficult issues that confront all who are concerned with the welfare of American higher education.

[2] *AAUP Bulletin*, Winter 1966, pp. 375–79.

The Role of Collective Bargaining

CHARLES COGEN

My MAJOR DISAGREEMENT with Professor Nisbet is that he fails to assign to the faculty any role in making conscious change in the state of affairs. He seems to have hope that impersonal evolutionary forces will create a balance and harmony of academic loyalties.

The fact that the term "professionalism" has been relegated to mean specialized service outside the classroom indicates that something needs to be done to restore the status of the professor who remains in the classroom. There are many ways of serving society, and one of them is teaching.

Professionalism in the broader sense, involving control of the various aspects of academic conditions, does not exist in all too many universities. Although the situation varies widely among colleges and universities, it is unusual for the faculty to have a high degree of control over academic conditions. The point here pertains especially to control over entry into the profession, with emphasis upon qualifications and training. It also relates to the practitioners' performance, which should be judged by their peers. Similarly, there are no basic criteria of good teaching. The teachers should—like the professionals in law, medicine, and clinical psychology—have a greater share in these various areas of control. All these are matters that may well fall within the jurisdiction of a faculty senate or council.

If, as Professor Nisbet contends, "the basic reason for the conflict in loyalties is the impact of government and foundation grants which distort university research," then some countermeasure must be proposed that will arrest this tendency and will restore the college and university to their basic purpose of education. This countermeasure must come from the faculty decisively acting to secure for the entire institution that set of conditions which would militate against the professor taking individual flight from classroom teaching and educationally related research.

It is here, in the broad area of economic welfare, that collective bargaining should play a major role. This is the field for the union. If the college teaching profession were organized and oriented so that the teacher in the classroom and the researcher both received adequate economic perquisites, there would most likely be a significant alteration in their status and, likewise, in their loyalty to their university.

Even salaries—generally reputed to be satisfactory—are far from being at an adequate level. This is clearly shown in the report on "The Economic Status of the Profession" in the Summer 1966 issue of the *AAUP Bulletin.* I would say that, judging by comparison with other occupations requiring similar or even less training, the statistical Appendix of that article indicates below-standard compensation. Strong corroboration appears in the *Monthly Labor Review* (March 1965), page 250. This is especially true for the public and church-related universities and for all categories of colleges. Further, it is also particularly applicable to those below the rank of full professor in every type of institution of higher education. There should be a basic salary schedule with a minimum annual increment.

Another area that requires serious attention is working conditions. In the first rank of considerations is work loads, that is, teaching load (hours) and student-teacher ratio (including class size). A sound basic program would be: for undergraduate teaching, nine hours with a maximum of 90 students, and for graduate teaching, six hours with a maximum of 60 students. The list of other types of working conditions that require attention includes leaves of absence, sabbatical leaves, adequate secretarial assistance, appropriate office space, and research facilities. Nonteaching duties, such as registration work, committee work, and advising duties, should also be brought into the realm of collective bargaining. Among other elements that should be included in negotiations is the great range of fringe benefits—health and hospital insurance, life insurance, retirement plans, travel funds for attending professional meetings, and research funds. And, not least, the teachers union should also see that promotions and other emoluments go to the teacher, as well as to the researcher.

Appropriate attention to all of these facets of teacher compensation would modify the prestige scale and give the teacher his proper status. It would also minimize the conflict between research and teaching staffs.

Finally, there is need for a formalized grievance procedure, with ultimate resort to an outside arbitrator. The use of such procedure would be a surer guarantee of the observance of tenure rights, academic freedom and nonpoliticalizing of the university.

Currently, the degree of consultation between administrators and teachers depends largely on the personality and educational philosophy of the president and the progressive or reactionary nature of the board of trustees. There is a definite need for institutionalizing collective bargaining. It is a significant device for resolving conflicting academic loyalties, because it brings personal gratifications that lead to loyalty.

The Nature of
The Academic Community

ROGER W. HEYNS

MOST OF US, probably, believe we have a clear understanding of the essential nature of the academic community. And perhaps we do. I shall not, therefore, in these remarks contend that we lack in our understand ing. But I will seek to show that among the members of our communities there is lack of agreement about some of the essential properties of academic life, and that this has been a major source of the news most frequently reported during the last two years from American campuses. Let me illustrate this point by recalling three types of scenes on a college or university campus. They happened on three different campuses but their counterparts have occurred on many others, and the phenomena to which they call attention are familiar to all of us, no matter where our institutions are located.

Scene 1: A large group of students has crowded into the outer office of a senior administrator—chancellor, president, vice-president, or dean. The group represents a variety of interests; it has been organized very quickly in response to a particular issue. The group has no designated spokesmen or leaders; indeed, the students earlier rejected the suggestion that some representatives be chosen to meet with the administration. The administrators present recognize a few of the students as having been active in political affairs on the campus but most have not been, and many of them are obviously very young. Several of the young women are holding babies in their arms.

The group has marched to the office from a central gathering point; the purpose is to protest a decision made by the university, to insist that a few questions be answered immediately, and to demand that the decision be revoked. The conversation becomes increasingly unproductive as one or two of the students become abrasive, caustic, and personal. This troubles some of the others and may even lead to some remonstrances on their part. After a period, the meeting breaks up inconclusively. It is uncertain what will happen next: the next step may be an impromptu sit-in, or the group may break up and await another day.

Scene 2: A faculty group has received a resolution from the student government insisting that the scope of student participation in decision making be increased. They want to be involved in "everything that concerns them." The students are emphatic that they don't mean they want to advise; they want to participate, to be a part of the deciding process heretofore reserved for faculty alone. The president of the student government defends the resolution, and the faculty begins to discuss the proposal. Mercifully, I terminate my description of Scene 2 at this point.

Scene 3: The president of the institution is visited by a delegation of students who have returned from a march to a town in Alabama. They demand that (1) the president issue a statement condemning Governor Wallace, (2) the president grant amnesty to all students from professors who insist that the students complete their assigned work on time in spite of their prolonged absence, and (3) the university stop its purchases from a paper company that proposes to build a new mill in that Southern city.

There are a multitude of issues in these academic episodes. Among them:

The first scene—the protest gathering—compels attention to the style and manner of academic life, especially as they are reflected in the techniques that members of an academic community choose to influence one another. It forces us to ask: What mechanisms do we have to resolve our differences and settle conflicts? The second scene—the faculty meeting on student participation—focuses on the governmental process of the academic community, that is, problems of power, authority, and responsibility. The third scene raises the question of the university as an instrument—an institution turned active agent for the immediate solution of social, political, and economic problems. What is the proper role for the university in connection with the issues of poverty, civil rights, and the Vietnam war?

I have raised more issues than I shall attempt to settle. I will make a few general comments before turning to my main thesis. It is obvious, first of all, that these issues are interrelated. In all probability they arise out of a common set of conditions. The consequences of war, the circumstances under which our students have been reared, the civil rights movement—these conditions help to create on our campuses a turbulence, a volatility, an excitement, and an uneasiness not felt before. Incidents such as I have described have a pervasive influence, even though the number of students in any one will be a minority, and even though there will actually be few such incidents.

STRAINS ON THE SENSE OF COMMUNITY

More than being the source of excitement and uneasiness, these problems have generated a serious concern among faculty members and administrators, as it becomes clear not only that these incidents strain institutions and their relationships but also that some fundamental issues are at stake. Academic communities have become polarized along many different lines: pro-students, anti-students; pro- and anti-activists; those who accept and welcome the techniques of influence that have come to special prominence in the civil rights movement and those who deplore this development—to mention just a few polarities.

In addition to creating divisions within the academic community, new strains have developed between educational institutions and the societies that support them. I do not see these as merely modern manifestations of the familiar restiveness of the society at large with academic freedom. Surely there are still those who would like to have students and faculty members screened or even silenced. But one could hardly refer to them as new strains. Nor has their influence been significant. The new strain I refer to is the concern of thoughtful persons with the possible effect on our independence of an unrestrained determination to make the university an instrument of social action. And such use of the university is indeed the goal of some of our restive but highly motivated students—highly motivated to action, that is, though not necessarily to analysis. And so our closest friends speculate worriedly about their ability to help us preserve our autonomy if the university assumes an active role in the political and social arenas.

There is a second new aspect to our *division* from our social support. There is, I believe, concern with our ability to resolve our own conflicts, indeed doubt about our ability to live an ordered, reflective life. Rightly or wrongly, although our alumni and friends have come to expect and even delight in outrageous experiments, they find some of our own *internal* activities uncongenial and, more importantly, inconsistent with our major purposes. I shall return to this concern later.

Although most of us have faced the kinds of problems I have been talking about, each of us has tended to respond to each on its own terms and with special regard for its unique set of surrounding conditions. Typically, administrators have acted, and then committees and study commissions have been appointed. But we are not developing principles that are *generally* useful or criteria to which faculty members and an informed public can refer. The considerations that have had the greatest impact have been political ones—political in the sense of the academic community itself. That is, the "best" decisions are held to be those that were the least disruptive. Administrative skill is measured by the degree of success one has in avoiding trouble, bringing disorder to a quick halt if it unavoidably occurs, in short, in keeping things quiet. Unfortunately, this kind of order-keeping in the academic community is terribly costly. It may not even be the best solution in the long run. In any case, much of our best talent—in administration and in the faculty—is being turned to maintaining the order of our common life. One test of the sophistication and maturity of our collective life must certainly be the amount of time we must spend in our governance. This is a test on which many academic organizations are getting lower marks now than they did a decade ago.

When we deal with the issues of conflict resolution, student participation, and a wide range of student activities, perhaps each of us has been guided by a conception of the university. But is that conception defensible? Is it sufficiently explicit so that it avoids giving the administrative posture an opportunistic and pragmatic quality that causes unease and simultaneously robs administrative decisions of the assurance that they require and the support they might otherwise gain?

I have doubts; hence my thesis: We, as members of the academic community, must state more clearly than ever before what we believe to be the essential nature of that academic community, the college or university. By an appeal to certain basic propositions about the nature of the university, these issues become manageable, the course of action becomes clearer, and the necessity of a common commitment to their resolution becomes more obvious. Our lack of clarity, our lack of agreement about the essential properties of the academic life has made us indecisive, uncertain, and divided.

Our lack of a common view about the nature of a university becomes readily apparent when we review some ideas which have attained currency on many campuses and are an important part of the intellectual apparatus of the actors in the scenes I described earlier. Let me list some of these conceptions of the university:

1. *The university is simply part of a larger political entity*. Its campus is an extension of the city streets. Its central mall is the university's Hyde Park. The city's ordinances set the standards of taste, or the permissible. The important fact about the student is that he is a citizen. He has a right to attend the university (clearly, if it is a state institution). The rights of all members of the university are most clearly spelled out in the U.S. Constitution. The rules that govern a student are those that operate with a citizen in court. The university is essentially a town meeting with each citizen having one vote.

2. *The university is divided into three power blocks*. These are: the administration (including the board of trustees), the faculty, and the students. The essential processes are those of power confrontations, of collective bargaining, and temporary coalitions.

3. *The university is an instrument of direct, social action.* It establishes goals, identifies issues, and marshals its resource for their solution. University policy must be evaluated according to the directness of its impact on the significant problems of the day. The buildings and the influence of the institution must be available for the programs of social activity selected by the members of the academic community.

4. *The university is an extension of the family.* Even as chestnuts go, this is an old one, but I mention it here because it has some novel touches these days. For one thing, the very groups that reject most vigorously the idea that the university is *loco parentis* show a continuing ambivalence about this. This is even true, for example, of the A.C.L.U. statement and the A.A.U.P. statements on academic freedom and civil liberties of students in colleges and universities. Even those students who oppose the doctrine most vehemently when they are focusing on its protective and restrictive aspects sometimes reveal an almost touching need for us to stand as parents, and thus as fit objects for a still uncompleted rebellion.

Another new feature is that the motivation of parents differs from what it was several generations ago, at least for some of them. In former days, parents were convinced that their well-reared and disciplined children would be destroyed by the freedom at the university. Now I believe that some of the most insistent parents are asking the university to assert more control because they are dissatisfied with the effects their own freedom and lack of standards have had on their offspring. There is an urgency about their concern that can be explained only as a desire that we do what has not been done, in contrast to the fear of former days—the fear that we would undo what had been done.

None of these four conceptions of the university is adequate. If any one of them were to be given a dominant role in our definition, serious harm could be done to our academic institutions.

This leads me inevitably to a very dangerous point. If I reject these, what view of a university would I propose that would permit a ready derivation about what a university should do with its issues of conflict resolution, student participation, and the social role of the university?

A UNIFYING CONCEPT

The nature of a university has been stated so often and often so beautifully that it takes a special audacity to attempt another, especially to members of the academic community. Yet I think we will all concede that each of the memorable statements has emphasized only a part of the complex institution we call a college or university. In spite, then, of the awe-inspiring precedents, I will submit some propositions that seem to me to have special relevance to the issues I have been discussing. They are offered to stimulate the academic community to decide what indeed it is and to tempt the members of those communities to consider their commitments to each other. Above all, my fondest dream would be realized if my attempt would dignify the topic. I think we must all concede that academic discussions on this matter in recent years have not been elevating and ennobling; often they have not even been possible. Although many of us are dissatisfied with descriptions of what a university is, our dissatisfaction has not necessarily spurred us on to define what it should be. And that is what I am arguing we must do.

But no more of this temporizing. What conception is it that I would advance? I would like to urge upon you the advantages of considering the university (or college) as a center of learning.

The university is a center of learning. The emphasis is on the activity. Faculty and students are partners in the process of learning. The two groups differ in sophistication, in the stage of development as it were. The difference is analogous to the difference between master and apprentice. Indeed this permits us to recognize the journeyman, the graduate student who partakes of the characteristics of teacher and learner.

In this conception, the teacher, the faculty member is the expert, not only in the content of his discipline, but also in the conditions of learning. It is he who is expected to select the content, the approach, the experiences that are designed to make most efficient the students' efforts to acquire the mastery of content and the acquisition of the necessary skills. Moreover, the faculty member sets standards, he motivates, he evaluates. In these roles he and his students are not equal partners, but they are partners in learning nonetheless. The student is an expert in his view of the learning situation. He is an expert on what he thinks, and what he thinks is often very relevant to how well and what he learns. This emphasis on cooperation in learning suggests that the classroom instruction has as yet unexploited potentials. Much more remains to be done to emphasize the common commitment of teacher and student to learning, and the need for joint efforts to create the optimum conditions for learning. There is no need to wait, for example, for the end of the year to get student opinion of courses. Indeed if they were obtained early and often, many useful changes could be made during the term, or if they could not be made, the reasons for that could be explained and understood.

The university as a center of learning gives, I believe, a different perspective to student participation in its government. Student participation is encouraged wherever it can improve the quality of the solution— in general terms, wherever it can assist to improve the learning environment. It is also justified when participation contributes significantly to student learning. I said "significantly" because we ought to be hard-headed about this. Most decisions in the academic community cannot be evaluated quickly, often not within an individual student's career at the institution. So it cannot be claimed that the student will learn a great deal this way. I pass over the values to be gained by working with peers, not because they are not real or useful, but because they are terribly inefficiently acquired. We have not typically made it our objective to train students in extracurricular affairs, for example, to be efficient managers, to delegate clearly, to communicate clearly, and so on. We could, but we do not; the learning potential in these situations is certainly not realized. Until they are, we can hardly defend student participation on these grounds.

What does "center of learning" say about the relationship to society? Several derivations are possible. The university is not an instrument of direct social action. Its task is to prepare men and women for intelligent and responsible social activity through sharpening their skills of data acquisition, analysis, and evaluation. If social experience is useful for learning, it is encouraged, under guidance and supervision as part of the learning task—not in response to collective guilt or impatience. When, as in the training of teachers and social workers, direct experience is necessary and useful to the process of learning, there is always an intellectual framework in which the action takes place; it is informed. Ideally, the skills that are used in these experiences are not the general skills of any human being (the student is not another body, as in the picket line) but skills of a student. The situations call upon him to acquire or develop proficiency in some tasks that are relevant to his role as a student. I recognize that direct experience with social and political problems is often a strong motivator, just as seeing a patient is a strong motivator to a freshman medical student. But there the contact is controlled; it is guided by the content, the attitudes, and the ethics of the profession. So too with our undergraduates.

There is a sobering thought here. Some of the motivation for direct action arises from the belief in the minds of some of our best students that their educational experiences are not related to the real problems—in themselves and in their society—that they feel most deeply about. I believe there is some validity in that indictment. And the most unfortunate consequence is that the students who believe this most fervently take an essentially nonintellectual and sometimes even an anti-intellectual approach to the problems they are concerned about. They feel free to discuss the most profound issues without doing their homework. They can discuss freedom and responsibility without having read Mill, or Milton, or Russell, for example.

The techniques of social change they adopt are not educational, but rather are those of social power. Their techniques of influence tend to become those of coercion and demagoguery rather than education and reason. I believe we have failed to invent learning situations in which these strong and honest motives are engaged in the pursuit of learning and skills that will make the person more effective in his efforts to solve the problems. We can be pleased with the motives and the concern; but I think we have been too indulgent with the lack of intellectual discipline that has characterized the expression of these interests. However, we have not provided disciplined alternatives in our learning situations. We had better start.

What about values and manners? The academic community ideally shares a reverence for the individual, a belief in his great worth and a moral commitment to maximize the likelihood that each member will realize his potential. We join in the protection of the institution from those outside, as well as inside, who would make it less attractive as a place to learn, or who would limit its effectiveness as a place of learning. The community embraces and exalts the reasoned, the examined life. It encourages the life of the mind, not because it rejects emotion and concern but because it knows that only disciplined concern is truly effective.

Recent events on many campuses compel me to expand a little on the emphasis in the community of learning on human dignity and the primacy of reasoned discussion. In the vignettes with which I began, the atmosphere is often poisoned by a basic disrespect for one's fellows, a disregard for their feelings, a disparagement of their motives. There are enormous costs in these scenes, and the bills are still coming in. It will not be possible to persuade able people to deal with students who have adopted these attitudes and these behavior patterns. But, of course, the greatest indictment is that they are out of keeping with the posture of mutual faith and respect that is necessary to learning. No one learns anything except bad habits in a hardened atmosphere.

Even if there were no hostility, there are other objections to these scenes, from an intellectual, educational standpoint. Shouting, name-calling, appeals to power, threats—these are not the techniques of the community of learning. Discussion, data collection and evaluation, reason—these are the ways of arriving at just and wise decision and of resolving conflict.

It is not only the campus community that stands to profit from a vigorous, disciplined discussion of the proper nature of the university. Let me mention, finally, one important part of the educational family that will benefit particularly. I refer to the governing boards, those most important buffers and interpreters. I believe the confusion within the community, to which I referred at the outset, has troubled these groups particularly, has made them less certain about their tasks as defenders and interpreters, has made them less ready to inhibit their natural and normal tendencies to intervene and administer. I am not an old hand at the care and feeding of boards, but I have had some opportunity to observe several of our able administrators who have had long experience in working closely with such boards. These are men with a long history of successful relations with their boards, and they report that in the last two or three years they have encountered increasing friction and disagreement with their boards. Most of this has arisen as a result of the kinds of problems I have been discussing.

That our board members and trustees should be concerned with matters of manners, taste, and style is no surprise. But they have become increasingly concerned about our ability to order our lives, dismayed at our lapses from the techniques of discussion and debate that we have told them is our mode of life. Most of all, however, they have come to be confused at our uncertain posture with respect to the university as a social instrument. If we support, or appear to support, the use of the university as an agent in the interest of student-selected or student-faculty-selected goals, then they begin to speculate about our claim to immunity and freedom from control. If the university is to be an agent, then its control is important, and they cannot be expected to be indifferent to the question of who is to be its principal. They are increasingly discontented with their passive role in the selection of social and economic goals, and with their time-honored role of protecting academic freedom.

Let me suggest but one way in which boards might be aided by being reminded that educational institutions are centers of learning. It seems to me that there is an emphasis here that the undergraduate is not the complete person, that for him to learn involves risks and the least risk is for him to fail a particular assignment. It means that penalties are evaluated in terms of helping the individual to learn rather than as punishments that re-establish the pride of the alumni in the power of the president.

We have come a long way from the time when our collective judgment was that students were apathetic and indifferent to the crucial problems of our time. None of us thinks that even now we have the amount of concern and involvement that is desirable. None of us is in the least reluctant to defend the interest and involvement of our students in these problems, or the presence on our campuses of student organizations led by students intent upon action by students. But it is ironic that our efforts to defend this territory are being handicapped by those whose commitment is not to academic values. This small group can be well contained by a reaffirmation of our central commitment to a center of learning.

This containment can be accomplished, I have suggested, by a reaffirmation of our values and our commitments. Perhaps more than clarity, we need the courage to assert for all to hear that universities are communities of learners; that they are devoted to the rational approach to problems, committed to preparation with participation encouraged primarily when it contributes to learning in a disciplined way; that their patterns of personal relations are based on mutual respect; their goals are the development of individual potential.

If we do this well, we will be able to help develop in our students a disciplined awareness of man's significant problems and his aspirations, and thereby increase, rather than decrease, the number of students who seek to give added meaning to their student life.

PART TWO

The Academic Man

The Future
of Teaching

WILLIAM ARROWSMITH

During the Roman Saturnalia even slaves were permitted to speak freely, even about slavery. I am here to speak, I suppose, for the classroom teacher, and I claim, *o decani praesidesque*, the ancient privilege of immunity for saying almost exactly what I think. I expect to be discounted as either innocent or impertinent, but that hardly matters. "So long as a man is trying to tell the truth," wrote John Jay Chapman, "his remarks will contain a margin which others will regard as mystifying and irritating exaggeration. It is this very margin of controversy that does the work. No explosion follows a lie."[1]

Let me say immediately that I am concerned here with only one kind of teaching, and I am eager to talk about it because it is the kind of teaching with which apparently too few administrators in higher education are concerned. I mean the ancient, crucial, high art of teaching, the kind of teaching which alone can claim to be called educational, an essential element in all noble human culture, and hence a task of infinitely more importance than research scholarship. With the teacher as transmitter or conductor of knowledge, as servant or partner of research, I have no concern. He is useful and necessary and, because he does the bulk of university teaching, it is important that his job be effectively performed and intelligently evaluated. But so long as the teacher is viewed as merely a diffuser of knowledge or a higher popularizer, his position will necessarily be a modest and even menial one. And precisely this, I think, is the prevalent view of the teacher's function, the view overwhelmingly assumed even among those who want to redress the balance in favor of the teacher. Is it any wonder then that the teacher enjoys no honor? For if the teacher stands to the scholar as

[1] Chapman, *Practical Agitation.*

57

the pianist to the composer, there can be no question of parity; teaching of this kind is necessary but secondary. So too is the comparatively subtler and more difficult kind of teaching that is concerned with scholarly methodology and the crucial "skeletal" skills of creative research. Only when large demands are made of the teacher, when we ask him to assume a primary role as educator in his own right, will it be possible to restore dignity to teaching. Teaching, I repeat, is not honored among us either because its function is grossly misconceived or its cultural value not understood. The reason is the overwhelming positivism of our technocratic society and the arrogance of scholarship. Behind the disregard for the teacher lies the transparent sickness of the humanities in the university and in American life generally. Indeed, nothing more vividly illustrates the myopia of academic humanism than its failure to realize that the fate of any true culture is revealed in the value it sets upon the teacher and the way it defines him. *"The advancement of learning at the expense of man,"* writes Nietzsche, "is the most pernicious thing in the world. The stunted man is a backward step for humanity; he casts his *shadow* over all time to come. It debases conviction, the natural purpose of the particular field of learning; learning itself is finally destroyed. It is advanced, true, but its effect on life is nil or immoral." [2]

What matters then is the kind of context that we can create for teaching and the largeness of the demands made upon the teacher. Certainly he will have no function or honor worthy of the name until we are prepared to make the purpose of education what it always was—the molding of men rather than the production of knowledge. It is my hope that education in this sense will not be driven from the university by the knowledge technicians. But this higher form of teaching does not die merely because the university will not practice it. Its future is always assured since human beings and human culture cannot do without it. And if the university does not educate, others will. Education will pass, as it is passing now, to the artist, to the intellectual, to the gurus of the mass media, the charismatic charlatans and sages, and the whole immense range of secular and religious street-corner fakes and saints. The context counts. Socrates took to the streets, but so does every demagogue or fraud. By virtue of its traditions and pretensions the university is, I believe, a not inappropriate place for education to occur. But we will not transform the university milieu nor create teachers by the meretricious device of offering prizes or bribes or "teaching sabbaticals" or building a favorable "image." At present the universities are as uncongenial to teaching as the Mojave Desert to a clutch of Druid priests. If

[2] Nietzsche, *Wir Philologen.*

you want to restore a Druid priesthood, you cannot do it by offering prizes for Druid-of-the-year. If you want Druids, you must grow forests. There is no other way of setting about it.

I am suggesting what will doubtless seem paradox or treason: There is no *necessary* link between scholarship and education, or between research and culture, and in actual practice scholarship is no longer a significant educational force. Scholars, to be sure, are unprecedentedly powerful, but their power is professional and technocratic; as educators they have been eagerly disqualifying themselves for more than a century, and their disqualification is now nearly total. The scholar has disowned the student—that is, the student who is not a potential scholar—and the student has reasonably retaliated by abandoning the scholar. This, I believe, is the only natural reading of what I take to be a momentous event: the secession of the student from the institutions of higher learning on the grounds that they no longer educate and are therefore, in his word, irrelevant. By making education the slave of scholarship, the university has renounced its responsibility to human culture and its old, proud claim to possess, as educator and molder of men, an *ecumenical* function. It has disowned in short what teaching has always meant; a care and concern for the future of man, a Platonic love of the species, not for what it is, but what it might be. It is a momentous refusal. I do not exaggerate. When the President of Cornell seriously proposes that the university should abandon liberal education so that specialization can begin with matriculation, and when he advocates this in order to *reconcile* the conflicting claims of research and teaching,[3] it should be obvious even to the skeptical that education is being strangled in its citadel, and strangled furthermore on behalf of the crassest technocracy. I find it difficult to imagine the rationalization of these salaried wardens of a great, ecumenical tradition, who apparently view themselves and the institutions they administer as mere servants of national and professional interests. A hundred years ago Nietzsche denounced the subservience of German universities to an inhuman scholarly technology and the interest of the Reich: "The entire system of higher education has lost what matters most: the end as well as the means to the end. That education, that *Bildung* is itself an end—and not the state—this has been forgotten. Educators are needed who have themselves been educated, not the learned louts whom the universities today offer our youth. Educators are lacking . . . hence the decline of German culture."[4] And what has happened in Germany is now an American story.

We too lack educators, by which I mean Socratic *teachers*, visible

[3] James A. Perkins, *The University in Transition* (Princeton, N.J.: Princeton University Press, 1966), pp. 43–45.
[4] Nietzsche, "What the Germans Lack," *Twilight of the Idols*.

embodiments of the realized humanity of our aspirations, intelligence, skill, scholarship; men ripened or ripening into realization, as Socrates at the close of the *Symposium* comes to be, and therefore embodies, personally guarantees, his own definition of love. Our universities and our society need this compelling embodiment, this exemplification of what we are all presumably at, as they have never needed it before. It is *men* we need, not programs. It is possible for a student to go from kindergarten to graduate school without ever encountering a *man*—a man who might for the first time give him the only profound motivation for learning, the hope of becoming a better man. Learning matters, of course; but it is the means, not the end, and the end must always be either radiantly visible, or profoundly implied, in the means. It is only in the teacher that the end is apparent; he can humanize because he possesses the human skills which give him the power to humanize others. If that power is not felt, nothing of any educational value can occur. The humanities stand or fall according to the human worth of the man who professes them. If undergraduates ever met teachers of this kind, then the inhuman professionalism of the graduate schools might have some plausibility; there would be an educational base. But nothing can be expected of a system in which men who have not themselves been educated presume to educate others. Our entire educational enterprise is in fact founded upon the wholly false premise that *at some prior stage* the essential educational work has been done. The whole structure is built on rotten foundations, and the routines of education have begun to threaten and destroy what they were intended to save. There is a very real sense, for instance, in which scholarship has become pernicious to literature; the humanities as presently taught are destructive of the past and therefore of the present.

I repeat: The teacher is both the end and the sanction of the education he gives. This is why it is completely reasonable that a student should expect a classicist to live classically. The man who teaches Shakespeare or Homer runs the supreme risk. This is surely as it should be. Charisma in a teacher is not a mystery or nimbus of personality, but radiant exemplification to which the student contributes a correspondingly radiant hunger for becoming. What is classic and past instructs us in our potential size, offers the greatest human scale against which to measure ourselves. The teacher, like his text, is thus the mediator between past and present, present and future, and he matters because there is no human mediator but him. He is the student's only evidence outside the text that a great humanity exists: upon his impersonation both his text and his student's human fate depend. For student and teacher alike, ripeness is all. The age of the student does not matter.

Men, not programs; *galvanizers,* not conductors. When students say that their education is irrelevant, they mean above all the absence of this man. Without him the whole enterprise is ashes, sheer phoniness. This is why students are so quick, and so right, to suspect a fatal hypocrisy in the teacher who lives without the slighest relation to what he knows, whose texts are wholly divorced from his life, from human life. What students want is not necessarily what they need; but in this case it is the students who are right and the universities that are wrong. The irony of the situation is enough to make strong men weep. Here, unmistakably, we have students concerned to ask the crucial questions —identity, meaning, right and wrong, the good life—and they get in response not bread but a stone. Here we have a generation blessedly capable of moral outrage, and it is the bitterest of anomalies that the humanities should be dying among students capable of moral outrage in a morally outrageous world. Almost without exception the response of the universities to this profound hunger for education, for compelling examples of human courage and compassionate intelligence, has been mean, parochial, uncomprehending, or cold. Above all, *cold.* The waste in sheer human incentive, in disappointment in matters where disappointment is destructive and fatal, is appalling. But what fills one with rage is the callousness of scholars, the incredible lack of human concern among humanists, the monumental indifference of the learned to human misery and need. Why, you ask, is teaching held in contempt? Because it has become contemptible by indifference. Teaching has been fatally trivialized by scholarship which has become trivial. What, I find myself wondering, would education be like if humanists and teachers had the courage of their traditions and dared to face their students as men in whom their studies and texts found worthy, or at least attempted, embodiment?

Such embodiment may be personal, rational, and contemplative, or activist and public. What matters is the integration of significant life and knowledge, of compassionate study and informed conduct. The teacher in this sense goes where the action is, where his example is most needed. Moreover, it is by going there that he can hope to recover the great, complex power of the text whose custodian he is. The point is important. We must at any cost find room in our universities for those who are capable of *living or acting upon a pure text.* Lacking such men, the student distrusts the teacher and the culture he represents; the culture is defeated in the teacher's failure. I am not suggesting that teachers must be heroes or great men, but they must understand greatness and desire it for themselves and others. Only so can they speak to the student's hunger for the same greatness. It is important, however, that our sense of human greatness find *varied* incarnation. One thing a student needs to know is how men cope with the vast, im-

personal chaos of modern existence. For most of us this is a matter
of daily improvisation. We no longer have the ability to cope together,
with a collective style based upon a common set of values, pagan, say,
or Christian; it is rather an individualistic *sauve qui peut*, requiring
educated hunchwork, luck, imagination, skill, and the habit of hope.
This present generation has experienced drastic change, and it therefore
has a drastic need for significant styles of coping, present and past
and as varied as possible. What is wanted is a repertory of convincing,
visible, and powerful life styles. And this the university should, as alma
mater, be able and happy to provide. It takes all kinds of men to make
a university—not scholars only.

For the scholar's example is no longer adequate to educate, though
at its best it may belong among the higher styles. His comparative
security, his cosy enclave of learning with its narrow departmental
limits, and his murderous preference for a single mode of the mind
(the discursive or methodological; do not call it "rational") with its
neat problems and solutions, his stunted humanity, all this strikes the
student as irrelevant and even repugnant. What he wants is models of
committed integrity, as whole as they can be in a time of fragmented
men. Admittedly such models are hard to find, and integrated men are
not to be expected. Hence it is essential that a student be confronted
with as many different, vivid modes as we can muster; from these he
may be able to infer the great, crucial idea of all true education—the
single, many-sided transformation of himself, the man he wants to be.
These men are hard to find because nobody is concerned to find them.
And meanwhile our universities are making them rarer.

One point should be made. When I say that scholarship no longer
educates, I am not thereby joining what Professor Bell calls the
"apocalyptic" faction against the exponents of order and reason. But I
also believe that the true stature of reason is no longer visible in technical scholarship, and that the academic sense of order is inadequate
because it is not related to the real chaos of existence. Finally it is
order and not instinctual anarchy that we want, and when I speak of a
style of life, I mean by style *controlled* passion, not the free play of
instinct. It is because reason and order have been so diminished in the
university that we require a repertory of models before we set about
constructing a curriculum. The days of the syllabus are gone forever;
we are not yet ready for a viable curriculum. General education has
failed, not because of its curricular inadequacy (though it *is* inadequate), but because men of general intelligence are not available to
teach it. It has ended up therefore in the hands of specialists who
always betrayed it in practice. If I had a campus to play with, my first
step would be to plant there, at any price, the six or seven charismatic

teachers of my acquaintance; their collective *aretē* would, I am convinced, create a curriculum that would truly, explosively, educate. But it is these men we must have, regardless of their academic pedigrees —prophets, poets, apocalyptics, scientists, scholars, intellectuals, men who sprawl across departmental boundaries, who will not toe the line, individuals as large as life, irrepressible, troublesome and—exemplary. Either we must make scholarship whole and ripe and human again, or we must import into the university every conceivable variety of active, shaping, seminal humanity we can find.

At present the latter course is probably the more practicable. By usurping the whole job of education and by claiming to represent the whole mind or the only part of the mind that matters, scholarship has had the effect of destroying what education, generously defined, might provide—the basis of a common culture. We have provided men with skills they cannot meaningfully use, and by so doing we have alienated the laymen of any coherent future culture. R. P. Blackmur comes pat to my point:

What we have, with respect to the old forms of our culture, is the disappearance of the man who, by his education, his tradition, and his own responsive life, was the layman to all the forms of his society. The mind no longer feels omniform or that it knows its own interest. We have a society of priests or experts who are strangely alien to the great mass movements which they presumably express or control.[5]

In the profession of the teacher lies one of the few correctives to the alienation that technical scholarship has conferred upon us, since, like the artist, only the teacher offers cultural skills in living and loving use.

But teaching will not easily recover its great, lost function. The forces arrayed—I will not say *against* teaching, but *for* research—are formidable indeed, composing a gigantic scholarly cartel. At its base is the department, the matrix of university power, protected from above by the graduate deans and administrators, who are more and more drawn from the research professoriat and therefore share its aims and ambitions. National structure is provided by the great foundations and the learned societies which form the American Council of Learned Societies. And now there is the new National Endowment for the Humanities, whose depressingly conventional initial programs (*inter alia* a grant for papyrological studies and historical bibliography) look as though they might have been designed by an unprogramed computer in collaboration with a retired professor of Coptic. Even the Woodrow Wilson Foundation, designed "to attract men and women to the profession of college teaching," now seems to be tailoring its standards more

---

[5] Blackmur, *The Lion and the Honeycomb* (New York: Harcourt, Brace & World, 1955), p. 189.

and more to the pinched professionalism of the graduate schools. There is also the Cartter report;[6] intended to assess the quality of graduate programs on the basis of informed opinion, it will almost inevitably have the effect of stifling innovation, if only because informed scholarly opinion is unadventurous and tyrannous as well as profoundly snobbish. My argument is this: At every level the forces making for scholarly conformity are immense, and the rewards of conformity high. If these forces are not directly hostile to teaching, they are certainly profoundly indifferent.

My point is not merely negative. If there is to be reform within the existing institutional framework, it must be radical. Teaching will not be restored by tinkering with the curriculum, by minor structural changes, or modest innovations in graduate degree programs. I offer the following observations as instances only; to my mind they represent the kind of profound structural reform that must precede real change. I believe they are practicable, but I offer them nonetheless with considerable pessimism, in the doubt that there is presently enough energy and leadership in the American university for it to be reformed from within.

ADMINISTRATION AND INNOVATION

Innovation, experiment, reform—these are crucial, and the pity is that, apart from a few noteworthy experiments, there is so little real innovation. Wherever one looks, there is the same vacuum of leadership, the same failure of nerve. For this I believe administrators must shoulder the blame, or most of it. It is idle to expect anything from the faculties, who are caught both in the hideous jungle of academic bureaucracy and their own professional lethargy. Nor can one look to the providential intervention of the foundations; they can perhaps fund imagination and courage, but they cannot, apparently, provide it. It is above all to local institutions—the colleges, the universities—that one must turn. They are funded by communities—states, alumni, student fees—and they therefore have a responsibility to the community that supports them, but above all to that general culture that I have identified with the ideal role of the teacher. But if community and faculty support is to be enlisted (and community tyranny to be avoided), there must be something more than mere management by administrators; there must be leadership, which means a sense of the whole endeavor. Chairmen of departments and deans have constituencies to represent; only the presidents and provosts can speak on behalf of the whole enterprise.

[6] Allan M. Cartter, *An Assessment of Quality in Graduate Education* (Washington: American Council on Education, 1966).

I believe that administrators fail to make anything like full, or imaginative, use of their power. As an ex-chairman I understand that administrators are not omnipotent, that hypocrisy and evasion go with the job. But I am not prepared to believe that presidents are powerless; too many instances of abuse of power convince me to the contrary. It is the margin of freedom that matters, and it is only with the failure of administrators to use this margin that I find fault. What is stunning is the universal torpor, the apparent dedication to the principle of *laisser aller*. If presidents are too harassed to provide leadership, what has happened to the provosts? Why are the deans so subservient to the departments, so supinely deferential to the research professoriat? Why don't administrators take the stump on behalf of their policies? There is, I suspect, only one answer, and it is not powerlessness, but lack of policies and ideas, and a long habit of prostration before success. A man cannot stump for programs he doesn't have, and this is why so many administrators talk such dreary rubbish. They have, quite literally, nothing to say. Alternatively, they are the prisoners of their origins, the professorial from which they emerge and whose assumptions and aims they share. Hence they conceive of their task as the encouragement of the *status quo* and, when confronted with the crisis of education, claim, like Clark Kerr, that chaos is positively good for us, or, like President Perkins, that we can reconcile teaching and scholarship by the simple device of abandoning liberal education.

THE COLLEGES

I can think of no more conspicuous failure of leadership than in the liberal arts colleges. With a few notable exceptions, the record of the college is one of failure, at least if judged by its own claims. Whatever else it may be, Socratic it is not, in faculty, in style, in results. This I take to be a matter of fact. Certainly it is hard to imagine a more damningly documented indictment of the liberal arts college than that of the Jacob study, with its bleak conclusion that, apart from three or four colleges, the effect of college teaching on student values is simply nil, zero, and that what small change occurs comes from the student subculture.[7] The conclusion is the more devastating because it is precisely on the claim to *teach* that the American college stakes its case. Here—in low student-teacher ratios, in college plans, tutorials, etc.—it has spent its money and ingenuity, and it is here that its failure has been spectacular. Why?

In my opinion, the colleges have failed as teaching institutions because they have been subverted from within. They have recruited their

---

[7] Philip E. Jacob, *Changing Values in College: An Exploratory Study of the Impact of College Teaching* (New York: Harper & Row, 1958).

faculties heavily from the major graduate institutions, and these recruits have inevitably altered the tone and finally the function of the colleges. There has doubtless been pressure from the graduate schools, but for the most part the colleges have consented to the process. And they are now in the ludicrous position of proudly claiming, on the one hand, that seventy-odd percent of their graduates go on to graduate or professional schools, and, on the other, of complaining that they are being turned into prep schools for graduate study. Gentility and snobbery have played a large part in this subversion, as well as the hunger for academic respectability which is now firmly linked to the business of research. Instead of cleaving to the Socratic pretensions and traditions, the colleges have tended instead to become petty universities, differing from the universities only in a slightly higher regard for the teacher and a corresponding tolerance of the student. If the wealthier colleges have managed to recruit able faculty, the poor colleges have fared badly, recruiting second- and third-rate Ph.D.'s, who for their part regard the college as an academic boondocks and lust for the day when they can return to the urban Edens of research. In the meantime they teach the only thing they know—technical expertise —and thereby both corrupt their students and refuse their Socratic opportunities. The colleges, in short, have yoked themselves to Pharaoh's chariot and, if they regret their loss of function, they have only themselves to blame. A handful of small colleges have dared to break the bond of snobbery and respectability that binds the college to the university, and they have done so simply by daring to profess the values they assert and finding teachers who profess them too.

Organizational energy and intelligence are crucial if the liberal arts college is to escape subordination to graduate education. I am, of course, in violent disagreement with those who believe that "the selective liberal arts colleges of the future . . . must become first-rate preparatory colleges for graduate education."[8] If we believe that the liberal traditions of the colleges are viable and that the college may have a higher function than feeding professional schools, then we must set about saving it. If I am right, the trouble with the colleges is that they recruit their faculties from uncongenial sources; the well is poisoned. By imitating the universities, the colleges have everything to lose and nothing to gain; neither their funds nor their human resources are adequate to the competition. My solution is dramatically simple. Let the colleges go into business on their own, *against* the graduate universities; let them form their own league as it were and train the kind of man they cannot expect to recruit from the universities. I am aware that such federations are in the air,

[8] Allan M. Cartter, "University Teaching and Excellence," p. 157 of the present volume.

and perhaps already exist; but I am emphatically not suggesting federation on the principle of beating the graduate schools at their own game. It should be a different game altogether, designed to produce men who do not think it beneath their dignity to educate others; men in whom the general civilized intelligence survives; humanists with a concern for men; scholars convinced that the world needs humane knowledge as never before. Ideally, I think, it would seek to involve its students in the real world, and it would surely seek real association with the vocations and professions. But its primary purpose would be to produce truly educated graduates as well as teachers to whom it could reasonably entrust the crucial task of providing models for those who wanted to become civilized men instead of scholars. I also believe that a formidable but generous enterprise helps to summon large behavior into being, and that the immense task of building institutions worthy of his love and learning might do much to create the kind of man who is missing. Enterprises which require humanity are the first prerequisite for a greater humanity. Men must use themselves significantly in order to grow. That is the law of all education, all growth. Why not apply it to education? We need new or renewed institutions; in the act of renewing them, we may renew ourselves.

Such institutions would surely not lack for students. Those who desire to study further but have no wish to be processed as professors are, I am convinced, far more numerous than is commonly suspected. The country is rich; leisure is available; educational expectations are rising. Far too many graduates of our colleges and universities feel, moreover, that they never got an education, and it is these who go on to graduate school in the hope of getting what they failed to get as undergraduates. It is graduate *education* they want, not graduate *training*.[9] This is why dissatisfaction with the graduate schools is so keen. There is simply no option available on the graduate level; everything is geared to professional training. And among those disenchanted with graduate school are precisely those from whom the colleges should in fact be recruiting their faculties—those students who are not averse to learning but who demand that it be given relevance and embodiment. It seems a cruel shame that such talent should go to waste or find no meaningful fulfillment at a time when it is so terribly needed. We are not so rich in the *higher* human resources that this source can be so tragically wasted.

Are there enough men to staff more than three or four such experimental "graduate" centers in the liberal arts? Probably not. But what matters is that there should be at least a handful of colleges in this country which dare to resist the conformity imposed by the research

[9] I am indebted for the distinction between "graduate education" and "graduate training" to Arthur M. Harkins; see "A Student's View of Academic Sociologists," *Kansas Journal of Sociology*, I, No. 1, 15.

cartel and to distinguish themselves by putting the teacher—and therefore the humanities—squarely at the center of the curriculum. Two or
three such places would, I am convinced, reinvigorate, perhaps even
revolutionize, American education simply by providing convincing examples of the daring and diversity we need. The logical place for them
to be established is either upon the existing base of the better liberal
arts colleges, or as a new "higher college" created by a group of colleges
acting in concert. Only by some such device, by striking at the source
of the trouble, can the traditional role of the college be protected and
expanded. It would be a staggering loss if the only institution of higher
education still committed to liberal education should be subverted by
the demand for professionals and technicians.

THE UNIVERSITIES

Teaching is notoriously worse off in the universities than in the colleges. Not only is the university traditionally more committed to pure
research, but it is particularly vulnerable to the pressures that have
eroded the teacher's status. Vast numbers of students, huge classes, intense competition for Federal funds and therefore for distinguished
research professors, political and professional pressures, all these have
operated to downgrade and even discredit teaching. But even in the
university it is the creative use of the margin of freedom that matters.
Something has been done, for instance, to give the multiversity a human
scale, through honors programs, emphasis on individual work, residential colleges, and so on. But helpful as these reforms are, they have not
succeeded in changing the imbalance. And this, I believe, is because
none of the reforms really touches the nub of the problem. And that is
the structure of the university itself, the way in which its physical organization determines its policies and precludes change and reform.
Certainly no real change in the status of teaching can possibly occur
without a radical change in the present power structure of the university.

Perhaps this is impossible, but I am not convinced that this is so.
At present the heart of university power is the department. It is this
departmental power that now so vehemently promotes research and is
hostile or indifferent to teaching. It is at the departmental level that the
evaluation of teaching is subverted, since chairmen apparently equate
research and teaching; it is there that publish-or-perish policies are
really promulgated; that the pressure for reduced teaching loads derives;
from there that graduate deans are recruited; that the demand for early
specialization arises, as well as the jealous specialism that fragments the
curriculum into warring factions. Put a mild and gentle man of broad

learning into a department chairmanship, and within two years he will either be murdered by his colleagues or become an aggressive and vindictive *mafioso* of the crassest specialism. The process can no more be resisted than the ravages of time. It is inexorable and destructive; and it is the remorseless tragedy of university politics.

This is why it is so imperative that some rival to it, some countervailing, antidepartmental force be created. Research is dominant now because teaching has no effective representation, no normalized political place or power, within the structure of the university. The departments are theoretically composed of teachers, or teacher-scholars, but actually they have been wholly captured by the research professoriat. The scholar has everything—the departments, the powerful committees, the learned societies, the Federal funds, the deanships, and the presidencies —and if he chooses to say that he finds teaching distasteful and unworthy of his abilities, who will say him nay? Who speaks for teaching here? Clearly nobody, except perhaps the students. If teaching is to survive within the modern university on terms of something like parity with research, it must somehow acquire institutional power. The teacher, like the scholar, must have a base, a position, a budget, students, an honored and normalized function. He cannot meaningfully exist in any other way. This, I am convinced, is simple political realism.

The obvious vehicle for such a countervailing force would be the so-called university professorship. For though this professorship is still an uncertain novelty, occupying a still undefined institutional position, it has usually come into existence because enterprising administrators felt the need for countering the effects of extreme departmental specialism. Thus, while the university professor may retain a departmental base, his appointment is a *university* one insofar as it cuts across departmental and even college lines. This "horizontal" professor has, of course, aroused the jealousies of departments, and they have frequently responded by cutting off the new professor's access to students. What is now needed, I believe, is a deliberate effort to expand and consolidate the university professorship with the hope of eventually creating a new professoriat of such power that it can challenge the supremacy of the research departments. I have no illusion that this will be an easy task, but the precedent exists and the principle has been established. It would seem folly not to follow it up. Clearly the problems of defining the relations of two such professoriats to each other and to the administration and students would be of exceptional and maddening difficulty, but I doubt they are insoluble. So far as function is concerned, it would seem natural to assign to the university professorship all those tasks at which the departments have proved themselves incompetent—the courses in general education, humanities, interdisciplinary programs, supervision of the teacher-oriented degree programs, and the like, and perhaps even the formal responsibility for evaluating teaching throughout the university. But its over-all concern would be with teaching, and with the training of teachers. It would therefore, I hope, display that broad spectrum of high and varied human skills that can significantly claim to be called *educational*, every conceivable great style of human existence and mode of mind side by side, the prophetic, the rational, the political, the scientific, the apocalyptic, the artistic. There would, of course, be an honored place in it for scholars too, but only for scholars whose scholarship educates. I suspect this proposal will strike most of my audience as fantastic, but so, when you think about it, is the present state of affairs: a vast educational enterprise built entirely upon a caste of learned men whose learning has no relevance to the young and even seems to alienate the young from both education and culture. It is a vision of madness accomplished.

PLURALISM

My argument would not be complete without a word about pluralism. Educators never tire of saying that ours is a pluralistic system and that pluralism is good since it accords with the nature of American society. I share this view, but my fear is that, where higher education is concerned, we are rapidly junking pluralism for monolithic uniformity. One can understand why this is happening, but it seems to me the process must now be resolutely opposed. If education is to become, as perhaps it must in part, an instrument of national policy, then we must have also institutions that still perform an ecumenical function, that speak for man rather than for the state or the nation. Professional training at the graduate level is now corrupting all higher education by ruthlessly expelling from the curriculum everything that does not conform to professional utility. By so doing, it is forcing the student—who may want to be more than merely a professor—into the streets and out of the culture. The student becomes marginal simply out of opposition to the elite which has expelled him. Alternatively, he responds by violent and often unintelligent assertions of those very values, especially freedom, which the university seems to have abandoned. His attempts at heroism thus become merely anarchic; he loses the skills of educated heroism, even while claiming to assert them. What we must have, unless we are prepared to abandon our fates to parochial technicians is precisely the pluralism to which we are committed. We need options, choices, alternatives; we need to honor the diversity of human skills and needs. We simply cannot afford, except at the cost of everything, to permit the range of realization to be narrowed to one small mode of the mind, and that a mode which seems to be incapable of compassion for any other mode, which seems, in fact, to have lost respect for humanity.

One final point. I expect to be told that I am actually meeting the problem of research and teaching not by reconciling them but by divorcing them altogether. That is my intention, and one which I am prepared to risk, since the only likely alternative is to make teaching the lackey of scholarship. I think we have reached the point at which slogans like "scholar-teacher" merely darken counsel; there may have been a time when that was a viable ideal, and doubtless some exceptionally gifted men still incarnate it. But by and large its vogue passes on to the professor the two functions which the university has inherited and which it cannot meaningfully reconcile. The realities of educational practice make it starkly apparent that no reconciliation can now occur except at the expense of teaching. And I am not prepared to incur that expense if I can humanly help it. This is why I urge you to consider freshly the wisdom of separating teaching and research, with the thought that significant teaching and fresh energy in academic institutions may eventually make scholarship human again, and that an invigorated scholarship may once again accept the burden of teaching as the source of its vigor and the test of its wisdom.

The Soundness of
The American Ph.D. Program

R. J. HENLE, S.J.

A LTHOUGH I am no longer a graduate dean, I still find myself believing that the basic pattern of the American Ph.D. is educationally and philosophically sound and is the best terminal education yet devised by any educational system. The strength of this program is, it seems to me, that it produces master knowers in a given discipline and that these master knowers arc so produced that, to greater or lesser extent, they are also creative masters of their own discipline.

"Mastery" as used here does not mean simply a knowledge that is "complete" with reference to any discipline, in the sense that it is materially complete, or embraces the whole range of fact, theory, law, and so forth within the discipline. By "mastery" and "creative mastery" is meant, rather, a kind of understanding and a kind of knowledge that puts a man in control of his discipline. In the above, I have not defined the basic strength of the doctorate program as lying in its preparation of persons to do research. By and large, it does so prepare people, but not because it is a professional research training program but because it produces people who have this kind of grasp of their discipline. This knowledge necessarily puts a person in a position to do research, for a true understanding and a thorough grasp of any law or theory in a discipline requires that a man have the same stance toward it as did its discoverer or its creator. To understand a theory fully, one must approach it through its origins and its evidences, must understand how it was constructed and on what base; and the processes are primarily identical with the intellectual activities of those who created and developed the theory.

PREPARATION FOR TEACHING AND FOR RESEARCH

By recognizing this basic purpose and effect for the doctorate program, we avoid the apparent dichotomy between preparing teachers

72

and preparing researchers. For quality education, a man must have the kind of grasp of his discipline just described, and this turns out to be exactly the kind of mastery of a discipline that he must have in order to carry on research in that discipline. Thus the doctorate program, as far as knowledge of the discipline goes, includes both preparation for quality university and college teaching and preparation for professional research within that discipline.

This reason, as well as others, permits arguments against any attempt to set up a different type of program for the preparation of college teachers. Granted that the doctorate program, as it is carried on in a number of our institutions, lacks some elements needed to prepare adequate college teachers; yet the *total* Ph.D. program is necessary to satisfy the knowledge demanded for the highest quality of university and college teaching. In my opinion, we should not consider some kind of special terminal degree—whether it be a doctorate or a special master's degree—for those who are going to teach in colleges and universities; we should continue to insist that it be a full doctorate.

Having said all this, however, I still feel that certain problems connected with the preparation of college teachers and with the operation of our graduate schools and their doctorate programs militate against the production of quality teachers.

Some of these problems have their origin in the meaning of the word "research." We have used this term to cover such a wide range of activities and such different sorts of activities that one must make distinctions under the general term if we are to talk reasonably about specifics. Not everything that goes by the name "research" constitutes the kind of training or the kind of activity that ought to be part of the doctoral program. I fear that many of the things now being done, particularly in some of the sciences in our graduate schools, are not really research in the sense that they give a man that creative and masterful grasp of his discipline, but only in the general sense that they involve solving a problem or adding to the sum total of knowledge or something of this sort. I suggest that we ought to make a careful study of the kinds of research that are being accepted as doctoral training in our graduate schools. This problem becomes all the more delicate and sensitive inasmuch as so much programed research now involves graduate students as research assistants, and it is out of this programed research that they are expected to get their theses and dissertations. This places a limitation on the educator who might not wish to have his student do a piece of programed research that is aimed at the solution of a special technical problem. Probably the cause here can never be completely won, but we must carry on a constant battle to ensure that the kind of research we require our graduate students to do is related to a creative and masterful grasp of the field.

There are two other basic difficulties with our current graduate school education. First of all, it is becoming increasingly difficult to maintain a program that gives the student a genuinely *reflective* grasp of his discipline; and, second, it is increasingly difficult to plan a combination of undergraduate general education and graduate education that enables the Ph.D.-holder to maintain a reflective understanding of his discipline within a perspective of modern culture and society.

With regard to the first point: The reflective grasp of a discipline alluded to requires that a person be able to step outside the discipline, look at it, and consider it reflectively and meditatively. There is an increasing hustle and bustle about our doctorate programs. In the science departments, there is the pressure to make reports, get out abstracts, publish articles, keep expensive instrumentation in action, and so on. The whole maturing process of genuine understanding of a discipline requires some quiet time, some time to mull and consider and meditate, some time to back away from the immediate problem, to take a large view. I fear that this kind of reflective consideration, of mulling and reflective discussion, has been reduced to an absolute minimum in many of our graduate departments.

The reduction is emphasized by the constant pressure to complete doctorate programs. Perhaps we ought *not* to try to speed up everybody to some kind of a minimal number of years. A slower process toward the doctorate may produce, at a critical time in a person's life, a deepening and mellowing of his understanding. It is true that after obtaining a quick doctorate a man may develop this further reflective dimension, but, as I see the world of scholarship and learning, it will likely be an unusual man who will do so. It is much easier for someone to do this when he is primarily concerned with his own intellectual growth: that is, prior to the completion of his doctorate.

The tendency to narrow the doctorate program to finer and finer areas of specialization and to push the disciplinary prerequisites down into the college can only increase the difficulty of giving the student a mature and broad grasp of the total culture of which his own discipline is only a limited and perhaps small part. He will certainly not understand modern culture if he does not understand the place of his discipline within it, and, further, if he cannot see his discipline in the broader perspectives of general culture, of philosophy, and of the ultimates of life, he will not even understand his own discipline. It has been said that a man who knows one language does not really know that: only if he learns a second language, so that he can approach his own language and see it as something in its own distinctive character, can he really come to appreciate it. The same thing is true of all disciplines.

The pressure to make the upper two years of the liberal arts college a preparation for graduate school has been growing. Although one of the functions of college education is to prepare students for graduate work, this has meant a pushing-down of general or liberal or broad education to the more immature freshman and sophomore levels of college. Hence, when a person has the very sophisticated and mature grasp of a single discipline, it becomes difficult to balance it against his own youthful and immature understanding of other disciplines and the totality of his culture.

These latter points really relate most strongly to the quality of collegiate education. I firmly believe that the college and university teacher should have the kind of knowledge of his discipline described above, but I am equally convinced that he must have a mature man's understanding—not a sophomore's view—of the rest of his culture, and this, many of the graduates of our Ph.D. programs lack.

THE VALUE OF THE TEACHING ASSISTANTSHIPS

Up to this point, I have been discussing the kind of knowledge that a college teacher needs, which is or is not supplied by the doctoral program. It seems self-evident that the primary requisite for good teaching is an understanding of the matter to be taught. On the other hand, I agree with the educationists who say that a thorough knowledge of one's subject is not adequate to ensure good teaching. In order to be a good teacher, one needs, in addition, certain natural gifts or abilities, which we do not know exactly how to produce. But even given these, there are a body of professional knowledge and certain professional skills that are not inherent in simply mastering a field and that a good teacher ought to acquire. I am not at all in favor of loading a doctoral program with a lot of courses in education, but I do think that the doctoral students ought to have carefully directed teaching experience and that a seminar in education might well be part of every doctoral program. Against this, some will allege that not everyone pursuing a doctoral program will teach, any more than everyone studying for the doctorate will engage in professional research. Just as I have argued that the research component of the doctorate program is essential simply to produce mastery of a field and therefore is essential to produce the good teacher, so I would argue that the kind of teaching experience I am talking about is necessary, or at least most beneficial, for a person who will engage simply in a life of research and scholarship. Communication of all kinds is, in some sense, identical with the process of teaching, and all scholars, all research people have lesser or greater need for communication, for the ability to express and discuss. Consequently, it seems to me that a carefully guided teaching experience ought to be an essential dimension of any doctoral program. This will slow up the program a bit, but, as I have already indicated, I am not too worried about a reasonable slow-up in the actual conferral of the doctoral degree.

This brings us to a point of the quality of education that results from using graduate students in undergraduate courses. It is almost impossible to make a universal judgment with regard to this. It is my opinion that, for the most part, a program of teaching for graduate students can be not only most beneficial to the graduate students themselves but also most effective in undergraduate teaching if it is properly organized and developed. The students must be admitted to this teaching only after they have done some advanced work in their field or at least have displayed a fairly good grasp in depth and understanding of their discipline. Preferably, therefore, the students should not teach undergraduates until after they have had at least one year of graduate study and graduate experience. They should be formally prepared for their teaching; they should be carefully supervised and directed. As they go along, depending on their competence and their achievement, they should be given more and more responsibility and freedom in the development of their teaching. Further, their program should be so arranged that they have adequate time to do a good job of preparing for teaching and adequate time to work with the students.

Some of the very best college teachers can, I think, be found in the group of advanced graduate students. They are at a time when their own intellectual life is being created and developed. They have a learning stance of their own. The basis of their discipline has not become tedious. Covering the field has not become routine. They are closer in years and interest to the undergraduate students. Very often they bring, therefore, an understanding and a sympathy and an enthusiasm to the undergraduate classroom that veteran scholars find hard to muster. Consequently, I think a combination of fully formed, mature scholars and younger scholars in their final formative stages is ideal for a college and university faculty, and I would regret seeing graduate students barred from undergraduate teaching. Of course, I am fully aware of the hard realities of life, and I know that, in many departments and in many graduate schools, the teaching experience is accepted as a necessary evil. Supervision is not given. Encouragement is not given. And recognition is not given. But it should be an exciting and inspiring part of both the undergraduate's experience and the graduate student's experience.

Who Teaches
The Teachers?

W. MAX WISE

THE CASE FOR CONSIDERING the preparation of college teachers was aptly put in a report of a conference held in 1949: "The American college teacher is the only high level professional man in the American scene who enters upon a career with neither the prerequisite trial of competence nor experience in the use of the tools of his profession."[1] This judgment, rendered in a summary of several days' deliberation on the topic, seems almost as pertinent today as it was seventeen years ago. Despite lively discussions of the responsibilities of graduate schools to help induct novices into the teaching profession and some evidence of increased interest in the problem on the part of employing colleges, in most institutions this interest is expressed vaguely and support is inadequately staffed and financed. Only a few institutions have, as yet, instituted programs to provide relevant experience to the embryonic college teacher.

Individual professors in the graduate schools often express interest in helping Ph.D. candidates obtain useful teaching experience but, with a few exceptions to which I shall refer later, the graduate schools have paid this matter little consistent attention. When they have been stimulated to do so by financing from outside sources, the interest has been short-lived and most of the innovations developed have disappeared after the outside financing terminated.

Discussions attempting to delineate reasonable responsibilities of the graduate schools for preparing their students for careers in college teaching have often been vague and polemical. Some members of graduate faculties argue that graduate schools have no responsibility in preparing for classroom teaching and that any attention given the problem distracts the graduate schools from their principal purpose—the preparation of the scholar. In like manner, proponents of the view that the

[1] Theodore C. Blegen and Russell M. Cooper (eds.), *The Preparation of Teachers* (Washington: American Council on Education, 1950), p. 123.

graduate schools do have a responsibility have also in the main been vague and polemical in their suggestions. Even while urging a reformulation of the purposes of graduate education, they have generally failed to focus sharply on specific actions that would improve the preparation of Ph.D. candidates for college teaching.

Several surveys of the interest and activities in the graduate schools in preparing college teachers sustain the observation that, although there is considerable concern in this matter, most graduate schools give it only incidental attention. A recent survey of graduate schools disclosed that fewer than half of the respondents reported any substantial programs.[2] Furthermore, there is no evidence of the quality of the programs that have been initiated.

Undergraduate colleges, too, have been slow to recognize their responsibilities in the initiation of the new faculty member into his professional duties. However, a few institutions have recently designed programs to provide the new teacher with help and advice from senior faculty.

A careful delineation of purposes and aims for graduate school and college programs is missing. Obviously, the American graduate school is indispensable to the improvement of American undergraduate teaching. It serves no useful function for undergraduate colleges to allege that graduate schools have diverted their students from careers in college teaching; nor is there empirical evidence to support this allegation. At the same time, it serves no useful function for graduate faculties to raise the objection that any attention to the preparation of college teachers will seriously dilute their scholarship. To do so is to misstate the possible effects of limited programs to prepare the prospective college teacher more adequately for his professional responsibilities.

RESPONSIBILITIES FOR INDUCTION

What is needed is a rational discussion of responsible ways in which graduate schools and employing colleges can agree to share the responsibility for inducting the new college teacher into the profession. In developing adequate programs, the following questions about professional needs should be taken into account:

1. Assuming that college teaching is largely an exercise in individual, if not idiosyncratic, professional behavior, does the typical graduate program of studies help the new teacher discover and develop a style of teaching that is likely to stimulate undergraduate students?

In most programs of study the graduate student develops very limited

[2] Survey by Peter Armacost and Diane Howland of the Association of American Colleges, "Preparing the College Professor for Liberal Arts Teaching" (Mimeographed).

perspectives of teaching. His experience consists largely of attending lectures and participating in seminars, but little chance to bring about stimulating classroom discussion. He has almost no contact with the use of teaching aids of any kind.

Having uncritically assimilated limited perspectives of teaching, the typical young teacher is prepared to spend his professional life replicating these experiences. Typically, the prospective college teacher has little or no opportunity to identify and develop a teaching style suited to his strengths and interests: he must discover and develop his style without help from either colleagues or students. He views with suspicion proposals which depart from these accustomed forms of teaching and ignores the overwhelming evidence of the inefficiency and waste that are apparent to even the casual observer. Much of what goes on in the classroom might be more effective without the teacher.

2. Does a typical program of graduate studies provide sufficient perspective for the prospective college teacher to deal with the individual differences among the students he will face, and does it provide an initial basis for understanding the range of motivations he will encounter in the students with whom he will work?

It seems clear that the typical prospective college teacher has little grasp of the variety of responses of students to undergraduate teaching. Furthermore, he has little awareness of the uses that may be made of different forms of teaching in order to establish a relationship with varieties of students, and he has little foundation for adapting both the level of content and the sequence of its presentation in order to facilitate learning in the classroom.

3. Does the content of Ph.D. study in a discipline provide a sufficient basis for the prospective teacher to select subject matter appropriate to the courses he will teach, and does it prepare him for the intelligent exercise of his responsibilities as a member of a college faculty which must make decisions about both purposes and procedures in the college?

Many faculty, especially young ones, appear to lack a clear and firm basis for the exercise of judgment about the priorities that are important to liberal education. They lack sufficient perspective to make judgments about inclusion of subject matter and about sequences that are appropriate to the purposes of liberal education.

There is, therefore, no deep mystery involved in the current educational malaise that prevails in many colleges, nor is it any wonder that crucial decisions about courses and curricula are often based on interests unconnected with the chief purposes of the colleges—preprofessional preparation of students and the special interests of faculty in narrow fields of study.

4. Does a typical pattern of preparation for college teaching—the Ph.D.—prepare prospective college teachers for the full and responsible exercise of freedom and initiative that is a distinguishing trait of the best college teachers?

Perhaps in no regard are new college teachers more deficient than in their lack of insight into the nature of the college teaching profession. They lack even the rudimentary concepts of the ethics of the profession and appear to lack workable hypotheses about the balance of freedom and responsibility which ought to be characteristic of their field of endeavor. Their understanding of the nature of academic freedom is extremely limited, and they are often unprepared to establish satisfactory professional relationships with their faculty colleagues, with the administrators of the colleges, and, perhaps most of all, with the students they teach. They have no adequate perception of the variety of American colleges and the diverse purposes they serve. Their first professional position is often, therefore, accepted without a clear recognition of the obligations to which they should be committing themselves in the particular college in which they accept a position.

Even this partial list of the deficiencies, apparent among most prospective college teachers, suggests the extent of the failure of the graduate schools and the colleges. It is up to the graduate school to take the first and very important steps to remedy these deficiencies. The employing colleges will have to assume a good deal of the burden for extending the initial work of the graduate schools.

THE TEACHING ASSISTANT: INTERN OR SERF?

A look at the present practices of the graduate schools in light of a tentative list of needs, such as that outlined above, drives one to the conclusion that the graduate schools have substantially failed their responsibilities. The chief means they use to help train new college teachers—the teaching assistantships (two-thirds of Ph.D. candidates hold these)—has generally also become a means for staffing undergraduate classrooms in universities that cannot find experienced teachers for this function. The primary purpose of the teaching assistantship is not, therefore, the induction of the new teacher into the profession but something quite different. It is little wonder, then, as Berelson noted some years ago,[3] that recent recipients of the Ph.D. judged their experience as teaching assistants to be the least helpful segment of their graduate study.

During the past two and a half years I have visited more than thirty-five graduate schools in the United States and have had opportunities

[3] Bernard Berelson, *Graduate Education in the United States* (New York: McGraw-Hill Book Co., 1960), p. 206.

to talk informally with teaching assistants in many of these institutions. I must report that, with a handful of exceptions, the morale of these teaching assistants is low. They believe they are being exploited by their institutions in order to meet the press of expanding undergraduate enrollments. They report that they get little help from senior faculty members on the teaching problems they encounter. They seldom report that they are treated as young colleagues by members of the regular faculty; instead, more frequently they report feeling that they are treated as individuals of low status employed to do work that no one else wishes to do. There are, of course, important exceptions to these observations, which I shall discuss below.

In general, teaching assistants are appointed by departments; however, little or no attention is given to the quality of the person appointed or the conditions under which he will work by the person responsible for undergraduate teaching—the dean of the college. While it is common practice to make one member of the department faculty responsible for supervising all assistants in a course, supervision may encompass as many as a hundred assistants or only one. The extent of supervision ranges from casual initial meetings with them to outline the general structure of the course, to highly productive and continuing relationships between the department faculty and the assistants.

The universities, in their need to staff elementary courses, have thoroughly abused and prostituted the chief means of training prospective college teachers—the teaching assistantship.

Berelson reports that Ph.D. candidates spend a considerably greater proportion of their time in teacher training (that is, as teaching assistants) than do prospective secondary school teachers. Thus, the question is not really whether time spent in helping induct new teachers would distract from serious scholarship, but rather what kind of carefully delineated, limited experience would give the most help to the prospective college teacher.

Universities tend to view the teaching assistantship as a form of financial aid to the Ph.D. candidate who cannot otherwise finance his study program. In fields where there are sizable amounts of other forms of financial aid—research contracts, and the like—the teaching assistantships are given to graduate students judged to be of somewhat lower quality than those selected to hold research assistantships. This is particularly true in the sciences where the teaching assistants are usually assigned the onorous duty of supervision of laboratory work.

In some universities teaching assistants are virtually required to hold such appointments over a two- or three-year period without regard to whether extended experience is likely to promote the development of a good college teacher. The institution's main aim in such instances obviously is to satisfy its need to staff freshman and sophomore courses. In only a few universities have I found any attention paid to the development of sequential experiences for the teaching assistant in which during the first year he undertakes minor responsibilities in close collaboration with a senior professor and during a second or third year assumes more substantial responsibilities either for the same course or for more advanced courses.

The point here is that the university officers who carry general responsibility for the quality of undergraduate teaching are almost never directly involved either in the selection of the teaching assistants or in the development of useful and productive activities to help them improve their teaching ability. That is, the presidents and the deans of undergraduate colleges in the universities often have little or no contact with the teaching assistant programs. In many institutions I have visited, these officers have been unable even to say how many students hold teaching assistantships. They seldom speak knowledgeably of the processes of selection or supervision. Only recently—and as a result of considerable student reaction and public interest—have many of these general university officers begun to address themselves to this important aspect of their institutions.

Yet in a few universities I have visited quite the opposite conditions prevail. In these universities teaching assistants have high morale, they feel they have adequate opportunity to confer with senior faculty as problems arise in their classrooms, they feel that their senior colleagues look upon them as important junior partners, they are assigned adequate space to carry out their preparation for courses and to confer with individual students, and, above all, they feel that most members of the regular departmental staff are interested in them as initiates into the teaching profession.

TUTELAGE FOR NEW TEACHERS

In a few universities carefully developed plans for the preparation of prospective college teachers have been developed. Such plans usually assure the student financial aid over a four- or five-year period during which he will combine study for the Ph.D. with a substantial amount of teaching. In most cases the Ph.D. candidate engages in part-time teaching over a period of two years. During his first year of teaching responsibility he works under the close supervision of a senior faculty member but has an opportunity to lecture and to lead class discussions with help and supervision from his senior colleague. In the second year he assumes more responsibility for a course. Having been assured of financial support for the entire period of the Ph.D. program, he is able to give attention to the first teaching experience without the distraction of financial worry. In the best of these programs several members of the departmental faculties work closely with the teaching assistants and display an obvious interest in helping them develop their teaching abilities.

But the developments I have described above are confined to very few of our universities, and they require extraordinary leadership from the deans of the graduate schools and the deans of the undergraduate colleges, as well as the president.

It would be naïve to believe that all or even most of the members of our graduate faculties in the major universities are willing to undertake any sizable commitment of time and energy to help induct young people into the profession. Yet I believe that a substantial number of professors in the graduate faculties do feel an obligation to the teaching profession. Berelson reports that among his respondents on graduate faculties 40 percent would increase the attention paid to the training of college teachers but an additional 41 percent felt that the present emphasis was sufficient. Only 6 percent of his respondents would reduce the amount of attention given to the training of teachers.[4] Thus, the usual characterization that graduate faculties are filled with individuals who are antagonistic to helping induct young people in the college teaching profession appears a gross exaggeration.

But if graduate faculty members who are disposed to accept this responsibility are to be effectively mustered in the enterprise, the general university officers must exert leadership that has obviously been lacking in most of the universities I have visited. Unless they use their influence and their financial resources to support and increase the interest of the graduate faculties in this matter, little achievement can be expected.

In summary:

All too often, . . . policy concerning the use of teaching assistants is dominated, not by a philosophy of education, but by considerations extraneous to educational objectives. Specifically, there seems often to be a tacit conspiracy between the Graduate Dean and the central administrative officers at the expense of the true interests of the students, both undergraduate and graduate. Graduate Deans and Graduate Faculties are, too often, more concerned with recruiting and supporting graduate students, than with training them in the art of teaching. In this they are frequently abetted by some of the departments. Likewise, the central administrative officers, who are often trying to do more than they can do well with available resources, are more than occasionally attracted by the budgetary advantages of using teaching assistants to staff some of the larger courses. They, too, are often abetted by the departments.[5]

[4] Berelson, *Graduate Education in the United States*, p. 206.
[5] John Perry Miller, "The Teaching Assistantship: Chore or Challenge?" *Ventures Magazine* of the Yale Graduate School, Fall 1964.

During the past few years the Danforth Foundation has awarded grants to five universities which proposed to effect substantial modifications in the system of teaching assistantships. In each instance the universities proposed to convert the assistantships into more appropriate initial experiences for prospective college teachers. Although it is too early to make substantial comments on the effects of these programs (three have just begun and the other two have been in operation only a short time), initial reports indicate developments thus far.

The History Department of Washington University, St. Louis, has developed a four-year Ph.D. program with the following elements:

1. Toward the close of the first year of graduate study students visit discussion sections of history courses taught by members of the department. These brief visits are followed by discussions of problems in teaching that have been raised by the visits. In the summer following the first year of study, the students prepare for teaching assignments by spending full time in reading. Toward the close of the summer they meet with members of the history faculty in a two-day conference on teaching and graduate preparation.

2. During their second and third years the graduate students teach under supervision in two history courses. In addition to accepting considerable responsibility for the discussion sections of these courses, the graduate students lecture two to four times a year. In one course they also supervise honors theses and, in addition, assist in preparing the examinations offered in the courses.

3. All members of the History Department faculty participate in supervising the work of the teaching assistants.

In an interim report on the program, the faculty of the Department of History reported that "The pilot program, which combines training in teaching, training in research and writing, acceleration, and a rational plan of financing graduate study, has proved to be realistically conceived and deserves to be continued." The program places primary reliance upon student observation of classes, consultation with instructors, and summer reading in preparation for teaching assignments as the principal methods of training prospective college teachers.

Under a grant made to the Graduate School of Yale University several departments have initiated new forms of teaching assistantships. In describing the program, the dean said:

The new Yale program of teaching interns, which becomes effective in several departments this fall, is based upon four propositions. First, the faculty has a responsibility to initiate the more promising graduate students into the art of teaching. Second, this is best done by providing graduate students with limited supervised teaching experience under the guidance of experienced faculty. Third, this experience must be viewed as an opportunity open to those of proven intellectual competence and teaching promise, rather than as a chore necessary for financial support. Fourth, there should be available to the student who wishes it the wisdom of those who are wrestling with issues of higher education as teachers, researchers, and administrators.[6]

In a brief and interim discussion of the first year's experience it appeared obvious that the grant has stimulated more thoughtful consideration of the nature of the initial teaching experience appropriate to the Ph.D. candidate. In a science department the usual teaching assistantship—which involved supervision of laboratory sections—has been converted into a more substantial initial teaching experience with a responsibility for discussion sections of the course. In addition, faculty in other departments appeared to be accepting supervisory functions in more substantial ways than had previously prevailed.

Obviously, a university *can* radically alter the typical pattern of teaching assistantships. In general, the problems are not so much a matter of reformation of graduate education as they are of stimulating effective leadership by general university officers and departmental chairmen. If these administrative leaders wish to exercise initiative, they can usually find sufficient faculty who are willing to undertake new and more appropriate responsibilities.

A second type of experience available to the graduate student who aspires to become a college teacher interrupts his graduate study for a year or so during which he accepts an appointment as a full-time instructor at an undergraduate college. This practice is common in American higher education and, although graduate faculties usually oppose the break in residence, for many Ph.D. candidates it appears to be a necessary intermission in their intensive studies during which they recover their enthusiasm for completing the degree. A year or so as a full-time college teacher gives them a sense of productivity and accomplishment not always available in a full-time graduate program.

Although a careful study and assessment of the results of an interim period of full-time teaching is still lacking—so far as I know—my impression is that such initial teaching activities have a certain advantage over the typical graduate assistantships in universities.

In the first place, new teachers holding appointments are often looked upon as junior members of the college faculty, a status not customarily available to teaching assistants in the university. In the second place, the instructor is able to devote nearly full time to the problem of developing course materials and teaching skills. He is not required to balance teaching responsibilities against activities associated with his pursuit of the Ph.D. Thus he is free to deal with both the

[6] *Ibid.*

intellectual and the psychological problems that he encounters in a first teaching position.

Here again, however, the quality of help available to the novice is largely the result of fortuitous and unplanned associations with members of the college faculty. In only a few colleges are there serious and continuous discussions of the responsibilities of the institution to the new teacher who holds a brief appointment. Yet the possible rewards of this type of initial teaching experience appear very considerable: since the instructor on limited tenure is not subject to the pressures of graduate study or the political activities in which non-tenured members of a faculty are almost inevitably engaged, he is much more open to thorough discussions of his methods of teaching and of the ways of presenting course material. Therefore, at least in theory, a brief appointment holds great promise for a painstaking exploration of the problems of initial teaching. But if these possibilities are to be exploited, members of the college faculty must recognize, as few have to date, an obligation to the induction of new people into the teaching profession.

My impressions of the experience of Woodrow Wilson interns—post-master candidates who accept one-year teaching positions in colleges—is that the degree of help they receive from their institutions varies widely. Such variances are probably typical of the full range of appointments of this type.

Antioch College has recently developed a form of teaching internship that differs somewhat from the pattern outlined above.

Nine interns will serve one-year appointments as teachers, after which they will take positions in other colleges. Most of them have completed the Ph.D. and the others are in the final stages of their study programs. Senior faculty members supervise their teaching, and plans have been made for active discussions not only of the problems which the intern faces in his courses but also of the more general problems facing American faculties. Each intern will carry approximately a half-time teaching load.

Antioch was apprehensive about obtaining a sufficient number of high-quality applicants for the program, especially since the remuneration is below that of other teaching jobs for which they might qualify. In fact, a very substantial number did apply and their quality was judged to be high. This example suggests that more than a few new college teachers would welcome an opportunity to participate in an internship program of this type.

In an informal memorandum Antioch reported that:

We have recruited types of teachers who would qualify for beginning appointments at instructor or assistant professor level. We expect the terminal professional degree (M.F.A. in arts or Ph.D. in other fields), or doctorate except for dissertation, prior teaching experience, and exceptional promise for teaching.

We have appointed this year nine such associates, all of whom we regard as exceptionally well qualified. In some fields (foreign languages, biology, etc.) we found it most effective to pinpoint our search and explore a small population of prospects intensively. In most other fields (especially philosophy, music, art) the array of outstanding candidates was large, and we had to interview numerous persons for each position in order to choose fairly among the candidates with excellent papers.

Among the . . . candidates with strong interest in college teaching, our concept and plans evoked great enthusiasm.[7]

A third type of initial experience for new college teachers involves the help which some institutions provide to new appointees to regular positions on the faculty. Some colleges plan a brief orientation period for new faculty, but few provide any continuous supportive relationships calculated to help the new teacher with the difficult first experience in the classroom.

Fortunately, a few colleges have taken a more constructive view in this matter and provide a quasi-internship during which the new appointee carries less than full-time faculty responsibilities and works closely with one or more senior faculty colleagues.

In addition to the three general forms of initial teaching experience calculated to induct the novice into the college teaching field which have been outlined above, conferences and workshops for new college teachers have been conducted. Examples are those sponsored by the North Central Association of Colleges and Secondary Schools and by the Association for General and Liberal Education. Reports of these conferences and workshops do not thus far, it seems to me, present clear evidence of their effectiveness. It appears that a considerable advantage may accrue to the new teacher in the opportunities to associate with new teachers and also experienced teachers from other colleges. Whereas problems of evaluation of teaching and of personal and professional relationships often inhibit frank discussion of teaching within a single college, conferences and workshops may permit a freer atmosphere for professional intercourse.

We appear to be in a period of increased interest in and concern for the quality of undergraduate teaching in American colleges. Clearly, new and different approaches to the induction of new college teachers into their careers should be developed, but, equally clearly, considerable improvement in teaching could be effected if present practices were more thoughtfully developed and if a higher level of cooperation between the universities and the colleges were evolved.

---

[7] This report is based on a memorandum from Morris Keeton, vice-president for academic affairs, Antioch College.

GUIDELINES

Assuming that the teaching assistantship will continue to be widely used in the universities, more attention will have to be paid to the following matters:

1. If teaching assistantships are held for more than a single year, the assistants should progress from minor to heavier responsibilities as time proceeds. Thus an initial teaching assistantship should introduce the candidate slowly to the problems of college teaching: the initial experience should consist substantially of observation and limited responsibility for lecturing and leading discussions. If the assistant moves into a second year, he would then be prepared to assume considerably more responsibility.

2. Teaching assistants should, in the course of their experience, have an opportunity to participate directly in various forms of teaching. Their activities should not be confined to the supervision of laboratory work or the grading of papers, but should also include opportunities to lead discussions and to lecture.

3. Careful attention should be given to the proportion of the Ph.D. candidate's time that is consumed by his teaching responsibilities. Limitation of the assistant's obligations to teaching should be studied carefully in relation to his obligations to progress toward the degree. In several universities I have visited, it is obvious that candidates are seriously impeded in attaining the degree by the amount of teaching they are required to do as teaching assistants.

4. Unless the departmental faculty looks upon teaching assistants as junior colleagues and unless the university administration makes adequate provisions for work space and accords them a degree of status, most graduate assistants will assume that the position is directed more toward staffing introductory courses than to inducting them into a profession that is highly regarded by the faculty.

Clearly, American colleges must assume a fair proportion of the responsibility for inducting new teachers. In order to discharge their full responsibilities, colleges should:

1. Assign reduced teaching loads to new and relatively inexperienced faculty during the first term or year.

2. Give selected senior members of the faculty responsibility for working with new members of the faculty.

3. Arrange cooperatively with other colleges for seminars and workshops to be conducted by outstanding leaders. Reports of seminars such as those conducted by the Commission on Liberal Arts of the North Central Association should provide constructive suggestions for further developments of this kind.

Associations of universities, graduate schools, and colleges can, I believe, exert leadership to improve on the present programs of preparation of college teachers. I recommend that the Association of American
Colleges, the Association of American Universities, the Council of
Graduate Schools, and other interested associations, perhaps under the
leadership of the American Council on Education, act immediately to
initiate a series of activities to provide information and encouragement
to individual colleges and universities that wish to develop such
programs.

I should like to close on a theme mentioned early in this paper.
Little will be gained if discussions of the training of college teachers
are conducted in the polemic style that has marked—and marred—so
much of the discussion to date. There is clearly no requirement to
alter in any radical way the graduate schools or the attitudes of graduate
faculties. Much can be accomplished within the already-present major
commitments of the graduate schools. But general university officers
will have to provide much more thoughtful and continuous leadership
if programs are to be developed that will have any extensive usefulness.
Universities and colleges should develop cooperative plans for the
induction of new college teachers with careful delineation of responsibilities of each. Such plans *can* be developed without undue burdens
on either kind of institution and at great profit to American higher
education.

Commentaries on

Who Teaches the Teachers?

JOHN W. ATHERTON,
JAMES I. ARMSTRONG, JOHN E. KING

Expectations and Responsibilities
of the Employing Colleges

JOHN W. ATHERTON

THE QUESTIONS RAISED by Max Wise in "Who Teaches the Teachers?" are provocative. Probably we would all agree that just as curious man came last to the disturbing study of himself, so do college and university professors come last, if at all, to any discussion or study of their own teaching activities. The matter is too close to home. Who is to judge? Administrators? Students? Colleagues? On what grounds? For what nefarious purpose would any such study be used? How can something so elusive and so personal be measured, weighed, evaluated?

All of us know the objections, and yet we know too that somehow students and professors meet, and that something called teaching happens. How can we improve the effectiveness of this endeavor? This is our proper and pressing question. As the president of Pitzer College, the newest of the Claremont cluster, a college in process of building a new faculty in the behavioral sciences and humanities, a faculty whose primary responsibility will be undergraduate teaching, I should like to comment on two parts of Max Wise's paper: (1) What the undergraduate college may ask of the graduate school. And, (2) in more detail, what the college should be prepared to do itself in orientation or training on the job.

What do the colleges want from the graduate schools? I mean here colleges wherever they are—a solitary unit, in a cooperative group like Claremont or Santa Cruz, or as the undergraduate component of a large university. First, I suppose, we want that guarantee of mastery of subject marked by the doctorate. In this statement we have already made the assumption that some doctorates are better than others; that is, some schools give us men better qualified in the subject-matter

90

specialty than others do. The ratings, the reputations of the graduate schools are there, both published and by word of mouth, shifting somewhat from year to year as departments of anthropology, or chemistry, or English change, grow old, or are renovated. But competency in a specialty is relatively easy to measure, though, as we know, in very short supply.

Second, we would like our young doctoral expert to come to us having taught a class or two. We are happy if he has been a teaching assistant who has had a freshman section of English composition, or handled a laboratory section for old Professor X in biology, or read some papers for an advanced course in sociology. He has seen a student from a teacher's point of view, we hope, and has some dim notion of the problems that may arise when one tries to turn research expertise into communicable knowledge. This teacher characteristic we sometimes get from the graduate schools, but, as Max Wise knows, the chance of the new teacher having it is no better than fifty-fifty, and it is never there by design.

And finally, I think we would all like but, in my experience, *never* get a young man or woman who has in some way learned something about the history and variety of American and European educational institutions, their aims and problems, their organization and structure, their rights, privileges, and obligations. I never glimpsed this world in my graduate days at Chicago, and none of the young teachers coming to us have seen it either. Max Wise mentioned this glaring omission, and I should like to recommend it to the graduate schools as a part of every doctor's bag of tools.

Thus far, all that I have said we want is minimal, in theory obtainable, and thus can be a matter of record in placement office credentials. But beyond and above this training the colleges would like the graduate schools to send us humane and creative men and women, qualities that no accumulation of credits or training can ever guarantee.

We have our new faculty member. We have read folders, held interviews, visited graduate schools, sent department heads to meetings —we have competed with other always wealthier and better-equipped institutions who do not scruple to bribe our prize candidate by suggesting he have any teaching duties at all—we have our new young faculty member on the campus in September. Now what should *we* do?

We should, and I am sure most of us do, induct the new colleague into his full rights and privileges of faculty status. The history and purpose of the employing undergraduate college should be explained, the organization of the faculty, the responsibilities of a teacher and scholar made clear. Equally important, the new faculty members should be made aware of the admissions policies of the institution and the resultant abilities and backgrounds of the students he will teach. And, most important of all but, I am afraid, almost uniformly neglected, our new colleague should have help, advice, counsel designed to encourage him to develop his own best skills as a teacher.

Far too often our new faculty member learns political skills before teaching effectiveness: he learns committeemanship before the Socratic method; he learns that recognition and promotion come from grants and articles rather than classroom performance. And he responds according to the message he perceives, no matter what may be written in faculty manuals about the college's devotion to good teaching.

This then simply returns us to a problem. Let me finish by sketching a possible solution.

First of all we must, as a profession, begin to mean what we say when we claim that we care about good teaching. Our department heads, our appointment-promotions-tenure committees, our administrators—whoever it is who recommends promotions—must begin to reward good teaching as we now reward publication and grant collection. This means, second, that we must begin to learn something ourselves about what good teaching is, and to this end we must be prepared to start our own campus programs for discovering, fostering, and rewarding teaching.

I propose that the undergraduate college vindicate its claim that it values good teaching by deliberately supporting it with a program which will involve the faculties of all departments in ongoing analysis, discussion, and research in the art and science of teaching. Any such program must be ongoing, must not stop and start with the happenstance of grant funds or shifting interests of deans or department heads, because the teaching that a college does needs constant evaluation and rejuvenation to serve its central educational function. And such a program must involve analysis, discussion, and research.

We must start with what we have, with a curriculum made up of courses. This is the case material for analysis and discussion. We need to examine collectively what happens in Psychology 1–2 and French 67. What is included; what is left out? What read and what examined? What discussed in class, lectured about, or actively performed in a laboratory? Is the aim a body of systematic knowledge? a repeatable mental skill? a heightened awareness of beauty? How are the hoped-for results tested? We start with what we are already doing, examine it, and discuss it with one another.

Against some background of what is already happening in our classes, we may begin a few experiments that, potentially, have value beyond any one course. But unless the new techniques we try are evaluated and reported back to our collective and ongoing program, they will (as they too often do now) remain trade secrets or talismans of an esoteric art. Analyze, discuss, experiment, evaluate, all these our program should do.

I can hear objections at once. An administrative device to force conformity. A stifling of creativity. An invasion of professional privacy. A blow against academic freedom. Clearly there are dangers. And just as clearly such a program can be useful only if it proceeds in an atmosphere that promotes open and receptive discussion, rather than defensiveness and fear. Here the administrative framework of the program is vitally important.

Such a program, it should be noted, avoids the stale teaching-versus-research argument, familiar to all of us. Research funds and research time are both becoming more readily available. There seems little danger that "research" will be slighted. But teaching is the process by which research is transmitted, findings are reported, and methods are refined and tested. We need to pay some conscious attention now to the effectiveness of this transmission and how it may be improved and extended.

Who Teaches the Teachers What?

JAMES I. ARMSTRONG

LET ME REVEAL MY PREJUDICES at the start by extending the question which Max Wise asks in the title of his paper. It may be useful to inquire not simply "Who teaches the teacher?" but "Who teaches the teachers what?" A good many educators might respond quickly with the answer "How to teach": that is, the question really being asked is "Who teaches the teacher how to teach?" In such case, then, the colleges and the graduate schools need to think very carefully before they launch into programs designed to teach graduate students how to teach.

Indeed, it may no longer be a popular view, but I am disposed with John Perry Miller to think of teaching as an art, and as such I would hesitate to make too-ambitious claims about programs for teaching Ph.D. candidates how to teach. If we mean initiation, induction, guidance, advice, opportunity to develop one's own style, then the problems raised appear in a more reconciling light. I assume these aspects are what Max Wise has in mind, and his paper seems to be sensible, sound, and stimulating. My comments will, therefore, either amplify or modify his general thesis that more can and must be done to assist new college teachers to take up their professional responsibilities with as much satisfaction and as little waste as possible for teacher and student.

Concerning the role of the graduate school in the initiation of teachers, I read with relief two sentences of Max Wise's last paragraph:

"There is clearly no requirement to alter in any radical way the graduate schools or the attitudes of graduate faculties. Much can be accomplished within the already-present major commitments of the graduate schools." In my judgment what the colleges want most from the graduate schools is a person with a good command of his discipline—a high professional competence—and one with scholarly aspirations. By and large the graduate schools, as now constituted, award degrees to people of this kind.

Unquestionably, more attention can and should be given to the preparation of graduate students for teaching, but even here some of the shortcomings of the graduate schools may be exaggerated. I would not so readily derogate programs of graduate study as valuable pre-teaching experience. Lectures and seminars in the seventeenth and eighteenth years of formal education may prove exceedingly useful to a prospective teacher qua teaching. The student is often a sensitive observer of his teachers. Rather than assume that the typical young teacher will assimilate uncritically limited perspectives of teaching— whoever knew an uncritical student!—why not expect with Plato that the young teacher will develop his own style through nemesis or a creative imitation of his teachers. The future "good" teacher will be master of imitation; the lesser one will copy his teachers, transmitting imperfectly their style and prejudices, which is only to say that graduate students differ in ability, both actual and potential. The preparation and oral delivery of seminar papers can be a good instrument for guiding graduate students in effective presentation of material. But more important than the techniques of presentation is the intellectual engagement with other minds through the discourse (I might have said dialectic) of seminars, the sharpening of the mind to work handsomely within a methodology. There is no better preparation for teaching than a live grasp of one's subject and therewith an intense, contagious enthusiasm for it that will nourish communication and scholarly aspirations.

Under the section heading "Tutelage for New Teachers" Max Wise cites three types of experience available to the graduate student who aspires to become a college teacher. Two of these seem to me unexceptionable, but I have grave misgivings about the virtue of even limited recourse to the third alternative, which involves the interruption of graduate study for an appointment as a full-time instructor at an undergraduate college. My reservations derive from my observations both as a graduate dean and as president of a liberal arts college. I firmly believe that the advantages are more apparent than real, and I am not optimistic or even very sanguine about a graduate student's "recovery of his enthusiasm for completing his degree" by this method.

The teaching experience will be real; indeed, so demanding will be his teaching commitments that there will be room for little else (family, social life, student counseling) and no time for his dissertation. The intermission becomes a full-fledged departure—even a flight—from graduate school, and in some cases the dissertation becomes an evil spirit forever turning the sweet of teaching into a bitter of a limited future.

> Take but degree away, untune that string
> And, hark! What discord follows.

Instead of the advantages of colleague status, there arises a shadow of inferiority and a massive rationale explaining the failure to complete the degree. All sorts of unhappy consequences may then follow. Incidentally, the Antioch teaching interns cited by Wise are *expected* to have earned their terminal professional degree. On balance, it seems to me, the argument for teaching experience gained through an intermission from graduate study ought not to be pressed whenever the expectations lead toward the Ph.D. degree. The dissertation fellowship program of the Woodrow Wilson National Fellowship Foundation sponsors the preferable course: complete the Ph.D. degree; then seek a teaching appointment. Within the graduate school, the course of study and teaching assistantships that are wisely conceived and administered with an eye to teacher initiation appear to be a better response to the need.

Max Wise is right in observing that colleges and universities do not do enough to help induct the new teacher. They should do more. What and how much are quite open to exploration. Although the American college teacher is the only high-level professional who enters his career as an "amateur," this may be a function of our view that teaching is, in final analysis, a very individual, personal activity. Even the most rigorous social scientist, committed to measurement of results, will concede that evaluation of teaching can hardly be definitive.

Having said this, I am fully convinced that evaluation of teaching—what is effective and what is not—must be undertaken. How can it not be in a college whose primary mission is teaching? Not only will evaluation be a test of the effectiveness of the whole educational program, it will also be a criterion upon which decisions affecting the advancement and promotion of individual teachers will be made. All the more reason, then, to assist the novice in those areas of teaching where the senior teacher can point the way. We owe it to the novice to tell him something of *our* expectations.

Max Wise has suggested some of the ways in which colleges and universities might help the newly appointed instructor—orientation periods, quasi-internships with reduced teaching load, conferences. What I would like to add is the importance of taking full advantage of the *first year* of an instructor's appointment. During that year he is more open, more amenable to suggestion, for he feels less any sense of scrutiny in the early period of teaching when his novice status appears to justify the mistakes of inexperience which he fears he will make. The young teacher will not see the assistance offered as a veiled spy system calculated to assess him; rather he will be grateful for the guidance proffered. A senior professor may even legitimately and safely overcome the great taboo of the teaching profession and be welcomed into the classroom of his junior colleague.

Whatever solution or program be found, there is one inescapable consequence: The colleges and universities are going to have to face increased costs. The senior professor who is asked to give guidance to the new teacher will soon ask for some reduction in his student teaching load. Contrary to what I suppose to be the prevailing practice, a new teacher should be given a lighter teaching load during his first appointment. Moreover, an administrator's time will undoubtedly be involved. The inevitable costs are there. Foundations are not going to finance a general effort among colleges and universities to improve the induction of teachers into the profession. Once again, in the interests of education, the institutions themselves will have to find the operational funds. But find the funds we must and will where the cause is a good one, for there is the doctrine that educational institutions are infinitely tough and resourceful and not easily disappointed of their legitimate needs.

The Need for In-Service Programs

JOHN E. KING

THAT THE GREAT GRADUATE SCHOOLS of our country do not have programs geared to the preservice preparation of college teachers does not really bother me. What does disturb me is that so many of the able young graduate students emerging from these schools obviously have somehow become indoctrinated with the idea that undergraduate teaching is not as important or as rewarding as graduate teaching or research. I doubt that they had such patterns in their thinking before they entered the great graduate schools.

It really cannot be expected that a great graduate school can produce a person who will know how to teach in college. Even doctors, engineers, and lawyers probably have to learn how to be doctors and lawyers and engineers after they actually start in the profession. And they are produced in professional curricula which at least purport to prepare them to practice. It seems reasonable, however, to expect that graduate school administrators and graduate professors should be able to produce a climate in their institutions within which undergraduate teaching would not be compared invidiously with other kinds of work in which their doctoral students might eventually engage.

Those who administer undergraduate institutions have probably become timid about trying to develop in-service programs to help our new teachers. We have usually welcomed them, introduced them, made sure they have a faculty handbook, and pointed out that the entire resources of our institution are at their disposal. Then we explain that most of the orientation and breaking-in of new faculty by its very nature, actually takes place within the departmental situation. Possibly a better job was done in the years before Pearl Harbor when a president or dean might fire a beginning teacher for "poor teaching" as easily as he might chase a dog out of a building. There was a greater supply of beginning teachers then, and the president or dean had more fire power, literally and figuratively.

Now that we have come to admit that we are unsure of what "poor teaching" is, and now that the supply of beginning college teachers is so limited, and now that the president or dean may likely point out his lack of control of the situation in the first lecture to the new faculty members, we are going to have to be very ingenious in order to bring about improvements. Mr. Wise makes four suggestions about how graduate schools might improve the preservice preparation of college teachers. Each suggestion is constructive and unlikely to be considered by graduate deans as intended "to alter in any radical way the graduate schools or the attitudes of graduate faculties."

Another device that works well in some graduate schools consists of a seminar—with or without graduate credit—conducted by the graduate dean or someone else of stature that is open to all teaching assistants who are doctoral candidates. This seminar is usually one semester in length, with weekly meetings and a program of lectures developed around the role of the college teacher in the United States. The lectures are given by faculty members of the university and perhaps an invited outside person or two.[1]

Mr. Wise's three suggestions for in-service education of new college faculty members are also worth study and use. His first suggestion—to assign reduced teaching loads to beginning college teachers while they are learning the ropes during the first term or year—will probably be given serious consideration and then gravely discarded by most de-

[1] Robert H. Bruce, dean of the Graduate School, University of Wyoming, has been conducting such a seminar for fifteen years and can supply outlines of the program.

partment heads and deans who find it easier to assign a full load to a new faculty member before he becomes aware of the possibilities of not having a full teaching load.

Better times may be nearing. Among the graduate schools, even the great ones, and in undergraduate colleges the word is coming out not only that college teaching is rewarding, but also that deans, presidents, trustees, parents, taxpayers, and legislators are willing to do their best to reward good college teachers.

The training of college teachers is a good area for foundation activity. There should be seminars, conferences, special study groups, retreats, attacks, all kinds of opportunities for college teachers—beginning, four- to six-year, prime-of-life, and over-the-hill—to keep learning to teach. We can help them realize the importance of their roles in this day of the open-door college, the second-time around institutions, the junior colleges, the small private colleges, the state colleges, and of days of heavy pressure that we place on most of our young people to succeed in college.

Who Teaches the Older Teachers?:   Additional Views

To COMPLETE THIS DISCUSSION, the question "Who teaches the *older* teachers?" should at least be raised. The rapid growth of knowledge has necessitated the "retooling" of professors in small institutions. Keeping abreast of one's discipline has become increasingly difficult, particularly at colleges with small departments and limited library resources. Programs at university centers, summer institutes, and superior laboratory facilities available during the summer for teaching scholars will help in this endeavor. But the need is not alone to help rusty professors, although this may be fundamental to improving college teaching. Older teachers who have become rigid may refuse to accept new knowledge and techniques of teaching and learning. They must be given opportunities to explore innovations with other college teachers through seminars, summer institutes, and the like. Leave programs for faculty are usually geared to research of "something productive."

Opportunities for faculty to learn new teaching techniques as well as to re-examine their teaching style would provide opportunities for improving the knowledge about teaching. For if classroom teaching is to be improved without waiting for a complete new generation of teachers, an effort must be made to teach the older teachers.

The Professor
And His Roles

LOGAN WILSON

THE BASIC PATTERNS of behavior among professors in the campus milieu have undergone no great alteration, and many of the problems of the profession a quarter of a century ago are still with us today. In making this assertion, I do not maintain that there have been no significant changes. Indeed, there have been. Higher education is not only an enlarged activity today, but also a more important enterprise. A corollary of this is that teachers, scholars, and scientists are more important figures on the current scene.

I shall analyze salient characteristics of the present-day academician and the ways in which he and his roles have changed during the last two decades. Specifically, I shall be revisiting *The Academic Man*, which I authored in 1942.[1] Let me review briefly my frame of reference for considering the professor and his roles. I looked at the formal and the informal organization of the university in terms of a typological individual. Factors having to do with recruitment were considered, and the academic hierachy was viewed as it affects the student and apprentice, the staff member from the lowest to the highest rank, and the professor administrant—as I then chose to call him. My book deals with problems of academic status in successive chapters on status appraisal, professional status, and socioeconomic status. Shifting from the anatomy to the physiology of the profession, the third section of the book deals with academic processes and functions and attempts to show the interrelations of prestige and competition, and of prestige with regard to the teaching and research functions. The last part gives conclusions.

My original reasons for choosing major universities as a focus of inquiry were that (1) these "wield the most influence in setting the pattern of higher learning," and (2) "it is only such centers which yield the kind

[1] New York: Oxford University Press, 1942; reprinted, New York: Octagon Books, 1964.

of uniformity in which we are interested." With the growth in size and complexity of institutions of higher education in recent years, the pattern, of course, has become more prevalent, and I believe that the uniformities described are more commonplace.[2] In focusing on the influences brought to bear on the academician as a creature of his environment, perhaps I anticipated what was later called the "organization man" of corporate enterprise.

THE ACADEMIC HIERARCHY

Although my inquiry did not attempt to follow academicians from the cradle to the grave, I did look into all available information concerning the social origins and backgrounds of those who are drawn into college and university work. The findings revealed, as was to be expected, that intellectually superior individuals form the recruits. Because of the inherent nature of advanced teaching and research, I am sure that this will always be the case, but whether the academic profession has been able to hold its own in recruitment alongside law, medicine, engineering, not to mention business and industry, is another matter. Certainly, until the last few years of marked improvement its comparative bargaining position worsened during the intervening period, both because of low salaries and because of increased job opportunities for Ph.D.'s in non-academic endeavor.

The situation I described then—the overproduction of doctorates in some fields, the "slave markets" held at annual meetings of learned societies, the frantic individual quests for $1,800 instructorships—is today completely reversed. Prospective employers of all sorts now search out individuals possessing advanced degrees.[3] In short, even individuals with unexceptional records confront a seller's rather than a buyer's market for their talents, so that the problem of most graduate schools today is that of increasing their production rather than that of finding jobs for those who have been highly trained.

Another aspect of this changed market situation is that the fledgling academician is much less likely to begin his climb of the academic ladder on the bottom rung. If he already has his Ph.D. and has had any teaching experience at all, he is, in many institutions, likely to start his ascent with the rank of assistant professor. Furthermore, if his performance measures up to the average, he is less likely to remain as long in the

[2] More than half of all the students attending senior-grade institutions are now enrolled in these larger, more comprehensive universities. Also, the "university syndrome" is more conspicuous today than it was a quarter of a century ago.

[3] See the more recent studies by Theodore Caplow and R. J. McGee, *The Academic Marketplace* (Garden City, N.Y.: Doubleday & Co., 1958); Paul Lazarsfeld and Wagner Thielens, *The Academic Mind* (New York: Free Press, 1958); and David G. Brown, *Market for College Teachers* (Durham: University of North Carolina Press, 1965).

intermediate ranks before achieving a full professorship. Viewed institutionally, the effect in many places is that the occupational "pyramid" has given way to something resembling a square. This changed configuration indicates, both individually and institutionally, that higher ranks are being more freely assigned in order to pay higher salaries—particularly in the lesser institutions.

Although I have no comparative evidence, I suggest that a consequence of this easier vertical mobility is a lessening of tensions in the lower academic ranks, to which I made frequent reference in my 1942 commentary. Likewise, I would guess that gerontocracy in faculty government of university affairs is less prevalent today.[4]

As for university government, I think it has, in general, become a more discrete rather than a more diffuse process. Despite proclamations by faculty groups regarding the desirability of wider participation in basic concerns of administration (or governance), the increased size and complexity of university operations has necessarily resulted in a more intricate division of labor. As departments and divisions have multiplied horizontally, so has administration grown vertically. Structure has adapted itself to function: deans, associate and assistant deans, and other specialized officers of administration have assumed new assignments or are taking on responsibilities formerly spread among faculty individuals and committees.

In most institutions the faculty still has virtually complete jurisdiction over all matters pertaining to the curriculum, but even in this instance it has been suggested by the late Beardsley Ruml and others that teaching would be improved and teachers better paid if this authority were shared with others, including trustees. Faculty attitudes toward encroachments on their traditional spheres are, of course, hardly less hostile than they once were. Yet, it should be acknowledged that there is a certain ambivalence of sentiment in view of the reluctance of many teachers to be burdened with committee work and other tasks not having to do directly with teaching and research. One source of cleavage between faculty and staff is that many of the faculty look upon money spent for administration (beyond a bare minimum)—including "overhead allowances"—as money that otherwise would have gone into their own salaries.

All in all, I think it can be maintained paradoxically that the administration of universities and of many colleges is both more and less democratic than it once was. Even though the president continues to be the most important single officer in any institution, the man himself is much less commonly the father image, the authoritarian leader, and the king pin who formerly dominated the scene. Both he and the trustees are

---

[4] I suspect, however, that faculty politicians may be no less active in faculty governance.

likely to be too busy in promotional work and fund raising to engage in much overt interference with the faculty. Thus, by default, educational leadership in the strict sense of the term can be more readily assumed by members of the faculty than in bygone days. Now as then, unfortunately, the ablest teachers, scholars, and scientists are too often unwilling to take much time away from their specialized pursuits to devote to the problems of the institution—and of higher education—as a whole.[5]

ACADEMIC STATUS

As I reflect on my 1942 observations about the academic hierarchy, it seems to me that either I overemphasized its influence as a conditioner of behavior then, or else it has become less significant as a factor now. Also, it is possible, to be sure, that experiences that are sharply outlined for those directly involved may become blurred from a more distant and detached perspective. In any event, if I were redoing my original inquiry, I should certainly pay more attention to the effects upon the academician's attitude and behavior of such structures as the department, the college or professional school, the graduate school, and special arrangements for teaching and research.

With the growth in the size and complexity of universities, the department as an entity undoubtedly assumes greater importance for the average faculty member. In a large university, for example, the English department may have more members than comprise the entire faculty of a small liberal arts college and may contain virtually all of their professional concerns. It and the field of specialization, rather than the whole institution, may thus be the occupational "universe" of the scholar or scientist. Moreover, I think there are noticeable attitudinal differences between individuals in the humanistic studies and the physical sciences, the fine arts and engineering, education and the medical fields, and so on. Some of these differences stood out quite clearly in faculty reactions to the 1965 student episodes at Berkeley. (I should like to see a study of the "young Turks" on faculties to ascertain whether they more typically emerge in some departments than in others.)

Since 1942, graduate education has loomed much larger in the university picture. Assuming that the holders of the baccalaureate who go on for advanced degrees will rise from the present 19 percent (up from 12 percent since 1959) to 25 percent in 1975 as a proportion of the total enrollment in all institutions, it becomes apparent that this level of academic activity is now and will be much more significant than it once was. In addition, in some institutions there is also the heightened significance of postdoctoral work.

Among the special arrangements for teaching and research, to which I

[5] See Cartter, "Future Faculty: Needs and Resources," Table 6, on p. 132 below.

alluded earlier, the campus-based research institute or center should be mentioned as an important, largely postwar development. Before the war they were few, but their number is now estimated as exceeding 3,000 in approximately 200 universities. Berkeley has more than 80 and a recent count at the University of Michigan disclosed 146. These centers, as Cartter has said, "fall outside the usual educational chain of command." Some of them have very large budgets, involve persons from many departments and schools within a university, and represent a complete reorganization of traditional disciplinary approaches to problems, both theoretical and applied.

To the professor, attachment to a research center often provides a degree of freedom and flexibility which is not easily duplicated in the educational institution proper. To the university, the existence of such centers often aids in attracting distinguished scholars. This is a two-edged sword, however, for the allegiance of the faculty member is divided between center and department, and the retention of faculty may be as much a function of continuing university grantsmanship as it is of the quality and climate of the education enterprise.[6]

If research activity were motivated solely by the desire to seek the truth and if teaching followed entirely from the wish to diffuse it, there would be no problems of academic status. My analysis of status does not make an opposite assumption, but it does employ a motivational scheme in which the employee's status is necessarily of great significance both to him and to the institution. Twenty years and more ago there appeared to be a good deal of uncertainty, confusion, and misgiving surrounding the whole matter of status appraisal. Those who may have to engage in a lot of this kind of personnel evaluation will come to realize that it still involves what is known in navigation as "blind reckoning." Recently, as I reviewed an American Council on Education publication titled "Policy and Practices in Faculty Evaluation,"[7] it struck me that, insofar as precision of method is concerned, not much progress has been made of late. Along the lines of an unprintable limerick, it looks as if many administrators are still not clear about who is supposed to do what, with which, and to whom when it comes to evaluating faculty performance.

During the last decade or two, many university professors have become heavily involved in research and public service. In response to pressures from business, industry, and government, they are even more frequently in their laboratories, secluded in their offices, or even away from the campus altogether for considerable amounts of time. Thus, one hears complaints about the neglect of undergraduate teaching and the divided

[6] Cartter, "Graduate Education and Research," Background paper for the American Library Association Conference on Education and the Nation's Libraries, Airlie House, March 29–30, 1965 (Mimeographed).
[7] By John W. Gustad, *Educational Record*, July 1961, pp. 194–211.

loyalties of faculty between their traditional assignments and these enlarged functions. Institutions of higher education in general and universities in particular are now deeply involved in the most basic problems of our era, and Mr. Chips has almost disappeared from the campus scene. What the Germans term *Gemeinschaft* has been displaced by *Gesellschaft,* as the spirit of a homogeneous community gives way to the depersonalization of a heterogeneous society.

As Clark Kerr mentioned in *The Uses of the University,*[8] there are lower teaching loads, larger classes, and more use of substitute teachers for regular faculty. The choice of faculty members is more often based on research accomplishment than on instructional capacity. Between 1940 and 1960, our national investment in research and development grew by 3,714 percent, and the participation of our institutions in this vast phenomenon has inevitably affected them.

There is a rising tide of grumbling everywhere, and especially in the larger universities, about the lack of attention to effective teaching and the absence of systematic means of teacher improvement. In some instances, of course, careful study is being given to such pedagogical aids and devices as closed-circuit television, teaching machines, and what not, but the most essential element—the human ingredient in the person of the teacher himself—is largely ignored or taken for granted. A few universities, it is true, do have procedures designed to evaluate and improve beginning teachers, and some use crude student-rating devices for all teachers; to the best of my knowledge, however, there is not a major institution anywhere that has made a strenuous, across-the-board effort continuously to evaluate and better its teaching productivity in the same way virtually all of them appraise their research output.

Contrary to expert as well as popular opinion, the proportion of Ph.D.'s on most faculties has increased rather than declined. But relief from teaching has come to be regarded as a reward for accomplishment and one of the highest status symbols. Everywhere, of course, there is lip service to the importance of good teaching; yet in few places is there really systematic and rigorous attention to reinforcing, rather than obstructing, the values institutions claim to uphold in this regard. The average faculty man's research gets criticized and evaluated; not so his teaching, for his classroom is still regarded as being sacrosanct.

In my opinion, both faculty and administration must accept blame for the fact that consultantships, outside research grants and contracts, and publications score more points in the ratings of academicians than does dedicated and effective teaching. The much-discussed publish-or-perish dictum, however, is in actuality more fiction than fact in the average institution. More than a decade ago I made a detailed analysis of the

[8] Cambridge, Mass.: Harvard University Press, 1963.

published research of three institutional faculties in the university system with which I was then associated, and I found that on one campus 71 percent of the faculty had neved published an article and 90 percent had not published a book; corresponding figures for the other two campuses were 40 percent and 90 percent, and 29 percent and 66 percent. More recently I had a tabulation made of the published writings of approximately a thousand faculty persons in a different university system and found that 32 percent had not published any articles and 71 percent had not published any books.

Among the 2,000 cases in these two samples, let me add, were some individuals whose personal bibliographies exceed in volume the collective output of a sizable proportion of all the rest of their colleagues. Since the data to which I refer were collected from large universities (both A.A.U. members) and not from small colleges, they lead me to conclude that allegations about the emphasis upon research and publication as *the* cause for neglect of teaching are unfounded. Other evidence I have seen reinforces my surmise that in all except a few leading institutions less than 10 percent of the faculty accounts for more than 90 percent of all published research. In brief, if the publish-or-perish dictum were fact rather than fiction on most campuses, the average professor would be dead.

Although our nation undoubtedly needs more genuinely distinguished, research-oriented universities, I doubt that the number can or should exceed forty to fifty. The kind of research that contributes to the advancement of knowledge should be a major emphasis in perhaps two hundred of our institutions, but I believe that on most campuses it is sufficient to expect the average faculty member to keep abreast of his field. Because talent for really creative research and writing is apparently a very scarce capability, it seems logical to conclude that time and energy would be put to better use if most academicians were encouraged to give more attention to their teaching. An urgent problem for the administration as well as the faculty, accordingly, is to find out more about the nature of effective teaching, establish means of identifying and rewarding it, and cease giving mere lip service to its importance.

In reviewing my whole treatment of academic status, it seems to me that my least satisfactory section is the one having to do with professional status. My frame of reference was too largly confined to one organization, the American Association of University Professors. Although this is the one academic organization (excluding the American Federation of Teachers) that includes all kinds of specialists and most closely parallels the trade union or the broad professional associations in other fields, my present opinion is that this association is less important to the average university teacher than his scholarly or learned society.

For the typical chemistry professor, for example, I suspect that the

American Chemical Society is closer to his perennial concerns. Correspondingly, this would be true of the American Sociological Association, the Modern Language Association, and dozens of others. Through participation in the activities of these societies rather than in those of other types of associations (e.g., A.A.U.P., A.F. of T., A.H.E.), the academic man gains professional recognition by reading papers, being on committees, chairing sections, serving in offices, and otherwise rising to prominence. To use a labor union analogy, it would be the *craft* rather than the *trade* unions that are of most significance in determining an individual's status in the academic world.

Members of the academic profession in the 1930's and early 1940's typically considered their socioeconomic status as being depressed. Little did they realize that they were enjoying relative affluence compared with the deterioration to follow during almost two decades of inflation. The average salary figures I cited then have in many instances more than doubled, to be sure, and even the purchasing power of academic incomes has improved. However this may be, per-capita incomes in the whole society have increased at an even greater rate.

Within the last six or seven years, there have been marked improvements almost everywhere, and even though these gains have been less widely proclaimed than the previous losses, the total incomes of many professors in large universities, as well as in some of the more affluent small colleges, are considerably higher than the public is aware. To be eligible for an "AA" rating under the A.A.U.P. scale for 1965–66, for example, an institution must compensate its full professors at an average rate of $23,290. Because of consultantships and other paid services in science and engineering, in the professional schools, and in a few other areas, the outside incomes of many scholars and scientists are appreciably more significant than they once were. (The effect of this and its wide variation by fields has been to enlarge the disparities between and within institutions and thus afford a new basis of disquiet in the academic profession.)[9]

[9] Although I commented on outside earnings in my 1942 book, it contained little information about fringe benefits for the faculty. One good source of data on this subject is William C. Greenough and Francis P. King, *Retirement and Insurance Plans in American Colleges* (New York: Columbia University Press, 1959). Another is Mark H. Ingraham's *The Outer Fringe: Faculty Benefits Other than Annuities and Insurance* (Madison: University of Wisconsin Press, 1965).

In reviewing this latter volume, Allan Cartter comments: "And what a grab-bag it is! Sixty percent of the institutions queried are landlords for faculty families, 15 percent are mortgage brokers, 93 percent of private colleges provide tax-free scholarships in the form of tuition waivers, 75 percent provide emergency medical treatment to faculty and families, one-fourth grant personal loans to employees, two-thirds pay moving expenses for tenure appointments, one-third provide discount purchasing services on appliances, food, and the like. Others, in varying numbers, provide family bonuses for children, free faculty lunches and morning coffee, free baby-sitting services, two-thirds of foreign travel expenses, and run holiday camps for faculty families. Over half of the institutions have regular sabbatical leave policies, and others have informal-leave-with-pay arrangements. Six hundred institutions provide faculty parking

As to image and reality of the professor then and now as a person, I noted in 1942 that in the hotel lobby or lounge car it was difficult at a glance to differentiate the professor from the doctor, lawyer, or business-man. Today I would note that the traveling professor goes by jet plane and has little spare time to tarry in hotel lobbies. He is still more likely than his counterpart in medicine, law, or business to wear crepe-soled shoes, a tweed jacket, and occasionally to have a beard, but, unlike his earlier counterpart in the academic profession, he is seldom a reclusive scholar whose activities are confined largely to his own campus. Even more than most professional workers today, he is a frequent participant in meetings, conferences, and other collective endeavors that draw him away from the classroom, library, and laboratory, not only to distant cities in this coun-try but also to remote parts of the world. In brief, I think it can be said that in many fields the professor has ceased to be a vaguely respected but unappreciated figure as he emerges in the role of the expert and true pro-fessional whose knowledgeability has become a highly valued commodity.

ACADEMIC PROCESSES AND FUNCTIONS

Turning now to considerations of academic processes and functions, it should be noted that my earlier analysis ties both individual and institu-tional competition to the quest for prestige as an ultimate value. The competitive processes I described then seem to me to be about the same at the present time, or, at least, to be no less intensive. As Berelson's study has shown, the leading institutions of a generation or so ago are still in the main the leading universities today.[10] Yet there have been some changes. The University of California, for example, is no longer just one of the top five or six universities; it now vies with Harvard for pre-eminence in first position.

Although major centers of advanced study and research are somewhat more numerous than they were a generation or more ago, the material and human resources required to build and maintain a truly great university are perhaps even more difficult to come by. Among the reasons are the explosion of knowledge, especially in scientific and technical fields, and the considerable investments required to effect further explosions. To be sure, graduate study and research have undergone notable improvements almost everywhere, but even so I suspect that qualitative differences be-tween the best and the worst universities are greater now than ever before.

---

spaces. Some, like Princeton, house half their faculty in university-owned property or in houses where the university has advanced all the money and requires no payments on principal."

No single institution, of course, provides *all* these services. Cartter estimates that these benefits may easily add up to $6,000–$7,000 a year, perhaps even $10,000 before taxes for the family at the "right institution" and with two children in college.

[10] Bernard Berelson, *Graduate Education in the United States* (New York: McGraw-Hill Book Co., 1960).

Curiously enough, some of our Federal policies and practices widen this gap by concentrating grants in institutions that are already strong while others narrow it by deliberately attempting to encourage a geographic and institutional spread of activity.

The national need for greatly increased numbers of highly trained individuals and for more creative endeavor in all sorts of spheres suggests that in the future many of these matters cannot be left to chance or to local determination. Under such circumstances it is indeed likely that interinstitutional cooperation and coordination, either on a voluntary or mandatory basis, will become more prevalent.

Student-teacher relationships are still central concerns in major universities, but the proportional amount of time the contemporary professor gives to classroom or laboratory teaching has steadily dwindled as the emphasis on research has increased. In fact, it has been sardonically noted that some professors in some universities appear to do no regularly scheduled classroom teaching anymore. Professional novices even—when their bargaining power is enhanced as unusually promising researchers—have been known to insist on teaching loads not in excess of three to six hours per week. As I stated elsewhere, the same inadequacies in evaluating and improving teaching that were the subject of debate several decades ago seem to me still to persist. Despite sporadic efforts here and there to improve teaching, the situation in most places can still be aptly described as one of laissez faire. My earlier generalizations about the comparative prestige of superior teachers and superior researchers are likewise valid today.

As I review what I originally had to say about prestige and the research function, my present judgment is that I overstressed the influences of ulterior motivation on research itself. Certainly now, and perhaps even then, there is less cold calculation about what a project may or may not do for the professional advancement of the individual directly involved. In the more dynamic fields of knowledge, research is currently so integral a part of what goes on that the young scholar or scientist of even average ability is likely to have a fairly wide range of choices among worthwhile possibilities for involvement, either working with others or on his own. Furthermore, many research projects today necessarily require team effort and leave less latitude for the virtuoso or solo performer.

Throughout my treatise on *The Academic Man* there is an emphasis on the social determinants of his behavior. This is to be expected in "A Study in the Sociology of a Profession," as the book is subtitled. The mode of analysis I employed did succeed, I still think, in getting at the sources of personnel stresses and strains in the university as a social system. Flaws in the scheme of coordinating effort, giving of precedence to means over ends, institutionalized evasions, and conflicts between nominal and real ends are all, without question, at the root of many problems besetting the academician in his workaday world. The logic of sentiment and the logic of efficiency still need to be more unmistakably identified as such.

However all this may be, I find that I am less prone to be an adherent of social determinism than I was twenty years ago. Perhaps it is because during the interim I have come to know personally enough academic men in many kinds of contexts to realize more fully the importance of subtle and little understood variables in human behavior.

PART THREE

College Teachers: Quantity and Quality

Future Faculty:
Needs and Resources

ALLAN M. CARTTER*

In the first few moments of flight, an unprepared astronaut might reasonably anticipate that things were going from bad to worse. With adequate preparation beforehand, however, he would know that the gravitational pressure would soon diminish as the rate of acceleration decreased, and that he could look forward to weightless flight once a constant speed outside the gravitational field of the earth had been attained.

Higher education in recent years may be likened to the unprepared astronaut, for the rising rate of expansion of college enrollments has strained both physical facilities and human resources. It has sometimes been forgotten that once the rate of increase in enrollment begins to decline, the new demands imposed by each successive college year will ease considerably. We have looked ahead to the early 1970's for so long that, now as we approach them, we tend to lose perspective. There is, indeed, some cause for concern about the next several years, but the long view clearly indicates that the present academic year represents the peak of our difficulties, and that the situation is likely to improve over the next decade. This paper focuses on the adequacy of the supply of college teachers in this longer time span, but its moral is equally applicable to buildings, equipment, and other more or less fixed resources.

THE LAST DECADE

If one had polled educators a year or two ago to ask them whether there would be sufficient numbers of adequately prepared teachers to man the colleges over the next decade or two, nine out of ten would probably have said there would not be. In the words of several distin-

* The author is indebted to Robert Farrell for computational assistance in preparing the faculty projections.

guished observers, there was "a disastrous shortage," a "serious crisis" in which the nation was "standing virtually paralyzed" facing "a major national scandal"; only "heroic efforts," "crash programs," and new degrees short of the doctorate could alleviate the worsening situation.[1] One estimate from the U.S. Office of Education predicted a cumulative deficit of 121,720 faculty members with doctoral degrees by 1974. No relief appeared to be in sight.

In the fall of 1963 the Commission on Plans and Objectives for Higher Education of the American Council on Education undertook a

TABLE 1: *Distribution of Faculty by Highest Degree, Private and Public Colleges and Universities,*[a] *1950–51—1962–63*

Type of Institution	Year	Percent Distribution			
		Doctor's	Master's	Bachelor's	Professional
Colleges:					
Private (N = 438)	1962–63	35.4	47.0	12.0	5.6
	1958–59	33.7	46.9	13.0	6.4
	1954–55	32.5	47.5	14.8	5.2
	1950–51	29.7	49.0	19.2	2.1
Public (N = 196)	1962–63	33.5	52.5	9.3	4.7
	1958–59	32.0	53.4	10.8	3.8
	1954–55	30.1	58.4	9.9	1.6
	1950–51	23.2	63.7	12.4	0.7
Total (N = 634)	1962–63	34.5	49.4	10.9	5.2
	1958–59	33.0	49.6	12.1	5.3
	1954–55	31.6	51.6	13.0	3.8
	1950–51	27.3	54.4	16.7	1.6
Universities:					
Private (N = 67)	1962–63	43.8	26.8	12.0	17.4
	1958–59	40.7	28.4	14.1	16.8
	1954–55	40.0	36.8	14.6	8.6
	1950–51	37.3	37.7	20.5	4.5
Public (N = 80)	1962–63	44.9	31.9	10.0	13.2
	1958–59	41.7	34.8	13.0	10.5
	1954–55	40.7	38.7	13.5	7.1
	1950–51	36.0	43.5	17.3	3.2
Total (N = 147)	1962–63	44.5	29.9	10.8	14.8
	1958–59	41.3	32.4	13.4	12.9
	1954–55	40.4	37.9	13.9	7.8
	1950–51	36.6	41.0	18.7	3.7

[a] Excluding faculty in schools of medicine, dentistry, and veterinary medicine.

Source: *American Universities and Colleges* (Washington: American Council on Education, 1952, 1956, 1960, 1964).

[1] For a sampling of such views, see: President's Committee on Education Beyond the High School, *Second Report to the President* (Washington: Government Printing Office, July 1957), p. 30; Earl J. McGrath, *The Graduate School and the Decline of Liberal Education* (New York: Bureau of Publications, Teachers College, Columbia University, 1959), pp. 26–27; Oliver C. Carmichael, *Graduate Education: A Critique and a Program* (New York: Harper & Bros., 1961), pp. 132–33; and Russell M. Cooper, "College-Teaching Crisis: Has the Graduate School Done Right by the College Teacher?" *Journal of Higher Education,* January 1964, p. 6.

preliminary study of the current data on teacher supply and demand. Although the results were not conclusive, they indicated that the magnitude of the problem might not be as great as was previously supposed.[2] In the fall of 1964 the commission devoted further attention to future needs for faculty. The result of this study was a paper reviewing the experience of the 1953–63 period, and indicating that just as everyone thought things were getting worse, the situation had in fact improved.[3] Table 1 summarizes the findings for all faculty (full time and part time) of 781 accredited institutions reporting faculty data from 1950 through 1963 in successive editions of *American Universities and Colleges*. For each type of senior institution, the percent of faculty with the doctorate rose steadily from one four-year period to the next. The combined total of doctorates and professional degrees (the latter often being the highest degree appropriate for a field of study such as medicine, law, library science, and social work) is dramatic for the university sector.

A recently completed Office of Education study now corroborates these findings.[4] Of the full-time instructional staff in four-year institutions, 50.6 percent held the doctorate in the spring of 1963. Table 2, which compares these findings with those of a similar study by the National Education Association ten years earlier, reveals a marked improvement. Thus the prediction of the distinguished Committee of Fifteen ten years ago that "to expect that by 1970 the proportion of college teachers holding the Ph.D. degree will have declined from the

TABLE 2: *Percentage of Full-time Instructional Staff with Doctoral Degrees, 1953–54 and 1962–63*

Category of Institution	1953–54 (N.E.A.)	1962–63 (O.E.)
Public universities.....	44.0	58.4
Private universities....	51.9	59.6
Public colleges........	30.7	42.6
Private colleges.......	35.2	42.7
All institutions........	40.5	50.6

Sources: 1953–54: *Teacher Supply and Demand in Degree-Granting Institutions, 1954–55*, N.E.A. Research Bulletin (Washington: National Education Association, December 1955), p. 138.
1962–63: "Doctorates among Teaching Faculty," Paper presented at the annual meeting of the American Educational Research Association, Chicago, Feb. 11, 1965, Table 3.

[2] See Harold Wolozin, "How Serious Is the Faculty Shortage?" *Challenge*, June 1965.

[3] A. M. Cartter, "A New Look at the Supply of College Teachers," *Educational Record*, Summer 1965, pp. 267–77.

[4] As of the date of writing, the 1963 study of college faculty (COLFACS) has not been published. A preliminary report was presented at the Feb. 11, 1965, annual meeting of the American Educational Research Association, "Doctorates among Teaching Faculty."

present 40 percent to 20 percent is not statistical hysteria but grassroots arithmetic"[5] has been proved surprisingly incorrect. (In all fairness to the committee, it should be pointed out that the Federal Government was spending then only about $25 million to support graduate students either through fellowships or through research assistantships; this figure has risen to over $300 million for fiscal 1967.)

The failure over the last decade to assess correctly current trends can be attributed to several factors, all of which compounded the errors. First, the National Education Association series that showed the percentage of new teachers holding the doctorate was mistakenly interpreted to reflect incremental changes in the doctorate-faculty ratio. In fact, however, it overlooked the number of teachers, hired by colleges in previous years, who later completed the doctorate. Thus, although only 26.6 percent of new teachers hired in the 1953–65 period possessed the doctorate when hired, the ratio of teachers (newly employed and already in service) awarded the doctorate to all new teachers hired (with or without the Ph.D.) was .44:1 for the 1954–64 decade. That is to say, over two-fifths of the new doctorates in teaching were overlooked.[6]

A second major factor is that college teachers with the doctorate more frequently continue in an academic career than do those not having the doctorate. Thus even if new doctorates in teaching as a percentage of new teachers hired remained at 44 percent, total faculty with the doctorate would tend toward a level of 50 percent or more. Meager evidence from a study of only one academic year (1962–63) suggests that the "quit rate" for nondoctorates is about 7 percent per year, as contrasted with only 3 percent for doctorate holders.

A third factor contributing to the incorrect assessment of trends was the frequent assumption that the necessary replacement rate for college faculty is 5 percent or 6 percent.[7] This figure was commonly divided into an estimated 2 percent for deaths and retirements, and 4 percent for faculty members who leave teaching for nonacademic employment. The 1964 Commission on Plans and Objectives study found that over the past decade the combined death and retirement rate was approximately 1.8 percent (varying from a low of .47 percent in biochemistry

[5] Report of the Committee of Fifteen, *The Graduate School Today and Tomorrow: Reflections for the Profession's Consideration* (New York: Fund for the Advancement of Education, December 1955), p. 7.

[6] For an elaboration of the point see Cartter, "A New Look at the Supply of College Teachers," Table 4, p. 274.

[7] Both the N.E.A. (Research Report 1959-R10, pp. 50–54) and the Office of Education (*Projections of Educational Statistics to 1973–74*, OE-10030 [1964], p. 26) used 6 percent. *Teachers for Tomorrow* (New York: Fund for the Advancement of Education, 1955) and David G. Brown in *The Market for College Teachers* (Chapel Hill: University of North Carolina Press, 1965) used 5 percent.

to a high of 4.37 percent in classics) and the net outflow of doctorates from academic employment was only .11 percent.[8] In this latter case it appears that the gross outflow of senior staff with the doctorate was about 3 percent, but that this was almost exactly balanced by a similar number of senior staff who each year re-entered the teaching profession. The difference between the frequently assumed 6 percent replacement rate and the actual rate of about 1.9 percent makes a sizable difference of about 40,000 doctorates over a decade.[9]

Finally, in the past, most forecasters have been overly pessimistic in their estimates of the number of doctoral degrees to be awarded in the future. As Table 3 indicates, the projections of the mid-1950's all assumed an actual decrease in doctorates over the next five years. The Office of Education's 1955 and 1964 projections have proved much too low. The latest (1965) revision, which raises the estimates for the early 1970's by almost 50 percent over the estimates of the preceding year, seems much more realistic.

THE NEXT TWENTY YEARS: AN AGGREGATE VIEW

In an exploratory paper last fall, the writer advanced some estimates of likely trends in faculty supply and demand ahead to 1985.[10] For the present paper these estimates have been further refined, and restricted to four-year colleges and universities. The reason for omitting junior colleges is twofold. First, junior colleges now employ only about 2 percent of new doctoral degree holders. (Less than 7 percent of the new faculty members hired by junior colleges possess the doctorate.) And second, although the Office of Education's recent (spring 1963) study of college faculty provides a good benchmark for the four-year colleges and universities, it does not include junior institutions.

Before analyzing actual trends, I would like to emphasize one factor often overlooked in discussing the future need for teachers. The "re-

[8] A recent study by Bolt, Kolton, and Levine ("Doctoral Feedback into Higher Education," *Science*, May 14, 1965, pp. 918–28) found the death and retirement rate to be 1.6 percent for scientists and engineers, and the net replacement rate for transfers into and out of academic employment to be negative (i.e., a larger number of older doctorates entered teaching than left).

[9] Replacement rates can be stated in gross terms—i.e., approximately 5 percent for deaths, retirements, and departures for nonacademic employment combined—but then the supply of teachers must be expanded to include senior doctorate holders and other persons returning to teaching. The faculty-forecasting models used by the N.E.A., the Office of Education, the Fund for the Advancement of Education, and others have considered only newly hired faculty (from graduate school or first-time teachers) as part of the supply, and therefore the appropriate replacement demand must be cast in *net* terms so as not to distort the true market situation.

[10] Cartter, "The Supply and Demand of College Teachers," Paper presented at the American Statistical Association meeting, September 1965. See A.S.A. *1965 Social Statistics Section Proceedings*, pp. 70–80, or *Journal of Human Resources*, Vol. I, No. 1.

TABLE 3: *Comparison of Doctorate Production Projections, 1965–85, and Actual Trend, 1955–64*

(Thousands)

Year	O.E. 1955 (1)	T.T. 1955 (2)	C.H.R. 1954 (3)	Actual (4)	O.E. 1964 (5)	O.E. 1965 (6)	A.C.E. 1965 (7)	N.S.F. 1964 (8)
1954–55...	8.5	7.1	7.0	8.8				
1955–56...	7.6	6.6		8.9				
1956–57...	6.9	6.6		8.8				
1957–58...	6.1	6.6		8.9				
1958–59...	7.0	6.8		9.4				
1959–60...	7.5	7.1	6.6	9.8				
1960–61...	7.6	7.5		10.6				
1961–62...	7.5	7.8		11.6				11.7
1962–63...	7.9	8.2		12.8				
1963–64...	8.0	8.9		14.5	13.2			
1964–65...	8.0	10.0	9.0	16.5	13.6	15.3	15.1	
1965–66...	8.4	9.9			14.1	16.0	16.1	
1966–67...	9.0	10.4			15.4	17.0	16.8	
1967–68...	10.3	11.0			16.7	18.6	18.0	
1968–69...	9.7	14.4			17.6	20.6	19.5	
1969–70...	9.6	13.8	12.0		18.3	21.6	21.4	20.8
1970–71...					19.8	21.7	23.2	
1971–72...					21.8	23.3	26.0	
1972–73...					23.6	27.6	28.9	
1973–74...					24.3	32.5	31.5	
1974–75...						31.9	33.6	36.4
1975–76...							35.7	
1976–77...							37.9	
1977–78...							40.4	
1978–79...							43.6	
1979–80...							46.0	56.6
1980–81...							47.9	
1981–82...							49.7	
1982–83...							51.6	
1983–84...							53.2	
1984–85...							54.7	70.7

Sources:
[1] Early U.S. Office of Education projection, as reported in *Teachers for Tomorrow* (New York: Fund for the Advancement of Education, 1955), p. 59.

[2] Projection from *Teachers for Tomorrow*, p. 59, which was based on a projection of college graduates and application of methodology used by Oxtoby, Mugge, and Wolfle.

[3] Estimated from Dael Wolfle, *America's Resources of Specialized Talent: The Report of the Commission on Human Resources and Advanced Training* (New York: Harper & Bros., 1954), pp. 42, 43.

[4] Actual doctorates awarded; compiled from *Earned Degrees Conferred by Higher Educational Institutions* (U.S. Office of Education).

[5] From *Projections of Educational Statistics to 1973–74* (U.S. Office of Education, OE-10030, 1964), p. 12.

[6] From *Projections of Educational Statistics to 1974–75* (U.S. Office of Education, OE-10030-65, 1965), p. 21.

[7] Projections made by the author; see A. M. Cartter, "Graduate Education and Research," Background paper for American Library Association conference, March 29, 1965.

[8] Projections from *Comparisons of Earned Degrees Awarded, 1901–62, with Projections to 2000* (National Science Foundation, NSF 64-2, 1964).

placement demand" for teachers dying or retiring is, obviously, a function of the size and of the age distribution of present faculty. *However, the "expansion demand" depends upon the rate of expansion of total enrollment.* A rising rate of enrollment growth requires a larger absolute number of new teachers each year; a declining rate means a decline (in absolute terms) in the number of new teachers needed annually.

These principles are illustrated in Figure 1. The upper line represents a hypothetical enrollment level over a twenty-five year period. The three lower lines indicate the associated demand for new faculty. The replacement demand rises gradually after the fifth year, for as the total faculty gets larger, a greater number of teachers either die or reach retirement age.[11] The expansion demand is zero during the first five years of stable enrollment. However, in the next five years (period B) it rises abruptly to about 10,000 new teachers a year to meet the enrollment expansion of 200,000 students per year.[12] During the third five-year period (C) when the rate of expansion rises to 400,000 students a year, the expansion demand jumps to 20,000 annually. During the fourth period (D), as the total system expands at a slower rate, the demand for new faculty actually drops and returns to the zero expansion demand level when enrollment again levels off (period E).

This analogue to the economists' "accelerator" model is highly relevant to the recent college experience. The decade of the 1930's and the brief 1950–52 and 1959–62 years look rather like period A in Figure 1, whereas the mid-1950's and 1962–65 are closer to period B. The 1965–68 years parallel period C, but the 1970's promise a gradual slowing down in the rate of expansion (an inevitable consequence as attendance ratios get closer to the 100 percent level for college-age youth) and an absolute decline in the number of new teachers required annually. Too frequently when discussing public policy toward higher education, we have visualized a continuation of the first three periods in Figure 1, and have failed to carry the analysis through to its predetermined conclusion.

Turning to the real academic world, Figure 2 reviews the experience of the last decade and projects ahead to 1985. It may be well, first, to enumerate the assumptions made in arriving at these estimates. Although these assumptions appear to fit the facts as they are presently known and are now predictable, obviously major changes in the pattern of support for graduate education, in the technology of teaching, and in the competing demands of other forms of employment will alter the actual growth path.

The key assumptions on which the projections are based are:

1. That there will be no change in the incremental student-staff ratios. Projections are based on the experience of the 1955–63 period. The incremental ratio is held constant at 17.2:1, implying a rise in the

---

[11] Actually there is a considerable lag in the response of the replacement demand to an expanding faculty, for most of the net additions to the faculty are young when first appointed. However, the principle is illustrated in the simplified model in Fig. 1.

[12] For the sake of illustration, a 20:1 incremental student-staff ratio is assumed.

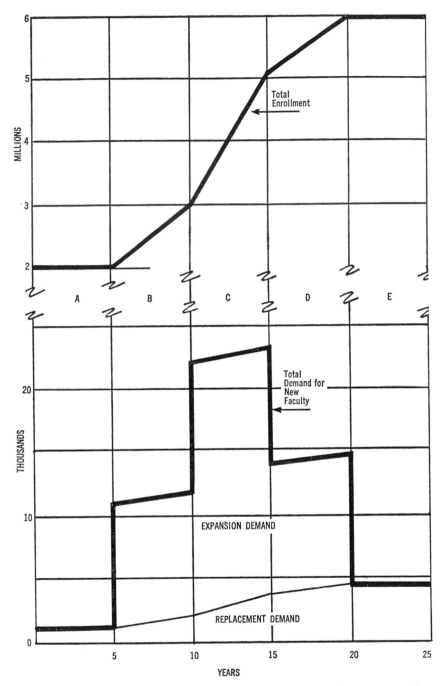

Fɪɢ. 1: Model illustrating relationship of demand for new faculty to student enrollment.

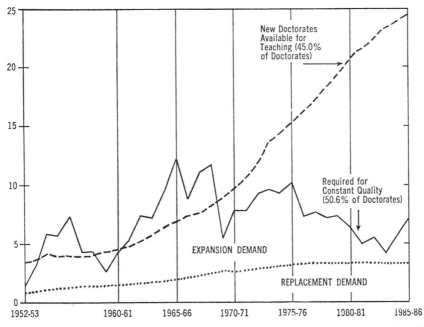

Fɪɢ. 2: New doctorates available and required to maintain constant quality of faculty in four-year colleges and universities: projections to 1985–86.

average student-staff ratio from its present 14.5:1 to about 15.9:1 by 1985.

2. That the ratio of full-time to part-time teachers will remain constant at its average for the last decade. As Table 4 (see page 129) indicates, full-time teachers comprise approximately 83 percent of the total full-time equivalent instructional staff.

3. That the combined death and retirement rate of doctorate-holding teachers will remain constant at approximately 1.8 percent per year until 1975, and then gradually decline to 1.4 percent by 1985. The decline is attributable to the gradual shift in the age distribution of faculty as younger members come to constitute a larger proportion of the total.

4. That the "net transfer rate" (the number of doctorate holders who leave academic employment, minus the number of senior doctorate holders who enter [or re-enter] teaching, divided by the total number of doctorate-teachers) is not more than .2 percent per year. This figure approximates the last decade, but could change substantially if the level of academic salaries relative to remuneration in nonacademic employment were to alter.

5. That enrollment and doctorate projections (given in the Appendix table, page 135 are accurate. The enrollment projections assume that the present "attendance ratio" for college-age youth will rise from its cur-

rent level of about .42 to .60 by 1985. Doctorate projections foresee a rise in annual degrees from 16,500 in 1964–65 to approximately 55,000 by 1985. These figures about equal the current Office of Education projections through 1975, and fall about 20 percent below a National Science Foundation projection for the 1975–85 period.[13]

6. That approximately 45 percent of those awarded doctoral degrees seek employment as college teachers in four-year institutions. Over the last decade, according to the N.E.A. biennial studies, about 47 percent entered college teaching (2 percent of them in junior colleges).

Although the six assumptions represent many "ifs," they are based chiefly on the experience of the last decade. As illustrated in Figure 2, they suggest the following conclusions about the general market situation for doctorate-teachers. For the immediate future—1966 through 1969—highly qualified college teachers will remain in short supply. For the next several years after that, until about 1976, the number required annually to maintain the present percentage of doctorates on senior college full-time faculties will remain about three-fourths the number of new doctorates available each year. ("Available" is defined as 45 percent of new doctorates; thus three-fourths is about 34 percent.) From about 1976 onward, however, the annual number of potential doctorate-teachers promises to far outstrip the number required to keep faculty quality constant. If the estimates prove correct, by 1977 *every* new teacher hired could have the doctorate and still the academic world could not provide employment for more than 45 percent of the new degree holders.

These conclusions are appropriate if one wants merely to maintain the present quality of faculty (as measured by highest degree attained). Judging from our past experience and present aspirations, however, it is unlikely that we will remain content with present standards of teacher preparation. Figure 3, therefore, illustrates two possible alternatives. Curve A shows the requirements for rising quality of faculty based on an improvement of one-half of one percentage point per year in the over-all proportion of faculty with the doctorate; curve B is based on an improvement of 1 percent each year. Curve A is a reasonable target and approximates the experience of the last dozen years; curve B is probably a maximum goal, realizable only at the end of the 1970's. Some casual readers of my earlier paper on projections interpreted the results to mean that there would be a glut of doctorates beginning about 1970. This is certainly not suggested here, for only a

[13] See *Projections of Educational Statistics to 1974–75, 1965 Edition*, OE-10030-65 (Washington: Government Printing Office, 1965), and *Comparisons of Earned Degrees Awarded, 1901–62, with Projections to 2000*, NSF 64-2 (Washington: National Science Foundation, 1964).

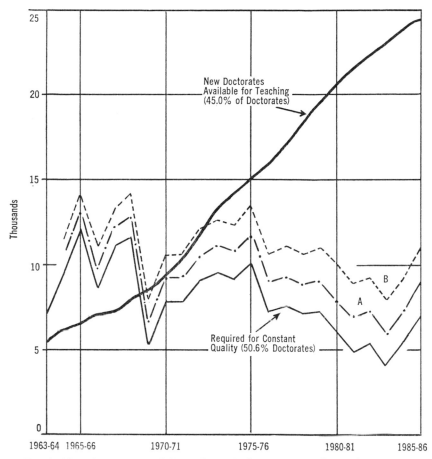

Fɪɢ. 3: New doctorates available and required: constant quality and rising quality models.

small number of distinguished universities are content with the present quality of their faculty, and in many fields—engineering, law, business administration, education—the doctorate is just beginning to be accepted as the most appropriate degree for a college teacher. If one can anticipate anything roughly akin to a condition of "glut," it would be sometime in the 1980's when there may be insufficient new openings in senior institutions to absorb more than about one in five of those receiving the doctorate. Yet, fifteen years from now the demands for persons trained at this highest level for business and for government and other nonprofit employment, not to mention junior colleges and various forms of continuing education, may be expanding so rapidly that colleges will still face strong competition in hiring.

Figures 2 and 3 provide an aggregate view of the projected market for college teachers. Such a summary, however, conceals continuing shortages in some fields of study and possible surpluses in others. Although a disaggregated view magnifies the problems of projection, the following section attempts to look more closely at several specialized areas of study.

SUPPLY AND DEMAND CONDITIONS IN TEN SPECIAL FIELDS

In an earlier paper I concluded:

. . . the aggregate data are better than [those] for individual disciplines. There are wide variations in the values of . . . coefficients from field to field, but the demarcations between fields are too fuzzy to permit the application of such a model with any degree of precision to individual disciplines . . .[14]

Although the conclusion, I fear, is still valid, I have attempted with some trepidation to apply the forecasting model to ten special areas. One must be cautious, however, in interpreting the results, for obvious reasons. The American Automobile Association is reasonably accurate in predicting the number of traffic fatalities likely to occur on Labor Day week end. However, they are much less accurate in predicting the level for each state, and predictions about which crossroads will be the scene and whose cars will be involved are impossible.

A second reason for caution is that a sizable number of teachers with the doctorate teach in departments other than the one in which they received their degree. Professors of religion frequently are found in philosophy departments, biophysicists in zoology or physiology, structural linguists in anthropology, statisticians in psychology or education, and so forth. With such flexible boundaries, and with the rather rigid classification categories used in reporting degree and faculty status, the errors multiply. To illustrate, one attempt to project faculty needs several years ago concluded there would be large deficits in every field except one; the exception was "miscellaneous," which, according to estimate, accounted for 2 percent of demand but 40 percent of supply.

A third problem lies with the assumption that each field of study maintains its share of the total teaching responsibilities: that is, if total enrollment doubles in X years, enrollments in English, economics, and astrophysics will also double. (One could make different assumptions, but they would be equally subject to error.)

A fourth difficulty—if any further caveats are needed to forewarn the reader—is the lack of knowledge of student-staff ratios in different fields of study. The over-all ratio may be 17:1, but does that ratio hold for home economics? nuclear engineering? physical education? [15]

Within the limitations imposed by these problems, the five parts of

[14] Cartter, "Supply and Demand of College Teachers," p. 78.
[15] In projecting annual needs, the incremental (rather than the average) student-staff ratio is the important variable, but the same limitation applies.

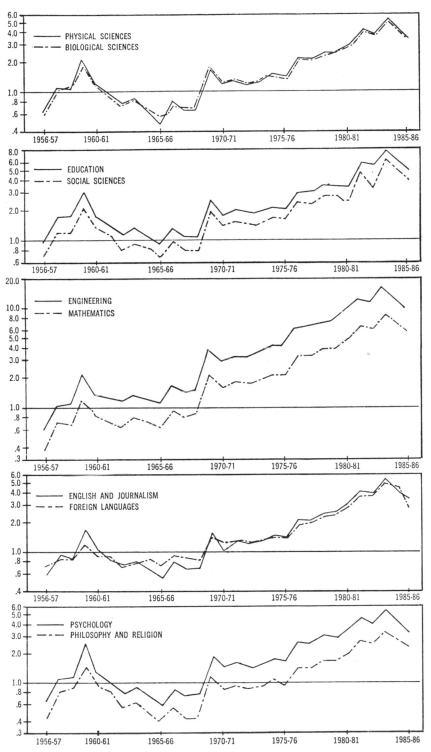

Fig. 4: Ratio of new doctorates available to new teachers with doctorate required to maintain 1962–63 quality level: projections to 1985–86, ten special fields. (Semi-log scale.)

Figure 4 illustrate anticipated deficits and surpluses in ten fields over the next twenty years. In these figures, fields are classified broadly, thus reducing the degree of possible error but also restricting somewhat the usefulness of the predictions. It should be emphasized that the term "surplus" in this context is used to measure doctorates potentially available for teaching in excess of the number needed annually simply to maintain the percentage of faculty with the doctorate at the 1962–63 level; when a surplus is indicated, there is a strong likelihood that the percentage of doctorate holders will rise over time.

Not surprisingly, in light of the aggregate model discussed earlier, all fields eventually rise to a level where faculty quality steadily improves. Perhaps of greater interest is the year in which a particular field makes the transition from deficit status. For engineering this year was about 1958. This is a field where the percentage of faculty with the doctorate was quite low earlier in the decade, where the new emphasis upon applied science is raising the sights of engineering schools in their hiring policies, and where the number of doctorates awarded is rising very rapidly. The physical and biological sciences will be among the last fields to move to rising quality status—in approximately 1969, and the projected surpluses will not be very sizable until the late 1970's. It is also one of the fields where the data are least trustworthy, since the only consistent attempt to determine how many doctorates entered (or continued in) college teaching after receiving their degrees is found in the N.E.A. biennial surveys, which limit their inquiries about the employment status of the doctoral awardee to the year following his graduation. Anyone familiar with the sciences today knows that a substantial proportion of newly minted doctorates take postdoctoral appointments for one to three years following completion of their degree, and that a sizable, but unknown, fraction of these postdoctoral fellows enter teaching after their fellowship period. Thus, the N.E.A. report that 25.6 percent of physical science doctoral awardees began a college teaching career is technically correct, but obviously understates the flow of young doctorates into teaching. If only one-quarter had actually gone into teaching over the last decade, the number of Ph.D. scientists on college faculties would have declined. Therefore, the projections shown in Table 4 are based on the assumption that one-third of the scientists who took research posts in universities immediately after graduation became college or university teachers within the next several years.[16] In this field, and in other fields where postdoctoral appoint-

[16] This assumption raised the percent of new physical science doctorates in teaching from 25.6 percent to 31.1 percent, and from 38.6 percent to 46.4 percent for the biological sciences. Some evidence supporting the assumption that a significant portion of university postdoctoral fellows enter the teaching faculty within several years is to be found in a review of National Register data. For example, the percent-

ments are common, the projections are open to a considerable margin of error. However, the assumption just outlined seems to fit well the experience of the last five to seven years.

Figures 5-A–D illustrate in more detail the projected relationship of doctorates available to those required from 1956 to 1985 for four major areas. English and journalism (Figure 5-A) appear likely to have a surplus in the 1969–75 period about sufficient to compensate for deficits in the previous five years. Engineering has a widening gap between doctorates available and required, suggesting either that the percentage of new doctorates in engineering who enter teaching will decline in the next few years, or that the percentage of teachers with the doctorate will rapidly rise.[17] Philosophy and religion appear to have difficult years ahead until the mid-1970's, although the combination of religion (which has a relatively high rate of turnover, as instructors move between academic and church appointments) and philosophy (where turnover is extremely low) may obscure the situation for the individual fields. The physical sciences (excluding mathematics) are projected at a modest surplus in the 1969–75 years (Figure 5-D), but may need these years to recoup losses in the late 1960's.

FULL-TIME AND PART-TIME TEACHERS

Over the last several years, and most notably since the disturbances at Berkeley in 1964, concern has been expressed about the heavy share of teaching duties performed by graduate students in the large universities. Unfortunately, without examining the archives of several universities, we have no adequate data to measure trends over more than the

---

ages of young Ph.D.'s in teaching and in basic research (about 90 percent university-based) in their first and second jobs were as follows in three fields in experimental biology:

	Biomedical Scientists	Biochemists	Other Biologists
First job			
Percentage in college teaching..	22.3	11.4	14.2
Percentage in basic research....	35.1	70.3	22.6
Second job			
Percentage in college teaching..	34.1	41.2	20.1
Percentage in basic research....	20.0	15.7	15.2

Judging by these data, the assumed one-third postdoctoral fellows entering teaching appears conservative. See Beverly L. Clarke, "Analysis of 1964 National Register of Scientific and Technical Personnel Data for Experimental Biologists," *Proceedings of the Federation of American Societies for Experimental Biology*, Vol. 25, No. 1, Part I (1966), pp. 169–74.

[17] In the 1959–63 period, the percentage of core engineering faculty with the doctorate rose from 33 percent to 45.5 percent, which is in keeping with the estimates in Figure 5-B. See Carl Borgmann, "The Ford Foundation's Role in Engineering Education," Paper presented at the American Association for Engineering Education College-Industry Conference, Seattle, Wash., Feb. 7, 1964.

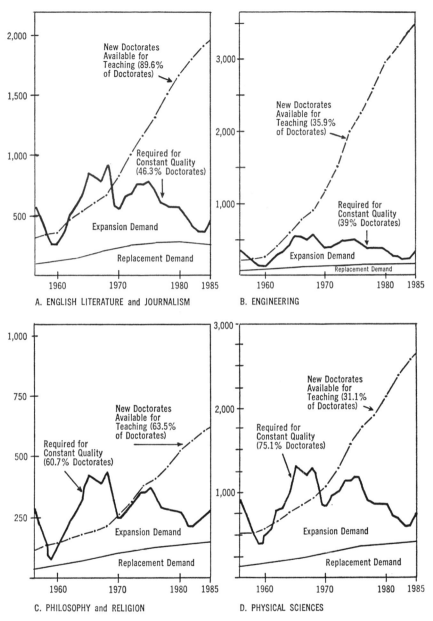

FIG. 5: New doctorates available and required to maintain constant quality of faculty, selected fields, actual 1956 through 1964 and projected to 1985–86.

last dozen years. The biennial surveys by the Office of Education since 1953 are summarized in Table 4, which shows full-time faculty and full-time equivalents of part-time and junior instructional staff. (The latter are presumed to be primarily predoctoral students.) The full-time equivalent figures for part-time staff were provided by the institutions themselves; I have assumed the f.t.e. figure to be 20 percent

TABLE 4: *Full-time Equivalent Instructional Staff, Four-Year Colleges and Universities, 1953-65*

(Figures [except percents] in thousands)

Year	Total F.T.E. Faculty	Full-time Faculty		F.T.E. of Part-time Faculty		F.T.E. of Junior Instructional staff	
		Number	Percent	Number	Percent	Number	Percent
1953............	145.6	120.9	83.1	19.4	13.3	5.3	3.6
1955............	158.5	132.3	83.5	20.1	12.7	6.1	3.8
1957............	184.4	154.6	83.8	23.0	12.5	6.8	3.7
1959............	197.0	163.7	83.1	25.6	13.0	7.7	3.9
1961............	216.4	178.6	82.5	29.6	13.7	8.2	3.8
1963............	247.9	204.6	82.6	32.8	13.2	10.5	4.2
1965 (estimated)...	293.8	241.0	82.1	40.0	13.6	12.8	4.3

Source: Figures computed from *Faculty and Other Professional Staff in Institutions of Higher Education, Fall Term, 1963–64* (U.S. Office of Education, OE-53000-64, Circular 794).

of the total number of junior instructional staff each year.[18] Apparently the portion of all teaching performed by full-time members of the staff dropped only 1 percentage point in the 1953–63 period.

The aggregate figures, however, conceal the fact that almost all junior instructional staff are to be found in the university sector. For universities alone, in 1963, 77.3 percent of the f.t.e. faculty were full time, 15.1 percent part time, and 7.6 percent junior instructional staff. There was also considerable variation among universities, the average being moderately higher for public institutions than for private universities. In Table 5, universities are divided into four categories, on the basis of the amount of teaching that is performed by junior instructional staff: 15 percent or over; 10–14.9 percent; 4–9.9 percent; and under 4 percent (the last category containing very few universities). Only those universities granting ten or more doctorates a year are included. In interpreting these percentages, one should remember that in most universities junior instructional staff have teaching duties only in the undergraduate college; thus, if undergraduate teaching comprised only 60 percent of all teaching effort, a figure of 15 percent junior instructional staff would imply that about 25 percent of the undergraduate teaching was done by junior staff. One cannot make the same assumption for regular part-time faculty, since three-fourths of them teach in professional fields, about one-half in the field of medicine alone.[19]

The figures by themselves prove very little, except that there is great

[18] F.t.e part-time faculty is 33 percent of the total number of faculty members in this category. The Office of Education also converts junior instructional staff to f.t.e. at 33 percent, but this seems too high in the author's judgment. The conclusion in the text would not be affected greatly by the O.E. assumption; f.t.e. junior instructional staff would rise from 6 percent in 1953 to 7 percent in 1965.

[19] For example, at New York University, of the part-time faculty of more than 2,000, 60 percent are in medicine and dentistry, and only 9 percent in arts and sciences.

TABLE 5: *Universities Grouped by Junior Instructional Staff as a Percentage of Total Full-time Equivalent Faculty*

University Category	Full-time Faculty		F.T.E. of Part-time Faculty		F.T.E. of Junior Instructional Staff		Total F.T.E. Faculty	
	Number	Percent	Number	Percent	Number	Percent	Number	Percent
15 percent and above.... (Indiana, Iowa, M.I.T., U.C.L.A.)	4,034	68.6	782	13.4	1,061	18.0	5,877	100.0
10–14.9 percent.......... (Arizona, Arkansas, California [Berkeley], Connecticut, Cornell, Harvard, Houston, Illinois, Kansas, Minnesota, Missouri, Nebraska North Carolina, Northwestern, Ohio State, Oklahoma State, St. Louis, Stanford, Washington [St. Louis], Washington [Seattle], Washington State, Wisconsin	22,151	73.6	4,312	14.4	3,612	12.0	30,075	100.0
4–9.9 percent............ (Other major universities)	58,716	78.8	11,658	15.7	4,062	5.5	74,436	100.0
Less than 4 percent....... (Columbia, Denver, Duke, Emory, Virginia, West Virginia, Yale)	5,666	84.4	870	12.9	184	2.7	6,720	100.0

Source: Computed from *Faculty and Other Professional Staff . . . , Fall Term, 1963–64.*

variation among universities. A graduate school which took its training of apprentice teachers seriously, and which encouraged its doctoral candidates to remain in residence until the dissertation was completed, would obviously have a high percentage of junior instructional staff, and we would applaud its efforts. On the other hand, a university which viewed graduate students as cheap labor and gave heavy teaching loads to many of its first- and second-year students would also have a high percentage of junior staff, but most observers would judge this an undesirable state of affairs. Too frequently the former case furnishes the rationale, and the latter case is the reality. The involvement of Berkeley teaching assistants in the 1964 demonstrations has helped to focus attention on the role of the "TA," and most universities today are re-examining their policies and practices. Control over the situation often lies with the individual department, but the administration's permissive policies have contributed to abuses in some universities.

As part of the biographical information collected in the recent survey of graduate education, each of the 4,000 respondents was asked to indicate how his working hours were divided in his present position, and how he "ideally" would distribute them. Department chairmen, understandably, found their administrative duties consuming about 50 percent of their time, and almost to a man they would like to cut this in half and divide the extra time between teaching and research. Table 6 shows the average proportion of time which senior and junior scholars spend on six categories of professional activity; it indicates, also, what they regard as the "ideal" allocation of time.

In reviewing Table 6, one should keep in mind that the respondents were selected on the basis of their being distinguished scholars teaching in the graduate school; thus they are not representative of all university faculty. They could be expected to devote a larger share of their time to graduate instruction than their typical colleague, and they probably devote more of their time to research than does the average professor.

Interestingly, the senior scholars both in engineering and in the physical sciences wished to increase slightly the proportion of their time spent on teaching, and neither group wished to substitute graduate for undergraduate teaching. The junior scholars, particularly in the humanities, social sciences, and biological sciences, wished to reduce substantially the time spent on undergraduates, and to increase their research time by about half. In most instances, they seemed to choose as their ideal the pattern which their senior colleagues were currently following.

One distinguished economist used to argue that the optimum teaching load was positive, but only slightly above zero. There was little evidence of this attitude in the returns: not more than a handful of

TABLE 6: *Actual and Ideal Distribution of Time for Professional Activities of Graduate Professors: Averages*

Field and Category	Average Percentage Distribution[a]						
	Instruction		Total	Research and Writing	Administration	Other Professional	Other
	Undergraduate	Graduate					
Humanities							
Senior scholars: actual	25	29	53	23	16	6	2
ideal	21	30	50	35	8	6	1
Junior scholars: actual	38	24	61	20	13	5	2
ideal	29	27	56	33	6	4	1
Social sciences							
Senior scholars: actual	25	26	51	23	17	8	2
ideal	22	28	50	35	7	7	1
Junior scholars: actual	34	24	58	24	10	6	2
ideal	25	26	51	36	5	6	1
Medical-related biological sciences							
Senior scholars: actual	21	27	48	29	16	6	1
ideal	18	28	46	40	8	6	1
Junior scholars: actual	20	28	48	38	8	4	2
ideal	16	27	43	47	5	5	2
Biological sciences							
Senior scholars: actual	20	27	48	28	16	7	2
ideal	18	28	46	39	8	7	2
Junior scholars: actual	28	25	53	33	9	4	2
ideal	20	26	47	43	5	5	2
Physical sciences							
Senior scholars: actual	18	28	46	25	18	8	2
ideal	18	29	48	36	8	7	1
Junior scholars: actual	26	31	57	27	9	5	1
ideal	23	30	53	37	4	5	—
Engineering							
Senior scholars: actual	19	28	47	18	23	10	2
ideal	20	30	50	25	13	11	1
Junior scholars: actual	27	32	60	19	12	9	1
ideal	26	31	57	27	6	11	1

[a] Percentages may not total because of rounding.

Source: Averages calculated from survey responses reported in Allan M. Cartter, *An Assessment of Quality in Graduate Education* (Washington: American Council on Education, 1966).

the 4,000 scholars indicated that they would like to spend all of their time on nonteaching activities. In almost all fields the senior scholars were relatively content with their current teaching responsibilities, and wished primarily to reduce committee assignments and other administrative chores in favor of more research time. There is little evidence in Table 6 of a desired "flight from teaching," although comparisons over time with similarly selected samples of respondents would be required to see what the actual trends are. Just as universities usually define their optimum size as being about 10 percent larger than their present size (whether that be 5,000 or 40,000 students), so scholars may project as "ideal" what they feel is realizable within the next several years.

CONCLUSIONS

The future conditions of supply and demand for college teachers, if the preceding estimates are borne out, have many implications for the management of higher education. If one is a young college teacher, this is obviously a good time to be alive; and the late 1970's will be a good time to have achieved tenure. Shortages over the next several years will continue to stimulate—and perhaps even to hasten—the upward movement of academic salaries. For the first half of the 1970's colleges and universities will be attempting to recoup ground lost during the late 1960's, so that even though large annual deficits in the doctoral supply are unlikely, upward pressures on salary levels will probably continue. The succeeding fifteen years, however, may tell a different story: it seems predictable that good teaching positions will be more difficult to find then, and that market pressures, which for many years have tended to compress salary differentials among the ranks, will be alleviated. After 1970 colleges can begin to be a bit more selective in their hiring policies, and nonacademic employers are likely to find it somewhat easier to lure new Ph.D.'s.

If, during the 1970's, nonacademic salaries improve relative to the pay of college teachers, some of the assumptions in the preceding forecast must be altered. For example, a decline in the relative attractiveness of college teaching will tend to increase the rate at which teachers move to nonacademic employment and to decrease the flow of senior doctorates into teaching. Thus, the net transfer rate may rise from the assumed .2 percent to perhaps 3 percent or 4 percent. This would not only make more room for young new teachers, but also represent some economy to the colleges. During the last decade many programs have encouraged older professors to continue teaching beyond normal retirement age; it is likely that fifteen years from now there will be a gradual movement toward earlier retirement.

In an earlier essay I concluded:

No head count of teachers can tell us how high the standard of teaching is; the possession of an advanced degree will not convert a poor teacher into an exciting and dedicated one. Just as many of the colleges and universities should be more concerned than they have been with the quality of education provided by their institutions, so should the graduate schools become more concerned with the preparation of their students for careers in college teaching.

If this [essay] accomplishes anything, I hope it will lay to rest our recent over-riding concern with quantity, and permit us to turn our attention to the really important problems of quality in higher education.[20]

Prior to World War II most Ph.D. graduates entered college or university teaching; today this is still true in the humanities and, to a large extent, in the social sciences, but only about a third of those with science doctorates anticipate teaching careers. If the projections in this article are even approximately correct, by the early 1980's only a small minority of the successful doctoral candidates will embark on academic careers. Thus, just when the clamor for the graduate schools to devote more attention to the preparation of college teachers is greatest, teaching promises to become a career concern for a declining proportion of graduate students. Thus, current efforts to build teacher preparation into the graduate school curriculum would seem to be inappropriate if such a program were applied to all students. If this view is true, two conclusions seem to follow. Either (a) graduate schools should begin to think of a "track" system, perhaps beginning after the first year of graduate study, or (b) special training in teaching skills should be relegated to an immediate postdoctoral period. Spokesmen for the liberal arts colleges have long complained that the graduate schools were not turning out the right kind of scholar for college teaching. One could as well argue the reverse: that such colleges have been derelict in assuming that the doctorate was a "finished product" stamp, and that they must take the responsibility of preparing the journeyman for eventual master teacher status. Fifteen or more years ago the Ford Foundation supported a program in a number of liberal arts colleges, permitting a fraction of the newly employed teacher's time to be utilized as a postdoctoral fellowship in college teaching. In retrospect it appears to have been the right program at the wrong time, for the major emphasis in the early 1950's was on improving the research skills of that generation's Ph.D. candidates.

We have come a long way since the 1930's, when Abraham Flexner could complain that few American universities were real institutions of higher learning, that they were dominated by "the mere teaching function," too concerned with teaching boys (undergraduates) rather than with the important task of educating men (the training of scholars in

[20] Cartter, "A New Look at the Supply of College Teachers," p. 277.

the graduate schools).[21] And, at an annual meeting of the American Council on Education in 1937, A. C. Roseander complained bitterly that the greatest weakness of American higher education was that it was so student-oriented, the faculty so involved in nursing undergraduates, that scholarly endeavors and the pursuit of knowledge—the only truly creative role of the university—languished. Today's swing of the pendulum calls for new solutions to perennial problems; perhaps the facts, views, and discussions in this volume, both at current stresses and future prospects, will be instrumental in pointing out rewarding avenues to explore.

APPENDIX: *Projections of Enrollment, New Teachers with Doctorate, and Doctoral Degrees, Four-Year Colleges and Universities, 1965–85*

(Enrollment figures [cols.1–3] in thousands)

Year	Total College Enrollment	F.T.E.[a] Enrollment in 4-year Institutions	F.T.E.[a] Enrollment Increments	New Teachers with Doctorate Required for Constant[b] Quality	Doctorates Projected
	(1)	(2)	(3)	(4)	(5)
1965–66	5,570	3,988	457	12,148	16,100
1966–67	6,007	4,230	242	8,880	16,800
1967–68	6,538	4,589	359	11,034	18,000
1968–69	7,097	4,967	378	11,675	19,500
1969–70	7,263	5,074	107	5,233	21,400
1970–71	7,583	5,285	211	7,819	23,200
1971–72	7,905	5,489	204	7,748	26,000
1972–73	8,304	5,743	254	9,063	28,900
1973–74	8,728	6,015	272	9,621	31,500
1974–75	9,116	6,262	257	9,138	33,600
1975–76	9,556	6,543	281	10,083	35,700
1976–77	9,830	6,704	161	7,232	37,900
1977–78	10,121	6,877	173	7,541	40,400
1978–79	10,388	7,027	150	7,053	43,600
1979–80	10,670	7,187	160	7,251	46,000
1980–81	10,900	7,312	125	6,406	47,900
1981–82	11,047	7,377	65	4,935	49,700
1982–83	11,229	7,464	87	5,436	51,600
1983–84	11,330	7,495	31	4,043	53,200
1984–85	11,522	7,584	89	5,407	54,700
1985–86	11,820	7,737	153	6,939	56,200

[a] The part-time, full-time student mix is assumed to remain stable over the period covered (part-time equals approximately 29% of total enrollment). Full-time equivalents (f.t.e.) are derived by adding 40% of part-time students to full-time enrollment estimates. Junior college enrollments are excluded.

[b] Implicit assumptions are: (1) the incremental faculty-student ratio will remain constant at the 1963–64 level of .048, (2) the ratio of new doctorates to new faculty remains constant at the 1963–64 level of .506, and (3) the faculty retirement and mortality ratio remains stable at .019 through 1974–75, and then declines to .016 by 1985–86.

Sources: Col. 1: The 1965–66 total college enrollment figure is from *Opening (Fall) Enrollment in Higher Education, 1965*, OE-54003-65 (Washington: Government Printing Office, 1966). The enrollment projections are based on Series IV of Allan M. Cartter and Robert Farrell, "Higher Education in the Last Third of the Century," *Educational Record*, Spring 1965, pp. 121–24.

Col 5: Projection is from Allan M. Cartter, "Graduate Education and Research," Background paper for American Library Association conference, March 29, 1965.

[21] See Flexner's biting essay, "American Universities as Institutions of Learning," *The University in a Changing World*, ed. Walter M. Kotschnig and Elined Prys (London: Oxford University Press, 1932), pp. 121–24.

Commentaries on

Future Faculty:
Needs and Resources

BERNARD BERELSON, A. W. DENT,
CARL BORGMANN

The Effect of Quantity on Quality

BERNARD BERELSON

THE UNDERLYING ISSUE of public policy in regard to higher education these years is suggested by the title "Future Faculty: Needs and Resources": it is the effect of quantity on quality. All the major problems in higher education today and tomorrow can be directly traced to the impact of numbers upon the goals, purposes, programs, capacities, and competencies of the institutions of higher education. This country is moving toward a position of "requiring" higher education for a very large proportion of its young people. What does that mean for the system? And in the consideration of college teaching, what does that mean for the size and character of college and university faculties?

Allan Cartter has performed a service to higher education by taking another hard look at "the numbers problem" of faculty in higher education. To my mind his contribution centers in his review—by applying the skills of economic analysis—of what the next years are likely to bring. There are still some lessons to be learned from the mistaken prognoses of the last decade and before, mainly having to do with the effect of self-interest upon objectivity, or ends justifying means—traits that the academic world deplores in Madison Avenue and college sophomores but is slower to recognize at home. There is something to be gained by detailed breakdowns by discipline or region but, as Dr. Cartter points out, they are more problematic and they may not be susceptible of efficient application. Finally, through no fault of his own, Dr. Cartter has less to tell us about quality except insofar as the Ph.D. and the teaching assistantship reflect that factor. If the academic community has not been able over the years to get a firm hold on the elusive matter of quality, we can hardly expect our author to solve the problem. But with regard to the numbers ahead, Dr. Cartter has given us a fresh view, and a valuable one.

With regard to quantity, an uninformed observer from the outside could hardly fail to be surprised at how rapidly the score appears to change in the numbers game. After all, only a few years ago the headlined crisis in higher education was the actual or imminent shortage of qualified faculty, that is, Ph.D.'s; today the "crisis" is to find places in the graduate schools for all the applicants; and soon, according to today's analysis, the crisis will be "overproduction." These so-called crises are either testimony to the vitality of the system or a comment on the commentators—probably something of both. Normally, large and complex systems like higher education do not change that rapidly, and thus a more moderate view might come closer to the target: we were not that badly off in the 1950's and we may not be quite that well off in the 1970's. Dr. Cartter has been ingenious in carrying through this economic analysis of what a plateau of college attendance, if it materializes, could mean to faculty supply. As he himself points out, a shift in the proportion of high school graduates who go on to college, or in faculty salary scales in comparison with competitive salaries off the campus, or in staff-student ratios could affect his projections. I personally think, for example, that the proportion of students going on to college will increase. But I also think Dr. Cartter is basically correct that the great concern about numbers which has characterized the recent period was, and is, misplaced, and that whether we will have enough faculty is a less critical question these days than what "enough" will consist of.

In one sense, of course, we in higher education shall never have enough: we shall never have enough highly trained and impeccably qualified, brilliant and dedicated, inspiring and imaginative scholar-teachers who simultaneously stir the undergraduates in introductory courses and make breakthroughs in research—and all at a price we can afford to pay. We shall never have enough of them any more than any other profession or occupation has enough of their counterparts. Such talk seems to me less than useful and it can be a positive disservice to serious consideration. There simply are not enough such paragons in existence; as an economist once said to me, that is like complaining that in all those respects there aren't more people four standard deviations above the mean! I myself have often wondered whether we ought not to aim instead at the goal of having every college student come into direct contact with just one first-rate man in each of the four major branches of knowledge—to get a deep sense of what the life of the mind in that field is like—and, for the rest, be exposed to solid, disciplinary competence. If we could achieve that level, it seems to me we would have sufficient cause for gratification.

Moreover, I take it as a positive good that all the best Ph.D.'s do not end up on college and university faculties: there are many other important enterprises in this complex society and it is a major contribution to the intellectual well-being of the country that highly trained academic intelligence applies itself in business, government, and professional life as well as in higher education.

With regard to quality: What do we really want by way of college teachers, and how can we get whatever that turns out to be? It is something of a commentary, I think, that quality of faculty usually gets defined as the proportion who have the Ph.D. degree. By that measure (by and large I accept it as a useful one) we are now doing better than ever before, and according to Dr. Cartter's analysis the upward trend is still very much in process. But its use does serve to direct attention to certain implications.

As a major example, take the question of teaching assistants. Dr. Cartter points out that a substantial proportion of undergraduate teaching at some large universities is done by teaching assistants, and other responsible estimates are even larger than his. The teaching assistantship system has long been a sore point in higher education. It has always been a convenient target for disaffection but is even more so today because the whole enterprise is bigger, more visible, and hence more vulnerable. Why is it that we show relatively little concern about a doctoral candidate who gets to or through his prelims and gets a full-time job teaching undergraduates in a liberal arts college when we are very much concerned about another doctoral candidate who gets to and through his prelims and gets a part-time job teaching undergraduates at the university? For that matter, do we really know whether either young man isn't a better teacher of undergraduates than the full professor everyone says he wants in that classroom—leaving aside for the moment the fact that the system cannot afford to have him there? Are we all going to feel more comfortable about the matter once these young men have one or another version of the new intermediate degree?

In any case, it appears that one almost inevitable effect of quantity on quality in higher education will be an even greater variety and diversity within the system than now exists. Indeed, one can argue that range of quality is a necessary and desirable way to handle the problem of "mass" higher education: it is one of the costs of the goal. Moreover, it is not only cost but also return. This large and complex society needs a range of trained people at a variety of posts, and variety offers one way to get such positions filled better than they otherwise would be, better both in liberal education and in professional-vocational training. In this regard, therefore, we can applaud the decentralized control of higher education, appreciate the social and personal consequences of the diversities that result, relax somewhat about the range of quality and purpose, and only wish that the issues could be better recognized and understood by everyone involved.

There are serious implications in all this for the graduate school and for the system. For the graduate school the implications impinge on admission policy and with the process and the content of doctoral training. These two are interwoven. Admission policies are still tied to an earlier era when graduate schools thought they needed more and more students —many are called though few are finished. Is that the most efficient process today? Or could a large proportion of doctoral students finish "with their class" if the universities willed that to happen? Does the new intermediate degree provide a way out? Must the universities have large numbers of graduate students around, whether they finish or not, in order to provide teachers for undergraduate classrooms and research assistants for the professors' projects? Can training in teaching be rationalized so that it is less of a chore and more of an experience, or is the whole idea a perpetual will-o'-the-wisp?

Just as we will never have "enough good teachers," we will never have enough money either, and that mundane factor is of course closely involved with considerations of quantity and quality. Indeed, it is a major reason for the diversity that exists within the system. In the end, the society will probably pay what it thinks higher education is worth, and in the long run that is how it should be.

For American higher education should be judged on its results, like any other institution that contributes to the public welfare. As representatives of the system, we should be quite prepared for it to be appraised on its merits. I believe that it would measure up well against other institutions of the society, against an international standard, against temporal or even absolute standards.

I say "measure up" and therein lies a central problem. The basic questions about quantity and quality of college teachers may not really be settled—if they ever can be—until we have some sound analysis of outcomes. Measurement of the outcomes of higher education is extremely difficult, given all the seemingly intangible values involved, like acquisition of knowledge and skills and problem-solving ability, or the development of critical thinking and aesthetic taste and intellectual zest. But does not the system have the responsibility to push ahead with a constant effort to measure the social return against the social costs? The likelihood that a final answer will not be found does not mean that partial answers are precluded. And recent inquiries into the economic returns of a college education gives some reason to think that such intricate problems can be successfully attacked. At the least, such an effort should get us closer to questions of quality in higher education than we now are.

The United States is currently engaged in one of the greatest explorations in man's history: how to develop a good *mass* system of higher education. No country has ever tried to do this on such a scale and in such richness. There is every reason to believe that the effort will be successful, but in the long view the community of education and the society at large should recognize that such a goal is extremely difficult of attainment, that it simply cannot be realized all at once and all of a high-quality piece. This is the proper perspective, I should think, in which to view the problems having to do with the quantity and quality of college teachers.

Effect of Teacher Shortage on Small Undergraduate Colleges

A. W. DENT

DR. CARTTER'S PAPER regarding "College Teachers: Quantity and Quality" is an excellent review of past predictions and present realities. His prediction that we will have an ample supply of highly qualified college teachers within a decade is gratifying. However, the fact that we will continue to experience a shortage of Ph.D. teachers for the next few years is disquieting. I would like to address my comments specifically to this point: the effect of the teacher shortage on small undergraduate colleges.

As a rule, teachers with the Ph.D. degree select small colleges only when there are no estimable positions on the faculties of large universities. Even when small colleges are preferred, they usually serve as a sort of professional training ground or springboard from which the new Ph.D. hopes to begin—not end—his academic career.

Pointedly, there seem to be several disadvantages encountered by the small college when it attempts to recruit young Ph.D. teachers:

1. As Dr. Cartter points out, the most promising Ph.D. recipients are likely to be given extended postdoctoral fellowships by their degree-granting institutions immediately upon graduation. They will then be retained in the services of the large universities for perhaps two or three years before beginning their teaching careers as such. This arrangement is designed to relieve the chronic teacher shortage faced by the universities. Yet it functions to prolong the teacher crisis in small colleges.

2. Large universities will have prior knowledge of the quality of Ph.D. candidates simply because they have had experiences with them as students and teaching fellows. Thus these universities will have recruiting advantages not only in terms of quantity but also quality. In other words, it is to be expected that the universities will attempt to relieve their teacher shortage by attracting the cream of the crop of their teaching fellows who desire to become full-time faculty members. In too many instances, therefore, small colleges must recruit their teachers from among the less-qualified of the Ph.D. recipients.

3. Small colleges can hardly compete with large universities with respect to faculty salaries. The most basic reason for this is the simple fact that universities usually receive a rather significant portion of their faculty salaries from research grants. Actually, the higher-ranking uni-

versities are sometimes referred to as "research centers." At this point small colleges are disadvantaged. They must emphasize teaching, while research is a secondary function. They receive relatively little research money that can be appropriated for faculty salaries. Besides, the salary ceiling is considerably lower for the small colleges, even though in some instances the beginning salary may be comparable.

4. Universities generally have more prestigious academic reputations than the small colleges. Since it is well known that the prestige of the institution tends to rub off on the scholar, it stands to reason that the most ambitious new Ph.D. will be likely to choose the university instead of the small college even when all other advantages are held constant.

5. Studies have shown that the main reason why many students still choose small colleges instead of undergraduate colleges in large universities is their desire to receive personalized instruction from full-status faculty members. In essence, the student-teacher ratio in small colleges must necessarily be kept lower than that expected in large universities. Small colleges, then, need to attract a proportionately larger number of new Ph.D.'s than the large universities if they are to keep pace with them during the next few years. This assumes that the small colleges are now as adequately staffed as the large universities. Since, of course, this is not the case, the small colleges are at an additional disadvantage in the recruitment of Ph.D.'s. They must first improve their faculty to the level of the university faculty.

6. Dr. Cartter observes that non-Ph.D. teachers are likely to leave the teaching profession and accept jobs in the nonacademic world more often than are Ph.D. holders. Here again the small college is at a disadvantage precisely because it has, as a rule, a much larger proportion of non-Ph.D. faculty members than do the universities. They are, therefore, more vulnerable to the recruiting practices of industry and government.

In conclusion, I would like to mention that the predominantly Negro colleges encounter all of the difficulties associated with the chronic faculty shortage that Dr. Cartter has pointed out. Further, these problems tend to be much more acute for the predominantly Negro colleges. Generally, these colleges are even smaller than the average small college, and they are usually economically poor. This adds up to an alarming fact: many of them will not be able to compete with large universities and high-status undergraduate colleges for the best-qualified teachers. Difficult as this problem is, I hope that through our collective wisdom we will be able to find means to help these very deserving colleges compete effectively in the teacher market.

I have at least one promising suggestion: We must find ways of greatly expanding study opportunities for teachers now in the small colleges, and particularly those in the predominantly Negro colleges, who have already given evidence of their dedication to teaching in these colleges.

Faculty Needs and Resources in Engineering

CARL W. BORGMANN

IT HAS BEEN REFRESHING to have had Dr. Cartter's analyses, in papers and speeches, of a problem that has had more study and has yielded more cries of "wolf!"—including a "coyote" or two from me—than almost any other academic topic during the past fifteen years. The dire predictions have been refuted by events, but we did not know precisely why until we had Cartter's scrutiny. Now we find that higher education is an amazingly adaptable system. Our predictions swing wildly, so that now we appear to be faced with another explosion—a Ph.D. explosion. If we believe the newest predictions, holders of the Ph.D. will become a drug on the market and the problem will be to find suitable occupations for the Ph.D.'s who cannot get teaching jobs. To get a faculty job after the next few years, the bright young Ph.D. may even have to agree to teach an undergraduate course or two!

As Cartter is careful to point out, counting degrees is fun but is not a complete measure of faculty needs and resources. Further, the lumping of colleges and universities and the use of undergraduate enrollments as the sole criterion of numbers of faculty needed is not completely satisfying. The graduate programs of universities have been experiencing a growth which, relatively at least, equals the growth at the undergraduate level; and graduate education is costly in faculty time needed per student. Finally, many forecasters appear to be biologically and mathematically illiterate. Few appear to know that a growth curve is S-shaped and that the achievement of infinity is an unlikely end. These factors, coupled with the certainty that our academic mores will drive all fields and all schools toward a faculty composed totally of "card-carrying" members, temper my fear that holders of the doctorate may sell apples for a living. It may be a worry for my grandchildren, but not for me.

I sympathize with Cartter as he attempts to analyze the real dimensions of the teaching assistant problem. Not only is it impossible from present data to get even an estimate of the numbers involved, but also the use of teaching assistants by departments and institutions varies from full classroom responsibility through supervised laboratory instruction to paper grading. I suspect that one would generally find that only in those departments that are striving to build a doctoral program rapidly is the use of graduate students as instructors more prevalent than it was, say, thirty years ago. In the science area, I suspect that mathematics is the greatest offender, if "offender" is the proper word.

Cartter, with proper warning about the dangers, has given some forecasts of the faculty situations during the next twenty years as they may be experienced in a few broad academic areas. To these, I can add a few observations about the engineering fields. We made surveys of the national engineering faculty in the spring of both 1959 and 1963. The returns approached census proportions in that we collected data on more than 95 percent of the faculty from all schools, whether accredited or not, that offered a degree in any field of engineering. It is well to remember that when one discusses engineering faculties, only a relatively small number of institutions are involved—225 in all and approximately 175 with one or more departments accredited. Further, few engineering departments or colleges are parts of institutions offering only the baccalaureate degree. The first survey was preceded by an eight-year period during which the numbers of doctorates in engineering granted per year remained nearly constant at a level of approximately 600. Further, these eight years encompassed the frantic first years of the space effort and a period of very rapid growth of support for research and development, when doctorates in engineering were in great demand by both Federal agencies and industry. These are the facts we gleaned:

By 1963 the total faculty had grown by 2,240 individuals or by 20 percent of the 1959 figure. Its composition each year, broken down into arbitrary, but useful, categories, is given in Table 1:

TABLE 1: *Composition of the Total Engineering Faculty*

	1959	1963	Difference
Core* faculty..............	8,200	9,060	+ 860
Peripheral* faculty..........	1,200	1,070	− 130
Adjunct and postretirement faculty.................	2,100	780	+1,510
Teaching assistants.........		2,830	
Total.....................	11,500	13,740	+2,240

    * The full-time faculty was divided arbitrarily into a group (core) considered to be committed to academia and another group (peripheral) composed of all full-time instructors under thirty-three years of age who were also pursuing a graduate program at the institution of employment.

The core engineering faculty was considered to be the key group to examine, and the following statements refer to it.

First, the core faculty grew by more than 10 percent, and the proportion holding the doctorate increased from 33 percent to over 45 percent. Translated into numbers, some 1,400 more individuals had the doctorate in 1963 than in 1959, but closer examination indicates that only 1,060 of these had received doctorates in engineering. Mathematics and the physical sciences were the doctoral fields of most of the other 340.

Engineering, however, has many specialties, and the proportions of doctorally trained faculty in them vary greatly. If one considers only the more common academic specialties, the doctoral percentages in them range from 85 percent in chemical engineering to 31 percent in industrial engineering. While all the principal specialties showed an increase in doctorates, the lowest relative improvement occurred in aeronautical engineering. Of course, this was the field in which there was the greatest competition for trained personnel from space and defense employers.

Even though our definitions of categories eliminated many of the younger teachers from the core group, nearly half of the faculty in it were under forty years of age in 1963 and two-thirds were forty-five years or less. Of the latter group, 52 percent had the doctorate and another 16 percent reported that they were seeking it. It was surprising to find that even among the older members of the under-forty-five group (those thirty-eight to forty-five), 11 percent were striving for academia's Grail. Further increases in the amount of academic training of the nation's engineering faculties appear to be assured. Reassurance can be taken from the fact that in 1959 the number of doctor's degrees granted in engineering was 647 and by 1965 the figure had grown to 2,124—a 330 percent increase—with no signs yet of a diminishing growth rate.

It is more difficult for me to offer facts in the natural sciences. From readings and from unstructured observations made over the past few years, it is my impression that the most serious faculty problem exists in the fields of physics and mathematics at our nonuniversity colleges. At all but a few such institutions it is apparently difficult to recruit and retain in these fields faculty who are capable of offering a major strong enough to serve as sound preparation for graduate study. This is not to say that the teaching of physics and mathematics is generally poor in such institutions; rather, it is increasingly difficult for them to provide the variety and level of coverage that are required of applicants by our leading graduate schools. There are, however, other demands for physics and mathematics offerings in the nonuniversity colleges than preparation for graduate school. They have—or should have—a major place in the education of the liberal arts major, and they are essential as tools in the modern biological and social sciences. Perhaps the faculty best suited to meet these needs might be qualified by criteria that are alternative to the Ph.D. and that are both acceptable to academia and educationally sound. I predict, however, that such criteria—particularly that of acceptability to academia—will be most difficult to achieve.

Demands for Doctorates: Some Dissenting Views

IF DR. CARTTER'S PROGNOSTICATIONS are accurate, one can feel some sense of comfort; if they are inaccurate, the results can be disastrous. This appraisal can be self-defeating if it encourages general apathy and reduced government support for graduate training and facilities. Further, a change in conditions can substantially alter Cartter's conclusions. Has sufficient attention been given to: (a) future changes in student-faculty ratio; (b) the increasing demand among nonuniversity employers for qualified personnel holding higher degrees; (c) a more rapid growth in graduate enrollment than in undergraduate enrollment, which would result in a decline rather than a rise in faculty-student ratios; (d) the possibilities of heavy commitments of faculty to serve in a variety of assignments abroad? Dr. Cartter seems to treat the university as a static organization, performing only its traditional roles. Yet the demands made by society (and, therefore, the government) for a host of new functions and services have increased dramatically. There seems to be almost no limit to these demands and probably no way for higher education to escape them since there is nowhere else for the government to turn. The effect of absorbing these new functions will be to create a larger need for Ph.D.'s and cause a continuing problem of the quantity and quality of college teachers.

PART FOUR

Teaching and Learning

University Teaching
and Excellence

ALLAN M. CARTTER

THE LAST TEN YEARS, beginning with Sputnik, represent a period when the overriding concern of higher education has been with research and graduate education. For the next decade, however, as can be predicted from the evolving policies of Federal agencies, private foundations, and the universities themselves, and as is underlined by the current spasms of student unrest, the primary concern of college educators will be with teaching. Just as the postwar university had to rediscover its mission of "creating the future" through scholarly and scientific research, so today we must again turn our attention to the primary educational function of the university.

The pursuit of excellence, to use the fashionable phrase, implies a concern with the *quality* of teaching—although "quality" here can be interpreted in two rather different ways. We might want to know what the contribution of teaching is to the reputation for excellence an institution earns; alternatively, we might seek to determine the contribution of teaching to a more narrowly defined (but perhaps more meaningful) concept of excellence, encompassing the nature of the student's educational experience during his period of residence at the university. Let me briefly comment on the first of these interpretations, since it is a somewhat easier question to speak to, and then turn to the more important aspect of teaching.

As far as an institution's reputation is concerned, the quality of teaching is probably most important to a small college which envisions as its task primarily the transmission of knowledge and the development of those qualities of mind and spirit which will enhance man's *Humanitas* (in Karl Jaspers' words). Reputation, although it may lag a decade or two, is made by the impact the institution has on its students. Such an impact is cumulative, as word is passed from one student generation to another. The eminence of such schools as Swarthmore, Amherst, Reed, or Grinnell is a gradual accretion. Perhaps we tend to place too much emphasis on the percentage of their baccalaureates who go on to graduate school or achieve professional eminence, but these are indicators of real accomplishment. Once a school has won such a reputation, it tends to be self-selective, attracting primarily those students who are endowed by native talent to confirm that reputation. This has both its good and its bad results, as David Riesman has pointed out in speaking of the lag in reputation:

. . . the quality of a school changes faster than its clientele recognizes; and colleges that have developed a novel or more demanding program cannot get the students to match it, while other institutions that have decayed cannot keep away students who should no longer go there. . . . And the result can be tragic, not only for misled students, but for imaginative faculty and administrators who may not live long enough to be rewarded by the appearance of good students attracted by those changes.[1]

Universities, on the other hand, seem to live within the aura of their over-all reputation. I seriously doubt that Harvard, Michigan, or Berkeley merit their excellent reputations on the basis of the quality of their *undergraduate* teaching. Events over the past year in Berkeley would support this view; riots may be beneath the dignity of Harvard Yard, but I suspect that undergraduate teaching is no longer the secret of Harvard's success. The fact that Harvard undergraduates are a very select lot and that Cambridge somehow endows the student with the capacity for self-learning undoubtedly accounts for the continued high reputation of its undergraduate college.[2] At the other extreme, I have learned to have a high regard for the graduates of several public and private universities which do not have the same national prestige but which seem to turn out more than their share of baccalaureates who are successful in later careers.

Current efforts to develop national assessment programs hold out the hope that we will be able to develop one device—imperfect though any standardized measure may be—to assess the educational impact of a college on its students. I, for one, would not be surprised to find that, given their human and capital resources, many of the most prestigious colleges and universities do a rather poor job; the high caliber of their graduates may be almost entirely a function of the talented students

[1] Riesman, *Constraint and Variety in American Education* (Garden City, N.Y.: Doubleday & Co., 1958), p. 5.

[2] The Harvard Crimson *Confidential Guide to Courses* notes that a reader may be tempted to conclude: "that the College has a surprisingly large number of poor or abysmal [undergraduate] teachers. This is an old complaint, but Harvard has long maintained that teaching ability is only one, and perhaps minor, quality to be considered in a potential professor." See 1965 ed., p. 2.

they attract, rather than of what the college does for them during their four years of formal education.[3]

In the absence of any technique for assessing the relative quality of undergraduate teaching, I would suggest the uncomfortable conclusion that a *university* which wishes to win national acclaim must do so first in its graduate and professional schools; if it wins a good reputation for Ph.D.'s, it will then attract the kind of undergraduates who will later justify its eminence as an undergraduate institution. As far as external reputation goes, good teaching in a university without an eminent graduate school earns its reward primarily in heaven.

The second concept of excellence, ignoring worldly fame, is concerned only with what an institution does for the students who happen to cross its threshold. This view is what John Gardner refers to in his volume on *Excellence:*[4] the pursuit of the most meaningful educational experience within the context of an institution's objectives, student body, curriculum, and degree level. In this sense excellence is both a state of mind and a way of pursuing objectives: it is the desire to do the very best possible job with the resources at hand. Most of the more than 2,200 institutions that are not Harvard have little to gain by merely wishing that they were. Each college has an important role to play, and it wastes its talents and resources if it does not try to perform that role as effectively as possible.

SOME CURRENT TRENDS IN UNDERGRADUATE EDUCATION

Concentrating on this second aspect of excellence, there appear to be a number of developments today which have important implications for the structure of undergraduate education and the collegiate learning environment. This article is a brief review of some of these trends, and of various obstacles to the improvement of undergraduate teaching in the university.

The anticipated rise in college enrollments needs little comment, except to stress that we have been concerned for so long with the tidal wave of the late 1960's that we sometimes forget that undergraduate enrollments are likely to continue to climb to something like 15 million by the year 2000. Thus, if all existing institutions doubled in size during the last third of this century, even then we would still need about 1,000 new four-year institutions and perhaps as many as 2,000 new junior colleges to handle the projected expansion. Much attention has

---

[3] Alexander W. Astin concludes from a study of National Merit finalists that Northeastern men's colleges are "underproductive" in sending students on to the Ph.D. See "Differential College Effects on the Motivation of Talented Students to Obtain the Ph.D." *Journal of Educational Psychology,* February 1963, pp. 63–71.

[4] New York: Harper & Row, 1961.

been devoted to new institutions over the last several years, but numerically they do not yet loom large on the higher education scene. For example, the vast increase in college enrollments from 1940 to 1964 was accommodated primarily by existing institutions; only 12 percent was accounted for by institutions founded since 1940. Fewer new colleges and universities were founded in the 1930–60 period than in any previous thirty-year period since 1840. The peak period, interestingly, was 1870–1900; there are 491 accredited institutions existing today which were founded then, as compared with 143 four-year institutions and 184 junior colleges founded in the 1930–60 years. Over the last several years the rate has jumped considerably, but it should be noted that only 59 percent of the institutions added to the Office of Education *Directory: Part 3* during the last twenty years were still in existence in 1964. Thus a count of additions to the directory overstates the growth rate.[5]

But the important point is that in the last several years, new institutions have been springing up at an ever more rapid rate. And it is the institution which starts from scratch that has the best opportunity to learn from the past and to be truly innovative. As one major university president recently noted: "If you are going to innovate, you better do it the day before you hire the first faculty member."

A second major trend discernible today is that we are finally coming to recognize the relationship between scale and the individual's sense of identification: we are at last launching an attack on the impersonality of the large institution. Certainly this is nothing new: Oxford and Cambridge have prospered with the college system since the twelfth century. In this country Harvard and Yale are today identified as early proponents of the small residence college, although it is within the memory of living men that Yale turned down its first offer of funds for establishing the college system, only to find that Harvard accepted it with alacrity. But it is really only during the last five years that the largest universities have begun to recognize the need for such a system. The example of Santa Cruz shows that such an organizational pattern is much simpler to establish when starting fresh rather than when trying to remodel an existing campus. Looking back ten years from now, we will probably view many of our major universities today as monolithic monstrosities, for we have memorialized in concrete or brick our earlier lack of concern with students as individuals. As one observer recently

---

[5] Of the institutions which dropped out of sight, 27 percent merged with other colleges, 29 percent ceased operations, 40 percent were dropped from the directory because they failed to meet even the minimum standards for inclusion (acceptance of transfer credits by three accredited institutions), and 4 percent lost their listing for other reasons. See A. M. Cartter and Robert Farrell, "Higher Education in the Last Third of the Century," *Educational Record*, Spring 1965, pp. 119–28.

remarked, architectural beauty and variety come close to being psychological necessities in the learning environment; all too few of us have taken this point very seriously in the past.

A third trend, related to the preceding, is the rediscovery that living is a learning experience itself. As President Fels of Bennington used to assert, the total college is the teacher. Too frequently we, on college staffs, have had an overriding concern with the fifteen hours a week the student spends in class, and too little interest in the other 97 waking hours he has at his disposal. The residence hall, the college within the university, even the fraternity house can be important elements in the education of a college student. But on too many campuses, if a faculty committee worked for a year to come up with the most self-defeating educational setting possible, they could improve little upon present arrangements. If I may use as an example one private university I have known well—and it is a reasonably good illustration, being a well-endowed institution which traditionally emphasizes undergraduate education—every dormitory (including the new men's dorm built in 1962) was of the noisy unbroken long-hall variety, rooms were overcrowded, the library had about one working space for every eight undergraduates and one library carrel for every three graduate students, the student had to drive to some dingy bar a mile away to have a beer, and until the faculty vociferously protested several years ago, there was not even a decent bookstore within twenty blocks of the campus. These liabilities have been, or are now rapidly being, changed; but it is an irony that one could not have created an environment less conducive to the stated educational objectives of the institution if one had tried. This case is by no means unusual; until very recently few colleges or universities were much concerned with what went on outside the classroom, provided student behavior did not publicly offend the morality of the community.

But we are rediscovering the value of collegiate residence just at the time when the national trend is toward the student's living at home. The community college is today the fastest growing sector of higher education, and too frequently its advocates present it as a cure-all for higher education's growing pains. The community college's accessibility may be a virtue, but it is won at considerable sacrifice to the quality of the educational experience. I would argue that two-thirds of the value of attending college is the residential experience: the loosening of ties with family and community, and the consequent broadening of intellectual horizons and cultural traditions. Attending college at home can be too comfortable; most students need to be shocked from their accustomed modes of thought, and this can best be brought about if they leave home.

Too frequently the community college pattern is sold on the grounds of economy. Actually, it involves many hidden costs. A recent California study indicated that students who commuted fifteen miles or more to college spent more on living costs and transportation than they would have on collegiate residence. In a city such as New York, where the average commuting student spends nearly two hours a day on bus or subway, the real cost differential (if the commuting time could have been spent either on a speeded-up academic program or at a job) is slight. Though the student lives at home, and colleges need not borrow large sums for residence halls, these savings are more apparent than real and frequently do not compensate for the loss of a meaningful educational experience.

In Great Britain, the Robbins Committee noted in its report (1963) that before World War II about 60 percent of university students lived at home; by 1963 only a third were living at home while attending university, and the committee's recommendation was that this figure should be reduced to about one-fifth. Too little attention in this country seems to be accorded the educational value of college residence.

Despite my general reservations about commuter colleges, I would suggest that the experiments now underway at Monteith College (Wayne State) and New College (Hofstra) are among the most promising innovations of this decade. If we *are* to have more commuting students in the future, then those universities which seek imaginative ways of providing a sense of community to the part-time or non-resident student should be praised and encouraged.—Whenever I am tempted to object to some current trend I am reminded that the Bavarian Medical Association in the 1850's passed a strongly worded resolution condemning railroads as a great physiological and psychological danger to mankind. To have the scenery swiftly moving by at speeds of twenty or thirty miles an hour would, they were convinced, dazzle and derange passengers. Their solution was to build along all the rights-of-way high fences, painted in some neutral color, to prevent loss of eyesight!

Another rediscovery of the past decade has been that students can learn on their own quite successfully. Until recently, the possibilities of independent study—and our Cambridge and Oxford friends would be surprised to hear that there is any other way for an adult to learn— have been explored only with the superior student. But even for capable students, the innovative path has not always been easy, for I can recall a heated university faculty debate where it was successfully argued that honors programs and advanced placement were terribly undemocratic. A more enlightened view holds that all students should be not just encouraged, but positively goaded into intellectual exploration as far as their interests and capacities can take them. The new experiments with universal independent study during some period of one academic year, and frequently during each of the four years, may set an improved pattern for the future. The standard commencement ceremony, with its invitation to a lifelong self-education, has too often been an initiation ceremony for which the initiates had no real preparation.

Boswell quotes Dr. Johnson as saying: "Lectures were once useful, but now when all can read and books are so numerous, lectures are no longer necessary." Few academicians, in the intervening years, have taken Johnson very seriously. Yet, in light of the development of excellent textbooks in most fields since the war, much of the lecturing done today is unnecessary. In the words of the Hale *Report on University Teaching Methods*[6] in Britain, many university lecture courses today are "the worst kind of spoonfeeding." According to the report, students in England judged the humanists to be the worst offenders, charging that many ill-prepared, badly presented lectures deserved to be missed. Hale concludes: "Over-indulgence in lectures should be classed as a drug addiction on the part of both the giver and the receiver."

Using talented manpower as "talking books" is a shameful waste in most of our colleges and universities today, and tends to keep the student a permanent adolescent. The student's umbilical cord must be severed upon graduation in any event, and we should take the responsibility of playing midwife at an earlier stage. If independent study can help accomplish this end and can release faculty time for more seminars and tutorials, where the student can actively participate in the dialogue, it is a worthy objective. Our chief occupational hazard is that the easiest thing for most of us to do is lecture. Yet most college lecture courses lack the intimacy and personal relationship necessary for a real learning experience, and many do not even have the advantage of organization that a good book has.

I will only mention in passing improvements in teaching technology and in curricula. In the contemporary discussion of innovations these two tend to get too much emphasis as it is. "Teaching technology" strikes a false note in the humanistic ear, for it seems a mismated phrase, almost an oxymoron, like "the mechanics of poetry" or "the art of key-punching." The onslaught of electronics and publishing firms threatens to create a new teaching technocracy; but perhaps, like educational television ten years ago, which was supposed to displace most college professors within a decade, this new gadgetry will soon find its place in a properly supplemental role. While the advantage of giving the most sophisticated Ph.D. student at M.I.T. speedier access

[6] University Grants Committee (London: Her Majesty's Stationery Office, 1964).

to technical data is indisputable, it is hard to fathom why a college freshman should want, much less be permitted, to tune in the Library of Congress at whim on his own electronic console. The one major virtue of the new "preserving jar" technology is that it allows the student to perform certain relatively routine exercises at his own convenience, instead of having to march lock-step through formal laboratory periods. But many teachers in American universities would share the sentiments of R. M. Ogilvie, tutor at Balliol College, Oxford, when he recently complained:

That a large number of extremely able people should be supported at vast expense of public money simply to facilitate the communication of facts and knowledge to students would be both uneconomic and inefficient. . . . There may well be a case for building cramming shops where information and knowledge can be retailed, but are we to call them universities? [7]

Curricular reforms are a somewhat higher order of innovation. Whether we fully agree with his recommendations or not, all of us must be grateful for Daniel Bell's serious and thoughtful analysis of contemporary liberal arts curricula. But even in discussions of the liberal arts I would venture that we are too frequently tempted to place greater emphasis upon the subjects taught than upon the object desired. Liberal education depends less upon a curriculum than upon the character of the teacher and his ability to place the subject matter in the larger context of man and his dominion over the earth. Too frequently we assume that a balanced diet of specialized courses taught by illiberal professors will somehow magically produce a liberally endowed student.

It is a common practice today to complain that the liberal arts colleges are in decline, that they are caught between the upward thrust of the secondary school and the downward reach of the graduate school. As students come better prepared in fundamentals—in modern foreign languages, mathematics, and science—many functions of the old freshman year are removed. At the other extremity, much of what used to be done in the first year of graduate study has crept into specialized courses at the senior level. But there is nothing inherently evil in the high school's assuming some of the generalist functions previously performed in the early years of college, and the college's assuming some of the specialist functions previously assigned to the graduate school. This may represent a shift in functions which disturbs the organizational structure of higher education as it has been traditionally envisaged, but it can serve well the principles of both liberal and advanced learning.

Eight years ago, only about 12 percent of those receiving baccalaure-

[7] Ogilvie, "The Role of the Teacher," *The Expanding University*, ed. W. R. Niblett (London: Faber & Faber, 1962), p. 96.

ate degrees went on to full-time advanced study; last year, the figure was more than 20 percent. In 1961, when National Merit Scholarship Corporation queried all incoming freshmen in 250 colleges about their degree aspirations, nearly 60 percent said they intended to stop at the baccalaureate degree.[8] In the fall of 1965, when Astin asked all freshmen in 55 selected four-year colleges and universities participating in the American Council on Education data bank, only 36 percent expected to stop at the bachelor's level.[9] Whether or not aspirations become realities four years later, they do suggest the magnitude of the revolution that is taking place. If present trends continue, there will be more students in graduate schools before the end of the century than there were in undergraduate colleges in the late 1940's.

Obviously technical and economic necessity will demand increasingly specialized education in the years ahead, however much we may regret it; but at the same time political, social, and cultural necessity in the future will demand the continued strengthening of our human heritage. The selective liberal arts colleges of the future, I believe, must become first-rate preparatory colleges for graduate education. Clinging to the fiction that they represent the terminal years of formal education only obscures their real task; objecting to the trend toward advanced education only weakens their ability to do that task well. This trend, far from making the colleges subservient to the demands of specialized education, gives them a broader opportunity to offer a truly liberal education, since no longer are they required to turn out terminal students with a major in depth in a single discipline. The student going on to graduate school needs rigorous training in the fundamentals of his subject, but he needs less concentration in a single field than the student who ends his formal education at the baccalaureate level. The student going on in economics, for example, needs a good grounding in theory and in mathematics, but to spend two years branching out into labor economics, public finance, money and banking, international trade, and other intermediate-level courses is largely a waste of his time: he will have to do it all over again in graduate school. How much better to spend some of this time on political theory, history, philosophy, and literature—for he will never again in his formal education have the opportunity to roam as widely. The student naturally tends to overspecialize, and unfortunately many of his faculty advisers encourage him to do so. The independent liberal arts college, because it is (or should be) more self-conscious about its educational aims and values, is in a

[8] See Alexander W. Astin, *Who Goes Where to College* (Chicago: Science Research Associates, 1965), p. 15.

[9] See Robert Panos and Alexander W. Astin, "The Profile of Entering 1965 College Freshmen," *College and University* (in press).

better position than is the undergraduate college in a large university to counter the student's uninformed propensities.

SOME OBSTACLES TO THE IMPROVEMENT OF
UNDERGRADUATE EDUCATION

Many factors inhibit the improvement of undergraduate education; and the literature on higher education is paying increasing attention to the difficulty of measuring teaching proficiency, the nature of the faculty reward system, the gap between learning theory and practice, and so forth. Attention here will be devoted to several other broad constraints.

Innovation is not a natural propensity of academic man: perhaps it is in the nature of the beast that he tends to be an imitative animal who enjoys familiar routines. Also, the traditional faculty control over curriculum, requiring consensus and encouraging compromises and departmental trade-offs, is not always conducive to experimentation.

Martin Trow [10] notes that deans are frequently more hospitable to experiments and innovations than are faculty committees. Christopher Jencks [11] also argues that orthodoxy stifles imagination on most campuses. Several universities are attempting to overcome this innate conservatism by the creation of semi-autonomous undergraduate colleges within the larger university. Few of us have the opportunity of starting *de novo*, as does the Santa Cruz campus of the University of California, but Santa Cruz, Monteith, Oakland University, Livingston College at Rutgers, and several others, are among the more exciting ventures in higher education today; not only are they trying to find new organizational patterns within the college, but also they are exploring the value of breaking the large institution into purposely diverse parts. An entire university is understandably, and probably correctly, an entrenched entity opposed to radical change. Creating relatively independent sub-units with the specific intention of encouraging diversity and heterogeneity is an attractive alternative. The administrator with an innovative bent, the young faculty member stifled by his senior colleagues, the older professor who has always wanted to try something new may find such colleges within a university the answer to prayer. Last year, talking to the faculty long-range planning committee at the Johns Hopkins University, I suggested that instead of doing away with the undergraduate colleges, as some faculty members wished to do, the university should spin off four or five satellite colleges as contiguous parts of the university com-

[10] See Trow, "Undergraduate Teaching at Large State Universities," pp. 164–80 of this volume.
[11] See Jencks, "An Anti-Academic Proposal," *Educational Record*, Summer 1966, pp. 320–26.

munity. Each college might have a different curricular emphasis, each might have its separate fee structure—but each would have access to the resources of the university center. Such a system would be a kind of Claremont Colleges in reverse. The one limitation of Claremont, in my opinion, is that the power and initiatory force lie primarily with the five undergraduate colleges, and each remains just a little fearful of potential domination by the graduate center. True federation, rather than loose confederation (such as the many voluntary consortia now springing up), may be the prime requisite for success. Whatever the details of a particular system, giving a degree of curricular autonomy to sub-units within a university is one means of encouraging experimentation to improve undergraduate education.

A second obstacle to imaginative educational planning has been our sense that the possibilities for attracting high-quality faculty will become increasingly limited. For ten years we have talked of the deteriorating quality of college teaching staffs, and we have learned to live with an impending crisis. Partly as a result of this real or imagined constraint, much of the emphasis upon innovation in recent years has been of the "labor saving" category: educational television, taped lectures on instant recall, teaching machines, large lecture halls with improved audio-visual aids, and so forth. As I have argued in another paper,[12] a more optimistic view about the future availability of college teachers is now possible. One can foresee a time within the next ten years when the trend may be reversed and instruction will become more personal and individualized. We have already found that much of the new teaching technology is not particularly economical in dollars, although it does release scarce faculty talent. And however effective these technical improvements are for the purely informational and routinized aspects of learning, they may be called diabolically illiberal. (I use *diabolic* in the sense of "inhuman," although it could be argued that teaching machines are literally devilish: how many of today's students and teachers are latter-day Fausts?)

A British educator, in a recent paper given before a meeting of university teachers, succinctly summarized the necessary ingredients of liberal education:

One can only spread interest by personal contagion. One can only develop individualism by taking each person's work separately and seeing what are the particular needs of each individual. One can only inculcate integrity by dialectic, by direct, personal *ad hominem* argument.[13]

Given the will and the desire, one can obtain knowledge from the book, the television screen, the magnetic tape, but wisdom, understanding, and tolerance—the essential aims of liberal learning—are attainable

[12] Cartter, "Future Faculty: Needs and Resources," pp. 113–35 of this volume.
[13] Ogilvie, "The Role of the Teacher," p. 95.

only through personal confrontation of teacher and student. Interest, individualism, and integrity cannot be mass-produced; they result from the personal interaction of man with man.

Another obstacle to innovative development is one of attitude. As higher education continues to expand, a larger proportion of the students who come to us are without the family and community background which would provide them with intellectual curiosity and a strong moral sense. We are expected to give them a purpose to live for and standards to live by, to encourage those attributes of being which are associated with the cultured gentleman (even in an age of technical specifications when there are few jobs left for those with only gentlemanly qualifications). This aspect of liberal education is accomplished more by example than by formal teaching, and it places on us an increasing burden to be exemplars of the kind of world we would like to create.

At the same time, however—perhaps partly because of the postwar seller's market—the typical faculty member takes this responsibility less seriously today than he did a generation or two ago. As John Gardner notes in his essay on "The Flight from Teaching," "there is a whole generation of able young faculty members who never knew a time when affluence did not prevail. Thus it is hardly surprising that some of them exhibit an opportunism that startles their elders." Gardner concludes that "we should consider the possibility of formulating ethical standards to curb the crassest opportunism in grantsmanship, job hopping, and wheeling-dealing." [14]

Another aspect of faculty attitude is reflected in the publish-or-perish syndrome. A recent review of data for three fields of study revealed that about 90 percent of all major publications (books, articles in leading professional journals) originated in the top twenty-five Ph.D.-granting departments in each field. At the other extreme, a quarter of the doctorate-granting departments turn out less than one article a year.[15] Such evidence suggests that, except in a small number of leading universities, "publish-or-perish" is largely a myth popularized by the few poor teachers who, lacking the one credential for tenure appointment, did indeed perish when found lacking in the other. (In the most publicized cases, however, "perish" is a complete misnomer: the faculty member involved usually took a job at a higher salary and rank in a more congenial environment.)

But the root of the problem of faculty attitude is deeper than this.

[14] *Fifty-Ninth Annual Report of the Carnegie Endowment for the Advancement of Teaching for the Year Ended June 30, 1964* (New York: The Endowment, 1965).
[15] A. M. Cartter, *An Assessment of Quality in Graduate Education* (Washington: American Council on Education, 1966). See especially chap. 4.

The young faculty recruit is an impressionable person, and the two most important periods in his life are those that immediately precede and follow his getting the doctorate. Typically, as a graduate student, he pursued a degree in a large university which was itself caught up in catering to many markets and serving many masters, and therefore gave little attention to any one. It is puzzling that all two-hundred-odd graduate schools in this country assume this stance, and unfortunate that no single one has ever devoted itself exclusively to seeking students intent on an academic career and doing a really first-rate job of training them as teachers. Claremont probably comes as close as any to this model, and I think that the urge of liberal arts colleges such as Wesleyan, Reed, and Lawrence to become liberal arts *universities* stems chiefly from the strong desire to turn out the kind of teacher they feel is needed at the undergraduate level. Only now, in a few scattered places, are the graduate schools showing much concern for preparing the teacher-scholar, as someone slightly different from, but not necessarily opposed to, the research-scholar.

The undergraduate colleges must share some of the blame with the graduate schools. Too often when they hire new recruits, they assume that nothing more need be done to convert the student into an experienced and mature teacher. The completion of a formal degree does not create an instant teacher, and serious considerations should be given to the development of postdoctoral teaching fellowship programs within colleges and universities. New college teachers, even more than new automobiles, might benefit from a carefully designed "breaking-in" program.[16]

The physical growth of the typical university in recent years poses another obstacle to improved teaching, for contact between teacher and student is increasingly limited to the formal classroom. In many large American universities today it is not uncommon for the majority of seniors to graduate without ever having been inside a professor's home. It is refreshing that in England the Hale report on university teaching can still talk unashamedly about "the pastoral function" of teaching departments; it expresses concern that when departments grow to more than twenty or thirty, its members may lose the ability to sit around the commons room and discuss the individual student: his progress and problems, the additional reading assignments that he would most profit from, the subjects that might best be assigned for his papers, and so forth.[17] We too frequently pose the question of size as: How large can the university be without becoming too unwieldy an administrative unit? Rather, we might ask: How small can a university remain and still

[16] This point is developed more fully in "Future Faculty: Needs and Resources," p. 134.
[17] *Report on University Teaching Methods*, p. 25.

achieve the minimum critical mass needed for quality education? The scholarly reputation of a university may be directly related to its size, but the quality of undergraduate education tends to be an inverse function of size.

Another obstacle to the improvement of undergraduate education is one which is almost impossible to overcome: the department. Anything larger than St. John's College (Annapolis) obviously needs administrative sub-units, and the academic discipline may be as good a unit as any. The department is a useful device for specialized graduate education, but at the undergraduate level it is frequently an intellectual encumbrance. The undergraduate liberal arts college, which should be devoted to the principle of the unity of knowledge, is instead broken into a series of nearly independent fiefdoms. One writer once described the modern American university as "a city of God that is all suburbs," the administration, library, and heating plant being the only substitute for "downtown." Separate graduate and undergraduate faculties do not seem to be the answer, nor do larger departmental units (e.g., social sciences, humanities) work satisfactorily if the quality of graduate education is to be maintained. Perhaps the combination of the college or residence hall system with a departmental system is the best a large university can do: in such a situation the professor is drawn into closer contact with those from other disciplines in the college, and yet not cut off from his colleagues in his own field.

CONCLUDING OBSERVATIONS

The preceding observations have been posed as obstacles to the improvement of undergraduate teaching; perhaps they stress the negative too much. Encouraging and rewarding good teaching need special attention in the large university; excellence in teaching has gone unrewarded chiefly because we lack the means of adequate judgment. We review *curriculum vitae* of potential new teachers, we assess their published work, we request letters of recommendation evaluating their scholarly promise and personal character—but we seldom know anything about the new teacher's ability to teach. The situation improves little after he joins the faculty. We make judgments of our colleague's teaching ability, but they are largely impressions based on out-of-class contact, tinged by student comments and the occasional snatches of lecture which float over the transom. At the small and intimate liberal arts colleges, such impressions may be accurate enough to serve as a basis for recognizing and rewarding teaching ability. But the large university must make special efforts if it is not to lose sight of one of its major educational tasks and undervalue the role of the excellent teacher in the community of scholars.

At the same time, the teacher in the university has a somewhat broader responsibility than his counterpart in the small college, for he is expected to be an active contributor to the world of scholarship. In accepting the privileges of membership in the university community he obligates himself to be a participant in expanding the frontiers of knowledge. As one distinguished teacher reminds us, however, the chief value of research is "as fuel to keep alive the fire in one's belly and not foam to extinguish the sparks in other people." [18] The challenge to university administrators is to create an environment for learning that will not only fan the internal fires of faculty members, but will also encourage transmission of the flame to succeeding generations of students. Only through the accomplishment of both objectives can a university truly claim excellence.

[18] Ogilvie, "The Role of the Teacher," p. 93.

Undergraduate Teaching
At Large State Universities

MARTIN TROW

I n the past few years, there has been a growing feeling among many American educators that undergraduate education is not getting the attention and resources that it deserves. In the large universities this is usually attributed to the increasing and competitive demands of graduate training, research, and administration, both within and outside the university. Elsewhere the deficiencies stem from the speed and size of expansion, the absence of strong intellectual traditions, the paucity of resources, or the myriad other difficulties attendant on the creation of a system of mass higher education.

The heightened concern about undergraduate education takes many different forms.[1] One response during the past year has been the creation of a national Union for Social Science Teaching, which grew out of a conference of college and university teachers in the social sciences held in Boston in October 1965.[2] The union aims to improve communication among social science teachers, and to encourage and help support new ventures and experiments in social science teaching, in new or weak colleges as well as in the stronger liberal arts colleges and public and private universities. These notes, written for discussion at an early meeting of the union, address themselves to some of the special problems of undergraduate teaching encountered in the large state universities. The problems I am discussing are certainly not

[1] Some of this concern is reflected in two important recent contributions to the discussion of undergraduate education in American universities: Daniel Bell, *The Reforming of General Education* (New York: Columbia University Press, 1966); and *Education at Berkeley: Report of the Select Committee on Education* [Muscatine Report] (Berkeley: Academic Senate, University of California, March 1966). See also the essays in Lawrence E. Dennis and Joseph F. Kauffman (eds.), *The College and the Student* (Washington: American Council on Education, 1966).

[2] The chairman of the union is Professor Gresham Sykes, College of Law, University of Denver.

164

confined to the large state universities, but they are particularly acute there because of the special characteristics of their faculties, student bodies, and organizational forms. It may be useful to reflect on some of these characteristics, since they provide at once the stimulus to, resources for, and difficulties in the way of, reform of undergraduate teaching in these institutions.

Any such discussion of the large state universities must accept that those institutions typically invest much smaller resources in undergraduate teaching than do either leading private liberal arts colleges or the major private universities. For example, the introductory social science courses at the big state universities are often taught by one or two faculty members and a small army of teaching assistants in classes of five hundred to a thousand, whereas classes of that size are very rare in the leading private colleges and universities. A current *experiment* in undergraduate education initiated by Professor Joseph Tussman at Berkeley operates with a faculty-student ratio of 1:30, in order to be comparable in resources with the rest of the undergraduate program. Although published figures on faculty-student ratios at various types of institutions are somewhat misleading, it is also clear that the undergraduates—particularly the first- and second-year students—in big state universities get less of the regular faculty's time and energy than in leading private colleges or universities. The over-all paucity of faculty resources allocated to undergraduate teaching severely limits the kinds of reform that can be adopted. Either we must find ways to increase those resources, or we must attempt to invent effective forms of teaching predicated on low faculty-student ratios.

THE TEACHING ASSISTANT

The widespread employment of teaching assistants is the principal means by which large public universities currently try to compensate for the relatively small numbers of "full-time equivalent" faculty actually engaged in teaching undergraduates. Put another way, using teaching assistants is a way of enabling those institutions to commit relatively small resources of faculty time to teaching very large numbers of undergraduates.

The two most common alternative ways of maintaining a program of undergraduate education with a poor staff-student ratio are the imposition of a heavy load of undergraduate teaching on the existing staff, and large classes. State colleges without large graduate programs are known for their heavy teaching loads. Leading state universities, with some exceptions, have opted for large classes, naturally so in light of their interest in postgraduate training and research, necessarily so if men with such interests (and the scholarly distinction they earn) can be recruited in a briskly competitive market. Teaching loads in the leading state universities, even apart from the substantial number of faculty on part-time research appointments, are comparable to those of institutions with much more favorable faculty-student ratios. Nevertheless, unlike the faculties of many European universities, where the ratio of staff to students is even lower than at our state universities, we accept as important elements of undergraduate instruction both the existence of classes small enough to allow student discussion and questions, and the close scrutiny of students' written work by the instructor. But it is impossible in very large courses to give the student the advantage of this close attention without the use of assistant teachers whose time is devoted primarily to talking to students, in class and office hours. The TA's, then, fill the gap created by (a) a poor faculty-student ratio, (b) a research-minded faculty, and (c) the American conception of undergraduate education as involving some measure of direct contact between student and teacher.

Nevertheless, while the TA system has the appearance of inevitability arising out of scarce resources, it is a poor solution to the problem, both educationally and administratively. Teaching assistants are too often poorly motivated and resentful; they are frequently drawn from among the less able graduate students, the more so as research assistantships and free fellowships increase in number; they are burdened by their own educational and research commitments; they are not even getting good experience for the quite different problems they will encounter in their own teaching careers.

It is easier to condemn the TA system than it is to suggest ways of organizing undergraduate instruction in the big state universities without it. But if we are searching for ways to improve the quality of teaching in the social sciences, then in the state universities we could not do better than to begin with the TA system. We are so delighted to get someone to talk to students in introductory courses we scarcely inquire what they say to them. Yet my own belief is that while a routine, textbook-bound introductory course may not be greatly harmed by the TA-section system (if indeed it can be harmed by anything), creating a more ambitious introduction to the social sciences which depends on TA's for the major part of the direct interaction with students is quite another question. It is of course closely linked to the question of resources, as I have suggested; but I think it would be a pity if we design ingenious new courses, focused on stimulating problems and reading lists, and then ignore (as we largely do now) what goes on in the section meetings.

One response to all this will surely be the rhetorical question: This all may be so, but how else are the big state universities to teach very large numbers of undergraduates, support the bulk of their graduate students during part of their graduate training, and keep faculty teaching loads low enough to recruit and retain research-minded men? My chief objection to the TA system is that it prevents us from asking those questions seriously rather than rhetorically. And genuine improvement of undergraduate education at large state universities requires that we find some answers to them.

THE FACULTY

It is risky to generalize about the faculty members of large state universities, if only because there are so many of them, doing so many different kinds of educational jobs. But if we restrict our view to the faculties of the social science departments, we can make one safe generalization: these are men who by personal choice and university policy are primarily oriented toward research and graduate training, not toward undergraduate teaching. The difficult and often unrewarding conditions of undergraduate teaching at the big state universities are no secret. People deeply interested in undergraduate education are not likely to want to teach at a big state university; and, if there, they are likely to leave as soon as possible. Given the favorable job market of the past decade, the social scientist can usually find a job in the type of institution he prefers.

In the leading state universities, faculty are recruited and retained primarily on the basis of scholarly achievement or promise. It is a commonplace (and often a reproach) that in a large university, publication and the reputation that publication earns carry the heaviest weight in promotion and tenure decisions. This reward structure is hard to modify; it has behind it the powerful interests of both the institutions and the departments, whose reputations are, in a rough way and over time, products of the aggregate scholarly and scientific reputations of their faculty.

Even when the institution expresses an interest in rewarding teaching ability, identifying and assessing this ability is difficult. The size, heterogeneity, and rapid turnover of the student body, and the consequent absence of an undergraduate community in which enduring relationships and a dense network of communications among teachers and students can exist, make consistent and reliable assessments of teachers as teachers almost impossible. Men at leading state universities are typically ambitious for academic reputation and advancement. This motivation results in a climate of continual assessment, but it also generates a strong sentiment that assessments be "fair," based on universalistic criteria, and accurate. The evidence bearing on a man's teaching effectiveness is usually neither adequate nor convincing to the men (administrators or colleagues) who make the assessments. Consequently, reports of teaching effectiveness have little bearing on decisions about retention or promotion.

The difficulties are illustrated by the experience of one large state university which some years ago initiated a largely symbolic prize for excellence in teaching to be awarded annually to three or four young faculty members below tenure rank. After a few years the prize-awarding committees realized that their decisions depended more on the skill and persuasiveness of supporting letters than on consideration of teaching skills. Moreover, the nominations and awards usually went to men who had created some new course or curriculum, or who had devised some new way of linking labs and demonstrations to lectures. Thus, awards were being made not for "excellent teaching," but for persuasive accounts of educational innovations, which are quite a different thing. Such innovations were rewarded not so much because they were worthy but because they produced written evidence such as course outlines and syllabi. Skill and devotion in reading papers and talking to students produce no such evidence; popularity among students is more likely to be suspected as demagogy and showmanship than to be admired by colleagues.

But all this is less important than the critics of "publish or perish" believe. These critics, who range from John Gardner to the New Left, imply that the institution forces faculty members to write when they would rather teach, and that these pressures are largely external to the teacher and divert him from his real interest in the undergraduate. My own impression is that, in the matter of research, university teachers make more severe demands on themselves than their institutions do, and that interest in research and in their graduate students is their central motivation in academic life. The big university does not whip or seduce an unwilling body of teachers into research and publication; it recruits research-minded men, and then rewards them for doing what it hired them to do, thus reinforcing their inclinations toward research.

In any event, the majority of university teachers are certainly not interested primarily in teaching. When a sample of Berkeley faculty was asked recently, "What proportion of the faculty members here would you say are strongly interested in the academic problems of students?" only a third answered "almost all" or "over half," as compared with 85–90 percent of faculty members at three selected liberal arts colleges giving those responses. The faculty's judgments of their colleagues is closely reflected in their students' judgments of them: when asked the slightly different question "What proportion of the faculty members here would you say are really interested in students and their problems?" about a third of a recent graduating class at Berkeley answered "almost all" or "over half," as compared with between 50–60 percent giving those responses at seven public and private colleges (not universities). The Berkeley faculty does not think much of itself as a teaching faculty either: only 38 percent thought that "more than half" of their colleagues could qualify as "superior teachers," whereas between two-thirds and 90 percent of the faculty members at three selective liberal arts colleges thought of a majority of their colleagues as superior teachers. On the other hand, two-thirds of the Berkeley sample had published five or more scholarly or scientific papers, as compared with only a third at the most distinguished liberal arts colleges.

It is charged that university teachers are indifferent to undergraduates and take little interest in their undergraduate courses. Speaking of teachers in social science departments in large universities, I think it a fairer generalization that by and large they have a genuine though *limited* interest in undergraduate teaching. Among the many demands on their time—their own research, their graduate students and courses, departmental and university administration, public service and consulting service to governmental and scientific agencies—undergraduates usually do not get first priority, but neither are they at the bottom of the list. But the search for devotion to teaching as a sign of grace, to which we are led by the more evangelical critics of the large university, distracts us from asking *how* the university teacher discharges his responsibility to his undergraduates. Not surprisingly, he usually does this in ways congruent with his temperament, interests, and other work, by developing and expounding new ideas, and by criticizing the contributions of others. I believe that the typical social science teacher in a large university takes great pains in preparing his lectures for undergraduate courses. He works hard to find ways of communicating the perspectives of social science to naïve students; he chooses his illustrations with care; he continually reworks his notes to introduce new findings and fresh approaches. He is especially good at presenting social science as a process of discovery, emphasizing the provisional and tentative quality of all knowledge, of every formulation. Perhaps he rarely asks his students to reflect on the moral implications of what they study or to consider the meaning of these findings for their own lives. But he does raise such questions as: How do we know this? What is the evidence for that? and, closely related, How did someone come to find this out? Not surprisingly, these questions are the ones which he constantly asks about his own work and the work of others.

But this approach leaves something wanting as far as liberal education is concerned. At its worst it encourages passivity or a prematurely and narrowly professional attitude toward the social sciences. But the critics overlook some of its strengths: the breadth of substantive knowledge presented, the teacher's theoretical and methodological sophistication, his steady search for meaning in a welter of detail, and the morality implicit in the canons of evidence and the disciplined pursuit of truth. Any efforts to reform undergraduate social science teaching in the public universities might better be rooted in the real strengths of the university teachers than in the qualities that reformers wish they possessed.

Part of the motive for teaching, and many of its rewards, lie in the quality and character of one's students, and in the value that one places on those qualities. At some of the new experimental colleges, social science teachers of an evangelical bent look for signs of "enthusiasm" (in the religious sense) among their students; they talk of "turning students on"; they find rewards in the immediate response of students who move from apathy and cynicism to a passionate involvement with and moral indignation about social injustice.

Teachers tend to value in their students the qualities that they themselves possess. It is relevant, then, to observe that the teachers and the students at state universities are on the average less alike in those qualities than are students and teachers in most other kinds of colleges and universities. Except for a minority of deeply dedicated teachers, the university faculty member ordinarily gives serious attention to his students only when they are able, studious, and intellectually motivated or lively; or when because of their social origins or the status of the university itself, they are likely to be the future leaders of the society. The first of these motives operates at the highly selective liberal arts colleges, universities, and technical institutes, and in the graduate departments of state universities. The second was the dominant motive at the Ivy League colleges before World War II (when they were not highly selective academically). Both motives operate now at Harvard, for example, though the first motive is gaining steadily in importance. But neither of these conditions holds true at the undergraduate level of big state universities. Of course their enormous student bodies include both gifted students and future leaders, but the numbers in both categories are relatively small and are diluted by the large numbers of quite "ordinary" youngsters who will achieve neither wealth nor power nor intellectual distinction. Whether or not it should, this fact does affect the ordinary faculty member's degree of involvement with and energy spent in teaching undergraduate students. But this is not to say that he does not put a good deal of himself into his undergraduate *courses*.

STATE UNIVERSITY UNDERGRADUATES

Rarely do discussions of undergraduate teaching mention that some undergraduates are dull, many ill-educated and barely literate, others profoundly uninterested in their education apart from the cash value of the diploma, and still others downright hostile to learning that cannot justify itself by narrow conceptions of short-run practicality. Although these attitudes and qualities of mind are relatively rare in the selective liberal arts colleges and private universities (which recruit not only the most able, but also the most sophisticated youngsters of college age), the teacher in the big state university sees them in abundance. Any social science curriculum designed for that kind of institution must take into account two facts about the intellectual and cultural resources of state university students. First, on the average, they are academically less able, less motivated, and possessed of less of the common coin of intellectual discourse than are students in the selective private colleges and universities. Second, and equally important, the big state universities recruit a very heterogeneous student population, which includes substantial numbers of very able, highly motivated, and culturally sophisticated students as well as large numbers less well equipped for higher education.

Berkeley furnishes a good example not only because of its size—27,500 students, of whom 17,000 are undergraduates—but also because of its heterogeneity. Even the casual visitor is struck by the variety of types he sees: youngsters fresh out of high school, almost stereotypes of the mass media's conception of clean-cut middle-class American youth; serious-minded graduate students in their late twenties and early thirties, some with families of their own; the political activists, the bohemians, the alienated in search of an identity, all these groups can be found on the Berkeley campus.

Equally startling are differences in degree of sophistication and scope of knowledge. A recent survey showed that one-fourth of the freshmen entering Berkeley could not name the Secretary of State, in contrast with less than 10 percent of the freshmen entering three selective liberal arts colleges. Only one in ten of the students entering the state university reported owning more than seventy-five books; at the three selective liberal arts colleges, between a fifth and a third of the students owned that many. Half the freshmen at the university owned fewer than fifteen books, as compared with 20–30 percent at the three colleges.

Taking the Scholastic Aptitude Test Verbal Profile as a rough measure of academic potential, we find even more dramatic variations. Thirty percent of the freshmen entering Berkeley in 1960 had SAT Verbal scores of over 600. In contrast, the figures for Harvard, Stanford, Cal. Tech., and M.I.T.—four major private universities which compete with Berkeley for faculty, graduate students, and research grants—are between 70 and 90 percent. These four private institutions admitted no more than 2 percent with Verbal scores of under 500; Berkeley, despite its being one of the more selective state universities, admitted nearly a third of its freshmen with scores of 500 or below.

But these percentage distributions hide one important fact: because of the size of its entering classes (5,000 freshmen are admitted each year), the *number* of highly able students at Berkeley is equal to the number attending the selective private universities. Conversely, the number of less-than-talented students entering the university annually far exceeds the number who enter some small, third-rate, backwater college. And all of these students—the gifted and the dull, the academically able and the deadbeats—inhabit the same campus, share the same classrooms, sit in the same lecture halls.

These comparative figures on SAT Verbal scores point to one important kind of variation in the Berkeley student body. But perhaps even more important, because more closely related to the character of the institution and more fraught with problems, are the variations in the students' attitudes, motivations, outlooks, and life styles. I once proposed a crude typology of student subcultures—"collegiate," "vocational," "academic," and "nonconformist"—which reflect different life experiences before entering college, different aspirations and plans, and different relationships to all aspects of the university. The ever-increasing selectivity of the prestigious liberal arts colleges and the leading private universities has led to a decline in the "collegiate" culture of fun and games, and also in narrow vocationalism at those institutions. Most of their students are highly able, have academic outlooks, and are committed to attending graduate or professional school; in addition, there is a leavening of intellectually oriented nonconformists in their student bodies.

But at Berkeley, as at other big state universities, students with collegiate or narrowly vocational orientations are in the great majority. Their attitudes and values, which permeate the world of the undergraduate, are a major force that the teacher either fights or ignores (more commonly the latter). In this respect, the big state universities do not differ from the four-year state colleges, or indeed, from most other colleges and universities in this country, except for the most "elite" private institutions. But they do differ from other less selective institutions in two ways: first, they also include large numbers of students who in ability, motivation, and sophistication resemble the students in the best liberal arts colleges; and, second, their faculties range considerably in interests and activities. State universities are not academic communities; they are collections of communities and aggregates of students. Some of our difficulties, not least in our efforts to teach undergraduate social science, arise out of our indifference to the nature of the complex societies that the university comprises.

The existing curriculum, especially at the introductory level, takes very little note of the diversity of the student body in the large state universities. If we are concerned with improving the quality and increasing the relevance of undergraduate social science teaching at these institutions, we might start by learning more about the diverse intellectual resources of our students, and then designing distinct programs and courses of instruction with these differences in mind. Some university departments already offer one set of introductory courses for prospective majors and another for nonmajors. My own belief is that a professed inclination to major in a subject is one of the least useful bases for distinguishing among students, quite apart from its tendency to encourage (and indeed require) a decision which most students might be better off postponing till the end of the second or beginning of the third year. Honors courses, typically offered only to majors late along in their undergraduate careers, do select, more or less, for academic performance and apparent motivation. But they do not meet the problems of the introductory course or of the place of the social sciences in liberal education. Surely we ought to be able to design courses for students who indicate a willingness to work beyond the requirements of the ordinary introductory course. Perhaps we could even attempt the more difficult task of designing a distinctive "introductory" course for students who are at home in the social sciences when they enter college, who have already read history, anthropology, archeology out of personal interest and curiosity. Such a course would be quite different from one designed for students whose whole conception of social science has been gained from high school texts in American history and civics, and to whom the modes of thought of university social scientists are utterly unfamiliar and bewildering.

Social science courses are currently differentiated in a variety of informal ways. Different subjects, through their reputations and images, attract students of very different abilities and motivations, and within subjects there exists a subterranean lore about "mickey mouse" courses that take little time or effort. A sociology department can attempt to reshape its clientele by introducing a difficult statistics requirement, in part to screen out girls with mild interests in social welfare. But generally, big university social science departments deal with diversity among their students by grading them rather than by teaching them differently.

Explicit recognition of diversity among students entails great, perhaps insoluble, difficulties. Apart from the problems of selection and differentiation (on what bases and with what instruments?), there are the problems attendant on concentrating the least sophisticated (*or* motivated *or* able) in one class. Who is to teach them? How is that task to be kept from being an onerous burden, the mark of second-class citizenship in the academic community? How will the draining-off of the more able (motivated, sophisticated) affect the less "endowed" students—a problem we are more familiar with in the guise of *de facto* school segregation? Even if it turns out that the problems presented by the heterogeneity of student bodies in big universities are too great to deal with except as we do now, this is something that reformers should know. Until we recognize and at least attempt to cope with the problems created by diversity, students at all levels of ability and sophistication will suffer from our indifference.

THE COMPREHENSIVE UNIVERSITY

We are dealing here with problems of "comprehensive institutions of higher education," problems that resemble those encountered in the far more familiar setting of the American public high school. By "comprehensive" I mean serving a very wide range of interests and abilities within the same institution. In this sense, while American higher education as a *system* is truly comprehensive (unlike most systems of higher education abroad), very few of its constituent colleges and universities are, and among these the big state university is the only major category. The selective private institutions are not "comprehensive," nor are most denominational colleges, or lesser regional private colleges, or the minor state and teachers colleges. The students in all these kinds of institutions are far more homogeneous in ability, interests, and educational values and orientations than are the undergraduate student bodies at Berkeley or Michigan or Indiana or Texas.

The faculty members of the academic departments of state universities have not advertised the comprehensive character of their institutions in part because many of them have tried to pretend that they are teaching in private universities run on public funds. Their salaries, teaching loads, faculty autonomy and self-government, graduate students, research support, leave policies, all support the illusion. The fantasy is really dispelled in daily experience only in relation to the undergraduates, and it can be sustained even there if one teaches them infrequently and impersonally, and as if they were all majoring in the subjects and planning to go to graduate school. (The illusion is also dispelled periodically by events arising out of the university's relations with its social and political environment, and most brutally at times of crisis.) But this illusion, whatever function it serves for the recruitment and retention of the faculty, does not serve the interests of the undergraduates, nor of good teaching of undergraduate social science. And it certainly interferes with our seeing the problems of undergraduate teaching in the state university, or of our doing much about them.

THE ORGANIZATIONAL PATTERNS OF LARGE STATE UNIVERSITIES

Our big universities seem to combine cumbersome rigidity at the college and university level with considerable freedom and flexibility at the departmental level. They have a tendency, as do other large institutions, to standardize rules and procedures and to impose them on everyone to whom they may legitimately be applied. It is difficult to introduce nongraded courses, for example, unless general university rules regulating their use have been established. In part, this situation arises out of the pressures for administrative convenience and consistency, in part from the feeling that all students should be subject to the same standards and procedures.

Yet procedures differ widely from department to department and from course to course. Elaborate bureaucratic rules governing registration, grading, credit requirements, and the like exist side by side with the variety of practices arising out of the autonomy of the teacher and the department. Faculty members justify this freedom by appealing on the one hand to the technical requirements of their own discipline—a matter on which they are the final arbiters, since the discipline is what they say it is—and on the other, to the vague but extensive rights and powers implicit in the notion of academic freedom. It is not always clear, therefore, where discretion lies, or what limits are imposed on its exercise, in decisions that affect the encounter of student and teacher. For example, departments vary greatly (though within limits) both in their "normal" teaching loads and in the proportion of the resulting teaching resources that they assign to undergraduate courses. The frequency of class meetings, nominally stipulated in the catalogue and related to the credit value of a given course, actually lies to a great extent in the discretion of the individual instructor. Grading procedures, by contrast, appear to be firmly fixed and enforced throughout the university, with a few clearly defined exceptions.

In part, the location of such decisions is a function of their visibility: the more visible, the less diversity permitted. In part, administrative convenience is the determining factor: the registrar must have grades. In part, relations with other institutions are involved: students who transfer or apply to graduate or professional school must have records of grades and credits that presumably have a common meaning. But these considerations are by no means the whole story; they merely point to broad questions about the location of and constraints on academic power and about the tension between the forces making for diversity and those making for standardization of rules and practices.

The individual faculty member frequently has considerable freedom because of the autonomy of the department and because other people, including his immediate colleagues, are usually ignorant of and indifferent to what he is doing. But this freedom is dispelled if he asks the institution to approve and support his innovations, as he must do if he is requesting additional resources or pushing for changes in formal requirements, course titles, or whatever.

To take a specific example of how these organizational patterns affect efforts to innovate and to revitalize teaching, a good deal of fresh thinking about introductory courses in the social sciences recently has centered on the value of interdisciplinary courses. But it is very difficult for faculty members to develop such courses unless they have the support of a dean of the college of letters and sciences (or its equivalent) as well as of a course committee, typically drawn from the college as a whole. Frequently, this committee is much less hospitable to experiment and innovation than is the dean; for example, a professor of French or chemistry may object to a new course in the social sciences on the grounds that it is not as "tough," and hence as professionally respectable, as the course it is intended to replace. Granted that departments and even institutions vary greatly in their receptivity to interdisciplinary courses, in most cases only the most determined effort by a group of deeply committed faculty members will suffice to get such programs started. Faculty members who are willing to support and even take part in such an effort will not invest the time and energy needed to fight the change through the machinery of the institution.

My own inclination is to suggest that we take advantage of departmental autonomy and flexibility by seeing if fresh approaches to undergraduate teaching can be developed by members within a single department. For even as some departments in the social sciences grow more narrowly professional and specialized, others, large and sprawling, make a virtue of their size by growing more catholic and flexible in their conceptions of their subject matter and thus become genuinely "interdisciplinary" within themselves. Or two departments working together might find ways of offering joint introductory courses within the existing curricular framework, using to the full their considerable freedom to introduce internal innovations. Whenever possible, large pronouncements to the world about their novel and experimental intentions should be avoided, since if every new approach is turned into a major "project" requiring exhortation, justification, and vote-getting, there will be very few innovations in the big universities. But by introducing such changes unobtrusively and by working within the existing course structure, innovations might become more frequent, casual, and informal, as well as easier to accomplish.

But all these considerations, which might be called the "tactics of innovation," deserve more thought, discussion, and perhaps even study. We must take into account the institutional patterns that such innovations are directed at changing or evading, since we are dealing with much more elaborate and usually more cumbersome administrative arrangements than are common in private colleges and universities. We may want to ask ourselves whether our enterprise calls for a direct assault on those arrangements or whether the freedom that we need to experiment may not more often flourish in the cracks between the flagstones.

IMPLICATIONS FOR THE TEACHING OF SOCIAL SCIENCES

If innovations in the undergraduate social sciences in large public universities are to have any value, they must take into account the special characteristics of those institutions and of their students and faculty members. In my view, the most important of these characteristics are:

1. A relatively poor faculty-student ratio;
2. A research-oriented faculty with a genuine but limited interest in undergraduate teaching;
3. A student body that is on the average relatively weaker and also far more heterogeneous in academic ability and motivation than the student bodies at selective private colleges and universities;
4. Organizational patterns that make curriculum revision and innovation fairly easy within departments and rather difficult across departments.

What do these characteristics imply about innovation and improvements in social science teaching in big state universities?

First, there must be an improvement in faculty resources allocated to undergraduate teaching. Whether one thinks of increased contact with students, or seminars, or field work, or guided study, or greater attention to course planning and design, it is clear that more faculty time is needed than is customarily provided for the introductory social science courses. This probably cannot be gained by rearranging teaching responsibilities or by increasing teaching loads or by exhorting university teachers to spend less time on research and more on teaching. Those who speak of a "flight from the classroom" seem to suggest that if that flight could be halted or reversed, undergraduates would get the teaching they need. However, I believe that inadequate teaching in the big state universities can be attributed more to the relatively small resources budgeted for undergraduates than to this alleged flight. It is not that teachers have withdrawn from undergraduate teaching, but that there weren't enough of them to begin with to do research, teach graduates, fulfill the many other demands made on them, and at the same time create and sustain an imaginative program of undergraduate teaching. It is my impression that formerly there was often a kind of division of labor within big social science departments: one group, often "local" in orientation, did relatively little research and writing but carried a disproportionate load of teaching, while another group, oriented toward the discipline, research, and graduate students, did relatively little undergraduate teaching. Gradually, the processes of attrition, self-selection, and selective retention have reduced the numbers of student-oriented "locals," and thereby created departments full of research-minded men for whom undergraduate teaching is a job but no calling.

Second, many able, motivated students attend big state universities, but the size and anonymity of those institutions dilute them. Thus, although they are present in every class, the instructor may not find out who they are till the end of the semester. (If the class is large enough and he has a reader, he never does.) Moreover, it is very rare for a student to have a given faculty member for more than one course: student attrition is high, departments large, faculty members very often on leave, and a constant stream of short-term visitors carries a significant proportion of the undergraduate teaching load. Under these conditions not only do the motivated and interested students have difficulty making contact with their teachers, but they also have trouble finding one another. The central problem lies not so much in the curriculum as in the ecology of intellectual life. It is the problem of bringing lively, curious students together, and of then putting them in touch with a teacher. It is the problem of creating the conditions under which teaching and learning can best go forward. Some students (perhaps the most sophisticated and highly motivated of all) can learn from books and distant lecturers and in isolation. But many need the support, stimulation, and correction of teachers and of other students. They need to communicate with people who share their questions and interests. But because they are lost in the crowd of students who do not have those interests, communication, both among students and between students and teachers, is greatly inhibited.

We need to find "concentrators"—devices that will bring together students with common interests and facilitate connections between these groups and teachers. Even on big university campuses, of course, students who share interests and outlooks do somehow meet one another, but the concentrators are few and feeble, especially for first- and second-year students. Residence halls are conspicuously inadequate for this purpose since they usually have little distinctive character and bring people together at random, and thus reinforce the interests of the "collegiate" subculture, the lowest common denominator of college student life. Political clubs and civil rights organizations do serve this purpose, as do the small third- and fourth-year classes for majors in a field. But the big introductory courses do not.

To achieve concentration, we might use instruments such as tests, grades, questionnaires, or interviews to group together students of special ability, motivation, or some other quality. Or we might permit students to group themselves through voluntary self-selection. Honors courses use both procedures, but they do not, of course, meet the problems of first- and second-year students. Moreover, they may be overselective, drawing only the highly motivated preprofessionals who regard the course as a kind of anticipatory socialization for graduate school, and skipping over those able and lively students who are not so clear about themselves or their futures.

Perhaps it would be possible to establish another kind of honors course, one based exclusively on self-selection and open to first- and second-year students. These students would not need to show a high aptitude for or commitment to social science; the only requirement would be that they take an interest in learning, as expressed by their readiness to take what is advertised as the more demanding of two options. I do not pretend that this is an adequate solution to the problem of the introductory course in the big state university. For one thing, it does not answer the question of what to do about "the others," the students who out of wariness or indifference or stronger interests elsewhere are inclined to take some courses without being taken by them. At present, such students are lectured at; they fill seats and blue-books; they receive grades and perhaps, eventually, diplomas; but they are not truly and deeply involved in the intellectual enterprise. Such students may need evangelists to inspire them. However, evangelists are conspicuously rare in the faculties of big universities. Perhaps if we put more resources into teaching them, many could be brought to see the pleasures and intrinsic rewards of learning.

Inevitably, the notion of concentration leads us to other problems: Is it wise to create more homogeneous subgroups within the university? What proportion of teaching and other resources should we allocate to the less able students (who need them more) and what to the more able (who want and will profit from them more)? What effects will segregation on the basis of common interest and ability have, both on the "elite" and on the "average" groups?

Moral dilemmas and questions of fact become intertwined. Our answers to these questions will be influenced by our knowledge of the educational effects of these practices. Moreover, the educational consequences of our decisions will be affected by a host of special circumstances: campus tradition, quality of leadership, location, size, recent events, the climate of ideas within and outside the institution, and so forth. Unfortunately, evidence about these matters is rarely available and is difficult and expensive to acquire.

Obviously, identifying the problems peculiar to large state universities does not provide clear directives for solving them. But we can at least take a first step by recognizing that the types of students at these institutions are far more varied than those at private institutions and that, because state universities are likely to become less rather than more selective, this heterogeneity will almost certainly persist. It is a characteristic we must recognize and deal with if undergraduate teaching is to be improved.

I feel more confident about the nature of the problems I have discussed than about any solutions I have suggested. I am more sure that the solutions will differ for different institutions than I am about what should be done in any one of them. But we need not—and should not —wait until we have more knowledge. One way to learn about the state university as a context for innovation is to innovate and see what happens. Let us by all means design new courses and new ways of teaching; let us try them out; but let us be sure that we follow them through and attend to their fates.

Innovations in
College Teaching

SAMUEL BASKIN

Most college teachers teach the way they have been taught or as the "system" prescribes that they teach. Generally this means they meet students in regular class sessions for a set number of times (two, three, or five per week, depending on the credit hours) over a set number of weeks.

Recent developments in the organization and content of the curriculum and in teaching methods are opening up a variety of possibilities for a new mix of resources for instructing college students. This paper reviews seven developments: independent studies; technology in instruction; content and organization of the curriculum; field experience as a way of learning; residence hall instruction; new instructional spaces; seminars for freshmen. It gives a brief view of the developments in a variety of settings.[1]

INDEPENDENT STUDIES

The idea that colleges use independent study in their instructional programs is, of course, not new, and a number of plans are described by Bonthius, Davis, and Drushal in *Independent Study Program in the United States*.[2] What is new is its position as a major development in college teaching. Independent study as a concept has long been regarded as the prerogative of the superior student in honors and tutorial courses. In its growing use, it is available to all students, and, further, it is available at the beginning rather than the close of the student's college career.

---

[1] For a fuller description of developments in undergraduate education, see S. Baskin (ed.), *Higher Education: Some Newer Developments* (New York: McGraw-Hill Book Co., 1965).
[2] New York: Columbia University Press, 1957.

The "January term" at Florida Presbyterian College, inaugurated in 1960, illustrates how many of the new programs seek to extend the opportunity for independent work to all students. The winter term is a special four-week period interposed between the fall and spring semesters. Classes are suspended during January, and the students, including freshmen, each undertake an independent study or research project. Intended to develop habits and skills for independent work, the program requires each student to undertake a problem growing out of either his own experience or suggestions by a professor. He is free to make the choice, and he may also decide whether his project is such that he will work with another student, a group of students, or by himself. A professor—again, of his own choosing—remains available for consultation and evaluation throughout the period. Each student is expected to put in about fifty to sixty hours a week and, at the close of the special term, present the results as a paper, short story, painting, product of a laboratory experiment, or the like. During the freshman and sophomore years, the student is encouraged to select a topic outside his major field of interest; during the junior and senior years, the topic is to be selected from within his field. Titles of some of the recent projects are: "Mathematics in Western Culture," "The Nature and Function of Symbols in Human Communication," "Studies in Tolerances of Marine Invertebrates to Variations in Environmental Factors," and "A Study and Analysis of the Works of Tennessee Williams." About two-thirds of the faculty regularly participate in winter term work. The other faculty members are free during this time to carry on their own research and studies.

Similar "winter term" programs are under way at several other institutions, among them Colby, St. Olaf, Macalester, and Bard. The programs at Colby and St. Olaf are primarily focused on general education for freshmen and sophomores. The Macalester program is primarily designed for juniors and seniors but is also open to freshmen. The winter half-semester at Bard—an outgrowth of the field period that runs concurrently with it during January and February—may be used either for work or for off-campus independent study.

The winter or January term, an increasingly popular program, is only one of several patterns that stress independence in learning. The trimester "break" for independent study at New College (Sarasota) permits the student to spend a full month in independent study between trimesters. In the new calendar plans inaugurated at Beloit and Kalamazoo Colleges, a student may spend a portion or all of one of his off-campus terms in independent study and research. Programs which excuse students from attendance in regular class meetings, but expect them to cover materials on their own, are in effect in a number of institutions including Antioch, Oberlin, Goddard, Carleton, Marquette, Colorado, and Michigan.[3] And in a program first inaugurated by Professor Sam Postlethwait at Purdue University (and now adapted by the University of Illinois at Chicago, Eastern Michigan University, Penn State, and Kansas State University), students taking courses in chemistry, biology, and other sciences work independently in the laboratory, using audio-tapes, films, workbooks, and other instructional materials.

In some regular-term programs the emphasis is on development of individualized curricula *early* in the student's career. Wayne State's Monteith College program incorporates a number of independent-study features into the basic general education courses of the early years, after which the student is expected to take the terminal segment of one of these without attending the discussion group meetings. In an experiment in individualized curricula, freshman year programs for special groups of students have recently been inaugurated at Allegheny, Colby, Colorado, Florida Presbyterian, Lake Forest, and Pomona. Although the students must demonstrate certain levels of accomplishment in the humanities, social sciences, and natural sciences, by the end of their second year they are free to chart their own goals and the means of accomplishing them. A faculty member, known as a preceptor, works closely with the individual student in his program planning. The First Year Program at Antioch offers freshmen a series of seminars, core presentations, or lectures, and resource materials for independent study (guides to instruction and self-directed study). Here, as in the programs described above, the student is free to plan his program without the customary grade and class attendance requirements. The structure for advising provides a faculty preceptor and two upperclass students for every fourteen freshmen.

TECHNOLOGY FOR INSTRUCTION

The new media and technology have aroused more controversy than any other pedagogical development of recent years. At issue is how the new technology—televised instruction, computers, programed courses, films, tapes, and other audio-visual materials—can be employed in teaching and learning, and whether these devices can be used to educate larger numbers of students without completely automating the educational process.

This is always a difficult tightrope to walk, for it is only too easy for us, in our desire to meet the problem of numbers and finances, to

[3] For a fuller report of these programs see "Better Utilization of College Teaching Resources," A Report by the Committee on Utilization of College Teaching Resources (New York, N.Y.: Fund for the Advancement of Education, 1959).

rationalize away all arguments about the importance of the dialogue between teacher and student as a significant component of the student's learning experience. Used in intelligent and sensitive balance, however, there is much that the new media and technology can offer in our organization of higher education, and while the warnings such as those voiced by Raymond Callahan in his *Education and the Cult of Efficiency* [4] dare not go unheeded, one might also argue that it is equally important that we not rationalize away every and any adventure in the use of technology, as a dehumanization of the learning process.

Many colleges and universities are using the products of technology as an integrated part of the instructional process in ways that extend the institution's instructional reach and provide individualized approaches to student learning. Several recent developments are described below.

Instructional television

Several institutions are using closed-circuit television to bring outstanding lectures to very large numbers of students and then supplementing these lectures with small-group discussions. The Center at the University of Miami in Florida is an example. The university's facility is equipped to televise lectures by closed circuit to as many as 1,800 students at a time and to rerun these lectures on videotape at any time. Key problems and issues growing out of the presentation are then taken up in small-group discussions. Similar programs are used at Penn State, where, in addition, a specially devised telephone system enables students to ask the lecturer questions, even though they are hearing him in another lecture hall. Stephens College has developed an elaborate Learning Center with a closed-circuit television capability to some 150 locations. The Universities of Texas and Wisconsin both use multimedia systems (slides, films, and other graphic materials) as part of their instructional television program.

Not all developments in television pedagogy are concerned with direct instruction. One exciting trend in teacher training is the growing use of videotape playbacks of live class meetings. For instance, in a project called "micro-teaching," Robert Bush and Dwight Allen at Stanford are videotaping brief teaching sequences, which are played back for analysis of teaching performance and style. The Hunter College teacher-training program has, for some years, employed a remote-control videotape facility that permits live classes to be filmed without a cameraman in the classroom. Antioch College is developing

[4] Callahan, *Education and the Cult of Efficiency* (Chicago: University of Chicago Press, 1962).

a series of videotapes, also filmed by remote control, for its programs of faculty orientation and improvement of teaching. Finally, several institutions in the Associated Colleges of the Midwest [5] are engaged in a teacher-training videotaping project which uses a mobile videotape facility that can be moved from institution to institution.

Cartridge-loading films

Many of the older media are being subjected to technological improvements that give them new forms, new applications, and vastly wider usefulness. For instance, with the new cartridge-loading films, which thread and rewind automatically, the student can consult a film as he would a book. The equipment: the film and a projector; the manipulations: inserting the cartridge and flipping the switch. Two examples of new series of films are the single-concept films in botany, zoology, cultural anthropology, and microbiology, made by the Encyclopedia Cinematographica, established a few years ago in Germany, and the physics demonstration films produced at the Ohio State University under the auspices of the National Science Foundation and the National Association of Physics Teachers.

Computer technology

A number of institutions are conducting experiments in the use of computer technology in instruction. As in other technological developments for education, the computer-based programs seek to give instruction to students to whom it might not otherwise be available. For example, I.B.M. is developing a program known as "Computer Assisted Instruction" which permits sending programed courses by telephone wire to any location in the country. Thus, a student sitting at a computer typewriter station anywhere in the United States can hook into and receive immediate feedback on a computer-programed course originated from the I.B.M. Research Center at Yorktown Heights, New York. Several universities, including Penn State, Florida State, and the University of Michigan, are currently tied into the I.B.M. program.

Still other developments in computer-assisted instruction can be illustrated: at the University of Illinois, Project Plato uses a computer-controlled system of slides, TV displays, and student response panels for teaching a number of students simultaneously while still allowing each student to proceed at his own pace; in the program being developed at Pitzer College, freshmen take at least one programed course, using computer consoles located in the residence hall; and in the projects at

[5] A grouping of ten Middle Western liberal arts colleges that have formed an association to undertake cooperative programs in higher education.

M.I.T. and at the University of California, Irvine, remote-control consoles provide access to a wide array of computer programs and banks of information.

Telelectures

The telelecture—pioneered at Stephens College and at the University of Omaha—offers students an unprecedented opportunity to listen to lectures and engage in discussion with scholars, statesmen, and other resource people anywhere in the world. The device is a simple adaptation of a telephone receiver: a microphone replaces the mouthpiece and a loudspeaker amplifies the message being received. For the cost of a phone call and a modest honorarium, speakers who would otherwise be inaccessible can talk to classes thousands of miles away. Visual materials to be shown may be mailed to the school in advance or—for the cost of an additional phone call—be transmitted by an electronic scanner for reproduction at the receiving end.

In an experiment supported by the Fund for the Advancement of Education, Stephens College has used telelectures to provide a number of outstanding courses to a group of ten other institutions. In an unusual "exchange program," a professor at Omaha lectured to his own class while students at other institutions listened in. In reciprocity, the cooperating schools broadcast lectures of their own faculty. Antioch uses the telelecture to bring presentations from various parts of this country and abroad to its campus; the University of Vermont offers 20 off-campus courses by telelecture to locations throughout the state; recordings of telelecture interviews are circulated from the library at Saginaw College, and Pace College uses the telelecture to call persons in foreign countries, in connection with its course in international relations.

Learning centers

Several institutions have built or are in the process of constructing learning or communication centers. These centers incorporate individual study, or "Q," spaces into the building design that permit automatic playback of lectures in audio and video form, using a remote control telephone-dial or push-button system. One such center, developed at Oklahoma Christian College, has 1,000 individual study carrels, with each student assigned his own study space. Each carrel is equipped with a telephone dial system, and the student simply dials a code number to get his choice of the more than one hundred lectures that have been audi-taped. The lectures are supplemented by workbooks and other problem-solving materials designed to involve the student actively in the lecture material. The center is regarded as an adjunct, not a substitute, for the college's regular instructional program. Although the number of class meetings per week may be reduced (usually by one), the student is still expected to meet with the teacher at regularly scheduled times. The center is open from 7:00 A.M. to 11:00 P.M. daily, and the student uses the facilities as he would a library.

An even more elaborate system is being installed in the six-story Learning Resources Center at the Oral Roberts University in Tulsa, Oklahoma. It will contain 1,000 study carrels, equipped for both audio and video reception. As planned, the system will offer a choice of study lessons previously recorded on motion picture film and slides and on video and audio tape. Similar centers, although on a considerably more modest scale, are being planned at Grand Valley College, Florida Atlantic University, the Oakland Community College, and several of the State University of New York institutions.

CONTENT AND ORGANIZATION OF THE CURRICULUM

While many of the new developments in undergraduate education focus on methodology and techniques, the organization and content of the curriculum are also coming in for significant reforms. The changes are marked by the extension of general education through the college years; a relaxation from rigid compartmentalization of disciplines and development of interdisciplinary studies; new programs in non-Western studies; and a concern for relevance through the study of contemporary issues and problems.

Comprehensive change

One theory in higher education holds that the interrelationships between courses become more obvious and learning is facilitated when integration of knowledge is stressed by entire faculties. St. John's College in Maryland, for example, expects all faculty to be able to teach a variety of courses on one model. Bowdoin encourages faculty to teach outside their home department—a social science course may be taught by a chemist. New College of Hofstra organizes its first-year studies so that students and faculty study together, with each faculty person responsible for a segment of the teaching.

In other settings entire curricula are being organized around an integrating theme. At Nasson, the New Division will reorganize knowledge according to its application to world order. The program at the newly opened Friends World Institute centers on the critical world problem of survival and uses the area studies technique. Students spend successive six-month periods during the four-year program in a different part of the world studying that civilization, its culture, politics and economics, its philosophy and religion, literature, history, geography, and language.

General education through the college years

General education programs developed to a more sophisticated level offer advanced students, perhaps competent in their own disciplines, opportunities to integrate concepts of different disciplines to a degree not possible earlier.

A curriculum at Rollins, begun in the fall of 1966, sandwiches specialized study between general education programs in the first and last years. The New College of Hofstra features a common core of academic experience combined with interdepartmental courses. Ithaca College supports a similar plan, but extends it to include cohesive specialization in the humanities, the social sciences, or the physical sciences. These programs, as well as those at Stanford, Monteith, Oakland University, and Florida Presbyterian—all of which require interdisciplinary senior seminars or colloquia—support the influence of general education throughout the college years.

Raymond and Monteith are two of the newer colleges heralding the approach of a major in general education. Although interdisciplinary and specialized majors can be arranged, the programs are coordinated to provide intensive general education leading to a bachelor's degree.

Interdisciplinary studies

Courses that cut across traditional—and often arbitrary—departmental boundaries are increasingly common. Humanities I at the University of Chicago requires students to read critical studies of the arts as well as study original works. The course also involves students in designing and executing their own art projects, composing music, and then writing about their experience in these endeavors. At Loretto Heights an interdisciplinary course in the humanities, now in its third year, affords to students otherwise unexposed opportunities to experiment in composing music, painting, or executing ideas in dance. Occidental College in its History of Civilization course and Columbia and Harvard in courses in non-Western civilization reach into literature, government, and philosophy as well as history.

Yale's Deductive Reasoning in Physics combines physics and philosophy. The Wabash-Beloit plan in chemistry, which integrates chemistry and physics into one course, is now offered in more than twenty institutions. Educational Services Incorporated, developers of the Physical Sciences Study Committee course for secondary schools, now has a college-level program in physics that delves into the integration of physics with other parts of our culture. Several colleges have adapted the chemical bond approach to advance interdisciplinary integration in chemistry. And the Commission on Undergraduate Education in the

Biological Sciences is developing a core program in biology in which study cuts across the traditional fields of biology to explore interconnections and underlying unity.

Interdisciplinary majors are also more frequent. At Muhlenberg College, a major in the natural sciences combines physics, chemistry, biology, and mathematics. And the American Society for Engineering Education is urging that, as undergraduates, students study engineering science and the liberal arts and then move on to one of the specialties. Other examples are the bilingual inter-American studies program at Cowell College of the University of California at Santa Cruz, the Asian studies program at the University of Hawaii, and the program in Latin American studies at the University of Florida.

Non-Western studies

Most colleges and universities now offer one or more courses or languages pertinent to the non-Western world, but according to a 1965 survey of the Association of American Colleges, only twenty colleges and universities require courses in non-Western studies. Students at New Paltz, Occidental, and Mills may take general education courses dealing with the non-Western world in a sequence over a two- or three-year period. Florida Presbyterian offers a junior-year core course on East Asia, and all juniors at Hanover take four such courses. Others, such as Cowell at Santa Cruz, Colgate, Western College for Women, and California State College at Hayward offer optional sequences in the freshman or sophomore year.

Student influence

In recent years students themselves have begun to seek an integration of the curriculum with the fabric of their daily life. Often their demand for "relevance" has produced a creative response. At San Francisco State, the autonomous, student-run Experimental College designs and implements its own curriculum, with students earning credit toward a degree in the regular college. Although most of the courses are student-taught, visiting scholars are hired (Paul Goodman for 1966) to lead studies in topics the students choose. At Berkeley, a major faculty study, stimulated by student protests, has led to the appointment of a vice-chancellor who is to implement an *ad hoc* curriculum conceived in response to compelling contemporary problems.

FIELD EXPERIENCE AS A WAY OF LEARNING

Baker Brownell has criticized American colleges for their failure to use the larger community as a resource for educating college students. His argument, stated broadly, is that higher education is "still treated not as life but as a preparation for life," that the cloistered campus is unreal, and that the typical college student has few opportunities to test his ideas against experience.[6] In such a setting, he argues, the student's development as a productive personality is delayed and the rate and amount of significant learning are reduced.

An increasing number of colleges, however, are making some form of off-campus experience a part of the undergraduate program. Illustrations are the research internship programs developed by the Associated Colleges of the Midwest; new programs of study abroad that combine field experience with academic work; and in several institutions, the new special calendar terms, such as those recently adopted by Kalamazoo and Beloit, that require students to spend a portion of their college program in some kind of off-campus experience.

Research-oriented programs

The Associated Colleges of the Midwest has initiated an Argonne semester during which students spend from ten to sixteen weeks as half-time research assistants at the Atomic Energy Commission's Argonne National Laboratories, with the other half spent in seminars and study guided by Argonne personnel and faculty from the Associated Colleges. The predication is that well-trained undergraduates can participate in a moderately advanced program of scientific research to their own benefit and that of the employing agency. In another program sponsored by the Associated Colleges of the Midwest, some thirty students are taking part in research studies at the A.C.M. Wilderness Field Station in Northern Minnesota, which offers an ideal opportunity for the scientific study of unspoiled nature. The project is manned by a botanist, a geologist, and a zoologist from member colleges. The studies benefit from the help given by the adjacent Quetico-Superior Wilderness Research Center, whose director and staff work with students and faculty of the A.C.M. project.

Experience abroad

The number of colleges sponsoring programs of experience abroad (for which the student earns academic credit) has grown from 50 in 1960 to 170 in 1966. Some of the programs offer options or combinations of job, field, and study for the student's foreign experience.

In the Princeton international studies program, students spend two months at various locations abroad in field work and research on a

---

[6] Baker Brownell, *The College and the Community* (New York: Harper & Row, 1952), pp. 35–38.

project of their own choosing. Columbia, Cornell, and Harvard collaborate in sending anthropology students to field stations in Ecuador, Peru, and Mexico. A period of study at Bryn Mawr's Avignon Institute is followed by a period during which students may join a nearby French archeological expedition. Sarah Lawrence offers a field experience program in Puerto Rico; also it often combines field work with its summer session and year abroad programs in France, Italy, and Geneva. Florida Presbyterian and New College at Sarasota encourage students to spend their interterm abroad on a job or in field or research work. Franconia College provides regular academic credit for participation in the Peace Corps and VISTA programs. The Goddard College French and Spanish comparative cultures programs provide for two months of life and work in French Canada or Puerto Rico, with related on- and off-campus project and seminar studies. Nasson's New Division will provide opportunities for community service in underdeveloped Latin American countries. And at Antioch, Kalamazoo, Beloit, and Keuka, job experiences pursued abroad are as much a part of the program as those at home.

Calendar revisions

Several institutions are adopting new calendar plans that encourage or require the student to spend some part of his degree program off campus. Illustrations are the new programs at Kalamazoo and Beloit Colleges.

The program at Kalamazoo, inaugurated in 1961, occupies a total of fifteen quarters, ten of which are on campus and five off. The student's off-campus activities include study abroad (usually in his third year), work, and independent study experiences. The Beloit calendar provides a period of under-class studies, when the student spends his first three quarters on campus; a middle-class period, when three of the student's five quarters are spent in an off-campus job, research, or study abroad; and an upper-class period, during which the student returns for three consecutive terms of on-campus studies.

RESIDENCE-HALL INSTRUCTION

The dormitory as a center for learning as well as living is a concept that several schools have sought to develop in recent years. These programs take advantage of the natural cohesiveness of the hall unit to achieve certain educational gains, for example, to develop closer student-faculty relationships, and to effect economies through the dual use of the dormitory for teaching and residential purposes. In several institutions, faculty office space, large-group teaching, seminar, and library spaces, and even laboratories are located in the residence hall itself. Three programs are described below.

In the House Plan at Stephens, 100 first-year students take all five of their freshmen courses in the residence hall in which they live. Five faculty members and a residence counselor serve as an instructional and counseling team for the group. Their offices are located in the residence hall itself, and there is much informal contact between the House Plan faculty and the students. Attractively furnished lounges can be used either as classrooms or for informal purposes. Libraries of paperbacks and key reference materials are maintained for student use, and facilities for bringing in televised lectures are also available.

Nearly 13,000 of Michigan State's 35,000 students are housed in living and learning units, seven of which have been built since 1961. Two additional units are under construction. Each hall includes a men's wing, a women's wing, shared dining and recreational facilities, plus classrooms, laboratories, faculty offices, resident advisers suites, conference rooms, a general purpose area, an auditorium, and a library. Taught by faculty from many different colleges and departments, most general education classes and a number of field courses are held in the residence hall. In the academic year 1964–65, some 43 departments offered 275 sections of 108 different courses in the in-hall academic programs. While the program is designed primarily for freshmen, about two-thirds of the sophomores choose to return. There are also some juniors and seniors.

Bowdoin is the first college to provide a living-learning center especially for seniors. Constructed at a cost of $3.5 million, the center contains space for 200 seniors. In addition to the regular study and living areas, the center contains lecture and seminar rooms, independent study space, a concert hall, offices for faculty and guest lecturers, and a library. Seniors take about a fourth of their work in the academic spaces of the center. The courses offered usually lie outside the student's field and, by their nature, cannot be presented within the traditional department structure; for example, a seminar on the social sciences is taught by a physicist or chemist.

NEW INSTRUCTIONAL SPACES

Winston Churchill has said, "We shape our buildings and they in turn shape us."

Experiments are under way in developing new physical facilities for teaching and learning. The resource centers at Oklahoma Christian College and Oral Roberts and the living-learning units at Michigan State University have been described above. Additional illustrations follow.

Classroom design

The new designs for classrooms and lecture halls often reflect the expectation that the communication media will occupy a major and essential role in classroom teaching. Electronic systems for registering students' responses have been wired into lecture halls at Miami, Texas, Illinois, and Penn State. At each station, push buttons that the student uses to record answers to multiple-choice or true-false questions give the teacher some access to student reaction. At the University of Indiana School of Business and at the University of Texas swivel movable chairs enable students to view three walls equipped with chalk and tack boards and projection screens. At Texas, audio outlets have been installed at each seat to facilitate discussion. At the University of Miami, Rensselaer Polytechnic Institute, and the University of Wisconsin, large lecture halls incorporate the newest technological devices.

Divisible spaces

Multiple use of what would heretofore have been specialized-use space is the object of many of the new designs. Classrooms at Illinois Teachers College North and Florida Atlantic can be used for large groups, small groups, or individual study. Delta College, by using movable walls and a system of closed-circuit TV monitors, can easily assign and reassign its spaces into walkways, lecture halls, seminar rooms, art displays, and lounges. The new theater-auditorium at Webster College in Missouri can be converted to small- or large-group classrooms.

Laboratories

At the University of Illinois, Chicago, campus the multiple-use "Roto-Lab"—a lazy-susan partitioned into three sections, like a pie sliced into thirds—is recessed into the wall between the lab bench and the storage room. While a student works with equipment mounted on shelves that face him, the other two sections face the storage room where an assistant may simultaneously be setting up equipment for later exercises.

Modular elements that fit around a central utility cabinet allow zoology benches to be converted to chemistry benches at the Southern Illinois University. At Drew, where needs do not warrant separate facilities for physics, biology, and chemistry, portable suitcase-like modules, which can be stowed along the wall, will replace the conventional bench-drawer as the student's equipment storage unit. Students from courses in all three areas may use the facility at the same time, and independent study labs can be packaged in a single drawer for use by several students during the course of a day.

Library design

Faced with a choice between a new library or a new classroom building, Centre College in Kentucky combined the two. The structure houses an audio-visual center, faculty offices, and seminar-lounges, as well as classrooms surrounding the library. During peak library occupancy, the classrooms are accessible as reading and working space. During class hours, they are sealed off from the library and can be reached only from an exterior hallway.

Florida Atlantic University has developed a computer-based library in which the library card catalogue has been replaced by a computer-produced catalogue printed in book form. The catalogue is available at various locations throughout the college, including instructors' offices and at certain central locations in the community. The University of California, Irvine, is planning to use pneumatic tubes to deliver materials from the central library to carrels at various remote locations on campus. Some of the carrels will also be equipped with computer consoles that give access to a central computer. And M.I.T. is planning a computerized library which it hopes will play a unique role in the student's educational process, with evaluation of the student's educational experience to be based in large part on what he has selected and read, rather than solely on the number of courses completed.

MAINTAINING THE DIALOGUE: SEMINARS FOR FRESHMEN

Most colleges organize their programs to give the student his seminar experience in the junior or senior year. This timing presumes that upperclassmen are better prepared for and can gain more from this kind of experience than underclassmen. Paralleling trends in independent study, freshman seminar programs are being offered in many colleges. Here, too, the intent is to give the student opportunity to acquire an experience in depth at the very beginning of his college career, in contrast to the large survey courses usually required of freshmen.

The best known of these programs is the one started at Harvard in 1959 and since adopted (1963) as a regular part of its curriculum. The seminars vary in nature: some are calculated to provide early experience of advanced work within a specialized field, others examine the nature of a broad area by treating in depth a sharply defined but representative subject, and still others aim to demonstrate the nature of a wide area by considering broad questions from the outset. All seek through a serious intellectual enterprise to associate freshmen in a close, provocative way with a distinguished scholar. Areas range from drama to politics; from philosophy and anthropology to the relationship of the individual to the cultural group in which he lives; and from the philosophy of life of the Navajo Indians to the origin, growth, and behavior of sunspots. The typical seminar is made up of eight to ten students who meet weekly, usually in the afternoon or evening, for two or three hours. Most involve some writing. A number meet informally for lunch and dinner, often with their professor. Several make considerable use of other Harvard faculty or speakers from the outside. Crucial to the development of student initiative, Harvard observers have found, is the voluntary and ungraded nature of the seminars.

Freshmen seminar programs have also been introduced in a number of other settings. Although they vary in organization and make-up (for example, use of a common theme for all seminar groups; mixing of groups to include upperclassmen in the freshman seminars; organization of seminars around student-initiated, rather than faculty-selected, themes), all emphasize involving freshmen in a small-group experience that places maximum emphasis on their participation in the initiation, study, and development of ideas. Among the institutions that have been using freshman seminars for some time are Mount Holyoke, Smith, Amherst, New College of Sarasota, Stephens, Monteith, Sarah Lawrence, Shimer, Goddard, Upland, and Loretto Heights. In more recently developed programs, Antioch, Colby, Colorado, Allegheny, Florida Presbyterian, Lake Forest, Pomona, stress freshman seminars as a key component on their new first-year programs. Stanford, in 1965, began a broad program of freshman-level seminars; and Recommendation 24 of the report of the Select Committee on Education at the University of California, Berkeley, recommends the initiation of a campuswide program of freshman seminars.

Concluding remarks

Still other developments could be added to this review, but the foregoing display something of the array of new curricular and instructional patterns that are coming into use in our colleges and universities. Some, like the developments in computer-assisted instruction and the learning centers, are relatively new; others, like independent study, off-campus learning, and residence-hall instruction, represent adaptations of ideas that have been around for some time.

Writing in the *Boston University Graduate Journal*, Richard S. Baer has this to say:

Broadly speaking, the professor of the future university will serve within it in three major roles: providing material for self-instruction by the students (i.e., films, tapes, programs for learning); advising students as to sources and helping them over difficult spots by individual or group conferences; and leading seminars, conducting investigations, or preparing lectures in which are treated the second general aspect of education mentioned, namely, the significance and relationships of the core material. The professor will no longer routinely and repetitively conduct classes in which core material is largely predigested and fed to students, who are then lulled into the belief they have been given all field content of importance. The predigested material which the professor prepares will be stored in the form of tape or film at the library. He will occasionally update it, but otherwise he progresses to the preparation of more study material.[7]

For some, these words may sound a somewhat ominous message. For others, they will be seen as having been long overdue.

Despite the programs described in the preceding pages, it is difficult to foresee to what extent the innovations will finally be adopted—*for habits in higher education die hard.* . . . This much, however, seems certain: the examinations of the curriculum and the explorations of new ways in teaching and learning now taking place reflect a welcome and much-needed turn in higher education. One can be hopeful that from them will emerge better students—and better teachers.

[7] Baer, "The Urban University of the Future," *Boston University Graduate Journal*, Spring 1963.

Commentaries on
Innovations in Teaching

ESTHER RAUSHENBUSH
ROBERT F. MC DERMOTT
NILS Y. WESSELL

Innovation and Educational Style

ESTHER RAUSHENBUSH

MY FIRST REFLECTION on reading Dr. Baskin's paper was that we should consider the different kinds of innovation described as a record of attempts to reconstruct college education in order to cope with both the new and the enduring problems, rather than merely as a record of various kinds of experiments. Otherwise, each of us who engages in one or another of the experiments is in some danger of separating it from the total design of education, becoming a specialist in one kind of innovation, closing our eyes to other forms on the grounds that they are more appropriate to other kinds of institutions than ours.

What has the Air Force Academy to do with a tutorial or conference system of the sweeping kind that Sarah Lawrence has? What has Sarah Lawrence to do with technological forms of teaching such as the Air Force Academy or Oklahoma Christian College uses?

A great deal. I suggest that a system of education that looks for the foreseeable future to using *only* ways of teaching that involve a one-to-one relation between teachers and students will be crippled if it closes its eyes and its attention to the possibilities for education which technology will continue to discover, and it is doomed because it will not be able to get or pay the teachers it needs; I suggest also that a system of education that gives students no opportunity for learning that lies in ongoing and regular interaction between teachers and students will give its students a truncated and distorted education.

We are in greater danger by far of the latter eventuality than of the former—although I think in just a little less danger than we were two or three years ago, before the students themselves reminded us that they are not ready to accept the depersonalization that is an obvious first consequence of dealing with them en masse.

I would like to comment on independent study and the importance of off-campus experience to education.

Much has been said about plans for independent study, much of it negative. It is frequently said that plans for independent study start with the assumption that self-education is an important experience; that studying independently is the way adults learn and students must continue to learn when they have finished their formal education, if they learn at all; that it frees the time of teachers and gives freer scope to intellectual inquiry; and that these plans end by demonstrating that without constant supervision students don't work, that they waste time, and that, to be effective, independent study demands more of a teacher, not less.

The great assets of independent study are those mentioned here: if a student, by the time he is twenty-one has not learned how to study independently, he has missed the most important ongoing discipline of education, because he is about to finish his schooling and his official connections with classroom teachers. A major goal of college teaching *should* be independent study. Where it most often fails is where there has been a sudden imposition of the demand that a student function with a high degree of intellectual independence for which he has had no reasonable preparation. To allow a student to spend the first two years of college in highly structured classes, with syllabus, lecture notes, regular quizzes and multiple-choice examinations, and all sorts of protective devices that make us sure that he has heard what we or the television set has said and has learned to say it too, and then, because he has made honor grades in performing this exercise, to turn him loose to engage in independent study is to court the disaster that many independent study projects report. Thus, in many places it is only the students who have learned to perform most perfectly in the least independent kind of learning who are permitted to undertake the most independent kind. I would not venture to say how many who have performed in a mediocre way in routinized learning might perform brilliantly, given a chance to ask their own questions and pursue them to the end, but I suspect there are many.

Most students coming to college have had little or no experience with independence of any kind. Most of them, although not all. While they cannot be expected to demonstrate independence in any convincing way as they enter college halls, a great many of them want it, hope for it, and respond when they are given an opportunity to exercise it. The best time to stir motivation, to sharpen and direct curiosity, to intensify the intellectual search is when a student first comes to college. The freshman year is a new beginning, that last best hope for thousands of young people that education can be an exciting and demanding experience. And it is the time when students in most of our colleges and universities experience the most formalized, impersonal, structured kind of learning.

Somewhere, and by some means, students should be given opportunity to discover questions to work on and to discover ways of working on them from the beginning, and I suggest that a most remarkable development of technological teaching would be the discovery of ways to stimulate and serve the personal, individual quest for understanding that is at the heart of significant education. I read that "computers . . . present lessons to students in such a way that each student receives a lesson uniquely tailored to his needs. He controls the speed at which he moves through the lesson and his performance determines what the lesson will be. Where he has difficulty, he gets help immediately, where he shows mastery he is moved ahead to more challenging materials." This will move the bright students along a given road rapidly and let the slow ones move slowly along the same road. They are certainly likely to learn better and more fully *what we have set them to learn.*

If in addition to this experience, which more and more of our students will have in college, we can begin at once to give them some opportunity to ask their *own* questions and seek their *own* answers, they may be really ready for independent study on a larger scale as they move along in time and maturity.

Independent study takes time. When any of us who are teachers engage in independent study ourselves, we find it takes time—often time we reluctantly allow teaching to interfere with. Students who have been prepared for large-scale independent study by having been given opportunities to learn how to engage in small-scale independent study should have expectations made quite clear, and opportunity equal to the expectations. If, as so many people complain, "independent study" takes too much of a faculty member's time, it is obviously not independent study, and the student has not been prepared for it on the scale expected. Independent study is not an easy way out. It can never be a way of saving teachers' time if it is not *also* a way of using students' time at the highest level. Like every significant accomplishment, it must be prepared for, and I suggest that if an institution is interested in developing programs of independent study, it is not enough to insert a number in a catalogue and say that students with a given grade-point average may undertake independent study. It must be built into the system from the beginning; it must be made part of a system in which a considerable amount of time is *not* spent in independent study; and students who have had no experience of independence must be helped to know how to use it. Independent study should not be looked on as an innovation or a device or a pedagogical exercise: it should take a student outside the orbit of being only a receiver of knowledge and educate him to the only kind of study that matters to a mature and thinking person. He may never become one, but we ought to give him this chance.

Off-campus or field experiences—like independent study, and, indeed, like certain of the discoveries and inventions of educational technology—recognize the obvious fact that in these times, and in the circumstances of our present life, college education can no longer be confined to a college campus. Oklahoma Christian College's thousand individual study carrels, where each student is assigned his own study space, would not have to have all those carrels on its own campus. Stephens College has extended the reach of its campus thousands of miles by telephone. In quite other terms, Kalamazoo College stretches its campus to cover Europe, not by telephone, wire, or radio beam, but by physical transportation. Field experience, like independent study, can be fearfully wasteful. But so can sitting in lecture halls.

Serious students have never questioned more seriously their purposes in being in college than they do now. Their anxieties and sense of dislocation often come from not being able to find the connections between their academic studies and the social, political, personal dilemmas, the violence and need they find in the world they inhabit. They see more of the world at an earlier age than students in any other generation, and the world they see is full of conflict and shifting values. It seems to me that the principal value of field studies and off-campus experience is to give them now, not ask them to wait until they have escaped the classroom, opportunity to observe and deal directly with the issues we talk about in our classrooms.

At the beginning I noted that we are in some danger always of adopting some innovation or experiment because we think it valuable in itself, or see somebody else working on it. Just as it seems to me the most important thing about independent study is that it be a growing experience, growing out of earlier experience and not suddenly imposed or granted, so I think the most important thing about off-campus experience is that it bear an organic relation to the educational style of the college that undertakes it. We are likely here to follow or create fashions, but a semester or a year in Europe or Puerto Rico or Appalachia, or in a social agency or a factory, means one thing if it grows out of one educational philosophy or style and quite another if it grows out of a different one. Students should not be asked to wait until they have done all the academic study, in the library and in the classroom and at their desks, that we want them to do before they have a chance to learn the meaning of some of this academic study by experience with places and events and people. But like any other form of innovation, the experiences a student has in field study will have meaning as they are knitted into the total fabric of his education, and are designed, not as a fascinating extra, but as a part of the design of the total fabric.

Technology for Instruction

ROBERT F. MC DERMOTT

WHEN THE Air Force Academy was established in 1954, the first efforts were—appropriately—concentrated on curriculum planning and development. With this focus, and unhampered by tradition, we did pioneer an evolution, if not a revolution, in service academy education. Our curriculum development has been based on an educational philosophy that every student should be given an opportunity and a challenge to advance academically as far and as fast as his abilities and motivation will carry him during the four years he spends at the academy. This philosophy led us to advanced placement of entering cadets, accelerated courses, overload courses, tutorials, student research, voluntary off-campus summer activities, academic majors, graduate-level programs, and cooperative master's degree programs with Purdue, Georgetown, U.C.L.A., and North Carolina State universities. All of these were pace-setting innovations in service academy education.

At the same time, with our concentration on curriculum development, we were wedded from the beginning—and still are for the most part—to the teaching methodology initiated by Sylvanus Thayer at West Point a century and a half ago: small sections of 14–16 students, homogeneous grouping of students in each course, the discussion method almost exclusively over the lecture method, almost daily recitations in each class by each student, and frequent testing. It was not until 1960 that the thrust of our efforts changed to concentrate on the implementation of the curriculum, rather than its definition. Since then we have made continuous deliberate efforts to create a climate for innovation in all areas of our program. We began instructional innovations to solve specific institutional problems.

One of the first problems to which we addressed ourselves was that of helping students accommodate to the work load expected of them. Out of much experimentation, we have developed an Academic Skills sequence, which is required of all freshmen. This consists of four segments of instruction, conducted over television, which teach the student how to study, how to use such resources as the library, reading improvement, and two sequences in typing—a beginner's typing course and a course for those who are more proficient. I might add that this

Academic Skills sequence evolved along with the uses of television for our instructional program. As a result, the whole Academic Skills course is presented from videotape and is distributed through the television medium to large groups of students, without the necessity of manning several rooms with live instructors. Two teachers administer this course using television, whereas, approximately 11 teachers would be required if the course were conducted in our traditional small-section manner.

One measurable result of the Academic Skills course that I can report to you is that the reading rate of our freshmen increases from approximately 350 words per minute to 930 words per minute and is accompanied by a slight improvement in comprehension.

Another development that occurred, really by accident, was the growth of the instructor-centered television concept. This concept we regard as "serendipity TV." We were unable, at the time we introduced television, to secure more than a minimum amount of equipment and operating capital. We determined to forge ahead—to use TV without a full production crew and to let the instructor control his entire program. As a result, we did startle some of the vested television interests in education with this instructor-centered concept, and we did get television in use for our instructional program sooner than anticipated.

Another development in the use of television has been the making of a portable, self-contained recorder and play-back unit in 1963. This we call Mimic, an acronym for Miniature Mobile Instructor-Controlled Television. We have been using this hardware for the recording and playing-back of student presentations in our public speaking program for the past three years, as well as for the recording and playing-back of presentations by our new instructors as a part of their preservice training each summer. We find these units to be not only effective in improving our student and instructor abilities, but also enthusiastically received and used by both teachers and students.

The foregoing are some earlier developments at the Air Force Academy. At present, besides the constant problem of improving the efficiency and effectiveness of our instructional program, we find ourselves faced with a nearly 80 percent increase in the size of our student body over the next four years. To cope with this increase and the enlargement of our facilities, we are currently conducting some instructional experiments and attempting to determine which technological innovations can be introduced into our program.

We are also conducting a comprehensive methodological study in the teaching of our general psychology course. The course is being conducted by holding the instructor-variable constant and varying the methods of teaching and the size of student groups. The student grouping is divided into two sizes—small and large—respectively defined as 15 cadets (our normal small section) and 75 cadets. The three methods are: (1) completely televised presentations; (2) lecture-discussion; and (3) pure lecture. There is nothing unusual about our study except that we do have excellent controls within the experimental design. Our class schedule is fixed. Absences are controlled. Students actually study during study time, and our learning environment is perhaps more controllable (with windowless classrooms, all rooms identical, and so on). The results of this study will be available in December and will be published.

I might add that the same experimental design is being used to conduct a smaller study with a portion of our military history sequence. These results also will be published.

Concurrently with our experimentation to reach solutions for specific institutional problems, we have some ongoing efforts in programed learning and some attempts to develop a systems approach to the teaching-learning process. One programed learning effort has been devoted to getting the teaching of place-name geography out of the formal classroom and to putting more of this responsibility on the student. In one experiment we used a printed program for geography homework and compared it with the normal text. We found that when the program was used, there was a 24 percent increase in student achievement and a 38 percent saving in the amount of time students devoted to the homework lessons.

In the basic sciences, the Department of Physics is using some of the audio-visual media for a variety of purposes. Video-taped demonstrations are being developed as an integral part of laboratory instruction, and 8-mm. cartridge, single-concept demonstration films will be made available to the students in other than the formal contact hours. An additional element in the array of presentational modes employed in physics is the use of random-access teaching machines to present some basic physical concepts to the students. The software (or programs) for these machines is being developed within our faculty and produced locally, and the machines themselves will be located in the dormitories so that students can have access to them during other than formal instructional periods.

So much for where we are at the moment. With the increasing impact of industrial technology on our sporadically developing instructional technology, I feel we must forge ahead in attempting to improve the instructional processes where we can. If we managers of education do not control the introduction of technological developments into the instructional processes, we may lose control of the process itself. Therefore, at the Air Force Academy, we are looking, with interest, at various means of putting more responsibility on the learners for their own learning. Individual learning stations, in carrel form, are in our planning. Such developments as the recently disclosed motion picture projection device, which can provide two hours of sound on film, in linear or random form with motion or single-frame capability, could well be a *major* development in providing students with random access to oral and visual information. Another promising recent development is the sound compression technique, which is now being marketed. This device can speed up or slow down recorded sound by as much as 50 percent in either direction. The implications here for introducing more efficiency in the presentation of information are great.

Finally, we have been looking at the embryonic development of the use of the computer for the presentation of instructional programs to students. We can see, at the moment, the development of two kinds of programs that use the computer. The first is a course in computer programing, to be taken by every freshman student at the academy. In this course, we are attempting to provide a large mass of information to a large number of students. It is hoped that after the cadet has completed this programed sequence, he will be able to capitalize on the computer to solve his math and engineering problems.

A second array of computer-assisted instructional courses will be employed in conjunction with our enrichment courses. Our experience in advanced and enrichment courses indicates that the classroom instructor spends a third to a half of the class period giving information to his class. The CAI program, in the enrichment courses, could permit the student to receive 100 percent of the essential course information before class and thus permit our instructors to deal with groups smaller than the traditional class size on a tutorial basis. We feel that the use of CAI, in conjunction with enrichment courses, will increase, rather than limit, the amount of meaningful instructor-student interaction.

Two of the deterrents to the use of CAI, at the present time, are: (a) the ability of the teacher-programer to communicate directly with the computer memory; and (b) the tremendous amount of time required for a programer to structure information in such a way that a student can interact with it "on line," as they say, with the computer.

At this point, let me summarize my feelings about "instructional technology." We, as a group, are charged with the managing of learning in our respective educational institutions. We are coping with technological innovations in all aspects of life. Our task, then, is to select wisely those innovations that, we feel, hold the most promise for the educational process throughout our country.

The Process of Innovation

NILS Y. WESSELL

TWO QUANDARIES beset college and university administrators concerned with innovation. The first concerns the process of innovation: getting it under way. The second concerns evaluating it: deciding what results, if any, have been achieved. Each poses some sticky questions, and each must be resolved if we are to do more than talk about innovation.

The claim that most innovations in colleges and universities have been introduced from the outside is supported by impressive evidence. We should not, however, sit back and assume that this must be the case. On the contrary, I believe that innovation that is generated within the institution by faculty members themselves is likely to be more significant in its effects, better tested, and longer lasting than change that is imposed by forces from without. Let us bless and accept enthusiastically such external influences, but let us not follow the counsel of despair which holds that only pressure from outside academic walls can affect the *status quo*.

I have in mind, not the Sarah Lawrences and the Antiochs with their relatively long tradition of giving a sympathetic hearing to new ideas, but the more typical college or university in which (too often) there seems to be an immediate and negative reaction to any notion that there might be different or better ways of achieving the institution's educational objectives. Institutions which have a history of innovation can provide models of innovative programs, but perhaps they are less likely to provide transferable experience with respect to the process of innovation. This seems to be true at all levels in our schools and colleges. Unless the new curriculum or program or technique is found in an institution closely resembling his own, the faculty member is not likely to believe that it has possibilities in his own case.

To illustrate my point, I must be autobiographical, much as I would prefer to be less personal. At Tufts University, an institution I served as president for thirteen years, we did embark on a program of experiment and innovation with strong faculty backing and participation. The history of this achievement may have useful implications for and applications to other institutions.

The only step in the process which was clearly identified with administrative initiative was the first one, the appointment by myself of a small Faculty Committee on Innovation and Experiment. It had that simple, yet bold title. It was composed of faculty who by their own behavior had clearly indicated either an interest in innovation or some degree of originality. Its existence and deliberations were given wide publicity and strong backing by both the administration and the

205

trustees of the university, although equal emphasis was given to the fact that it had the broadest of directives, so broad that in effect it was invited to "write its own ticket."

It met regularly for the better part of an academic year, invited both suggestions and criticisms, and took care to give audience to those who felt its mission was unnecessary. Some of the latter included those who believed that considerable innovation and experiment were already under way at Tufts as well as those who believed that conservation of traditional practice was more important than change.

Innovative proposals made to the committee ranged from highly specific new courses to a complete reorientation of the whole university. Wisely, in my opinion, the committee rejected both the piecemeal approach and the global approach, the first in the belief that it would bring slow if not tortured change, and the latter in the belief it would stand no chance of acceptance by the faculty as a whole.

It proposed instead the creation of an Experimental College whose administration and policies were to be in the hands of the faculty itself and whose charge from the faculty was as broadly defined as possible, the latter purchased at the reasonable price of a time limit of five years to this sweeping delegation of authority. Special, informal faculty meetings were arranged for the purpose of discussion and debate, not vote taking. When the formal meeting was arranged for final action on the proposal, reluctant or opposed faculty members were once again given full opportunity to present their views. That the protagonists had stated their case well was reflected in the fact that the only amendments to the proposal passed by the faculty were in the direction of greater liberality: opening the program of the Experimental College to all students, regardless of academic performance, and not setting limits to the amount of time a particular faculty member could devote to the work of the Experimental College.

The faculty committee's success was abetted also by the fact that it made clear that its goal was to put the Experimental College out of existence through adopting into the regular curricula in arts and sciences those programs and procedures found effective in the Experimental College. It won adherents also by leaving to the individual academic departments final decisions regarding programs of concentration although it was committed to encouraging innovation and experiments with respect to these too.

Existing traditional curricula and instructional methods were allowed to go their merry way, threatened in no direct manner by the Experimental College. In time, of course, it was hoped that such conventional programs and approaches would be influenced indirectly by comparison with the programs of the Experimental College.

Important also was the involvement of the student body through their own selected representatives. At first the student representatives were nonvoting members of the board of the Experimental College, but on the initiative of the faculty members themselves, they were given full rights and voting privileges. Although this decision could have been made at the outset, I believe it was a matter of wisdom to postpone it until such time as students' contributions were shown to be useful and their judgments sound. Thus, faculty members dubious about the involvement of students at this level could be told that a careful test had been made of the validity and the significance of their participation. In retrospect, I would say that an even better approach might have been to let the students know at the beginning that their full voting privileges were being considered and could come in due course (this is probably not an important matter).

I myself appointed the first faculty board of the Experimental College, but with the understanding that as staggered terms of the members expired, replacements would be made through a vote of the faculty. The program is now in its third year, and a majority of the members of the board hold membership by virtue of election by the faculty.

The board has final authority with respect to all degree requirements except those represented by concentration requirements, as mentioned earlier. While this exception may sound like a concession so great that wide innovation could be stifled by conservative departments, such has not proved to be the case. Interestingly, many innovations already under way before the creation of the Experimental College but woefully unpublicized in the college community benefited from the light of day provided by the Experimental College.

I will not recite the large number of innovations being tested under the auspices of the Experimental College, for I would concentrate on the process of innovation instead, but I can assure you that the spectrum is a broad one. The main bar to even broader and wider experimentation is the expected one—inadequate financial resources. Real momentum nevertheless has been generated, by the faculty itself, and is being sustained largely by the faculty, although the university administration and trustees do provide the important encouragement and assistance from the sidelines. Intriguing and amusing both have been the instances now coming to light of experiment and innovation almost secretly tried by individual faculty members, even by some faculty members who heretofore in the eyes of their colleagues were among the strongest advocates of the *status quo*. More predictable have been the excitement and the interest of the students, present even before their representatives had full membership on the board.

But what is the Experimental College accomplishing, and how can its achievements be measured? This is the second major concern of the college or university administrator who is the champion of innovation. Although some of the boldest and seemingly most effective of innovators care naught for appraising their pet projects, and while I share the conviction that the process of innovation is just as important as the results, evaluation of some kind is going on at all times, subjective and unreliable though it may be. To the individual scientifically or quantitatively oriented, the evaluation of the educational process and its outcomes is in a primitive state indeed. He would claim with real justification that even a theory of evaluation is yet to be developed. Others would go back even a step further and maintain that until we derive a set of goals for education generally, or for a specific curriculum in particular, it is futile to speak of evaluation. And if we insist that the end of education is the good life, how do we get even a modest degree of agreement with respect to what the good life is? If an important objective of a college education is the development of lifetime habits of independent study and continuing intellectual curiosity, how can these possibly be assessed over a period of time shorter than a lifetime?

In spite of these seemingly insoluble problems, I believe it is imperative that we make a start toward improving our ability to assess what we do. Bold is he who would claim that in our colleges there is not conspicuous waste in the resources used, whether they be human or material. While principles of cost-effectiveness might be difficult to apply in measuring the good life and the outcomes of education, clearly there are other objectives that can be tested by such principles. It would also appear to me that higher education is lagging behind secondary and elementary education in its concern for the full and efficient use of its resources. Many university administrators could profit by the example of secondary and elementary school administrators.

Some very simple steps toward improving evaluation could come first. A survey, for example, of present practices in the choice of materials used in the classroom by the college teacher, whether these are conventional textbooks, audio-visual materials of a traditional sort, or other kinds of equipment, would be extremely useful even though possibly disillusioning.

More difficult would be a research program intended to develop appropriate objectives and criteria for subject-matter fields as well as for the broader aims of education. If high among our concerns are the development of independent study habits, intellectual curiosity, the process of self-discovery, and joy in intellectual accomplishment, then let us be bold enough to say that we will attempt to learn whether these goals are possible of assessment and whether we can identify those educational experiences and methods which are positively related to their realization. Granted that only the ultimate fate of our civilization is the real test, we need not despair of uncovering and finding those signs which foretell survival or decay.

Let us try to develop also what might be called a taxonomy of evaluation, and determine the usefulness of each of the kinds of appraisal we already have or can develop. The taxonomy I have in mind ranges from such a simple thing as a long-distance telephone call, preferably over a distance greater than fifty miles, to an authority in a particular field, to a carefully controlled study of matched groups of students, to longitudinal, lifetime studies of the careers of individuals.

The psychologist concerned with learning theory is properly discovering the elementary and secondary school classroom and is developing a feeling of obligation to education. Let us persuade him to include the college classroom in his compass and let us insist also that we are interested in attitudes as well as skills, in approaches to learning as well as to the subject matter learned, in modifying the behavior of the eighteen- to the twenty-three-year-old in ways that will serve him at age thirty, at fifty, at sixty, and beyond as well.

Having preached in this fashion as a university president for more than a dozen years, I have finally come round to doing something about it. The new organization which I represent, the Institute for Educational Development, places top priority on the improvement of evaluation in education, on a program of research and development directed at the questions I have raised in these remarks. We admit to uncertainty, to ignorance, and to the likelihood of confronting as many failures as successes, though we think everyone in education has an obligation to submit his activities to forms of appraisal of their relevance and validity. How else can we plot the future course of education except by wasteful trial and error which may tell us too late wherein we failed?

The staff of our new nonprofit enterprise consists of psychologists, former school and university administrators, curriculum experts, persons knowledgeable about instructional technology, teachers, and businessmen. It will remain small in number of full-time professional staff, but will seek the cooperative involvement of individuals everywhere who have talent and interest to contribute. Certain of its activities will seek support through government agencies, others through foundations, and still others through arrangements with the growing number of commercial firms entering education.

A promising development in a related direction is represented by the recently established Center for the Study of Evaluation in Instructional Programs at the University of California, Los Angeles. I would urge those of you not acquainted with the program of this center to learn of its plans. It is engaged in research in the evaluation of *content* of curricula, *methods* of teaching, and the multiple effects of both on students. Investigation of cost-effectiveness of instructional programs is also under way. It goes without saying that there is more than enough for all of us to do.

I would enlarge on that statement as my general conclusion. In the encouragement of innovation in colleges and universities and in the evaluation of the results of innovation there is more than enough for all of us to do. Urgency attaches to our task also.

Research in Teaching:
The Gap Between
Theory and Practice

W. J. MC KEACHIE

GILBERT HIGHET WRITES in the Preface to his *The Art of Teaching,*

[This book] . . . is called *The Art of Teaching* because I believe teaching is an art, not a science. It seems very dangerous to me to apply the aims and methods of science to human beings as individuals. . . . Teaching is not like inducing a chemistry reaction: it is much more like painting a picture, or making a piece of music, or on a lower level like planting a garden or writing a friendly letter. You must throw your heart into it, you must realize that it cannot all be done by formulas, or you will spoil your work, and your pupils and yourself.[1]*

One cannot help cheering Professor Highet's call for commitment to teaching, but in practice the "art of teaching" is all too often based on naïve assumptions about students, teaching methods, and the nature of the student-teacher relationship. Art based on sound knowledge and well-honed skills is more effective in promoting student learning.

Teaching is like art in that it involves value judgments, and the means for achieving these values are complex. Research has revealed that many variables interact in determining teaching effectiveness. But it is the very complexity of the teaching situation that makes every bit of empirical information the more precious.

The basic question researchers have tried to answer is: What kind of teaching-learning situation is educationally most effective? This implies that the goals of education can be defined precisely enough to permit judgments about which of two teaching methods is more effective. Unfortunately, statements about goals are often so general that opinions

Author's note: Preparation of this paper was greatly facilitated by my participation in research sponsored by the U.S. Office of Education, Research Contract OE No. 4/10/001 with W. J. McKeachie, J. E. Milholland, and Robert L. Isaacson.

An excellent review of recent work in this field is found in Ruth E. Eckert and D. C. Neale, "Teachers and Teaching," *Review of Educational Research,* 1965, *35,* 304–17.

* The references are given at the end of the paper (see pp. 231–39).

211

about teaching effectiveness can only be impressionistic. The ultimate criteria of teaching effectiveness are *changes in students*—learning; movement toward educational objectives.

In thinking about college teaching, we professors have usually been most concerned about content. The Ph.D has been the teacher's certificate for working at the college level. It seems obvious that knowledge of subject should be necessary (but not sufficient) for effective teaching. This assumption, however, has never been checked, and, conceivably, students might become better educated by a confused or ill-informed instructor who motivated his students to clear up the confusions than by a professor with great depth of knowledge.

The emphasis on content has led to a distorted view of the role of the professor.[2] This view is that the professor's most important qualification is his knowledge and that the process of teaching involves communicating the professor's knowledge to students. This notion of the professor as a source of information—a walking encyclopedia—is really a carryover from the times when books were scarce and expensive, and oral transmission of culture was necessary.

Today the importance of the Ph.D. degree is as a symbol that the holder has achieved some degree of expertness in *learning* a scholarly field. His role in teaching should be as an expert guiding novices in developing the skills of learning his field. The professor's knowledge is a concomitant of his skill as a learner rather than the *sine qua non* for teaching.

What is the relationship between the instructor's learning skills and his ability both to teach these learning skills to students and to motivate students to learn? The whole area of content has been neglected in research on teaching.[3] We do not know the effects of misinformation, amount of information presented, level of abstraction, emphasis upon cognition versus motivation, analysis versus synthesis, didactic versus problem-solving approaches, or deductive versus inductive styles. Fortunately, programed instruction is beginning to give some attention to these variables.[4]

One can imagine that proposals for research on "professors' knowledge of subject matter" would not be greeted with enthusiasm by professors. It is thus not surprising that the beginnings of research on teaching have been in areas that are less personally threatening.

CLASS SIZE

The earliest research on teaching was on class size. Are small classes really more effective for teaching than large classes? The answer of the professor has generally been "yes." But the refreshing empiricism of the 1920's looked hard at many "self-evident truths" about human behavior.

Among them was the assumption that class size has something to do with educational effectiveness.

Among the first investigators were Edmondson and Mulder,[5] who compared the performance of students matched for intelligence enrolled in a 109-student class with students enrolled in a 43-student class in the same course in education. Achievement of the two groups was approximately equal, with a slight edge for the small class on an essay and the mid-semester tests and for the large class on quizzes and the final examination. Students reported a preference for small classes. The Edmondson and Mulder results at Michigan encouraged the Committee on Research of the University of Minnesota to begin the most comprehensive studies of class size ever undertaken. Fifty-nine well-controlled experiments, reported by Hudelson,[6] involved such widely varying subject matter as psychology, physics, accounting, law, and education. In 46 of the experiments, results favored the large classes. Although only eight differences were large enough to be statistically significant at the 5 percent level, six of the eight favored large classes.

Support for small classes, however, came from studies in the teaching of French conducted by Cheydleur [7] at the University of Wisconsin between 1919 and 1943. With hundreds of classes ranging in size from nine to 33, Cheydleur found a consistent superiority on departmental examinations for the smaller classes. Mueller [8] found similar results in an experiment comparing elementary psychology classes of 20 and 40 students. More recent experiments are also less favorable to large classes. Nachman and Opochinsky [9] found a small class to be superior to a large class on surprise quizzes, but the two classes were not significantly different on the final examination. In the Macomber and Siegel experiments at Miami University [10] significant differences favoring small classes were found on measures of change in misconceptions in psychology, on a case test of problems in a course in marketing, and on the measures of student attitudes toward all the courses. When retention of knowledge was measured one to two years after completion of the courses, in eight of the nine courses compared, small differences favored the small class.[11] Differences were also revealed in the more subtle and persisting outcomes in Feldhusen's [12] study showing that a small class in educational psychology produced more change in attitudes toward teaching than a large class.

Few of us are satisfied with achievement of knowledge if it is not remembered, if the student is unable to use it in solving problems, or if he fails to relate the knowledge to attitudes. If one takes the more basic outcomes of retention, problem solving, and attitude differentiation as ends, the evidence clearly favors small classes. Moreover, in almost all studies, students and faculty members tend to prefer small classes; other things being equal, high student and faculty morale is an asset.

As in most areas of research on college teaching, the initial interest in class size was empirical, and theoretical considerations came to the fore later. Social psychologists Thomas and Fink [13] reviewed research on face-to-face groups; they suggest that two types of input increase with increasing group size—*resource input* (skills, knowledge, and the like) and *demand input* (needs).

It is clear that the more members in the group, the greater the likelihood that some members will have resources of knowledge, intelligence, or other skills needed for the educational purposes of the group. It seems likely, however, that the amount of relevant knowledge and skills is limited, so that beyond some point additional students will contribute little that is not already in the group's resources. The group's utilization of its resources is constrained by the simple fact that (1) in large groups, a smaller proportion of group members can participate verbally, and (2) the larger the group, the less likely a given person will feel free to volunteer his contribution. As the size of the class is increased, the number of different demands or needs of members also increases. But it is unlikely that the instructor and class can meet increased, different expectations proportionately, since class time usually cannot be extended. As Stephan and Mishler [14] have shown, larger groups are more likely to be dominated by the leader, and the teacher can give less individual attention to each member. The research of McKeachie *et al.*[15] indicates that men high in the need for affiliation achieve well for teachers who take a personal interest in students; we might, then, expect such students to fare better in the smaller classes. Likewise, we might expect more frustration and dissatisfaction in larger classes unless they are relatively homogeneous.

In order to apply these general propositions to teaching, we need to ask such questions as:

In what teaching situations is amount of information in the group important? One might, for example, hypothesize that in most courses in which knowledge is the primary goal, the relevant information is contained in books and the instructor's head, and the amount added by students is likely to be inconsequential. On the other hand, if application is an important goal, amount of knowledge of application situations and of the conditions governing application contributed by students may well be significant; therefore, if Thomas and Fink's principles are valid, there may be groups too small, as well as too large, to be maximally effective.

In most courses there are several levels of goals—knowledge, critical thinking, attitudes toward learning, and so on. The teacher's task is to find a combination of methods that will achieve an optimal balance of all these. Unfortunately most teaching research has studied the effect of one method versus another painfully repeated day after day for a semester; thus little evidence is available on the relative effectiveness of differing combinations or degrees of flexibility in teaching methods. (Some studies on lecture-discussion combinations are reviewed in the next section.)

While many teaching methods can be used in large groups, probably teaching is confined more to lecturing than in smaller classes. The large class often reduces the teacher's sense of freedom in choosing teaching methods, assigning papers, and testing to achieve various objectives. Assuming that teachers have some repertoire of skills, anything that handcuffs them is likely to be educationally damaging. This is how edution is likely to be sabotaged by large classes.

What can we say about class size? It is a commonplace that the effect of size depends on the method used, and probably true that group size is less critical for success of lectures than of discussion. But analysis also suggests that the importance of size depends on educational goals. In general, large classes are simply not as effective as small classes for retention, critical thinking, and attitude change.

LECTURING

Lecture versus discussion

Research on the lecture method is almost as hoary as that on class size. In 1925 Bane published "The Lecture vs. the Class-Discussion Method of College Teaching." [16] In five experiments, he found little difference between the methods on measures of immediate recall, but on tests given one to six months later consistent differences favored discussion. Later studies similarly have found little effect on end-of-course achievement.[17] Ruja,[18] however, found that the lecture was superior to discussion as measured by a test of subject-matter mastery in a general psychology course. In the other two courses included in his experiment, no significant differences appeared in achievement or in changes in adjustment in any of the courses. When we turn to measures of more complex outcomes, the results favor discussion. Hirschman [19] compared the effectiveness of presenting material by dictation with presenting written materials followed by discussion and rereading. The reading-discussion method resulted in superior ability to identify examples of the concepts presented.

Barnard [20] compared the effectiveness of a lecture-demonstration teaching method with that of a problem-solving developmental discussion in a college science course. In this experiment the lecture-demonstration method proved superior on a test of specific information, but the discussion method proved superior on measures of problem solving and scientific attitude. Likewise, Dawson [21] found problem-solving recitation and lecture-demonstration methods to be equally effective in a course in elementary soil science as measured by a test of recall of specific information, but the problem-solving method was significantly superior as measured by tests of problem-solving abilities.

Other evidence favoring discussion emerged from the experiment of Elliott,[22] who found that students in his discussion groups in elementary psychology became more interested in electing additional courses in psychology than were students in a large lecture. Similarly Casey and Weaver[23] found no differences in knowledge of content but superiority in attitudinal outcomes (as measured by the Minnesota Teacher Attitude Inventory) for small-group discussions as compared to lectures.

What can we say about lectures versus discussion? Since discussion offers the opportunity for a good deal of student activity and feedback, it could be (according to theory) and is (according to research results) more effective than typical lectures in developing concepts and problem-solving skills. However, because the rate of transmission of information is slow in discussion classes, we would expect lecture classes to be superior in attaining the objective of teaching knowledge. Research results tend to support this generalization and probably are not more convincing largely because the knowledge tested on course examinations usually can be learned by reading the textbook.

The role of lectures

The lecture continues to be the most commonly used method of teaching in colleges and universities. Although it has been severely criticized, it still should not be rejected, for research has not dealt specifically with the strongest aspects of lecturing.[24] For example, although normally one should assign reading rather than lecture when the material is available in printed form, books or printed materials are not always readily available in an appropriate form. The lecturer may be able to choose from a book those elements most needed by his class and save student time by a concise presentation.

Moreover, a lecturer can be an effective guide to reading. By indicating the most important points, by posing questions with which students can approach their reading, by his own appreciation and interpretation of what has been assigned, the instructor can help his students develop the ability to read in his field. Presumably this role of the instructor is particularly important early in a student's entrance into a field. As the student gains experience, the lecturer can rely more and more on the student to get information from reading and cut down the proportion of time devoted to lecturing. Unfortunately in most courses the size of class and characteristics of the classroom lock us in so that such flexibility is difficult to realize.

As reading materials carry an increasing portion of the task of communication of knowledge, the lecturers' role becomes that of presenting new materials not yet in print. The lecture is the newspaper or journal of teaching; it, more than any other teaching, must be up to date.

Distribution of lecture and discussion time

Many universities and large colleges use a method of distributing class meetings between lectures and discussions. This administrative arrangement is supported by studies in psychology [25] and physics.[26] In general, the more course time devoted to recitations in proportion to lectures, the better is student achievement. The conclusion to be drawn from these studies seems to be that a combination of large lecture and small discussion sections is preferable to the common arrangement of several sections of unwieldy medium size.

To summarize: What is the role of the lecturer in higher education? The research results cited provide little basis for an answer. Nevertheless, they do not contradict and sometimes support the notion that the lecture is a useful way of communicating information, particularly in classes where the use of printed materials is impractical. A good deal of evidence, however, suggests that discussion is more effective than lecturing in achieving the more complex cognitive and attitudinal objectives.

DISCUSSION METHODS

The chief alternative to lecture is discussion. What theoretical concepts are apposite to the relative effectiveness of various types of discussion methods both alone and in combination with other teaching methods?

Active versus passive learning: Lectures usually place the learner in a passive role, and passive learning is generally less efficient than active learning. Bloom and his colleagues at the University of Chicago used recordings of classes to stimulate students to recall their thoughts during class.[27] As predicted, they found that more active thinking was stimulated by discussion than by lecture classes.

Practice and feedback: If students are to achieve application, critical thinking, or some higher cognitive outcomes, a reasonable assumption is that they should have an opportunity to practice application and critical thinking and to receive feedback on the results. Although teaching machines and mock-ups may also be programed to provide prompt and realistic feedback, group discussion permits presentation of a variety of problems that allow a number of people to gain experience in integrating facts, formulating hypotheses, amassing relevant evidence, and evaluating conclusions. In fact, the prompt feedback from the teaching machine may actually be less effective than a method in which students are encouraged to discover solutions for themselves with less step-by-step guidance.[28]

Motivation: A decade or two ago psychologists discussing motivation would have talked about reward and punishment and suggested that teachers look at the rewards for learning in the classroom. Rewards and punishments do play an important role in determining what we learn. But the revolution in motivation research and theory lies in new evidence that Man is naturally curious. He seeks new experiences; he enjoys learning new things; he finds satisfaction in solving a puzzle or developing a skill.

How does this generalization apply to learning in college? It is tempting to answer in vague phrases such as: "varied teaching methods," "posing new, but soluble problems," or "setting realistic standards of achievement." But we can go beyond this. One hint comes from studies by Berlyne.[29] He found that asking students questions, rather than presenting statements of fact, not only improves learning but also increases interest in learning more about the topic. Questions, he found, are particularly effective in arousing curiosity about things that are already familiar, and the most successful questions are those that are most unexpected. This checks with the finding that National Merit scholars describe the classes which influenced their choice of field to be ones where they didn't know what to expect next.[30] The interplay between familiar and novel may thus be a very significant factor in developing curiosity. Thus, the unsettling lack of certainty about "where we're going" may be one of the assets of the discussion method.[31]

Group variables

A final theory to be considered in discussion methods derives from social and clinical psychological studies of attitudinal and personality change. Failure to achieve some goals of learning may not be due to lack of intelligence or deficiencies in the materials presented but rather to emotional barriers in the learner. For example, a student of literature may fail to see the essential elements of a novel because it comes too close to his own problems; a mathematics student may have a block against mathematics; a history student may resist materials counter to his concept of American idealism; a potentially creative student may inhibit his intuitions because of insecurity.

Psychotherapists and social psychologists believe that expressing one's attitude in a non-threatening situation may help "unfreeze" the attitude. Group discussion may provide opportunities for such expression as well as give opportunities for members to express other attitudes that may be instrumental to meeting the individual's needs. Most attitudes influencing learning have some interpersonal antecedents and are stabilized by one's perception of the attitudes of other liked persons. Group discussion may facilitate a high degree of liking for the instructor and for other group members. It also permits more accurate assessment of group norms than is likely to occur in other techniques of instruction. In fact, while individual instruction is advantageous for many teaching purposes, group processes provide a real advantage in bringing about changes in motivation and attitudes. Lewin [32] showed in his classic experiments on group decision that sometimes change is easier for a group than for an individual.

Whether or not discussions actually are superior in these theoretical respects cannot be easily determined, for discussions range from monologues, in which occasional questions are interposed, to bull sessions in which the instructor is an interested (or bored) observer. Nevertheless, a good deal of research has attempted to compare the effectiveness of various discussion techniques.

Student-centered versus instructor-centered teaching

A wide variety of teaching methods are described by labels: "student-centered," "nondirective," "group-centered," and "democratic" discussion. They have in common the desire to break away from the traditional instructor-dominated classroom and to encourage greater student participation and responsibility.

Theoretically, student-centered teaching in its more extreme forms might be expected to have some serious weaknesses, at least in achieving lower-level cognitive goals. With the instructor's role as information-giver reduced, his role as source of feedback virtually eliminated, and his opportunity to provide organization and structure curtailed, it is apparent that a heavy burden falls upon the group member to carry out any of these functions that are necessary. Since student-centered teaching attempts to reduce dependence upon the instructor, it would be expected to diminish his influence as a prestige figure. However, this may be more than compensated for by increased freedom of expression and increased potency of group norms as sources of influence. I have reviewed the research on student-centered teaching elsewhere.[33] The results are not conclusive, but tend to support this theory. There seem to be few instances of loss in achievement of knowledge in student-centered classes. Students apparently can get information from textbooks as well as from the instructor.

In eleven studies, significant differences in ability to apply concepts, in attitudes, in motivation, and in group membership skills have been found between discussion techniques emphasizing freer student participation compared with discussion with greater instructor dominance. In ten of these the differences favored the student-centered method. The eleventh [34] had mixed results. Thistlethwaite [35] found that National Merit scholars check as one of the outstanding characteristics of the teachers who contributed most to their desire to learn, "allowing time for classroom discussion." Other characteristics mentioned included "modifying course content to meet students' needs and interests," "treating students as colleagues," and "taking a personal interest in students." However, in line with the earlier discussion of feedback, another trait mentioned was "providing evaluations reassuring the student of his creative or productive potentialities."

A recently completed, and as yet unpublished, study by a University of Michigan research group has also shown that psychology instructors whose students do best on tests of psychological thinking (with intelligence controlled) tend to be described as follows:

He listened attentively to what class members had to say.

He was friendly.

He was permissive and flexible.

He explained the reasons for criticism.

Things are explained clearly.

He is skillful in observing student reactions.

Both the Thistlethwaite and the Michigan results support the value of student-centered teaching for motivation and critical thinking.

The choice of instructor-centered versus student-centered discussion thus appears to depend upon one's goals. The more highly one values outcomes going beyond knowledge acquisition, the more likely that student-centered methods will be preferred.

READING, PROGRAMED LEARNING, AND INDEPENDENT STUDY

One of the newest developments in higher education which has received much less publicity than television and teaching machines but probably will have more long-term significance for higher education is the revolution in the use of printed materials, such as paperback books, off-prints of journal articles, facsimile or microfilm copies, and other duplicated materials. Not only is the student now able to own a richer variety of resources, but, in addition, the new open-stack libraries invite him to go beyond his assignments to books and journals giving other viewpoints and additional information.

In discussions of the remarkable values of bringing "master teachers" to all learners through television, we often overlook the fact that through books and printed materials the student can follow the teaching of a master teacher and, further, can choose from among a number of master teachers the one who best communicates to him.

An early study [36] found that students learned as thoroughly from reading material as from listening to it. The better students, moreover, profited more from reading than from listening. A number of other studies have compared printed materials with lectures, with results favoring print, at least with difficult materials. [37] However, the amount of research on books and articles as teaching media is small, considering their widespread use. There have, however, been studies of size of print, readability, and the effectiveness of illustrations. (Illustrations apparently don't contribute much to learning as measured by conventional tests.)

Programed Instruction

One of the newest developments in textbooks is the programed textbook, an instructional book that uses the learning-in-small-steps sequence of the teaching machine. Such books and pamphlets are often designed as adjuncts to conventional teaching materials.

The teaching machine is a device for presenting questions in a predetermined sequence and providing immediate knowledge of results to an active learner. The questions proceed in tiny steps from the simple to the complex and permit the learner to proceed at his own rate. With some machines, the student may, if he makes a series of correct responses, adjust the machine to skip some steps; if he fails items, they are repeated.

There have been two general approaches to the use of teaching machines. In the early investigations of Pressey and his students, the teaching machine was used primarily as a device to provide prompt knowledge of results of conventional testing procedures. As a testing machine, it was simply a supplement to conventional teaching methods such as lectures, discussion, and textbook assignments. The second approach, originated by Skinner and his followers, substitutes the teaching machine for other teaching methods: it is used either as the sole instrument of instruction or at least as a major method to be supplemented by the teacher. In some cases the "program" (the series of questions or statements presented to the student) is presented in a text or workbook, and "programed instruction" is now used to refer to any carefully sequenced presentation, whether by teaching machine, book, lecture, film, or television.

Some of the research evidence supports the use of teaching-testing machines as supplements to conventional instruction. In addition to Pressey's early work, Angell,[38] Peterson and Peterson,[39] and Stephens[40] found that knowledge of results on a quiz or special answer sheets was more effective when it was immediate than when delayed until the next class meeting. The research with Skinnerian types of programs has been less encouraging. Students do learn from the programs, but learning is generally slower than with conventional printed materials (but faster than lectures).[41] In some cases, achievement is higher for the programed learners,[42] and one must judge whether the extra investment in time is justified by the gain in learning. In other cases learning from programs is less than learning from conventional sources.[43]

The controversy about whether the student needs to make a response has largely abated. If the response itself must be learned, as in the teaching of typewriting or a new vocabulary, an overt response is required, but in most college courses the responses required are already in the student's repertoire and he learns more rapidly by not stopping to fill in blanks.[44]

Little research has been done to determine what kinds of students learn well or poorly from programs and what types of objectives can be achieved most efficiently. It might be expected that programs written so that every question is answered correctly by almost every student would bore most students, particularly those with strong achievement motivation, and this is affirmed by Moore, Smith, and Teevan.[45] A study by Lublin [46] found that performance was better with variable reinforcement or without reinforcement as compared with consistent reinforcement. A less expected but reasonable finding is that students scoring high on a sociability test do poorly with programed instruction.[47]

The furore about teaching machines and programed learning is subsiding, and research is beginning to clarify effective and ineffective uses.[48] Present programs are not panaceas for the problems of American higher education. For a while it appeared that programed materials might give educators a shortcut in the difficult problems of curriculum and course organization, but now it is recognized that writing a good program requires just as much scholarship as writing a good textbook.[49] Programing is hard work, and so far scholars seem less willing to write programs than books. As of now the number of good programs for college use is very limited, and programs adapted to computer-assisted instruction are almost nonexistent.

Programing has also suffered from a lack of evaluation. To many advocates of programed instruction, it has seemed self-evident that anyone who completes a program successfully has learned—he has achieved the goals of the program. Professors like to make this same assumption about their lectures; yet most of them have had the disheartening experience of finding that points made crystal clear in a brilliant lecture have not sunk into the awareness of their students sufficiently to be used in responding to an examination question. One of the problems for programers of college materials is that, in general, they are working at a level of conceptualization where the required response is only one of the class of related responses to a group of stimuli. Sometimes the programer provides irrelevant cues, to which the student learns to make the desired response; at other times the response required is irrelevant to the goals—simply indicates that the student read the frame, as when he is asked to fill in a trivial word.

Some program writers have recognized the importance of a separate testing of learning, but such tests frequently contain items or paraphrases of items from the program. Correct answers then are not accurate measures since a high score might be obtained by someone who has learned to respond to irrelevant cues or who has learned only the specific responses taught without grasping the principle or concept. Ideally, achievement should be measured by a test as different as possible from the program items.

The programed learning movement has had the healthy effect of forcing clarification of educational objectives. But after obtaining a precise list, the programed learning protagonists have tended to dismiss as unreal any objectives that were not specified at a level appropriate for programing and have, instead, prepared programs that had trivial objectives. Disillusionment with the movement has arisen in part when, once a program has been written, educators have too often discovered that what it taught was not really what their students needed to learn.

Despite these problems, programed learning is here to stay and will make a real contribution to higher education. Few teachers enjoy the role of drill master; yet drill seems necessary if students are to master certain necessary facts, schemata, and responses. Here, at least, is a task programs can perform, freeing the instructor for other functions. More than this is also possible. Computers can individualize instruction as printed programs do not. With computers, the motivational value of unexpectedness can be retained. Frase [50] has even experimented with the effects of varying praise and reproof upon programed learning for students differing in aggression, deference, and other personality characteristics. The Socratic dialogue, which was the rallying cry of teaching machine salesmen, can become reality. We have not yet explored the full potential of programing, for it is, in essence, simply careful, systematic educational planning.

Independent study

One of the advantages of programed materials is that they can be used with relatively little teacher supervision; they force the student to read carefully and actively. Thus the programed learning movement has looked for allies among the proponents of independent study. If one goal of education is to help the student develop the ability to continue learning after his formal education is complete, it seems reasonable that he should have supervised experience in learning independently—experience in which the instructor helps the student learn how to formulate problems, find answers, and evaluate his own progress.

Independent study has a strong kinship with the project method, which became popular a generation ago. The results of research are not particularly encouraging. One of the first "independent study" experiments was that of Seashore.[51] His course consisted primarily of guided individual study with written reports on eight projects, each of which took about a month to complete. Final examination scores, however, were no different for these students than for students taught by the usual lecture-discussion method.[52] In a study in a college botany course, Novak found [53] that students in conventional classes learned more facts than did those taught by the project method. Similarly, Goldstein [54] reports that students taught pharmacology by a project method did not learn more than those taught in a standard laboratory.

Unfortunately, measures of achievement such as those just noted are probably insufficient measures of the purported objectives of project instruction. Presumably the real superiority of the project method should be revealed in measures of motivation and resourcefulness. One morsel of support is Thistlethwaite's [55] finding that National Merit scholars checked requirement of a term paper or laboratory project as one characteristic of their most stimulating course, but most research on independent study has failed to find expected gains in motivation, learning, or even independence.[56]

As yet few studies have attempted to assess the unique learning of each group from classroom lectures and discussion or from additional reading.

The most favorable results on independent study were obtained in the experiments at the University of Colorado by Gruber and Weitman.[57] In a course in freshman English in which the group met only about 90 percent of the regularly scheduled hours and had little formal training in grammar, the self-directed study group was significantly superior to control groups on a test of grammar. In a course in physical optics, groups of students who attended class without the instructor (but were free to consult him) remembered fewer facts and simple applications, yet were superior to students in conventional classes in difficult applications and learning new material. Moreover, the latter difference was maintained in a retest three months later, although the difference in factual knowledge had disappeared.[58] An experimental class in educational psychology which met once a week with the instructor and twice a week in groups of five or six students without the instructor was equal or superior to a conventional three-lectures-a-week class in mastery of content, did more serious reading after the course, and tended to be superior on measures of curiosity. Beach [59] found similar results for self-directed student groups at Whitworth College: as compared with classroom groups, the self-directed groups were superior in quantity and quality of study, amount of required and non-required reading, and publications consulted in writing term papers. These are the kinds of results that are the objectives of independent study.

The experiment reported by McKeachie, Lin, Forrin, and Teevan [60] also involved contact with the instructor, in this case at least biweekly. The results suggest that the "tutorial" students did not learn as much from the textbook as did students taught in conventional lecture and discussion section classes, but did develop stronger motivation both for course work and for continued learning after the course.

Typically, knowledge of specific facts is not the major objective of an independent study program: what we are hoping for is greater integration, increased purposefulness, and more intense motivation for further study. That independent study can achieve these ends is indicated by the Colorado, Whitworth, and Michigan experiments. But the paucity of positive results suggests that we need more research on methods of selecting and training students for independent study, arranging the independent study experience, and measuring outcomes.

LABORATORY METHODS

The activity of the student and the frequent individualization of laboratory instruction should, theoretically, contribute positively to learning. However, information usually cannot be obtained as rapidly by direct experience as from abstractions presented orally or by printing. Films, demonstrations, ready-made drawings, and labeled photomicrographs may also short-cut some of the trial and error of the laboratory.[61] Thus, laboratory teaching would not likely have an advantage over other teaching methods in information gained; rather, the differences should be revealed in retention, in ability to apply learning, or in skill in observation or manipulation of materials. Unfortunately, little research has attempted to tease out these special types of outcome.

In experiments in physics and engineering, Kruglak[62] and White[63] found that students taught by individual or group laboratory methods achieved more than those taught by lecture-demonstration. In contrast, in studies by Balcziak,[64] Dearden,[65] and Trotter,[66] individual laboratory was combined with (1) lecture-demonstration, (2) combined demonstration and laboratory, (3) workbook, and (4) term paper in physical science, general biology, and home economics courses, and no significant differences were found between the methods as measured by tests of information, practical application, scientific attitude, and laboratory performance. Also earlier experiments[67] found no significant loss resulting from reduction of laboratory time or assigning one cadaver to four students rather than to two.

Bainter[68] found that a problem-solving method was superior to traditional laboratory manual methods in teaching students to apply principles of physics in interpreting phenomena. Lahti[69] also found problem solving to be superior to more conventional procedures in developing ability to design experiments. Because many laboratory teachers have been interested in teaching problem-solving methods, this may also be an appropriate place to note Burkhardt's finding [70] that students who are taught the calculus with an emphasis on the understanding of concepts learn concepts better than students taught with conventional emphasis upon solving problems. Although this finding appears to controvert the results of Kruglak, Bainter, and Lahti, actually all of them point to the importance of developing understanding rather than teaching solution of problems by routine steps. Whether or not laboratory is superior to lecture-demonstration in developing understanding and problem-solving skills probably depends upon the amount of emphasis placed on understanding of concepts and on general problem-solving procedures.

Simulation

As remote terminals of computers begin to sprout throughout the campus, I predict that simulation will replace television, independent study, and programed instruction as the glamour method in the 1970's. Simulation does not necessitate the use of a computer, but computers can provide rapid calculations and prompt feedback on the results of decisions. According to theory, the active participation, uncertainty about outcome, and prompt feedback should be motivating and effective for learning.

Presumably simulation can be used in almost any subject matter. For example, in science courses, the variables and equations of a theory can be programed into a computer and students given the task of designing experiments to run on the computer to test their hypotheses about "nature" as represented in the computer.[71] However, simulation is currently most used in teaching political science and business courses, although there are some educational games in courses in education and other fields.

"Games" or simulations are ordinarily intended to develop skills in making decisions, to give students understanding of the principal parameters of a field and of the complexity of interactions, and to develop motivation for learning. Although millions of dollars have been spent in developing simulations, I can find only two college-level studies evaluating their effectiveness.[72] In neither study was simulation more effective than other methods. This should not lead to the conclusion that the method should be abandoned. As we have seen in our evaluation of other teaching methods, the gap between theory and research findings has narrowed only as one was able to view the results of a number of studies. The studies to date should dampen the uncritical enthusiasm that often accompanies innovations, but the findings contain enough glimmerings of pay dirt to justify further research.

AUDIO-VISUAL DEVICES

Most higher education is verbal and conceptual. Words are wonderfully efficient substitutes for direct sensory experiences, but on occasion visual identification, discrimination, or eye-hand responses are important goals of education. In such cases, audio-visual aids may substitute for direct experience.

Television

The most widely publicized solution to teaching greater numbers of college students has been the use of closed-circuit television to bring a single teacher to several classrooms. Although some experiments were not sufficiently well designed to permit evaluation, there are probably more good comparisons of television and live instruction than of any other teaching methods. The results are also much more consistent than are any other comparisons. Of the 33 experiments at the college level in which controls were reasonably adequate, 27 produced greater learning in the "live" classes than in those taught by television.[73] Most of these differences were not statistically significant by themselves but their consistency is statistically significant. One can thus conclude that television is generally not as effective as face-to-face instruction.

The conclusion, however, isn't this simple. In the first place, goals of instruction are important. While television instruction seems to be inferior, on the basis of results on the types of measures used, there is still a hidden criterion problem that troubles most research on teaching. Television should be at its best in teaching visual recognition and form discrimination. The tests of achievement, however, are almost entirely verbal. Therefore, the results do not disclose whether television students are better able to recognize or evaluate some visual properties because these outcomes have not been measured. Where there are courses in which visual skills are important objectives, television might be expected to be superior to conventional instruction.

A second condition upon the simplicity of the conclusion that television is inefficient is the instructor. There is some evidence in both Army and college studies that certain instructors blossom before the TV cameras and actually are more effective than in their ordinary classes. Others, however, freeze when the camera red light goes on.

A third variable is the student, and a fourth is the instructional methods used. Complex interactions of these variables occur.[74]

Films

Like the advocates of television and teaching machines, educational film experts have been frustrated by lack of acceptance by college faculties. The only difference is that for the audio-visual aid protagonists the frustration has now subsided into a dull pain; after some forty years of experience they no longer cherish a vision of leading a revolution that will topple existing teaching methods. Films have found a modicum of acceptance; good films are available in most fields, and most professors are willing to accept their educational value (when used sparingly; the professor who uses many films still is assumed to be shirking his work).

Most of the research on educational films has been carried out by the Armed Forces or in elementary schools. Although it is not appropriate to review this research in detail, certain emerging principles seem relevant to our purposes: [75]

1. Students can learn from films, and usually do learn at least as much as from a poor teacher.[76]

2. Such learning is not confined to details, but may include concepts and attitudes.[77]

3. Outline material such as titles and commentary increase learning if a film is not well organized.[78]

4. For less intelligent students, repeating the film increases learning.[79]

5. Students learn how to learn from films; that is, students with previous experience with instructional films learn more than students without previous experience, especially students with little previous knowledge of the film subject matter.[80]

6. Presenting pictures is more effective than presenting words as stimuli in rote association tasks such as learning a foreign language.[81]

7. Participation increases learning.[82] In this study, active response with prompting and feedback was most effective on the most difficult material with the least motivated, least able students—a finding which probably has wide generality in teaching.[83] However, Ash and Carlton [84] found that note taking during a film was not effective. Snow, Tiffin, and Seibert [85] found that active, assertive students and students low in responsibility learn less well from films than live demonstration. It may be that such students especially need participation devices.

Language laboratories and tape recorders

Tape recorders are now convenient and relatively inexpensive tools available for teaching. Their original and most common use has been in language laboratories. Developed in the Army intensive language training programs of World War II, language laboratories multiplied rapidly in the postwar years and boomed under the financial impetus of the National Defense Education Act of 1958. The core of the language laboratory is the tape recorder, and, as Carroll [86] has noted, "This device can present foreign language sounds and utterances with accuracy, fidelity, and endless patience and do so with great flexibility and ease of handling."

With its emphasis upon prepared recorded sequence of stimuli with frequent opportunities for student responses, the language laboratory has close kinship to the programed learning movement. Language laboratories are now an accepted part of the college scene, and I was amazed to find no experimental tests of their value in college as I prepared this paper. One study of a senior high school class found that students who had the benefit of a language laboratory did less well in reading, vocabulary, and grammar than those without the laboratory experience.[87] On the other hand, the use of undergraduate student assistants to conduct laboratory sessions including films, acetate visuals, and language has been successful in saving instructor time with no loss and some possible gain in achievement at Antioch College.[88]

Other imaginative uses of tape recorders are in presenting oral questions in programed teaching,[89] in dictating comments about student papers,[90] in lecture-poster or slide presentation,[91] in an automated taped lecture programed question—filmstrip presentation,[92] and in recording lectures prepared by students as a technique for developing student motivation and active integration of material.[93]

Telephones

Cutler, McKeachie, and McNeil [94] and Davis [95] have shown that instruction can be effectively carried out over telephone circuits. The most imaginative use of the telephone has been to enable students to listen to and question a distinguished guest. The use of the telephone hour for students to interview the guest rather than to listen to him lecture maintains a high level of student interest and provides needed feedback to the guest.[96] In Hilgard's terms,[97] this is an example of successful invention in which the actual practice of education is probably ahead of theory, for theory alone would probably not have suggested this technique or predicted the high level of interest generated.

CONCLUSIONS

Where do we stand today with respect to teaching methods? Clearly, no one method is best for all goals, students, or teachers. Rather, what is the best method is a function of each of these variables.

When one looks at current learning theory, the gap between it and current educational practice appears tremendous. But this is neither the fault of the learning theorist nor the educator.[98] Educators *are* applying learning theory; the empirical wisdom of good teachers is generally consistent with learning theory so far as comparisons can be made, but learning theory cannot dictate educational practice because no learning theory deals with the complex interactions of the many variables affecting classroom learning. The very constraints necessary for laboratory experimentation limit the applicability of the research to the classroom. The programed learning movement failed to reach its goals as rapidly as had been hoped because the jump from laboratory to school gave rise to motivational and social-psychological variables that were controlled in laboratory studies. Notwithstanding, the research on programed learning is proving highly productive for education. No other stream of educational research has produced so many findings on issues both of theoretical and practical importance to education. As we have seen, theory is also beginning to have an impact on the direction of research on traditional problems of college teaching. The generalization that psychological theory has dictates for teaching that can be applied immediately with great profit seems to me about as true as that theoretical chemistry has rules useful to a good cook; nevertheless psychological theory can provide concepts that help college teachers analyze and interpret their experience.

Moreover, we do know more from theory and research on classroom teaching than we are usually given credit for.[99] We have seen fairly convincing evidence that differing teaching methods do make a difference in learning if one analyzes the different goals of education. Other things being equal, small classes are probably more effective than large, discussions than lectures, and student-centered discussions more effective than instructor-centered discussions for goals of retention, application, problem solving, attitude change, and motivation for further learning. Factual learning and these other kinds of learning are not positively correlated across teaching methods; thus the teacher must make value decisions about what he wants to aim for as well as strategic decisions about his means to these goals.

One implication of this finding is that one should expect to find a variety of teaching methods used in a college and that teachers should develop a repertoire of skills. With increasing knowledge about their particular strengths, we should be better able to match means and ends.

Further, more and more evidence shows that different teaching methods work well for different types of students. A direct implication is that a variety of methods be used in a college and in a course. One would hope that each student will be "turned on" somehow, somewhere during the course even though aspects of it remain relatively unprofitable for him. As I suggested in my discussion of class size, large classes constrain a teacher's ability to use the most effective methods. Another constraint is facilities. The nature of the classroom, the unavailability of audio-visual services, or the inadequacy of the library resources limits the instructor's flexibility.

With freedom to adapt teaching to achieve goals with the infinite variety of students, teaching becomes an art—an art that builds upon knowledge and skill. The very complexity of the teaching process is the source of its challenge to creative minds. Research can help to lay bare the deepest properties of our teaching while revealing to us more wonderful intricacies. As we gain in our understanding, our teaching will be illumined with new insight, delight, and mastery.

REFERENCES

[1] G. Highet, *The Art of Teaching* (New York: Alfred A. Knopf, 1950).

[2] My conception of college teaching is largely derived from the ideas of Roger Heyns.

[3] This point was stimulated by N. L. Gage's "Psychological Conceptions of Teaching," Paper presented Feb. 14, 1966, at New York University.

[4] For example, J. D. Krumboltz and W. W. Yabroff, "The Comparative Effects of Inductive and Deductive Sequences in Programed Instruction," *American Education Research Journal*, 1965, 2, 223–35, found that inductive and deductive methods were not differentially effective.

[5] J. B. Edmondson and F. J. Mulder, "Size of Class as a Factor in University Instruction," *Journal of Educational Research*, 1924, 9, 1–12.

[6] E. Hudelson, *Class Size at the College Level* (Minneapolis: University of Minnesota Press, 1928).

[7] F. S. Cheydleur, "Criteria of Effective Teaching in Basic French Courses," *Bulletin of the University of Wisconsin*, August 1945.

[8] A. D. Mueller, "Class Size as a Factor in Normal School Instruction," *Education*, 1924, 45, 203–27.

[9] M. Nachman and S. Opochinsky, "The Effects of Different Teaching Methods: A Methodological Study," *Journal of Educational Psychology*, 1958, 49, 245–49.

[10] F. G. Macomber and L. Siegel, "A Study of Large Group Teaching Procedures," *Educational Research*, 1957, 38, 220–29; *Experimental Study in Instructional Procedures*, Progress Report No. 2 (Oxford, Ohio: Miami University, 1957); *Final Report of the Experimental Study in Instructional Procedures* (Oxford, Ohio: Miami University, 1960).

[11] L. Siegel, J. F. Adams, and F. G. Macomber, "Retention of Subject Matter as a Function of Large Group Instructional Procedures," *Journal of Educational Psychology*, 1960, 51, 9–13.

[12] J. F. Feldhusen, "The Effects of Small and Large Group Instruction on Learning of Subject Matter, Attitudes, and Interests," *Journal of Psychology*, 1963, 55, 257–62.

[13] E. J. Thomas and C. F. Fink, "The Effects of Group Size," *Psychological Bulletin*, 1963, 60, 371–85.

[14] F. F. Stephan and E. G. Mishler, "The Distribution of Participation in Small Groups: An Experimental Approximation," *American Sociological Review*, 1952, 17, 598–608.

[15] W. J. McKeachie, Yi-Guang Lin, John Milholland, and Robert Isaacson, "Student Affiliation Motives, Teacher Warmth, and Academic Achievement," *Journal of Personality and Social Psychology*, In press.

[16] C. L. Bane, "The Lecture vs. the Class-Discussion Method of Teaching," *School and Society*, 1925, 21, 300–302.

[17] R. B. Spence, "Lecture and Class Discussion in Teaching Educational Psychology," *Journal of Educational Psychology*, 1928, *19*, 454–62; H. H. Remmers, "Learning, Effort, and Attitudes as Affected by Three Methods of Instruction in Elementary Psychology," *Purdue University Studies in Higher Education*, 1933, 21; R. W. Husband, "A Statistical Comparison of the Efficacy of Large vs. Smaller Recitation Sections upon Achievement in General Psychology," *Journal of Psychology*, 1951, *31*, 297–300; A. Eglash, "A Group Discussion Method of Teaching Psychology," *Journal of Educational Psychology*, 1954, *45*, 257–67; D. A. Leton, "An Evaluation of Course Methods in Teaching Child Development," *Journal of Educational Research*, 1961, *55*, 118–22.

[18] H. Ruja, "Outcomes of Lecture and Discussion Procedures in Three College Courses," *Journal of Experimental Education*, 1954, 22, 385–94.

[19] C. S. Hirschman, "An Investigation of the Small Group Discussion Classroom Method on Criteria of Understanding, Pleasantness, and Self-confidence Induced" (Master's thesis, University of Pittsburgh, 1952).

[20] J. D. Barnard, "The Lecture-Demonstration versus the Problem-solving Method of Teaching a College Science Course," *Science Education*, 1942, 26, 121–32.

[21] M. D. Dawson, "Lectures versus Problem-solving in Teaching Elementary Soil Sections," *Science Education*, 1956, 40, 395–404.

[22] Elliott, reported in D. Beardslee and R. Birney, "Summary of Conference on Research in Classroom Processes" (Unpublished MS, Department of Psychology, University of Michigan, 1951).

[23] J. E. Casey and B. E. Weaver, "An Evaluation of Lecture Method and Small Group Method of Teaching in Terms of Knowledge of Content, Teacher Attitude, and Social Status," *Journal of Colorado-Wyoming Academy of Science*, 1956, (4), 54.

[24] But reading's advantage of speed may be challenged by "speeded speech"—time compression of tape-recorded lectures. H. L. Friedman and D. B. Orr, "Comprehension of Speeded Speech as a Function of Practice," Paper presented at American Psychological Association meeting, Sept. 3, 1965.

[25] N. Lifson, P. Rempel, and J. A. Johnson, "A Comparison Between Lecture and Conference Methods of Teaching Psychology," *Journal of Medical Education*, 1956, 31, 376–82; M. J. Eash and C. M. Bennett, "The Effect of Class Size on Achievement and Attitudes," *American Educational Research Journal*, 1964, 1, 229–39; H. II. Remmers, "Learning, Effort, and Attitudes as Affected by Three Methods of Instruction in Elementary Psychology," *Purdue University Studies in Higher Education*, 1933, 21.

[26] O. E. Lancaster, K. V. Manning, M. W. White, and other members of the Physics Department, Pennsylvania State University, "The Relative Merits of Lecture and Recitation in Teaching College Physics," *Journal of Engineering Education*, 1961, 51, 425–53; R. Warren, "A Comparison of Two Plans of Study in Engineering Physics" (Doctoral dissertation, Purdue University, 1954 [*Dissertation Abstracts*, 1954, 14, 1648–49]).

[27] B. S. Bloom, "Thought Processes in Lectures and Discussions," *Journal of General Education*, 1953, 7, 160–69.

[28] G. M. Della-Piana, "Two Experimental Feedback Procedures: A Comparison of Their Effects on the Learning of Concepts" (Doctoral disserta-

tion, University of Illinois, 1956 [*Dissertation Abstracts*, 1956, *16*, 910–11]).

[29] D. E. Berlyne, *Conflict, Arousal, and Curiosity* (New York: McGraw-Hill Book Co., 1960).

[30] D. L. Thistlethwaite, "College Press and Changes in Study Plans of Talented Students" (Evanston, Ill.: National Merit Scholarship Corp., 1960).

[31] Having everything wrapped up neatly by the instructor may reduce motivation for further thought and work. See R. C. Craig, "Discovery, Task Completion, and the Assignment as Factors in Motivation," *American Educational Research Journal*, 1965, *2*, 217–22.

[32] K. Lewin, "Group Decision and Social Change," *Readings in Social Psychology*, ed. G. E. Swanson, T. M. Newcomb, and E. L. Hartley (2d ed.; New York: Henry Holt & Co., 1952), pp. 330–44.

[33] W. J. McKeachie, *Teaching Tips: A Guide-Book for the Beginning College Teacher* (Ann Arbor, Mich.: George Wahr Publishing Co., 1965).

[34] H. Guetzkow, E. L. Kelly, and W. J. McKeachie, "An Experimental Comparison of Recitation, Discussion, and Tutorial Methods in College Teaching," *Journal of Educational Psychology*, 1954, *45*, 193–209.

[35] D. L. Thistlethwaite, "College Press and Changes in Study Plans of Talented Students" (Evanston, Ill.: National Merit Scholarship Corp., 1960).

[36] E. B. Greene, "Relative Effectiveness of Lecture and Individual Reading as Methods of College Teaching," *Genetic Psychology Monographs*, 1928, *4*, 457–563.

[37] For a review of these studies, see F. R. Hartman, "Single and Multiple Channel Communication: A Review of Research and a Proposed Model," *Audio-Visual Communication Review*, 1961, 9, 235–62.

[38] G. W. Angell, "Effect of Immediate Knowledge of Quiz Results on Final Examination Scores in Freshman Chemistry," *Journal of Educational Research*, 1949, *42*, 391–94.

[39] H. J. and J. C. Peterson, "The Value of Guidance in Reading for Information," *Transactions of the Kansas Academy of Science*, 1931, *34*, 291–96.

[40] A. L. Stephens, "Certain Special Factors Involved in the Law of Effect," *Abstracts of Doctoral Dissertations*, No. 64 (Columbus: Ohio State University, 1953).

[41] N. H. Smith, "The Teaching of Elementary Statistics by the Conventional Classroom Method versus the Method of Programmed Instruction," *Journal of Educational Research*, 1962, *55*, 417–20.

[42] For example, see Joanna P. Williams, "Comparison of Several Response Modes in a Review Program," *Journal of Educational Psychology*, 1963, *54*, 253–60.

[43] For example, J. J. Wulff and D. L. Emeson, "The Relationship between 'What Is Learned' and 'How It Is Taught,'" *Student Response in Programmed Learning: A Symposium*, ed. A. A. Lumsdaine (Washington: National Academy of Sciences—National Research Council, 1961); chap. 30 reported that in learning the names of electrical circuits, students did better by studying alone than in learning from a structured program. Also see C. G. Zuckerman, G. R. Marshall, and S. Groesberg, *Research in the Automation of Teaching*, NAVTRADEVCEN 666–1 (Port Washington,

N.Y.: U.S. Naval Training Device Center, February 1961); J. F. Follettie, "Effects of Training Response Mode, Test Form, and Measure on Acquisition of Semi-ordered Factual Materials," Research Memorandum 24 (Mimeographed; Fort Benning, Ga.: U.S. Army Infantry Human Research Unit, April 1961); M. E. Feldman, "Learning by Programmed and Text Format at 3 Levels of Difficulty," *Journal of Educational Psychology*, 1965, 56, 133–39.

W. H. Bartz and C. L. Darby, "A Study of Supervised and Nonsupervised Programmed Instruction in the University Setting," *Journal of Educational Research*, 1965, 58, 208–11, found that *supervised* programed instruction was not inferior to formal instruction even though unsupervised programed instruction was inferior.

[44] A. A. Lumsdaine and M. A. May, "Mass Communication and Educational Media," *Annual Review of Psychology*, 1965, 16, 475–534.

[45] J. W. Moore, W. I. Smith, and R. Teevan, "Motivational Variables in Programmed Learning: The Role of Need Achievement, Fear of Failure, and Student Estimate of Achievement as a Function of Program Difficulty," Final Report: USOE, Title VII, Grant No. 7-48-0070-149.1.

[46] Shirley Lublin, "Reinforcement Schedules, Scholastic Aptitude, Autonomy Need, and Achievement in a Programmed Course," *Journal of Educational Psychology*, 1965, 56, 295–302.

[47] Barbara and L. A. Doty, "Programmed Instructional Effectiveness in Relation to Certain Student Characteristics," *Journal of Educational Psychology*, 1964, 55, 334–38.

[48] An excellent review of this literature appears in A. A. Lumsdaine and M. A. May, "Mass Communication and Educational Media," *Annual Review of Psychology*, 1965, 16, 475–534, and in more length in A. A. Lumsdaine, "Instruments and Media of Instruction," *Handbook of Research on Teaching*, ed. N. L. Gage (Chicago: Rand McNally & Co., 1963), pp. 583–682.

[49] For example, see J. D. Krumboltz, "The Nature and Importance of the Required Response in Programmed Instruction," *American Educational Research Journal*, 1964, 1, 203–9.

[50] L. T. Frase, "The Effect of Social Reinforcers in a Programed Learning Task," Nonr. 1834 (36), Technical Reports, No. 11 (Urbana, Ill.: Training Research Laboratory, University of Illinois, 1963).

[51] C. E. Seashore, "Elementary Psychology: An Outline of a Course by the Project Method," *Aims and Progress Research*, No. 153 (Iowa City: University of Iowa, 1928).

[52] Norma V. Scheidemann, "An Experiment in Teaching Psychology," *Journal of Applied Psychology*, 1929, 13, 188–91.

[53] J. D. Novak, "An Experimental Comparison of a Conventional and a Project Centered Method of Teaching a College General Botany Course," *Journal of Experimental Education*, 1958, 26, 217–30.

[54] A. Goldstein, "A Controlled Comparison of the Project Method with Standard Laboratory Teaching in Pharmacology," *Journal of Medical Education*, 1956, 31, 365–75.

[55] D. L. Thistlethwaite, "College Press and Changes in Study Plans of Talented Students" (Evanston, Ill.: National Merit Scholarship Corp., 1960).

[56] See W. J. McKeachie, "Research on Teaching at the College and University Level," *Handbook of Research on Teaching*, ed. N. L. Gage (Chi-

cago: Rand McNally & Co., 1963), pp. 1118–72. Also see R. E. Ulrich and S. I. Pray, "Comparison of Directed Self-study versus Lecture in Teaching General Psychology," *Psychology Reports*, 1965, *16*, 278, and P. W. Caro, "The Effect of Class Attendance and 'Time Structured' Content on Achievement in General Psychology," *Journal of Educational Psychology*, 1962, *53*, 76–80.

[57] H. E. Gruber and M. Weitman, "Cognitive Processes in Higher Education: Curiosity and Critical Thinking," Paper read at Western Psychological Association, San Jose, Calif., April 1960.

[58] M. Weitman and H. E. Gruber, "Experiments in Self-directed Study: Effects on Immediate Achievement, Permanence of Achievement and Educational Values," Paper read at Western Psychological Association, San Jose, Calif., April 1960.

[59] L. R. Beach, "Self-directed Groups and Student Learning," *Approach to Independent Study*, compiled by W. R. Hatch and Alice Richards, New Dimensions in Higher Education, No. 13, OE-50041 (Washington: Government Printing Office, 1965). Also see L. R. Beach, "Sociability and Achievement in Various Types of Learning Situations," *Journal of Educational Psychology*, 1960, *51*, 208–12.

[60] W. J. McKeachie, Yi-Guang Lin, B. Forrin, and R. Teevan, "Individualized Teaching in Elementary Psychology," *Journal of Educational Psychology*, 1960, *51*, 285–91.

[61] For example, see W. T. Stickley, "The Evaluation of a Film Program Technique for Self-instruction in Medical Pharmacology," *Dissertation Abstracts*, 1966, *26*, 4462; L. E. Taylor, "Ready Made Drawings with Relation to Student Achievement," *School and Society*, 1930, *32*, 371–74; and J. D. Novak, "The Use of Labeled Photomicrographs in Teaching College General Botany," *Science Education*, 1961, *45*, 119–31.

[62] H. Kruglak, "Experimental Outcomes of Laboratory Instructions in Elementary College Physics," *American Journal of Physics*, 1952, *20*, 136–41.

[63] J. R. White, "Methods in Engineering Laboratory Instruction," *Journal of Engineering Education*, 1945, *36*, 50–54.

[64] L. W. Balcziak, "The Role of the Laboratory and Demonstration in College Physical Science in Achieving the Objectives of General Education" (Doctoral dissertation, University of Minnesota, 1953 [*Dissertation Abstracts*, 1955, *15*, 2485–86]).

[65] D. M. Dearden, "An Evaluation of the Laboratory in a College General Biology Course," *Journal of Experimental Education*, 1960, *28*, 241–47.

[66] Virginia Trotter, "A Comparison of the Laboratory and the Lecture Demonstration Methods of Teaching Survey of Food Preparation for Freshman Home Economics Students at the University of Vermont," Abstract of research done for the doctoral dissertation at Ohio State University, 1960.

[67] R. E. Downing, "Methods in Science Teaching," *Journal of Higher Education*, 1931, *2*, 316–20; A. W. Hurd, *Problems of Science Teaching at the College Level* (Minneapolis: University of Minnesota Press, 1929); also, C. M. Jackson, "Experiment in Methods of Teaching Gross Human Anatomy," *Problems of College Education* by E. Hudelson (Minneapolis: University of Minnesota Press, 1929), pp. 444–49; V. H. Noll, *Laboratory Instruction in the Field of Inorganic Chemistry* (Minneapolis: University of Minnesota Press, 1930); V. H. Noll, "The Optimum Laboratory Emphasis in College Chemistry," *School and Society*, 1930, *32*, 300–303.

[68] Monica Bainter, "A Study of the Outcomes of Two Types of Laboratory Techniques Used in a Course in General College Physics for Students Planning To Be Teachers in the Elementary Grades" (Doctoral dissertation, University of Minnesota, 1953 [*Dissertation Abstracts*, 1954, *14*, 502–3]).

[69] A. M. Lahti, "The Inductive-deductive Method and the Physical Science Laboratory," *Journal of Experimental Education*, 1956, *24*, 149–63.

[70] Sara Burkhardt, "A Study in Concept Learning in Differential Calculus" (Doctoral dissertation, Columbia University, 1956).

[71] This technique was developed by the late Paul Fitts who used it in teaching his course Principles of Research Design in the Department of Psychology, University of Michigan.

[72] In the study by G. L. Hershey, L. V. Shepard, and J. D. Krumboltz, "Effectiveness of Classroom Observation and Simulated Teaching in an Introductory Educational Psychology Course," *Journal of Educational Research*, 1965, *58*, 233–36, participation in simulated teaching experiences was not significantly different in effect on knowledge, attitudes, and career plans from actual classroom observation (presumably a plus for simulation). In J. A. Robinson, R. C. Snyder, L. F. Anderson, and Margaret Hermann, "A Comparison of Simulation, Case Studies, and Problem Papers in Teaching Decision-making," Cooperative Research Project No. 1568 (Evanston, Ill.: Northwestern University, 1964), simulation was compared with case studies in a sophisticated study. Women high in need for power in the simulation groups developed more interest in the subject and read more than similar women in case study, and simulation tended to develop more interest generally according to three criteria; learning of facts or principles was not significantly different.

[73] For a detailed review, see W. J. McKeachie, "Research on Teaching at the College and University Level," *Handbook of Research on Teaching*, ed. N. L. Gage (Chicago: Rand McNally & Co., 1963), pp. 1118–72. See also W. Schramm, "What We Know about Learning from Instructional Television," *Educational Television: The Next Ten Years* (Stanford, Calif.: Institute for Communication Research, 1962); Schramm reports 13 significant differences favoring live teaching versus three favoring television.

[74] L. and Lila Siegel, "The Instructional Gestalt: A Conceptual Framework and Design for Educational Research," *Audio-Visual Communication Review*, 1964, *12*, 16–45.

[75] For a more complete analysis, see N. M. Miller, "Scientific Principles of Maximum Learning from Motion Pictures," *Audio-Visual Communication Review, Graphic Communication*, 1957, *5*, 61–113. Air Force research is summarized and integrated with concepts from programed learning in A. A. Lumsdaine (ed.), *Student Response in Programmed Instruction: A Symposium* (Washington: National Academy of Sciences—National Research Council, 1961).

[76] A. W. VanderMeer, *Relative Effectiveness of Instruction by Films Exclusively, Films Plus Study Guides, and Standard Lecture Methods*, Instructional Film Research Report SDC 269-7-12 (Special Devices Center, Office of Naval Research, July 1950).

[77] J. P. Kishler, "The Effects of Prestige and Identification Factors on Attitude Restructuring and Learning from Sound Films," Technical Report SDC 269-7-10 (Port Washington, N.Y.: U.S. Naval Training Device Center, Office of Naval Research, 1950); Marjorie S. Mertens, *The Effects of*

Mental Hygiene Films on Self Regarding Attitudes, Pennsylvania State University Instructional Film Research Program, Technical Report No. SDC 269-7-22 (Port Washington, N.Y.: U.S. Naval Training Device Center, Office of Naval Research, July 1951); C. F. Hoban, Jr., and E. B. Van Ormer, *Instructional Film Research, 1918–1950*, Pennsylvania State University Instructional Film Research Program, Technical Report No. SDC 269-7-19 (Port Washington, N.Y.: U.S. Naval Training Device Center, Office of Naval Research, 1950).

[78] D. S. Northrop, *Effects on Learning of the Prominence of Organizational Outlines in Instructional Films*, Pennsylvania State University Instructional Film Research Program, Human Engineering Report SDC 269-7-33 (Port Washington, N.Y.: U.S. Naval Training Device Center, Office of Naval Research, October 1952).

[79] C. L. McTavish, *Effect of Repetitive Film Showings on Learning*, Pennsylvania State University Instructional Film Research Program, Technical Report No. SDC 269-7-12 (Port Washington, N.Y.: U.S. Naval Training Device Center, Office of Naval Research, November 1949).

[80] A. W. VanderMeer, *Effect of Film-viewing Practice on Learning from Instructional Films*, Pennsylvania State University Instructional Film Research Program, Technical Report No. SDC 269-7-20 (Port Washington, N.Y.: U.S. Naval Training Device Center, Office of Naval Research, November 1951).

[81] F. F. Kopstein and S. M. Roshal, "Learning Foreign Vocabulary from Pictures vs. Words," *American Psychologist*, 1954, 9, 407–8.

[82] C. I. Hovland, A. A. Lumsdaine, and F. D. Sheffield, *Experiments in Mass Communication* (Princeton, N.J.: Princeton University Press, 1949).

[83] D. N. Michael and N. Maccoby, "Factors Influencing the Effects of Student Participation on Verbal Learning from Films under Varying Conditions of Audience Participation," *Journal of Experimental Psychology*, 1953, *46*, 411–18; D. N. Michael and N. Maccoby, "Factors Influencing the Effects of Student Participation on Verbal Learning from Films: Motivating versus Practice Effects, Feedback, and Overt versus Covert Responding," *Student Response in Programmed Instruction: A Symposium*, ed. A. A. Lumsdaine (Washington: National Academy of Sciences—National Research Council, 1961).

[84] P. Ash and B. J. Carlton, *The Value of Note-taking during Film Learning*, Pennsylvania State University Instructional Film Research Program, Technical Report No. SDC 269-7-21, November 1951).

[85] R. E. Snow, J. Tiffin, and W. F. Seibert, "Individual Differences and Instructional Film Effects," *Journal of Educational Psychology*, 1965, *56*, 315–26.

[86] J. B. Carroll, "Research on Teaching Foreign Languages," *Handbook on Research on Teaching*, ed. N. L. Gage (Chicago: Rand McNally & Co., 1963), pp. 1060–101.

[87] J. B. Carroll *et al. Annual Report, Committee on Foreign Languages, School and University Program for Research and Development* (Cambridge, Mass.: Graduate School of Education, Harvard University, 1960).

[88] "Experiment in French Language Instruction," Antioch College Reports (Yellow Springs, Ohio: Office of Educational Research, Antioch College, 1960).

The use of undergraduates to teach small groups proved spectacularly successful at Pennsylvania State University. Results were among the most consistently favorable of any experiment I have reviewed. See C. R. Carpenter, "The Penn State Pyramid Plan: Interdependent Student Work Study Groupings for Increasing Motivation for Academic Development," Paper read at the Fourteenth National Conference on Higher Education, Chicago, March 1959. Also, R. H. Davage, "The Pyramid Plan for the Systematic Involvement of University Students in Teaching-Learning Functions" (University Park: Division of Academic Research and Services, Pennsylvania State University, 1958), and R. H. Davage, "Recent Data on the Pyramid Project in Psychology" (University Park: Division of Academic Research and Services, Pennsylvania State University, 1959).

[89] H. C. Mahan, "Adjunct Programming of the Basic Psychology Course for Oral Presentation via Tape Recorder" (Abstract of paper presented at the Western Psychological Association, spring meeting, 1966).

[90] Reported by John Moore at faculty fall conference, Kalamazoo College, September 1965.

[91] R. E. Johnston, "Magnetic Recordings and Visual Displays as Aids in Teaching Introductory Psychology to College Students," *Audio-Visual Communication Review*, 1961, 9, 1–46; students in this experiment who were taught by the taped lectures achieved less than those taught conventionally. Also see W. J. Popham, "Tape Recorded Lectures in the College Classroom," *Audio-Visual Communication Review*, 1961, 9, A28–A29. The same technique has also been used at the Technical University of Berlin.

[92] K. U. Smith, "Audiovisumatic Teaching: A New Dimension in Education and Research," *The Behavior of Man*, by K. U. and W. M. Smith (New York: Henry Holt & Co., 1958).

[93] N. J. Webb, "Student Preparation and Tape Recording of Course Lectures as a Method of Instruction," *Psychological Reports*, 1965, 16, 67–72.

[94] R. L. Cutler, W. J. McKeachie, and E. B. McNeil, "Teaching Psychology by Telephone," *American Psychologist*, 1958, 13, 551–52.

[95] K. E. Davis, "Do Students Learn from a Telephone Lecture?" Paper presented at the American Psychological Association meetings, September 1963.

[96] There are hints of these reactions in both the Davis paper and the Stephens College experience: J. A. Burkhart, "An Experiment To Determine the Values of Using Amplified Classroom Telephone Interviews with Significant Individuals to Enrich Certain College Courses," Final Report, Registry Form Title vii, File 250, Sponsored under the Provisions of the National Defense Education Act of 1958 (P.L. 85-864).

[97] E. R. Hilgard, "Learning Theory and Its Applications," *New Teaching Aids for the American Classroom* (Stanford, Calif.: Institute for Communication Research, Stanford University, 1960).

[98] See E. R. Hilgard, Chairman, Yearbook Committee, *Theories of Learning*, 63rd Yearbook, National Society for the Study of Education (Chicago: University of Chicago Press, 1964), Pt. I, p. 404; A. Melton, "The Science of Learning and the Technology of Educational Methods," *Harvard Educational Review*, 1959, 29, 96–106; and A. A. Lumsdaine (ed.), *Student Response in Programmed Instruction: A Symposium* (Washington: National Academy of Sciences—National Research Council, 1961).

[90] And we have some promising analytic frameworks. For example, see L. and Lila Siegel, "The Instructional Gestalt: A Conceptual Framework and Design for Educational Research," *Audio-Visual Communication Review*, 1964, *12*, 16–45.

Commentaries on
Research in Teaching

ARTHUR A. LUMSDAINE,
N. L. GAGE, DONALD D. O'DOWD

Improving the Quality and Relevance of Research on Teaching

ARTHUR A. LUMSDAINE

IT IS QUITE EVIDENT that the amount of research on college teaching needs to be greatly increased even beyond the current unprecedentedly high level, achieved in part by strong support from Federal agencies. My comments, however, will be concerned with the qualitative requirements for the research. Here I mean the need to upgrade both its relevance and validity. "Relevance" refers to the extent to which the research deals incisively with important variables in such a way that the results can be translated into practice. "Validity" refers to the credibility or defensibility of the findings as reported in scholarly journals and in summary statements such as those presented by Dr. McKeachie.

When McKeachie says that the complexity of the teaching situation makes every bit of empirical information the more precious, one cannot disagree. But shouldn't the stress be only on the value of valid, relevant pieces of empirical information? Much that parades as research findings is more likely to obscure than illuminate the relationships actually operating in this complex kind of behavior.

My first thesis is that the quality of research—both soundness and relevance—would be improved by developing better dependent measures of the outcomes of teaching in terms of observed changes in students' behavior. Improvement is needed in measures of gains in knowledge and comprehension, as well as in the wide class of important but presumably "less tangible" outcomes such as interest, motivation, appreciation, enthusiasm, and the like. Progress in conducting useful studies of the independent variables that influence these latter outcomes will depend on the extent to which we can achieve behavior indices of the kinds of student activity that give direct evidence of having engendered understanding, appreciation, motivation, interest, and the like.[1]

I applaud most warmly McKeachie's emphasis on the need for more precisely defined goals and, thus, more precisely measurable outcomes, if research is to be useful. Better dependent measures of educational outcomes are a first requirement for improving the relevance of research on teaching. A special difficulty evident in some of the studies cited by McKeachie, is that the factor of cost is given insufficient attention. For example, in finding that a small class is (if it is) more effective than a larger one, the question is not phrased in terms of the realistic alternative, namely, how the money saved by using one large class instead of four small classes might be used to produce more effective results per dollar. This needs more explicit attention in the design of our experiments—in the way we phrase the questions that generate the experiments.

Given acceptable measures of the outcomes in which we are interested—and not just those for knowledge of facts—a second major requirement for useful research is unfulfilled in a number of studies of factors influencing the effectiveness of teaching. This requirement is for a clean design in which the effects of experimentally manipulated variables, and their important interactions, can be unambiguously revealed (distinguished from other sources of influence). Only thus can clear-cut and scientifically respectable statements about the causal relation between independent variables in the act of teaching and dependent variables be defined in the manner suggested above.

Experiments on class size suggest the need for better definition of independent variables. In a sense, class size is a secondary, rather than a primary, variable. Size, which can be readily measured and manipulated, is effective primarily because of other factors correlated with it—possibilities for discussion, differences in teaching style associated with those who teach in large or small classes, and the like. Often the size of the class is scarcely a factor *per se*; rather, it is the associated practices, which tend to be (but are not necessarily always) correlated with class size, that seem to be the effective primary variables. Why not more studies to attack these variables directly rather than through the correlative of class size, which as a variable has, it seems

---

[1] I have elaborated this idea elsewhere: see my chapters in *The Handbook of Research on Teaching*, ed. N. L. Gage (Chicago: Rand McNally & Co., 1963), and in *Teaching Machines and Programed Learning, II: Data and Directions*, ed. R. Glaser (Washington: National Education Association, 1965).

to me, somewhat the same status as time. Time and size are not effective causal agents in themselves, but only provide a context or milieu in which other variables operate. The aim of research on teaching is to obtain a more precise analysis and manipulation of these more fundamental variables.

A third requirement, sometimes overlooked, derives from the truism that there can be no science of the unique. The applicability of research (given the first two requirements) is limited by the extent to which the independent variables can be defined in operational terms so that they specify *reproducible* processes. To say that a particular "method" or "procedure" of instruction is reproducible means that its essential elements can be communicated (taught) to other individuals who are subsequently to employ them. Only then can we say that we can define operationally what it is we have done to produce the effects we have observed; and only then are we in a position to make useful assertions about the predictable effects of employing a particular procedure or of incorporating a particular principle in our teaching.

McKeachie's research summary contains several examples in which the independent variables are grossly defined as "methods"—"participation versus nonparticipation methods," "discovery method," "lecture method versus discussion method," and so on. But these so-called methods are not defined by operational procedures that permit reproducibility. Since there are variations within each method, unless well-defined sampling procedures are enforced (by which an adequately representative sample of implementations of a method might be denoted) no way is available, generally speaking, to establish that the difference revealed, if any, is attributable to the "method" rather than to the manner in which it was employed. A good film will always beat a poor lecture—and vice versa. The so-called lecture method employed in one fashion by one lecturer may be highly effective; in the hands of another it may be quite ineffective. The problem is to conduct investigations so that they can be employed as a basis either for selecting superior lecturers or for defining those elements of a lecture procedure that can be transmitted, with predictable results, to those to whom the procedures are to be taught. The use of such undefined terms as "class discussion method" and other method designations used as independent variables may have done more to obscure the truth (no matter how careful the formal design of the experiment) than any other single flaw in educational research. As a basis for inference, a method is a meaningless independent variable unless it is reproducibly defined according to the operations it actually embodies, or unless it is defined empirically by an adequate sampling of a relevant population of lecturers, discussion conductors, and the like.

A fourth crucial requirement for valid research on variables that govern effective teaching is *better standards of reporting*. We need greatly improved terminology conventions for differentiating findings according to the soundness and directness with which the reported conclusions follow as rigorous deductions from the evidence obtained. Here is largely chaos. I have commented elsewhere on the violation of elementary logical considerations—given the formal impossibility of proving the null hypothesis—of statements implying that the lack of significant differences between two procedures means that they were equally effective.[2] Yet the practice still goes on. The lack of sound rationale for determining the size of a practically consequential difference (sometimes referred to as the distinction between practical and statistical significance) is a related point. We may be tired of hearing about these things, yet we persist in a style of planning experiments and of reporting research that does violence both to the requirements of fruitful research and to the basic logic underlying permissible inferences from sample to population.

What is most needed, I suspect, is a definitive set of standards for research on teaching, formulated somewhat along the lines of those worked out by the Joint Committee on Programmed Instruction for the special case of evaluative data on the effects of self-instructional programs.[3] Such standards, with real sanctions enforced by the professional associations and journal editors, would go far toward clearing up the looseness and ambiguity that now prevails in reporting educational research. Both in summaries of research and in original reports, results of relatively rigorous studies are hopelessly confused with results of studies that have employed nonexperimental or otherwise inferior methods; and methodological requirements for sound inferences about the effects of variables are grossly violated. This is not the place to go into technical details, but I would contend that (possibly aside from the windfall of some genius in the definition and implementation of independent variables) the most critical need for fruitful research calculated to improve the effectiveness of teaching is to clear up the present state of methodological and related reportorial chaos. I believe it is no exaggeration to say that at present it is difficult indeed to know which reported "findings" are to be believed and which are not.

[2] See my chapter in *The Handbook of Research on Teaching*.
[3] *Recommendations for Reporting the Effectiveness of Programed Instruction Materials* (Washington: National Education Association, 1966).

The Need for Process-oriented Research

N. L. GAGE

PROFESSOR MCKEACHIE has reported on a much wider variety of topics than I can respond to in a brief commentary. Hence I shall restrict myself to three matters—class size, the lecture method, and discussion methods, subjects that fit together in an obvious way. To the degree that the lecture method is effective, class size may be increased; to the degree that it is ineffective and educational objectives can be attained better through discussion methods, class size must be kept down. The other matters that McKeachie dealt with—reading, programed instruction, independent study, laboratory methods, simulation, and various audio-visual devices—do not fit together quite so neatly and, in any event, do not bear so closely upon the issue of what the college teacher ought to do; they are instead ways of replacing or supplementing the college teacher.

WHY WE LECTURE

This trio of topics—class size, lecturing, and discussion—not only are at the heart of the college teacher's concern with his job but also have behind them several centuries of disputation. For the major question about the lecture method is an old one. Why should we lecture, when students can read and print is so cheap? Boswell's *Life of Samuel Johnson* reports the latter gentleman as commenting: "Talking of education, people nowadays got a strange opinion that everything should be taught by Lectures. Now, I cannot see that lectures can do so much good as reading the books from which the lectures were taken. I know nothing that can be best taught by lectures except where experiments are to be shown." Recently, a student voiced an up-to-date version of Johnson's criticism in a column titled "Our Absurd Lecture System" and stated that:

. . . the advantages of the written word—its permanence, its usually having been well-thought out, its availability in the sense that it can be read—over the spoken word being clear, it follows that, in an age when mimeograph machines, books, and paper backs are common and inexpensive, the spoken lecture is an archaic and inefficient mode of communication. . . . The clarification of assigned readings is another matter: It is the one defensible activity of the teacher-as-teacher, and it logically requires a dialogue between the teacher and student, and between student and student.[1]

A similar reaction can be found in a professional school: A news story reported that in January 1966 twenty-five Harvard medical students, feeling that their lectures were dull and a waste of time, petitioned

[1] *Stanford Daily*, April 19, 1963.

244

to be excused from lectures and laboratories for the rest of the year. Their dean granted his permission and the students were divided into groups of five to devise their own learning techniques with the help of volunteer faculty advisers. They were to take the same examinations as their eighty-one classmates but attend only the lectures that interested them. The news item ended, however, with a statement from Dean Ebert that "Harvard has no intention of abandoning the lecture system altogether." [2]

So a major question remains: Why should professors lecture? My answer is based largely on what might be called logistical rather than psychological considerations. It is often simply more convenient to lecture. Of course, sometimes a teacher does not consider his ideas, charts, tables, and illustrations to be well enough prepared or sufficiently settled in his thinking to justify the effort and expense of preparing a film or a printed document. But teachers are human and —more generally—given the choice between planning far enough ahead to make printing or filming possible and worthwhile, or letting things go and having to resort to a lecture and the blackboard, they are likely to choose the latter course simply because they are too busy or disorganized to do anything else. Largely, we must look in the realm of logistics rather than pedagogical effectiveness to explain the apparent anomaly that lecturing embarrasses but prevails.

CLASS SIZE

Let us turn now to considerations of class size. The investigations reviewed by McKeachie compared achievement in classes of different size, but we are not told what went on in those classes. Did the activities and processes of teaching and learning actually differ in the large and small classes? If so, in what way? If class size determines teaching method to some extent, what is the nature of the effect? It seems reasonable, as McKeachie surmises, that "probably teaching is confined more to lecturing [in larger classes] than in smaller classes." But there are ways in which teachers of even very large classes, of one hundred or more students, can arrange discussions among students. If so, would the differences between large and small classes disappear? Thus the issue of class size seems to be reduced to one of teaching method; size becomes relevant only insofar as it affects teaching method, which in turn affects outcomes.

One aspect of size is often neglected: the kind of *written*, as against oral, teacher-student interaction that is feasible in classes of differing size. In the tutorial system described by Highet, the student wrote an essay every week and, in a class consisting of one other student, discussed his essay with his tutor for an hour or so while the other student listened. Later in the week, the other student had his turn.[3] This amount of writing on the part of the student can be read by the instructor only when classes are tiny. Essay examinations and term papers can be read carefully by instructors in classes of more than 50 or so by only the most indefatigable instructor; typically, when classes become larger, graduate students take over, and we no longer have whatever benefit comes from having papers criticized by a mature scholar. Similarly, teacher-student conferences quickly become impossible as class size increases. Recourse to objectively scorable multiple-choice examinations, which have limitations as well as advantages, must increase as class size increases.

These matters of convenience and logistics, often disregarded in the research on class size, are probably what make teachers and students prefer smaller classes. Even if differences in measured achievement in large and small classes are not statistically significant, we should not overlook the typically unmeasured effects on teacher and student morale, comfort, access to one another, and ability to interact in writing as well as vocally. In short, research on class size can become more closely related to theory if it takes classroom activities and processes into account and does not confine "results" to the score on an examination of limited significance.

LECTURE VERSUS DISCUSSION

Research on the lecture method should probably be analyzed according to kind of subject matter. The lecture method may be more fruitful than discussion in fields that possess substantial agreement on major concepts, principles, and methods—in mathematics, the natural sciences, and engineering, as against the social sciences and humanities. The latter do not have and, in principle, may never have such high degrees of consensus. In the latter areas, the discussion method may well be found to be superior more often than the lecture method. It might be revealing if the dozens of studies cited by McKeachie could be categorized by subject matter or discipline to determine whether the trend of the results favors the lecture method in the high-consensus fields and the discussion method in the low-consensus fields.

Another distinction that might facilitate organizing the results of the research already completed is that among various kinds of outcome, such as knowledge, comprehension, and problem-solving skills. Lectures may prove better for the first, discussions for the last two.

In any case, the question must always be raised: Exactly what went on in the lectures and in the discussions? The research, as McKeachie

[3] Gilbert Highet, *The Art of Teaching* (New York: Alfred A. Knopf, 1950).

reports it, disregards the details of *process*. Insofar as results now available make any sense, they presumably reflect a wide variety of styles, techniques, skills, and other characteristics of a heterogeneous collection of lecturers and discussion leaders. To compare their final outcomes without looking in detail at what goes on within each method is something like trying to arrive at a generalization about the relative merits of two drugs of unknown but varying composition that are being used for the same or different purposes. Whether one is "better" than the other always depends on its composition and one's purpose in using it. Whether a lecture method is better than a discussion method similarly depends on what goes into the lecture or the discussion—what content and what processes—and on what one is trying to get students to learn—what knowledge, comprehension, skills, and attitudes. Only as we go deeply into the details of how the two methods are used will we begin to arrive at something more sensible than the usual comparisons of mean scores on final multiple-choice examinations.

An example of process-oriented research

This kind of investigation of process can be illustrated by a current research project under my direction at Stanford. Although it is being done at the eleventh-grade level in social studies classes, it could be replicated at the college level in classes of almost any kind.

To summarize briefly, we persuaded forty teachers each to deliver a fifteen-minute lecture on an article on Yugoslavia from the *Atlantic Monthly*. After the lecture, their students took a ten-item multiple-choice test of their comprehension of the lecture. The next day, the same teachers and classes did the same things, except that the subject matter was an article on Thailand from the *Atlantic*. On the third day, all classes heard a fifteen-minute tape-recorded article on Israel, and then took a test on it.

The class mean on the Israel test was used to adjust the class means on Yugoslavia and Thailand for between-class differences in ability. The class means on Yugoslavia and Thailand were also adjusted for teacher differences in the content relevance of the lecture, as determined by an analysis of the transcript of the lecture in relation to the items on the test. The remaining variance between the adjusted comprehension test means of the classes was considered to reflect differences between the teachers in what we were concerned with, namely, the intellectual style and process reflected in the teacher's lecture. Since all of the lectures were recorded on video tape, we were able to study and analyze both the verbal and nonverbal aspects of the lectures.

So far, it appears that two variables, out of about forty that have been tried, discriminate between good and poor lecturers as measured by the adjusted mean comprehension scores of their students. These variables are: (*a*) the degree to which the teacher uses phrases referring to cause, reason, and process, and (*b*) the degree to which the teacher's discourse follows a rule-example-rule pattern, that is, first stating a rule, generalization, or principle, then giving examples of it, and then repeating the rule, generalization, or principle. These two variables have been cross-validated on both the Yugoslavia and Thailand lectures. I offer them not as firmly established findings, however, but rather as examples of the kinds of variables being investigated.

If there is any theory underlying what I am suggesting as a fruitful way to do research on teaching methods, it is the following: We should work with much smaller units of teaching behavior and learning outcome, and with much more detailed analyses of what goes on in those smaller units. Perhaps a fifteen-minute lecture on the same subject matter, consisting of a five-page magazine article, is still too large a unit of teaching behavior to yield valid knowledge. Perhaps the mean score on a ten-item test of comprehension, adjusted for student ability and the content relevance of the lecture, is still too large and complex a dependent variable. But, compared with the massive, tangled, and unanalyzable units that have typically been studied in research on the lecture method, the discussion method, and class size, they are precise and manageable. And the possibility of conveniently recording teacher and student behavior on video tape, without disrupting classes, permits us to search for functional relationships by repeated analysis of the same behaviors rather than having to decide on our variables in advance and then measure or observe them on the run.

The path of progress in research on teaching, as in other fields, may lie in further analysis of smaller units that can be more intensively studied. With such units, we may find it feasible to apply behavior theory, modeling theory, cognitive theory, or any other kind of theory of learning and curriculum that may have promise for shedding light on effective teaching.

Closing the Gap

DONALD D. O'DOWD

DR. MCKEACHIE HAS PRESENTED an admirable summary of the current state of empirical understanding of the art of teaching. Each time I read a summary or commentary on this body of research findings, I am at once stimulated and appalled by the enormous areas that remain to be investigated. The luncheon conversation in a faculty dining room during one noon hour often produces more hypotheses about the teaching process than all of the accumulated research effort has been able to test. I have recently been encouraged to find that some fine, younger research men are being drawn to this area of investigation and promise to open new vistas in the near future.

In my comments, I wish to represent the point of view of the concerned public looking in on the teaching process in higher education and the research related to teaching. As a member of the public, I am disturbed and annoyed at the dilatoriness and timidity of higher education. How can a major social institution care so little about understanding its central function? It is evident that research into teaching is nonexistent in most universities and is only an incidental activity in others. The infinitesimal percentage of the higher educational budget devoted to research into educational results and the improvement of teaching is shameful. Higher education has failed to develop measures of educational outcomes. It has only the crudest means for determining its effectiveness in that facet of the enterprise, that is, in teaching, that requires the main expenditure of its resources. Higher education has permitted a key variable in the teaching process to remain shrouded from the eyes of research: the teacher who, as Dr. McKeachie points out, would not greet with enthusiasm research into his knowledge. Higher education, by its very resistance or inattention to the study of its major activity, has denied itself the very means by which it can improve. The colleges and universities by their traditional inaction deny to the teacher accurate evidence of the effectiveness of his effort—evidence that might motivate additional effort. By the same token, innovation, invention, and imagination in the teaching process are discouraged by the very privacy of the teaching situation. The teacher, ironically, denies himself the very elements of learning that he provides for his student—the knowledge of results.

This failure of higher education to put its house in order has been the cause of an unprecedented outcry in the past two years. I believe that a significant element in the so-called student rebellion is a growing realization that the university holds students to a much higher standard of performance than that to which it holds itself. The world of higher education is being accused by students of unfairness and, perhaps, even dishonesty. The contemporary student has an abhorrence of insincerity, whether it be clothed in the name of tradition or hidden in the caverns of the subconscious. As students become more aware of their rights and conscious of their power, very likely they will demand greater attention to their academic well-being. They are already very skeptical of any reliance on tradition as an excuse for avoiding an examination of the teaching relationship.

There are a number of areas in which the university can begin to act in studying the teaching process if it has the courage. Several decades of research have suggested that in the teaching process the interaction among the relevant variables—teacher, students, method, and so on—is often more significant than the effect of any single factor such as the teaching method. Certain combinations of methods, teachers, and students in specific subject areas represent the optimum learning situation. I believe that the most vital dimension in teaching is the relation between student and teacher. In particular, I suggest that the mental and emotional constitution of each party in the instructional process has a vital effect on teaching of the most subtle skills and attitudes. We must study the importance of the cognitive style, attitude pattern, and motive structure of both teacher and learner in maximizing educational gains. In order to do this, both parties must enter into the investigation and permit themselves to be participants in a study. In my experience, students are entirely willing to cooperate by participating in many forms of assessment, and, in fact, faculty, also, are willing to cooperate if they are asked. Given the opportunities inherent in large, multisection university courses, considerable understanding could be gained quickly by research into the interaction of student and teacher characteristics. I can foresee the time when the sectioning of students can be carried out with the knowledge that certain students can learn most rapidly and in greatest depth in one class with a specially selected teacher. Let us hope that selective sectioning will replace sectioning on the basis of a random number generator in the 7090. Timidity and tradition deter the university from confronting this and related problems. The university should outgrow this reluctance—soon.

The involvement of faculty in a research effort in depth will, I am convinced, serve to improve teaching. As faculty become involved in research about teaching, they grow more conscious of the student as a learner. They begin to make finer discriminations among students, to be more sensitive to student needs and more flexible in their approach to the teaching relationship. My observation has suggested that this effect of research has an impact on the seminar teacher, the lecturer, and even the laboratory instructor. Few people in higher education have had a better opportunity to see this effect than Dr. McKeachie, whose students have been involved continuously in research on the teaching process while teaching classes themselves, and, it has seemed to me, college teachers who have been through the Michigan psychology program are unusually aware of the teaching process. Ultimately, I hope that concrete research results will serve to guide faculty toward a continuous refinement of teaching technique and emphasis.

One aspect of the teaching situation that needs to be made an object of study is the emotional, or subjective, side. Traditionally, the classroom has been the arena for the unfolding of fact and theory. The teacher's commitment is to the rational, analytic, objective, empirical aspect of the world. However, in recent years the academy has been finding room for the artist, actor, musician, and other performers who are deeply committed to feeling and emotion as an integral part of their profession. May it not be that the teaching of the traditional disciplines could become more energetic through the use of teaching styles currently associated with the arts? This may be what we call "the exploration of values" in the traditional disciplines. Most of us can call to mind some of the truly powerful, character-forming teachers who have harnessed the emotional to the rational in their teachings. It may be possible to widen the province of the teaching art by a careful examination of what teaching in the arts can demonstrate to teaching in the academy.

Finally, it is in order to suggest that research in teaching should be a part of the academic endeavor of every college and university. This may require the establishment of an office for institutional research in many schools. This office should *not* be concerned with filling out Office of Education statistical requests, doing cost studies, space-utilization analyses, or Council questionnaires; rather, it should be devoted to pedagogical research, research into the teaching process. Perhaps this agency would more appropriately be called the office of teaching, instructional, or pedagogical research. The charge of this office should be to maintain a continuing series of investigations into the process of teaching, with the goal of seeking the optimum relationship between faculty and students by involving in the research all parties to the teaching process. The investment of one percent of the university instructional budget in studying the process of education might work wonders.

College Teachers
and Teaching:
A Student's View

MICHAEL DROSNIN

Toward the end of our senior year at Columbia, my roommate, reviewing his undergraduate career, noted the number of points at which he had disappointed someone—his parents or his adviser or his professors —in making decisions about his course of study. "You know," he remarked, "my father didn't get enough out of my college education."

My friend was hardly an expert on pedagogy; indeed, like most of us, he had some trouble handling his own four-year program. However, his quietly ironical comment was in many ways more revealing of "the gap between the generations" than is the expert commentary of educators. His father had wanted him to be a doctor; his adviser had suggested law; my roommate chose instead to be an English major, and, as far as I know, is now preparing to study the Southern novel in graduate school.

His case, if not representative, is at least symptomatic of the multiple demands confronting a student during his four years of college. And it raises the basic questions this essay seeks to answer: What are the expectations of the college student, how are these expectations modified by the values of the academic community, and how successful is the modern university in fulfilling them? Fundamental to this problem, of course, is the college professor and his relationship with his students. For to a great degree his success is their success, and his failure their failure.

The question of whether the liberal arts college any longer holds a meaningful place in society is a source of great controversy among educators. Jacques Barzun, provost at Columbia, recently warned that the four-year institution is facing an imminent demise. Its role usurped by the high schools below and by the graduate schools above, the college, declared Barzun, must find a new justification for its continued life.

It is significant that this debate has attracted scant student attention. For it is quite apparent that the average student spends little time during his college years seeking a justification for those years. This is a problem he tends to leave to those who write articles analyzing student concerns. To ask a student why he is going to college would seem to him as meaningless as to inquire why he eats or sleeps. It is a question which, in all probability, he has never seriously pondered, and which, to his mind, need not be answered. That he would go to college is an assumption that he has never challenged, and, most likely, that no one else has ever challenged. The central issue, in his eyes, is not whether he should go to college, but rather to which college he should go.

It is precisely the college freshman's lack of direction which enhances the influence of the university. Because the average student lacks clearly defined goals when he enters his undergraduate career, the professor's opportunity to reshape old ideals and inculcate new ones is increased. Indeed, one Columbia professor asserted to me that it was the college's role to substitute a new set of values for those the student had inherited from his previous environment.

But this, I believe, is a misunderstanding of both the college's responsibility and the student's desires. Ironically, it is a misunderstanding created by the students themselves. Recent campus protests criticizing the impersonality of the modern university have led many concerned faculty members to adopt the mistaken notion that undergraduates are seeking in the professor both a father and a friend. Actually, most students want neither; they are quite happy to have finally escaped parental domination and even parental guidance, and would rather find their friends among their contemporaries. What they want in a professor is, quite simply, a professor. And the problem of impersonality lies less in the formal line between student and teacher—a line most students would like preserved—than in the failure of the professor to perform well behind the lectern.

When today's student decries the lack of communication between teacher and student, he is likely to be attacking the breakdown within, rather than outside, the classroom. The lack of concern he finds disturbing inheres not in the limited nature of extraclassroom contact, but in the limited interest the professor displays in his classroom performance. Unsettling as it may be to instructors, most students would rather confine their relationship with most teachers to the few hours they spend together in class each week. The formal line between the teacher and the taught has the advantage of not obligating the student to spend time favorably impressing his professor beyond the regularly required course work. In the exceptional cases where contact outside the lecture hall is desired, it is likely that the professor will be accessible if only because it is also probable that the course will be one in which the student excels. The important thing is that the relationship be initiated by the student and that he not feel obligated to seek such a relationship with all, or even a significant number, of his teachers. Mr. Chips is no longer the ideal; I doubt if he ever was.

The lesson of Berkeley has been misinterpreted. What the student wants is not equality with his instructors, but the assurance that courses are offered and taught with the consumer in mind. And the freedom the student seeks is not liberation from traditional requirements, but latitude for independent and individual development.

To understand the expectations of the generation of college students of which I was until recently a member, one must recognize that we are a post-Kennedy generation. The transformation of aspirations effected by the late President cannot be overestimated. College students have always, I suspect, been caught between the conflicting pressures for material and for scholarly achievement, the former often parental in origin and the latter emanating from the academic community. With President Kennedy, a new third force was introduced: the obligation to benefit society. It is a force that has been strengthened by the civil rights and peace movements, both of which have placed the student in a new and significant role vis-à-vis the world outside his campus. For the present generation of college students, Kennedy was a vindication of youth, and the social protest movements created a natural conduit for the new sense of purpose he inspired. Today's student is no longer the passive recipient of his social heritage; he is an active force in shaping the new society.

This reorientation of student values has made the self-contained community of scholars an anachronism. And it has raised the question of whether the education our universities are offering is "relevant" to the problems of present-day America. Berkeley's Muscatine committee seeks to solve the question of relevance by introducing into that school's curriculum current affairs courses dealing with such contemporary issues as the emerging nations and the Viet Nam conflict. This is, I believe, a step in the wrong direction.

The offerings in a college catalogue need not parallel the headlines in the daily newspaper in order to be relevant to current problems. The curriculum need not be revised to deal with each new world crisis in order to be meaningful. The student does not abdicate his responsibility for self-education by matriculating in a university. The classroom is not the place to teach Crisis $1202x–1203y$. In this area, the newspaper is his textbook, the rally is his forum for discussion, and the visiting or resident expert is his mentor.

Many who raise the criterion of relevance seem to forget that the main function of education is to impart ideas which transcend the topical, and to develop in the student an understanding of the methodology which will endow him with the capacity for independent evaluation. The professor who is merely a transmission belt for factual data is of little value. And the test for relevancy is not time*li*ness, but time*less*ness.

The four college years constitute a brief liberation from the daily demands of society; they represent a unique period during which the individual's mind is sufficiently free and sufficiently developed that he may devote himself to intellectual advancement. Every endeavor which aids that advancement is relevant, and any which hinders it is irrelevant. The undergraduate course which most influenced my patterns of thought was one whose subject matter I have found applicable to virtually every other area I have studied. It was relevant not because it focused on the contemporary, but rather because it concerned itself with ideas which were not imprisoned by their chronological setting.

What the student seeks from college is a justification of the intellect. The college freshman has left behind him a society basically hostile to the unbridled pursuit of knowledge, and the senior will soon re-enter that hostile environment. The academic community has four short years to induct him as a member. In that time it must instill in the student a pride in intellectual achievement that will remain after graduation, so that when he leaves the community of scholars, he will still be a part of it.

PART FIVE

The Evaluation of Teaching Performance

Less Teaching,
More Conversation

HAROLD HOWE II

It is imperative that ways of improving college teaching be devised and evaluated. Merely lamenting the deterioration of undergraduate teaching, deploring the overemphasis on research at the expense of teaching, or regretting the poor preparation of scholars for teaching is futile.

THESE TWO SENTENCES appear in the statement setting forth a basis for discussing improving college teaching. From them, I take my text.

First, I would like to enter a mild reservation about the second sentence. For years, educators have urged that we find ways to measure a teacher's effectiveness. And for years, we have conceded that no one has yet done so. If we cannot measure teaching—weigh it, take its temperature, or otherwise appraise it—I question whether we should agree so readily that college teaching is headed downhill. Edward Gibbon, Henry Adams, and Henry Thoreau among many other notable men have deplored the boredom and waste of their college days. If undergraduate teaching has deteriorated, what has it deteriorated from? And I wonder when, if ever, scholars have been well prepared for teaching. Gregor Mendel, who discovered the laws of genetics, failed his teacher's examination four times and finally went into administration.

There is probably a moral there, but as an administrator, I absolutely refuse to look for it.

Education has always needed improvement and always will. I suspect that our collective consideration here stems not so much from the sad state of teaching as from two kinds of masochism: the first a typically American and probably Puritanical pleasure in flaying ourselves for real or imagined shortcomings; the second, an academic subspecies of this masochism that derives from the exalted position of research since World War II. Just as the sudden outpouring of Federal aid for the sciences after Sputnik produced a sudden sympathy for the "plight of the humanities," so has the dramatic university interest in research produced a guilt-ridden concern for college teaching.

But in offering this suggestion that perhaps we are not doing so badly after all, I do not mean to imply that we should stop worrying and begin instead to felicitate each other on what splendid fellows we are. For however well or poorly other teachers may have performed in other times, we can improve both the circumstances of teaching and the rationale for doing it in the first place.

Improving the circumstances of teaching is an institutional responsibility. If teaching today suffers by comparison with research, it is because colleges and universities have succumbed to external influences and relegated teaching to an inferior position. There is both money and prestige in many kinds of research today, and colleges characteristically covet both. In consequence, the scholar and the researcher are well rewarded by their disciplines and by their institutions with professional recognition and faculty advancement. This is as it should be.

Achievement should bring reward. But rarely does the achievement of the outstanding teacher bring similar recognition. If higher education institutions are serious about improving the quality of the teaching in their classrooms, they must demonstrate their interest in doing so by building an appraisal of teaching ability into their promotion procedures. They must make known to their own faculties as well as to candidates for appointment the fact that the institution values good teaching and will reward it in tangible ways.

This, of course, brings up the matter of evaluation, which has long puzzled the academic community. In this connection, I would like to mention an evaluation project begun a year or two ago by students at one Eastern university. For all its informality and lack of sanction by the university authorities, it still strikes me as having merit. The students passed out questionnaires to their fellows so that they could grade professors on their teaching performance. The disadvantages of such an evaluation are obvious: there is no guarantee that students will have sufficient maturity to distinguish good teaching from popularizing, or that they would not exploit such a grading system to reward lenient professors and punish strict ones.

On the other hand, we have the obvious fact that students do pay for the instruction they receive; they are not simply a necessary evil to be tolerated as part of the educational endeavor, but are the purpose of it. The opinions of those who eat the pudding certainly ought to be considered if we wish to know how the pudding tastes. On balance, it seems logical that the judgment of students should be considered as part of the process for evaluating teachers.

As another element of that evaluation, I think colleges should en-courage members of a department to criticize each other's teaching in a constructive fashion. The scholar and researcher are regularly exposed to such criticism by their colleagues throughout every discipline; I cannot imagine that members of a single faculty would be any more savage in their appraisals of a colleague's teaching performance than scholars often are in their evaluations of each other's research and publications. To guard against the possibility that internal politics might affect the objec-tivity of such judgments, colleges could bring in teams of evaluators from other institutions, as they do now to gain an outside opinion of a department's strength.

These suggestions all bear on the responsibility of the institution for encouraging good teaching. More basic than institutional responsibility, I believe, is the individual teacher's understanding of why he is teaching. It strikes me that the fundamental problem with college teaching is that there is too much of it, and not nearly enough conversation. There is too much information, and not enough inquiry; too many facts, and not enough explanation of their meaning.

Consider for a moment a typical college course in Shakespeare. In one semester, a student is expected to read between twelve and twenty plays. With diligence, luck, and a College Outline survey or other *aide-mémoire*, the student will be able to remember enough plot lines, heroines, and snatches of famous speeches to pass a test certifying that he has "taken" Shakespeare.

Yet for all this frenzied gallop through one of the ornaments of Eng-lish literature and Western civilization, the student may completely have missed the literary experience, which is the only justification for having Shakespeare in the curriculum in the first place. If in the thoughtful and leisurely reading of four plays, he experiences a shock of recognition at finding his own thoughts and emotions expressed in the words of another man, or finds a new world of thinking and feeling opened to him, he has laid the foundation for a lifetime of deriving the most profound sort of pleasure—and pleasure, after all, is what literature is about. If, on the other hand, he derives from his course little more than three hours of credit toward his degree and a modest packet of tag lines that he can drop into a bridge-party conversation, he has failed the course no matter how many plays he has read.

For all their railing against the trend toward utilitarianism in educa-tion, humanities teachers seem to me to have adopted many of the methods and goals of those they criticize. Liberal arts courses abound in reading lists. The purpose of such lists is sound enough; they try to ensure that a student will read at least a basic minimum of those works of our language that we commonly denote as excellent. But the implication of such lists is that the student should not only read them, but must "appreciate" them in the sickly sense that word has taken on. These books are all classics, the reading list proclaims, and if you don't like every one of them, there's something wrong with you. Rarely does a teacher candidly admit that he himself found some of the classics rather heavy going, and that Wordsworth, for example, has written some of the worst poetry this side of a finishing school yearbook. Rarely does a teacher point out that a distinctive book, like a distinctive human, has a personality to which the student's personality may respond or it may not.

In consequence, the teaching of literature and of the liberal arts in general takes on a utilitarian aspect. It contributes to that sort of intellectual bullying which characterizes the culture industry advertisements in any Sunday supplement. One ad proclaims, "You are not well educated unless you have read these books." Another asks, "Do you admire the Mona Lisa for the wrong reasons?" Another tells you to buy twenty volumes of Truth on the installment plan so that you will be an interesting conversationalist. The life of the mind takes on the nature of social insurance; it becomes a kind of intellectual mouthwash to protect you from offending, by making sure that you will not prefer a minor poet to a major, or admire either for the wrong reasons.

Requiring a systematic exposure to a significant part of a language's literature is necessary to the development of a student's critical sense. But vast quantities of reading that leave little time for understanding or for mature consideration pervert the educational process into little more than a breathless tour of intellectual landmarks. It is the teacher's responsibility not merely to point out those landmarks, but to help the student realize why they remain standing while other works have long since crumbled into oblivion.

Nor are the sciences exempt from this anxiety to "cover the material" and this failure to help students understand *why* we cover it. Just as we confuse reading with the literary experience and the record of history with the meaning of history, so do we substitute scientific data for the spirit of science. A student is told in chemistry that he will be "held responsible" for Mendeleev's periodic table, and, sure enough, his examination asks: What is the atomic number of hydrogen?

Knowing the atomic number of hydrogen is surely part of the professional kit of the scientist in chemistry or physics. But in teaching undergraduates, we are not dealing with scientists—not yet, anyhow. We are dealing with a mind that has a natural curiosity about some things, but must be awakened to inquiry about others. Why on earth should any sane and healthy undergraduate care *what* the atomic number of hydrogen is? It is at this point, I believe, that teaching at every level often reserves a natural cause-to-effect relationship, thus frustrating an instinct that makes the difference between passive indoctrination and active learning. We present the *results* of inquiry instead of trying to recreate the *process* of inquiry.

What, in other words, led Mendeleev to care about the atomic number of hydrogen? He was not interested in producing a chart to be memorized; he was interested in discerning a pattern in the behavior of certain chemical elements. What quality of mind led Charles Darwin to puzzle over the differing varieties of obviously related birds? What sort of temperament led Edward Gibbon to try to determine the causes for the decline and fall of Rome, or Plato to speculate on the relation of man's physical nature to his spirit?

The answer in each case is the same: a lofty curiosity that drives each of us to ask who he is and what his world is, where he and it came from, and where he and it are going. This is the abiding spirit of intellectual inquiry that unites every field of learning beyond our arbitrary divisions of man and nature into subjects and courses. It is the spirit of search that is built into every human, and the measure of educational failure in our age is the degree to which formal education manages to convert so much natural interest into baffled tedium. We have long assumed that students who drop out of school or college before completing their academic work—the phrase "academic *work*" is instructive—dropped out because they lacked ability. But in recent years, we have come to realize that what many dropouts lack is an ability to put up with rigid instructional procedures and arid educational content.

This is the basic failure of teaching: the failure to probe for the intellectual curiosity in every student and guide it in those directions that we have found over the centuries to be most important to a civilized and fulfilling life. And the basic problem confronting those institutions that wish to improve their teaching is to restore the spirit of inquiry that has been snuffed out in many teachers themselves.

Such a restoration requires, first, relieving the teacher of much of his responsibility for transmitting information; books do it better and cheaper; and modern media may improve on books for certain special kinds of information. The teacher should concentrate instead on arousing in the student that interest which gives information both relevance and appeal. A student who wants to know *why* will find out what, who, when, and where for himself.

It means re-examining some accepted administrative practices to determine whether they are dictated by sound educational practice or merely by custom and institutional convenience. This re-examination might lead, for example, to relieving the best students of any necessity to attend regular classes at all, so that the teacher will at once have more time for those students who are experiencing difficulty in their studies and more time for conference and tutorial work with able students. It might lead to a drastic revision of examination practices, so many of which attempt to evaluate in a quantitative way performances that are essentially qualitative in nature. And, it is to be hoped, it would lead to a reappraisal of our programs of graduate study, many of which merely extend the baby-sitting philosophy of education from a student's youth into his early maturity. Is it really necessary, for example, for a graduate student to spend a semester or more in a course on bibliography? I tend myself to believe that all a really curious student needs to know about a research library is where to find the librarian. To put the matter into its most homely form, where there is a will, there is a way. I think teaching too often concentrates on showing students the way before it has awakened in them the least desire to go there.

In sum, I believe that what teachers and their institutions must do to improve college teaching is to remember to renew the motivations that lead a man to teaching in the first place. Presumably every one of us was at some time struck with wonder or delight at the operation of a great mind probing the eternal human questions. The daily necessities of any kind of life can obscure with repetition and routine the deep pleasure that led us to choose a life of learning. Digging beneath the accretion of the years to uncover those old motivations will make us students again; and any good teacher must forever be a student.

Evaluation of
Teaching Performance:
Issues and Possibilities

JOHN W. GUSTAD

*As a nation—and a very education-conscious and statistic-happy one—
we do know a lot about some parts of our educational system. We know
how many teachers there are and how old and how tall they are; we have
reliable statistics on school buildings and how old and tall they are; we know
how many language laboratories are in operation; we can calculate to the
penny how much we are spending for education.*

*The only thing we don't know is what is produced by all these teachers,
buildings, laboratories, and dollars. We don't know what the students are
learning.*

Carnegie Quarterly, Spring 1966

It is paradoxical indeed that the academic world, ostensibly devoted
to the continuous search for evidence which can be brought to bear on
the solution of problems and the increase of knowledge, continues with
great equanimity to tolerate a system of evaluating its members wherein,
as this writer said earlier, "to call what is typically collected or adduced
to support evaluative decisions 'evidence' is to stretch the meaning of
that honored word beyond reason." [1] Almost a quarter century ago,
Logan Wilson said: "Indeed, it is no exaggeration to say that the most
critical problem confronted in the social organization of any university
is the proper evaluation of faculty services, and giving due recognition
through the impartial assignment of status." [2] The almost imperceptible
progress since then is eloquent testimony to the academic profession's

[1] John W. Gustad, "Policies and Practices in Faculty Evaluation," *Educational
Record*, July 1961, p. 208.
[2] Wilson, *The Academic Man* (New York: Oxford University Press, 1942; reprinted, New York: Octagon Books, 1964).

265

unwillingness or inability, or both, to do what is needed to develop adequate and equitable methods for faculty evaluation.

Not that evaluations do not go on continuously. As Clark has put it, "the truth of the matter is that such evaluations occur all of the time; each of us evaluates one another, makes judgments about the competence of individuals at all times. Sometimes these judgments are made on the slightest basis; under these circumstances we recognize the fact that the judgment we have made is not worth very much. In many instances, however, we do not realize how meager is the basis on which such judgments are made and sometimes rely far too much on information collected in a haphazard or chaotic fashion." [3] In a profession that prides itself on speaking only when the data speak, it is most strange that conferences on promotion and tenure are not as silent as a Quaker meeting in which no one has been moved.

Faculty members engage in an increasingly wide variety of activities, and decisions about promotion, salary increases, and tenure are based on their performance in a substantial proportion of these activities. What follows will be an examination of the problems and possible solutions with regard to only one—teaching.

What is a teacher?

Colleges and universities have many responsibilities, but there is one which they all share: helping students learn. To say this is in no way to depreciate research and scholarship, consultation, service, and other activities in which members of the academic community engage. Sometimes, however, these things appear to overshadow the task of assisting students in their learning.

If it is correct to say that a teacher is one who assists students to learn, several questions require answers. Among them is: With what kinds of learning is the teacher concerned? As Tyler has said: "Of course, not all things students learn in college are desirable so that the evaluation of college teaching is not simply finding out whether students have learned, but whether they have learned the things which the instructors were trying to teach." [4] In addition, the distinction must be made between student behavior and instructor behavior. That is, we need to know what the instructor is doing and what impact this has on students. Increasingly, the college teacher has come to feel that his job is to teach his discipline—or, more often, some small fragment thereof.

[3] Kenneth E. Clark, "Studies of Faculty Evaluation," *Studies of College Faculty* (Berkeley, Calif.: Center for the Study of Higher Education, and Boulder, Colo.: Western Interstate Commission for Higher Education, 1961).

[4] Ralph W. Tyler, "The Evaluation of Teaching," *Preparing College Teachers*, ed. A. D. Albright and John E. Barrows (Lexington, Ky.: University of Kentucky, and Atlanta, Ga.: Southern Regional Education Board, 1959).

He does not, as used to be the case, concern himself much with such matters as belief, discipline, or morality. Although some people talk about developing attitudes and appreciations, precious little has been done to find out whether they are effective in doing so and what evidence there is ought not lead anyone to feel very sanguine.

If a teacher is to assist students to learn, we need also to inquire into the necessary conditions for learning. Although educational psychology has been around for many years, its contribution to an understanding of these conditions leaves much to be desired. Bruner has recently tried to develop a theory of instruction,[5] but it is too early to know what effect he will have. There is a growing interest in learning about how college students learn, but we are far from knowing as much about this as we do about how white rats learn. Surely, motivation is involved, and it is sometimes felt that the teacher should not merely capitalize on the motivation already existing but should work to increase and channel it. The folklore of education is full of stories about teachers who, by one means or another, got their students to work hard. Praise and blame, setting high standards of performance, being a good guy, establishing rapport, being a hard grader, and being an exciting showman are a few examples of these means, but we really know little about how these work, under what conditions, and with whom.

If we are to get students to substitute (or acquire) new and, it is to be hoped, more appropriate ways of behaving, we must somehow get them, first, to recognize the need for new responses and then, second, try out alternatives until a good one is found. This investigation requires both motivation and the ability to help students choose among a variety of alternatives, to be a guide so that time is not lost needlessly in random exploration. Students need to learn to be autonomous in the sense that they be able to set their own standards of behavior and know, without having a teacher tell them, when they have performed well or achieved a satisfactory solution to a problem. They need, also, to learn to recognize problems without having someone else point them out. Disciplines have their own internal organizations, sometimes alternative ones within the same discipline (as, for example, several versions of learning theory). It is possible that a student on his own could discover these, but the limitations of time and the interests of efficiency are best served if the teacher helps him to see at least the broad view of the terrain.

These are a few examples of the kinds of things which we are dealing with as teachers. More are known, and even more are yet to be learned. Only as we pay attention to what we know and continue to learn what is needed can we hope to increase the effectiveness of the teacher's role

[5] Jerome E. Bruner, *Toward a Theory of Instruction* (Cambridge, Mass.: Harvard University Press, 1966).

as a person responsible for establishing optimum conditions for learning. Recent work by McKeachie [6] and Bugelski [7] are promising and helpful beginnings.

WHY EVALUATE TEACHING?

To some, the concern with improving procedures for evaluating teaching seems nothing less than the expression of an obsessive-compulsive neurosis. Those who have learned to use the darkness for their own purposes will probably not welcome the light. And, as Dressel has said, "there are those professors who, knowing full well that they could do better, interpret academic freedom as inclusive of the privilege to teach as badly as they wish. . . ." [8] Certainly, a system or set of procedures which brings their deficiencies to light would be a threat.

Gage has identified three important reasons for evaluating teaching. [9] There is, first of all, the necessity for providing a basis on which a number of administrative decisions can be made, decisions about promotions in rank, increases in salary, and the granting of tenure. These decisions must be made, are being made, will continue to be made. It would seem only reasonable to try to make them as accurately and as equitably as possible. Clark has summarized this view succinctly: "Whenever we make a decision to retain a faculty member, or to let him go, we determine the nature of our college faculty for years to come. And when we decide whom to recognize and whom to reward, we modify the distribution of time and activities which is spent by members of our faculty." [10] The longer we continue to operate in our present manner, the less control we have over the shape and direction of the institution.

The second reason for trying to measure teaching effectiveness is that the information generated provides a basis for self-improvement by the faculty. Just as students need feedback in order to correct errors, so also is feedback essential to faculty members. If the quality of the information is poor, chances for improvement are correspondingly reduced. As Tyler has said, "Hence, the development of a sound body of guiding concepts and principles in teaching is largely dependent upon means for evaluating teaching so that our principles have been tested rather

[6] W. J. McKeachie, "Research on Teaching at the College and University Level," *Handbook of Research on Teaching*, ed. N. L. Gage (Chicago: Rand McNally & Co., 1963).
[7] B. R. Bugelski, *The Psychology of Learning Applied to Teaching* (Indianapolis, Ind.: Bobbs-Merrill Co., 1964).
[8] Paul E. Dressel, "The Current Status of Research on College and University Teaching," *The Appraisal of Teaching in Large Universities*, ed. W. J. McKeachie (Ann Arbor: University of Michigan, 1959).
[9] N. L. Gage, "Ends and Means in Appraising College Teaching," *The Appraisal of Teaching in Large Universities*.
[10] Clark, "Studies in Faculty Evaluation."

than resting upon personal preference, or upon unsystematic impressions." [11]

The third reason given by Gage has to do with the need for a criterion that can be employed in research on teaching and learning. What we know is pitifully small compared with what we ought to know, and research efforts have been severely hampered by the lack of any even reasonably valid and reliable measures of outcomes. Once we have those, we will be in a position to move ahead with the research which will, some day, permit us to know enough to do our jobs better.

For the present and for some time in the future, it is altogether likely that the kinds of measures we develop to serve each of these three purposes will be somewhat different. More will be said about this later, but it is true that we require a higher level of measure reliability, for example, when dealing with individual cases (as in determining promotions) than we do when dealing with groups (as in certain kinds of research). The measures used by an individual instructor in studying his own teaching may be substantially different from those used for other purposes. In the long run, it is likely that we shall see a convergence to the point where the same measures can be used for all three purposes. We should not, however, await that millennium.

THE PRESENT STATE OF AFFAIRS

Five years ago, this writer reported on a survey of policies and practices in faculty evaluation.[12] In preparation for the present paper, the American Council on Education again surveyed member institutions with a slightly revised questionnaire. Although not exactly comparable, enough similarity exists to permit making some comparisons. Table 1 shows the rankings of certain sources of information according to their importance as defined by frequency of utilization. The category "Universities," it should be noted, is the least comparable between the two surveys. In the 1961 survey, each university submitted only one report; in 1966, the several major divisions (arts and sciences, business, engineering, agriculture, and education) each submitted reports. The 1966 rankings for universities shown in Table 1 refer only to colleges of arts and sciences. It should also be noted that, since the number of items included differed, small differences in rankings should not be considered important. At best, Table 1 provides a rough comparison.

Despite difficulties of comparability, certain major trends are evident. There has apparently been a substantial decline in the use of systematic student ratings. Equally substantial has been the decline in the use of classroom visitation as a means for obtaining information. On the other

[11] Tyler, "The Evaluation of Teaching."
[12] Gustad, "Policies and Practices in Faculty Evaluation."

TABLE 1: *Comparisons by Rank Orders of Sources of Information Employed in the Evaluation of Teaching*

Source	Universities[a]		Liberal Arts Colleges		Teachers Colleges		Junior Colleges	
	1961 (N=130)	1966 (N=110)	1961 (N=272)	1966 (N=484)	1961 (N=29)	1966 (N=133)	1961 (N=25)	1966 (N=128)
Chairman evaluation	1	1	2*	2	1	1	6*	2
Dean evaluation	6	2	4	1	3	2	—	1
Scholarly research and publication	4*	3	—	5	5	4	4*	15
Colleagues' opinions	2	4	5*	3	4	3	2	7
Informal student opinions	11*	5	1	4	—	6	—	5
Committee evaluations	11*	6	15*	8	12	9	4*	12
Grade distributions	7	7	11*	6	—	7	10*	6
Student examination performance	13	8	7*	9	6	10	9	9
Enrollment in elective courses	4*	9	10	11	—	13	6*	14
Systematic student ratings	15*	10	5*	12*	9*	15	3	11
Self-evaluation	9	11	11*	10	9*	11	1	10
Course syllabi and examinations	14	12	11*	7	2	5	8	4
Alumni opinions	3	13	7*	12*	—	12	—	13
Classroom visits	10	14	2*	15	7	8	—	3
Long-term follow-up of students	8	15	9	14	8	14	—	8
Informal methods	15*	—	11*	—	9*	—	—	—
Student behavior	15*	—	15*	—	—	—	—	—
Other	17	—	17	—	—	—	10*	—

* Rank shared with another source.
a College of arts and sciences only.

hand, the utilization of committee evaluations and the analysis of grade distributions have markedly increased in popularity.

Informal student opinions and evaluations by deans and chairmen are still frequently used methods. The question remains: What kinds of data do students, deans, and chairmen have available for making such evaluations? Students, of course, are regular observers, but, as noted above, classroom visitation has become less frequent, a fact that leaves one to wonder where chairmen and deans get their information—unless it be from informal student opinions. The same question applies to committees.

Table 2 shows the percentage of institutions employing rating forms (whether completed by students, colleagues, or administrators) or other special techniques in the evaluation of teachers and also the percentage reporting research on the instruments used. As noted above, use of systematic student ratings as a technique has declined substantially during the past five years. What is particularly striking—and what may well

TABLE 2: *Frequency of Use of and Research on Rating Forms or Other Special Techniques for Evaluating Teaching Competence*

Type of Institution	Percent Reporting	
	Use	Research
Junior colleges.............	30.3	0.0
Liberal arts colleges.......	23.9	0.6
Teachers colleges.........	21.3	1.5
Universities:		
Arts and sciences......	26.2	4.8
Business..............	21.3	1.7
Engineering...........	17.3	3.8
Agriculture...........	33.3	3.2
Education.............	23.4	5.0

account for decreased use—is the almost total absence of research on the validity of the instruments that are used. Lacking sound information about their validity, their use could be expected to follow the path of a fad: great enthusiasm followed by disillusion. What little research there is tends to agree that the reliability of these instruments is generally satisfactory. Their validity, in the absence of validation, is another matter.

CHARACTERISTICS OF GOOD MEASURES

We are dealing with the measurement of human performance. Contrasting the measures now employed with the body of research and theory available on measurement, we are in much the same position as the crusty New England farmer who told the eager young agricultural agent, "Shucks, sonny, I ain't farmin' half as good as I know how to *now*." Although there remain very difficult theoretical and technical problems in the domain of measurement, we do have a substantial body of knowledge that could be put to work to our immediate benefit.

Any measure must have validity. That is, it must measure what it purports to measure. Establishing this validity by one of several possible methods is in many respects the most difficult problem of all. Although there are several alternative approaches,[13] most of the work done to establish the validity of measures has related the measures to one or several criteria. Tests of scholastic aptitude, for instance, have typically used grades as a criterion on the assumption that intellectually superior students will, on the average, get better grades. Admittedly, there is a circularity involved here; nevertheless, these tests have proved to be useful over the years.

Since the validity of measures is so often established by relating them to criteria, it is obvious that criteria are themselves of prime importance. Astin has distinguished between the conceptual criterion and criterion performance. The former he defines as "a verbal statement of socially relevant outcomes based on the more general purposes or aims of the sponsor." With regard to this, he says, "One distinguishing characteristic of the criterion . . . is its essentially *ecological* nature. In contrast to a purely psychological construct or trait, a criterion variable usually refers to a relationship between the person and his environment. It is, in fact, difficult to speak of 'standards' of performance or of behavior as being 'desirable' without also defining the social context in which the behavior occurs." [14] The conceptual criterion, in other words, is a value judgment having to do with socially desirable outcomes as, for instance, good teaching.

The criterion performance, on the other hand, is "any observable event which is judged to be relevant to the conceptual criterion." [15] The relationship between the conceptual criterion and criterion performance he describes as follows: "Since conceptual criteria are rational rather than empirical, the relevance of a criterion performance can be judged only on rational grounds. To illustrate: changes in a student's achievement test score (criterion performance) constitute a measure of 'effective teaching' (conceptual criterion) only if one is willing to *assume* that the student's score is an important or socially relevant variable to be manipulated by the teacher."

---

[13] American Psychological Association, "Technical Recommendations for Psychological Tests and Diagnostic Techniques," *Psychological Bulletin*, No. 2.

[14] Alexander W. Astin, "Criterion Centered Research," *Educational and Psychological Measurement*, Winter 1964, pp. 807–22.

[15] *Ibid.*

Measures of criterion performance are sometimes both simple and readily available as in the case of piece work on a factory assembly line. More often and particularly in the case of complex tasks, they are very difficult to assemble. The practice of medicine is a good analogy. That is, just as a good teacher is supposed to have beneficial effects on his students' learning, so a good physician is supposed to help his patients to get well. Before we can assess this, however, we have to know how sick a physician's patients are at the outset and what their condition is after treatment. Take the situation of many of the most distinguished physicians: because patients are referred to them only when in dire straits, their cure rate may be lower than that of a witch doctor.

The same problems are encountered when one tries to assess teaching effectiveness. Presumably, a good teacher does have beneficial effects on his students. One must, however, inquire into the capabilities of his students. A faculty member in a college with high admissions standards faces a substantially different problem from one in an institution with an unselective admissions policy. Similarly, a faculty member teaching only elective courses has different problems from one who faces classes made up largely of students who are there only because they must be.

Criteria are measures and must be evaluated with the same care as other measures. Brogden and Taylor [16] have outlined some of the problems which affect adversely the validity of criteria. There may, for instance, be criterion deficiency: significant elements of the behavior under consideration may have been omitted. The use of an income criterion to measure competency of physicians is an example. While it may be true that the better physicians tend on the average to earn more money, there are too many exceptions—as, say, physicians on university faculties, in government service, or serving as missionaries—to permit earned income to become the sole measure of effectiveness.

Equally troublesome is criterion contamination: inclusion in the criterion of extraneous elements. To cite a special case, invalid inferences may be made on the basis of appearances. For instance, a man may be judged to be a good mechanic because he has an impressive set of well-maintained tools and talks knowledgeably about his work. In other words, he "looks like" a mechanic. Another kind of contamination arises from the presence of a halo effect. Here, a general impression—as of liking—is permitted to affect judgments of an individual on other, often unrelated, traits. Halo is not always bad, as Bingham has shown, [17] but it is a constant source of difficulty unless it is recognized.

[16] H. E. Brogden and E. K. Taylor, "The Theory and Classification of Criterion Bias," *Educational and Psychological Measurement*, Spring 1950, pp. 159–86.
[17] Walter V. Bingham, "Halo, Invalid and Valid," *Journal of Applied Psychology*, April 1939, pp. 221–28.

A third difficulty encountered in criterion development is scale unit bias, an effect created by unequal units being used to measure criterion behavior. Without considering the statistical details of this problem, suffice it to say that using a rubber yardstick whose various segments have different degrees of elasticity produces serious distortions.

The fourth difficulty Brogden and Taylor identify as criterion distortion. It acts much like scale unit bias but concerns improper weighting of various components of the criterion. Criterion behavior is almost always a complex of elements. Assigning of weights must be done accurately lest what are really important behaviors be slighted while less important (although perhaps more accessible) ones be overestimated.

Thorndike has classified criteria as ultimate, intermediate, and immediate.[18] The ultimate criterion for the teacher would be his long-term impact on the student's behavior. Such behavior, however, is frequently almost inaccessible to measurement in that it is so intertwined with extraneous or uncontrollable variables that it cannot, itself, be used as a criterion.

In such cases, resort is usually made to the use of an intermediate criterion. The practice of medicine is again a good example. If we cannot determine to our own satisfaction how the physician actually affects his patients, we *can* find out how well he did on his specialty board examinations. Using this intermediate criterion as a measure, we must still admit to not knowing how performance on the specialty boards relates to being a good physician, but, on rational grounds, there ought to be some relationship. In judging teachers, however, using results on the final oral examination for the Ph.D. would probably be unsatisfactory since, for one thing, almost nobody fails, and variability is a requirement for any measure.

The immediate criterion is usually the most accessible and the least useful. To become a physician, one must graduate from medical school. Grades earned in medical school are available, but as a criterion, they are at least *two* steps removed from what we are really interested in. If teaching effectiveness is the ultimate criterion, then the immediate criteria might be such things as a faculty member's holding the Ph.D., his years of experience, the amount he has published, and so on. As one goes from the ultimate to the immediate criterion, convenience and accessibility increase as relevance and importance decrease. To the extent that we simply describe the faculty member and his credentials, we are dealing with an immediate or, at best, intermediate criterion. To the extent that we can measure changes in students' behavior (on rele-

[18] Robert L. Thorndike, *Personnel Selection* (New York: John Wiley & Sons Co., 1949).

vant variables), we are dealing with the ultimate criterion. If we are in a position to use an ultimate criterion, we can afford to abandon the others.[19]

The second requisite for any measure is that it possess satisfactory reliability. What constitutes "satisfactory" depends in part on the circumstances in which the measure will be used. Reliability is frequently described as having to do with the consistency with which a measure operates, but this is a misleading characterization. Actually, reliability has to do with the amount of error in a measure; thus, the higher the reliability, the less the amount of error present. To put it another way, the question is: Can we *count* on the measure? A high degree of reliability is essential when measurements are to be used in individual cases. Even when comparing groups, it is generally true that, although a lower reliability coefficient can sometimes be tolerated, in many instances negative results—a decision that the groups are not different—were arrived at erroneously because the reliability of the measure employed was such that real differences were obscured. Upon subsequent research with better measures, the differences have come to light.

Measures must also have variability. A test which everyone either passes or fails is useful only in extremely limited circumstances. This is one trouble with the Ph.D. oral examination. Only those who are almost certain to pass are permitted to take it, and instances of failure are so rare as to be minor scandals when they happen. At the same time, everyone who has had substantial experience with such examinations knows that there *is* variability in performance. The difficulty is that our measure—pass-or-fail—does not show it. One respondent to the 1961 survey noted wryly that his college apparently had nothing but excellent teachers on its faculty.

Finally, measures ought to be as "pure" as possible. That is, there are times when one can add apples, oranges, and bananas and get a number that is useful. Generally speaking, however, it is best not to be in the position of the purveyor of sandwiches made up of equal portions of rabbit and horse: one horse and one rabbit. We have gone along for years talking about intelligence even though we know that intelligence tests measure a complex of traits. Certainly teaching is a complex of many interrelated activities. There are complicated interactions among students, teachers, techniques, and content that need to be studied. *Some* teachers can use *some* techniques with *some* students when dealing with *some* subjects. Particularly for research purposes, we would be

[19] Relating a measure to a criterion is the most commonly used method for establishing its validity. There are, of course, other approaches, but there is not time here to do more than acknowledge their existence. Recent work, for instance, has made use of construct validity rather than criterion-oriented validity, an approach which may hold some promise for educational research.

well advised to know quite precisely *what* we are measuring even though, for some purposes, we will wish to combine scores into a composite. The work of Barr *et al.*[20] and Ryans[21] on secondary teachers are good examples.

SOME COMMENTS ON PRESENT TECHNIQUES

Table 1 showed a rank ordering of the kinds of information used in judging teaching ability. Before considering some alternatives, it seems worthwhile to comment on present practices. Considering all types of institutions, the evaluations of chairmen and deans are most frequently used. The problem is, as one respondent in the 1961 survey put it, that "the dean is supposed to know, but he isn't supposed to find out." It is entirely possible, even likely (else how could higher education have managed to remain in confusion and not slip into utter chaos?), that many chairmen and deans do make "proper" decisions. An analogous situation exists in clinical medicine where experienced physicians can and do respond to subtle cues and arrive at correct diagnoses. They themselves are often unable to explain how they do it.

Perhaps it is the ability of chairmen and deans to make what at least the majority of their faculty members regard as correct judgments that permits them to survive and prosper in office. Their judgments may not only be perceived as equitable but actually *be* so. Perhaps. The question remains: On the basis of what kinds of information do chairmen and deans make their judgments about teaching competence?

Looking again at Table 1, it would appear that the opinions of colleagues and informal student opinion are the primary bases. Even so, we are still at some distance from understanding what is involved. Although colleagues frequently have closer relations among themselves than they do with their chairman or dean, their opportunities for direct observation (note the substantial decline in classroom visitation) are minimal as far as teaching behavior is concerned.

As for students, they are probably reasonably good sources of information *when they are asked the right questions*. In the present conditions of academia, they are virtually the *only* direct observers. Ratings based on observations can be useful provided *competent* observers are involved.

To ask beginning students about the instructor's knowledge of his field is probably of little value. These students could, however, report on their own degree of interest (although it remains to be shown how this relates to what and how much they learn), whether the instructor

[20] A. S. Barr *et al.*, *Wisconsin Studies of the Measurement and Predicting of Teacher Effectiveness* (Madison, Wis.: Dembar, 1961).

[21] David G. Ryans, *Characteristics of Teachers* (Washington: American Council on Education, 1960).

motivated them to do more than was required, whether he got them interested in taking more work in that department, and so on. If the questions are well phrased, students can probably make pretty good estimates of the instructor's effects on *them*. In addition, one might be willing to say that *one* valid outcome of good teaching ought to be that students enjoy the experience. Certainly, the contrary proposition would be difficult to defend.

Similarly, colleagues can probably give fairly reliable information about things that may be indicators of good teaching, at least as intermediate criterion measures. Such things as a faculty member's tendency to talk enthusiastically about teaching, to try out new ideas for course organization or teaching methods, and to evidence his intellectual vitality could be related to his effectiveness as a teacher. We need to find out, but colleagues are at least a promising source of information.

In the universities and in the liberal arts colleges, committees are increasingly in use. The same question must be raised with regard to them as with chairmen and deans: What is the basis for their decisions? Unless the committee has access to sound information, about all it can do is to serve to spread out the onus associated with an unpopular decision and to prevent individuals from operating unfairly.

SOME ALTERNATIVE APPROACHES

Dressel has suggested several possibilities which would appear to merit investigation.[22] One is to examine the correlations between scores on scholastic aptitude tests and grades attained in course. This approach assumes that a good teacher will succeed in getting the best efforts from his students; in effect, the motivational component, which now accounts for so much of the variance, would be removed and only the effects of intellectual ability would remain. In other words, those instructors having classes where the correlations are very high could be judged to be effective. The principal difficulty with this approach, however, is that it could easily penalize instructors who go out of their way to assist students having special difficulties since such assistance would affect the course grade and thus lower the correlation.

As another possibility, Dressel suggests the use of delayed measures of retention in addition to the conventional end-of-course examinations. It is to be hoped, of course, that what students learn will stay with them, and it is sometimes assumed that better teachers will have more lasting effects. While this approach should be investigated, it raises problems of the relationship between what students know and the individual instructors concerned.

[22] Dressel, "The Current Status of Research on College and University Teaching."

A third and related approach involves the study of students' performance in advanced courses in a sequentially ordered series. A professor who teaches the calculus is in a position to judge how well students have mastered analytical geometry. Although there could be some difficulty in attributing learning to particular instructors, this does not appear to be an insurmountable problem.

A fourth method suggested by Dressel is simply to count the number of students who decide to major in the department. One must know, obviously, the extent to which students were interested in the discipline prior to their enrollment in the course. Also, if they have taken several courses in the department, the problem of attributing effects to a particular instructor is encountered again. It could also penalize instructors in certain of the less exciting courses. Statistics and experimental psychology, for instance, are usually not as popular with students as abnormal or child psychology.

Classroom visitation is another approach that has never received the attention or systematic analysis it deserves. If we must admit that students have their limitations as competent observers, then it seems reasonable to permit individuals with special competence to see what is taking place. Academic tradition, of course, is opposed to this, and the notion is widespread that the professor's classroom is his castle. The schedule of visits would have to be arranged so that an unbiased sample of observations could be obtained, and the frequency of visits would have to be large enough to reduce or eliminate stage fright. In addition, the ground rules would have to be carefully spelled out in relation to purpose of the visits. That is, visits by a colleague who would then report to the instructor in private in the interests of assisting him to improve his teaching would be viewed differently from visits designed to obtain information to be used in administrative decisions. Another problem with this "device" is that, if done right, it would be time consuming and therefore expensive. Nevertheless, it should be considered seriously.

Dressel's final suggestion is to study the growth of students in relation to course objectives. Rarely do instructors specify in detail the things they hope to accomplish. In the absence of a detailed statement of objectives, it is impossible to develop measures capable of producing results that will reveal how well the students have done in achieving the objectives. Words such as "understanding" and "appreciation" are often used in course descriptions, but rarely can one find examination procedures that are even minimally adequate in assessing these abstractions. Involved also is our whole grading system. Most instructors who work with classes enrolling thirty or fewer students learn a great deal about their students, often about their understanding and appreciation. Yet the present grading system requires that they grind up all that they know and present the registrar with a single letter grade. Grades tell us approximately as much about a student's development as an IQ score does about his intellectual status.

Tyler has suggested another approach.[23] On the assumption that first-hand, direct measures (ultimate criterion) are for the moment unavailable, he proposes that we turn to a less direct approach and assess the extent to which the conditions of learning as we now understand them are present (intermediate criterion). We could try to find out what, if anything, the instructor does with respect to motivation. If learning takes place when previous responses have been shown to be unsatisfactory, how does the instructor make this clear to students? One who is learning needs guidance as he tries to select new responses that are adequate, and we could see what the instructor does in this regard. The student needs appropriate materials with which to work; some instructors are more diligent and more imaginative than others in providing them. There must be time to practice new responses, and the amount of time required will vary from one student to another. If new responses are to become effective, satisfaction must be derived from them. Students differ in the kinds and timing of reinforcement to which they respond optimally. If there is an optimum sequence, the student must know it and practice it. Students need to learn to set standards for their own behavior, and to know for themselves when they have accomplished what they set out to do. Some instructors seem to do this well, but others appear to prefer to maintain a relationship of dependency.

One great step forward could be taken immediately. It is the development of adequate devices for measuring student progress toward course objectives. (It can be said that the teachers' examinations *are* the ultimate criterion since the teacher is the one who establishes the goals. To feel comfortable with this, however, teachers' tests stand in need of great improvement.) The tests need not be of any particular type. For some purposes, objective tests are quite adequate. They have the advantages of scoring economy, higher reliability (provided they are well constructed), and wider sampling of areas of information and judgment. They also have distinct limitations. For some purposes, essays are preferable even though they require the time of an expert to score them and, even under the best conditions, possess less reliability. We should also look into various methods for measuring attitudes since we proclaim loudly our concern with them. There *are* ways to assess students' ability to comprehend, to solve problems, to deal with novel issues, and they need to be perfected. The theory and technology of measurement is sufficiently advanced so that all of these things *could* be done *now*.

[23] Tyler, "The Evaluation of Teaching."

At least initially and perhaps permanently, the testing of student progress toward course objectives will require more time than we have been spending on studying outcomes (criteria), and, since time is costly, it will require more money. The entire educational world is going to have to make some hard decisions. Either we continue our present haphazard methods of finding out what students learn and how faculty members contribute to this, or we undertake the very substantial but technically possible steps needed to improve the system in the interests of improved education and more equitable evaluation.

"THERE IS A NEED FOR FURTHER RESEARCH"

It is one of the ineluctable traditions of academia that Ph.D. theses must conclude with a statement—however worded—that although the particular thesis has identified some of the problems and arrived at certain conclusions, there is a need for further research. In the nexus of problems with which this paper has been concerned, there is also a need for further research, a lot of it. Unless we are willing to say that these matters are ineffable and not merely recondite, the traditions of the academic world would seem to require that we go to work as we have thus far not done.

The theoretical and technical problems, awesome though they are, are less a deterrent to our going ahead than is the paradoxical willingness to tolerate a patently inadequate system. No one really doubts that students do learn—some, more than others—but we do not know how much more or how much more effectively they *could* have learned under other conditions. No one doubts that some instructors are more effective than others in assisting students to learn, but we have little more than a body of folklore to guide us in helping instructors do their jobs better and to help us decide how to allocate rewards equitably.

Students can and do learn without the aid of teachers, but they probably learn more and perhaps differently with their assistance. The evaluation of teaching consists in finding out what contribution the teacher makes to what the student learns. If we are to have sounder bases than we now have for administrative decisions, if we are to improve the practice of teaching, and if we are to have a criterion for use in the research which may some day lead us to a viable theory of instruction, we must be able to assess that contribution which the teacher does make to learning.

It is not so much that what we are doing is demonstrably bad. Rather, we are demonstrably ignorant about entirely too much of what we are doing. At least as much as our students, we need to learn which of our teaching practices are appropriate and adequate and which are not so that we can learn to do better. To this end, we need to be able to set standards for our own behavior. We need to do, in short, what we are asking our students to do. But this should not be too much to ask of a profession made up of men and women who have chosen to spend their lives learning.

> *Some are bewilder'd in the maze of schools,*
> *And some made coxcombs nature meant but fools.*
>   *Alexander Pope, Essay on Criticism*

The Evaluation of
Teaching Performance

NEILL MEGAW, BILL J. PRIEST,
JAMES A. JOHNSON, EDWARD JOSEPH SHOBEN, JR.

The Dynamics of Evaluation

NEILL MEGAW

DEAN GUSTAD cannot suppress a certain incredulity. And no wonder. As he says, the past quarter-century has brought "imperceptible progress." And to compare evaluation procedures in 1961 with those in 1966 is to see again that the more things change, the more they remain the same. We have all felt that incredulity: Is it not unaccountable that so many people so openly committed to enlightenment should for so many years put up with such ignorance about a procedure so close to the heart of their common endeavor?

It may be time to stop being surprised, however, for it is really not so strange: We have not made any progress because we do not want to. Many of us have spoken in public of the urgent need to identify and reward good teaching, but a quarter-century of inaction speaks louder than words. I believe this massive resistance will continue until we have honestly faced the human motives behind our common inaction.

Let me attempt a quick sketch of the main faculty motives. First, the ignoble ones: fear and laziness. The nightmarish fear of being declared incompetent, or at least shamefully inexpert, affects only the less-able teacher, but a lighter version, a competitive nervousness about one's ranking in relation to one's rivals, may extend to the highest level of faculty ability. Unheroic feelings, certainly. But understandable, and strong beyond dispute. Why are they so rarely taken into account, then? When a college or university president speaks of the need to evaluate teaching in his institution, how often does he emphasize that the evaluation procedures *must* incorporate safeguards that preclude public humiliation of weaker teachers? How often does he emphasize that there are too many different kinds of good teaching for any numerical ranking of competence, and that the object is not to expose weakness but to study different kinds of effectiveness, reward them, and use them as alternative models by which the less proficient can be helped to become more proficient? Without such emphasis, the administrator may be trying to win general support while threatening the self-respect of half his faculty.

Laziness, though less intense than fear, is more endemic. Not a general, undifferentiated laziness, however—most teachers put in a long working day—but a special laziness of the experimental spirit: reluctance, in short, to consider *new* patterns of overwork. Like fear, this motive is not confined to the academic world, and logic has proved a feeble weapon against it everywhere. You cannot persuade to large new efforts a man who prides himself on a familiar fatigue. Not, that is, unless you provide him with released time and a plan of work for that released time which gives him a clear start in a new direction. These have not often been provided.

No case is being made here for perpetual capitulations to small-mindedness. I have conceded the existence of ignoble faculty motives because I wish to examine next an honorable faculty motive, and I hope to do so without being discounted as an apologist. Also, though I shall not attempt a parallel sketch of administrators' attitudes, I hope you will concede that these two include weakness as well as courage, hypocrisy as well as honesty. As I said at the beginning, there are human reasons for our long inaction; too much righteous indignation about the less attractive of these may very well ensure another quarter-century of failure.

The honorable faculty motive for resisting change is loyalty to the idea that what goes on in the classroom is vastly more complex than any definition of it, and that its chief values reside in this complexity. It is not that our teaching performance is complex beyond description; Dean Gustad's analogy to the physician locates accurately enough the level of complexity, although we are concerned with extending health rather than merely restoring it. It is rather that the ways in which the subject and the student's mind can come together profitably are so many as to make even an elaborate definition of course objectives seem appallingly reductive. Evaluative methods based on an oversimplified list of desiderata not only threaten the teacher himself with shame or strange new efforts, but also they threaten the central values of the educational experience he is devoted to. We would rather have the rich though undefined experience than a definition of it which will then serve as the model for a much reduced experience.

Some of the evaluative methods proposed involve objective measurements. The best of these, the proposal most warmly urged by Dean

Gustad, is that we develop a much more carefully discriminated and internally weighted definition of course objectives, matched with an equally careful measurement of student achievement of those objectives. The logic of beginning here seems impeccable; the catch is that the weighting of secondary, tertiary, and even more remote objectives is so difficult as to ensure that they will be dismissed from consideration. True, the teacher who is planning a new course must, himself, have at least primary objectives in mind; there is no other way to give the course form and select the materials. And he also recognizes that he must satisfy student and institutional needs for some measure of student achievement, and that logically these needs should be related as closely as possible to the course objectives. But what teacher takes this framework seriously, this rickety guesswork skeleton, as the true heart of his course? The real life and substance of the course is what happens all around this wretched synopsis-in-advance. Of course, some gains can be made by improving evaluation procedures, but only provided we do not take them too seriously as indications of the success of that educational experience. When Dean Gustad speaks of this reform as constituting a "great step forward," he seems to suggest that we can work backward from better measurements of the student achievement of these primary, simple objectives to a valid judgment of the teacher's effectiveness in general, and presumably beyond that to a widespread improvement in teaching. As I see it, this train of evaluation places far too much faith in definitions and examining devices, and promises a long wait indeed before the machinery meets with general approval.

I am so deeply skeptical about the potential of objective measurements that I am tempted to find our only hope in subjective measurements: that is, intelligent guesses about a teacher's effectiveness by trained comparative observers in the classroom. But how can one be optimistic here? For this takes us back to that notorious classroom door.

One way to open that door is by force. Most of us would agree that nothing very useful would come of that. The advantages would be whittled away by obstruction or distortion, and heavily counterbalanced by lowered morale. Moreover, if reliable judgments are to be passed, the unwelcome observer would need to return for many visits; these unwelcome visits would be every bit as expensive as observation by a welcome visitor.

The matter of costs is, I think, the key to the classroom door. Once it is fully grasped that an inexpensive system of observation can produce only snap judgments, that the door *cannot to any good effect be opened cheaply*, a possibility emerges. If administrators can see their way clear to a substantial continuing investment in observation to the extent, say, of about 3 percent of the total faculty salary costs, it might be possible to develop a suitable instrument in a specially defined institutional committee on instruction. To ensure faculty confidence in its competence, impartiality, and tact, such a committee would need to be faculty-elected and large enough to provide repeated observations by a number of visitors. (On a rough guess, I arrived at the 3 percent figure by postulating, for a faculty of 300, a committee on instruction with 27 members on one-third released time, for an equivalent of nine full-time salaries, or 3 percent of 300.) To ensure administrative confidence that committee members would not become self-seeking or try to usurp authority for tenure and promotion decisions, such a committee should be clearly separated from the administrative and faculty body responsible for those decisions: that is, the committee on instruction would submit appropriate findings on teaching effectiveness, and these reports would then take their place among other relevant considerations. Such a committee should also have open lines of communication with the students. Finally, though it is unwise to be too specific without knowledge of the local situation, probably such a committee would produce recommendations other than simply those directly involving salaries; its most important suggestions might be for changes of teaching assignments, leaves for refresher studies or for the development of new courses, early or delayed retirement, and changes in the curriculum or in conditions or methods of study at the institution.

If many such committees could be established, would their functioning be enough? It would be a great advance, no doubt; but to think that it would be *enough* might be to fall into the old error of underestimating the resistance. Perhaps what is required for a general improvement of teaching is nothing less than a basic alteration of incentive patterns within higher education. This is a much larger matter, involving public attitudes, government support, changing work patterns, salary scales, academic freedom, and faculty participation in institutional governance. But one alteration of the pattern of incentives could be effected quickly: we could try to give the superior teacher some measure of that professional visibility now enjoyed by the successful publishing scholar. If the good teacher could achieve recognition outside his own institution, much of the publish-or-perish fuss would vanish overnight. One conceivable solution would be to establish a system of disciplinary and regional or even national awards for excellent teaching. The process of selecting candidates at both institutional and higher levels would stimulate an unprecedented discussion of effective teaching.

I have outlined one possibility at the institutional level and one beyond it. Regardless of their specific merits, these give some idea of the scale of action that I believe is necessary if the next quarter-century is not to be as disappointing as the last. Significant common action must not be deferred until we have constructed a theoretical basis for it that wins general acceptance; that would take forever. Rather we must act first in as enlightened a way as we can manage together, trusting that this action will stimulate the continuing discussion needed to strengthen our theoretical grasp on the problem.

We already have a basis for action, some not too imperfect ideas or hunches about what distinguishes effective from ineffective teaching. And we should know by now the two extremes to avoid: on the one hand, the monistic ideal of the Great Teacher, replete with every imaginable human and scholarly virtue, a polymath for all seasons. The other extreme to avoid is the flabby latitudinarianism which says that education is so complex that every kind of teacher is valuable in one way or another—in short, that we are all good fellows. Between these extremes, moreover, we already have in mind at least tentative typologies of different kinds of superior teachers for each of the major disciplines and each kind of institution. Theoretical deficiencies in these working typologies can be repaired as we begin making larger numbers of comparative observations in the classroom. In the meantime, we could do worse than to rely on simple human judgment. The last twenty-five years proves that we can do worse.

Classrooms: Castles or Learning Laboratories

BILL J. PRIEST

THE EVALUATION OF TEACHING performance has fundamental implications for administrative personnel in higher education. Administration at all levels has a responsibility for quality control in education; teaching is the principal avenue through which formal education takes place in any institution; and, therefore, administration must give major attention to attaining and maintaining high-quality instruction.

Education has a product: training that prepares individuals to achieve their general and specific goals. Admittedly, there are differences from other types of production, but the differences do not excuse us from a continuous effort to improve our product. Efforts to improve our product—the quality of instruction—are frustrated by the de-emphasis given to the importance of quality teaching by the very institutions that train faculty for higher education. This de-emphasis of quality teaching is one of the glaring deficiencies in our educational system. Training in teaching methods, skills, and techniques is the exception rather than the rule in university graduate schools which produce prospective faculty. Schools of education are currently in disrepute, and academic cliques are centered on research. They are offended by suggestions that they give formal training in teaching skills, organization, and methods. Presumably instructors learn by observing their research-oriented graduate professors. For men of science, this is an astounding way to learn a profession. Such a system relies only on natural ability, word of mouth, alertness, and incidental experiences that may contribute to good teaching. It assumes there is no organized body of knowledge on the subject worth including in training programs.

With this attitude prevalent among institutions ostensibly producing teachers and among many of the so-called teachers they produce, highly selective recruitment of faculty members becomes the major means for obtaining superior teaching. Recruitment has the potential of getting the proper material to do the job, but having the material still does not assure the quality of production sought.

If an administration is discharging its responsibility, it must assure the maintenance of high-quality instruction through continuous evaluation of the work of faculty members.

A number of issues concerning teacher evaluation are raised frequently by academicians opposed to such evaluation. Some advance the fallacious argument that direct oversight of instruction by qualified personnel is an invasion of professional privacy. Evaluation is an inherent element of any organized effort to achieve a goal. We must submit to and cooperate with rational types of evaluation or be evaluated by ludicrously shoddy means. A large percentage of professors have convinced each other that they are unique and therefore not subject to evaluation. This is sophistry. The argument that teaching is too complex and subjective to be measured, and therefore not an appropriate subject of measurement, is also illegitimate. A large percentage of our measurements in the total order of things are inexact and imperfect, but to conclude that this makes any attempt at measurement improper is ridiculous. The answer is to do as well as we can and work hard toward improvement of measurement techniques. Teaching is too important to be exempted from measurement. Any admission that we cannot differentiate between good teaching and bad teaching is an admission that we are hopelessly confused. The argument that rewarding superior teaching creates ill will and actually reduces over-all teaching effectiveness is true only to the extent that the system accepts and reinforces this myth by submitting to it. If we establish that (1) there will be evaluation, (2) compensation will be geared to superiority as determined by such measurement, and (3) the techniques employed and criteria used will be such and such, we can breach the wall and begin progress toward improving measurement, rather than haggle over whether academicians are "above" this sort of accountability.

There is need in higher education for a segment of personnel who are experts in upgrading teaching. They should be part of the administrative machinery of colleges and universities, and they must recognize the complexity and subjective nature of evaluating the interaction of personalities. The assumption should be made that good professors can be made outstanding, and mediocre ones made good, through group and individual in-service training. Just as research papers now get critical reaction from the best researchers, so should the quality of teaching undergo close scrutiny by qualified kibitzers (for example, a whole series of lectures could be recorded on video-tape and become the basis of a critique by a qualified teacher).

If resistance to upgrading the quality of teaching through evaluation of instruction continues, institutions may resort to having outstanding professors tape lectures, and let teaching machines take it from there. The student-teacher ratio could go to 250:1 in the process of eliminating high teaching costs for low-quality teachers.

If educators are in fact responsible for developing the growing edge on the frontiers of new knowledge, they must include themselves with the rest of mankind, rather than attempt to perpetuate a high priesthood that follows a separate set of rules tailor-made by them and for them.

Instruction: From the Consumer's View

JAMES A. JOHNSON

PROFESSOR GUSTAD'S PAPER on the "Evaluation of Teaching Performance: Issues and Possibilities" is beautiful but also a bit terrifying. It is thoroughly researched, academically sound, and quite concise. But it leaves me, as a student, feeling empty. The rules of the game seem to be set. The players have been selected. The referees have donned their shirts, and the only remaining task is the methodology of recording why some win and some lose. This leaves me quite empty.

To me, there is a flaw in the game which is implicit in this paper. The general assumption, though not completely consistent, is that the process of teaching can be divorced from the process of learning. By what is *not* talked about, Professor Gustad assumes that teaching occurs largely in the classrooms, that most teaching takes the form of lectures, that at least a large part of teaching is concerned with the transfer of knowledge from professor to student, and that the determination of the significance of the material to be presented is decided upon largely by the faculty member teaching the course.

This all leaves little room for change. If all that can be changed in the teaching-learning formula is a few books in the syllabus, some subtleties in class-side manner, and the order of lectures, I see little reason for pursuing the highly complex task of finding an evaluation system for teachers which is *more just* than the one that teachers continually use on their students. Professor Gustad eloquently documents the inadequate present research. But he also speaks with his silence to the real problem in teaching *and learning* in higher education. Professor Gustad, and the vast majority of teachers along with him, are not willing to take the all-important risk. The risk is simply facing the question: What will be the effect of what I am teaching upon students who are trying to learn?

I do not claim to speak for all students, but let me articulate my own philosophy insofar as it pertains to the evaluation of teaching. Students are being treated too much as budding academic specialists and not enough as full human beings who are already making decisions in all spheres of knowledge. Faculty must become more interested in helping students *use* as well as remember knowledge. And students must become more confident that academic learning can be good in itself as well as useful in living. For this to happen, faculty members and students are going to have to sit down—for much longer periods than either anticipate—and talk about the teaching-learning experience. This cannot be done exclusively in student-faculty committees. It must be done in conjunction with every course. The one or two weeks invested each semester in assuring effective communication will pay off in the same way that it does in every other field of human endeavor. If we value higher education, we must value research—applied as well as pure—on what we value. This statement obviously applies to education itself.

No one questions that faculty members know more about their subject matter than students do.

On the other hand, a teacher must often listen to a student to find out whether or not he is learning. As one student from Yale University has recently said:

It is often the individual student who best knows whether or not he is learning.

It is the student who knows best when he cannot understand or already knows what is being discussed.

It is the student who knows when a course is stimulating him to learn more about a subject or whether it is boring him to death.

It is the student who can best formulate those fundamental and personal questions so bothering him that he cannot readily proceed to other academic matters.

It is the student who can best evaluate when he is beginning to integrate the process of learning with the problems he continually confronts in life.

If educators really want to evaluate teaching performance, they must be prepared to deal with the questions implied in the above statements. If they want to find the answers, they must be willing to involve students and encourage honest answers. If they want to improve teaching (and, as students like to say, learning) performance, they must be willing to accept student questions and answers that are not always consistent with the assumptions about teaching in Professor Gustad's paper or in most teaching in colleges and universities today. *Faculty teaching subject matter cannot be confused with students learning subjects that matter.*

Current attempts by students to evaluate courses and teachers do have many of the shortcomings that Professor Gustad points out. With a few notable exceptions, students have also limited themselves to old and, I contend, outdated assumptions about teaching imposed implicitly or explicitly by the faculty. However, on the basis of my experience with the National Student Association and in visits to a large number of campuses in the past year, I question Professor Gustad's statement that there has been a decline in attempts by students to evaluate courses and teachers. Just the opposite: I have witnessed a steady and marked increase. The area of the highest number of requests to the N.S.A.'s Student Government Information Service during 1965–66 was student course and teacher evaluation—more than a hundred. It is my estimate that there are approximately four hundred such programs currently in effect.

This high interest and activity is encouraging to me, but not for the reasons that most faculty and administrators might expect. The existing student programs of course and teacher evaluation are not effectively improving either courses or teachers. The few programs that have been published may help students avoid especially boring or disorganized professors. But no program is significantly influencing decisions on promotion and tenure. Yet student course and teacher evaluation programs are encouraging. They represent the first attempt of students on many campuses to state their intention to force the institution to confront the problems of student learning. And on some campuses, traditional student course and teacher evaluation programs have led students to propound new questions that they have really felt but not formulated, and sometimes have even led them to begin educational experiments of their own.

In conclusion, I would like to stress that the evaluation of teaching performance is crucial to the future of higher education. *But* just as important as continuing to perfect empirical procedures and data collection is a strong effort to open what, unfortunately, seem to be new questions: specifically, how student learning relates to faculty teaching.

There are a number of practical ways in which this exploration might proceed:

First, the hundreds of existing student course and teacher evaluation programs should be encouraged to continue and grow. Sustaining current student interest in their own education is crucial. Such programs should be moved as close as possible to decisions regarding curriculum design and faculty evaluation, for they will not only produce information about student response to decisions, but also encourage broader student interest and participation.

Second, student experiments in building their own courses, as in the free universities, should be strongly encouraged and carefully watched for hints regarding teaching and learning innovations that might facilitate vigorous student response from a broader segment of the student body. The student-run Experimental College at San Francisco State College would be particularly valuable to try to understand.

Third, serious attempts should be made to find audio-visual replacements for many of the information-giving functions teachers now perform. I shudder a bit at this suggestion, not because I think that television and film cannot be as effective as most of the present live lectures, but rather because *I fear that faculty time won by mechanization will not be given to students.* Increasing the number of seminars, tutorials, and other personal student-faculty confrontation is the *only* basis on which I would accept audio-visual teaching.

Fourth, all courses should have formal classes stopped for a week about half way through the semester or quarter. This time should be spent in serious discussions devoted to understanding what the teacher has taught, what students have learned, and how learning might be improved in the rest of the course. It is my hunch that such deliberations will often be so shocking an experience for students and faculty that a trained educator who has had experience in group dynamics will have to come in to facilitate the discussions.

Fifth, there should be more research, but, for the most part, it should be applied rather than pure. The goal of the research should be action rather than analysis. Instead of merely trying to evaluate the teaching and learning experience, the research should be designed to create a number of alternatives that a specific course might use to improve itself.

None of these suggestions calls for additional money, although I am sure an ingenious administrator could find a way to use them to obtain additional financing. What the suggestions *do* call for is an honest commitment to what students have heard educators all say so beautifully: a quality education. The only result that can be expected from continued lip service is millions of students well practiced in the same art. I am sure that is not the quality of education which any of us want, and there are an increasing number of students who will refuse to tolerate it.

Gimmicks and Concepts in the Assessment of Teaching

EDWARD JOSEPH SHOBEN, JR.

AMONG THE MANY POINTS made in Dr. Gustad's provocative review of the issues bound up with the evaluation of college teaching, three related concerns seem to call especially for italics. These concerns have to do with the role of psychometric concepts and procedures in the assessment of teaching performance, the utility of various evaluative devices in attempts to improve instruction, and the remarkable lack not only of any comprehensive theory of teaching but also of any definitional conception of it that gives unity and meaning to our realm of discourse.

The most significant member of this rather unholy trinity, of course, is the last. Although it is beyond doubt that men have somehow taught one another ever since the primate brain acquired the propensity for speech, and although the psychology of learning (in contrast to teaching) has achieved a high degree of elegance and at least a significant level of power, there has been little investment of conceptual thought in the teaching process itself. One need not take the extreme position that theoretical clarity is an absolute prerequisite to adequate measurement to be worried about this state of affairs. Indeed, our experience with electricity in physics and with intelligence in psychology argues persuasively to the contrary. Neither electricity nor intelligence has yet been defined with anything like desirable precision, but both can be evaluated in ways that are extremely useful in a variety of both theoretical and practical contexts. Nevertheless, in the domains of our examples, there have at least been some guiding ideas and some basic operations that have facilitated the development of units and techniques of measurement that have proved their value. Little, if anything, in the way of comparably influential notions seems to have grown up around the complex act of teaching. It seems to be one of those things the nature of which everybody "knows" but nobody can articulate.

One suspects that this lack of conceptual riches is not irrelevant to the fact that teaching—at the college level, at any rate—is simply not a very interesting topic. It is probable that the problems of teaching take up very little time in faculty conversations or in the meditations of professors as they contemplate their instructional responsibilities. The logic of their disciplines certainly does. It may be that the matter of dramatics —how to open sleepy eyes, draw nods of assent, provoke laughter, and so on—also does. In the one case, there is a web of intriguing issues having to do with the very business of the trained scholar. In the other, there is the immediate feedback of a live audience. But neither a logical organization of subject matter nor an excited or attentive classroom defines teaching; that is, neither is in itself a demonstration that students have been helped to learn what the teacher wanted them to learn.

Another way of making this point is to suggest that students can learn to come willingly or unwillingly to an instructor's class, but not to do well on his examinations. They can learn that he is a witty and informed person, but not to become fascinated with his subject. They can learn to memorize what he says when he inflects his voice in a particular fashion, but not to generate the strings of logically related propositions that he does. And because the issue of what he does in the classroom that promotes these myriad learnings that he has *not* intended is both personally threatening and conceptually uninteresting, he is not likely to give much attention to it. (The fact that the rewards for his doing so are also unlikely to be very significant is relevant here, too, but that is another story.)

Can the notion, then, of teaching as an aid to the accomplishment in others of predetermined learning yield much nutriment when analyzed conceptually? At the very least, it suggests that the *predetermination* of the learning to take place is crucial. Whether it involves the correct spelling of *mischievous*, the discovery that the joys of *King Lear* are somewhat more durable than those of *Batman*, or a growing sense of the relevance of intellect to the solution of human problems, the act of teaching requires the establishment and communication *in advance* of the necessary outcomes in student response. It follows that both the processes of learning and the means of evaluating it must be geared specifically to those outcomes. The assessment of a teacher's performance, therefore, must be attentive to such matters as the clarity with which goals are initially outlined and the congruity of fit between those goals and both the requirements laid down for students and the nature of the examinations by which the mastery of those requirements is measured. It undoubtedly makes a difference whether one goes to the professor himself, his colleagues, or his students for the evidence here, but evidence germane to this *idea* seems important. If we are still a long way from a theory of teaching, we have at least begun an analysis of the teaching act in terms of its conceptually significant features and their entailments; and this analytic enterprise is likely to interact profitably with our efforts at faculty evaluation, both enlarging the scope and precision of our analysis and giving greater cogency to our direct observations, rating devices, and questionnaires.

This argument—the total character and implications of which have only been hinted at here—brings us to our second point for italicization. Almost two-thirds of Dr. Gustad's presentation deals accurately and insightfully with the techniques and principles of measurement. Sophistication in this arena is of vital importance, and the niceties of psychometric methods are too infrequently considered when vital decisions are made on our campuses. Nevertheless, they are not a path to salvation, and they can become subtle barriers to the effective consideration of prior or at least concomitant issues. The jargon of the computer engineers is happily applicable. Their term GIGO, referring to the processing of information, translates as "garbage in, garbage out" and means simply that if inadequate information is fed into a computer, the machine feeds out comparably inadequate answers. The same principle holds in the present discussion: Methodological excellence, while never irrelevant, is no substitute for either conceptual cohesiveness or conceptual range; procedural precision, while always of merit, never successfully replaces thought. For instance, a questionnaire or rating scale which reliably and validly appraises lecturing is probably quite irrelevant to a course in which the primary goal is increased skill in critical thinking about literary issues or greater inventiveness in the solution of engineering problems. Because neither critical thinking nor creativity is a spectator sport, the oratorical brilliance of the professor is likely to be quite subordinate to his skill in managing situations in which students can find some graded and guided experience in the exercise of these capacities. If there is to be meaning in our *assessments* of teaching, then there must be meaning in our *conceptions* of teaching.

Here we come to our third point. Given the present state of the teaching arts, the issues bound up with the improvement of college teaching may be a little like those reflected in the Queries of the Quaker persuasion. It is not important that they be settled soon, but it is fatal to stop thinking about them. One purpose of faculty evaluations—the provision of information on which to base improved performance—is certainly an attractive one, but one that may be better fulfilled obliquely than directly. If a professor is bluntly rated as a less than satisfactory instructor, his guides to improvement are hardly well specified; if he is charged with having a weak voice or an unusual manner of dress, he is likely to dismiss the whole appraisal as trivial; and if he is characterized as giving overly difficult examinations, he can understandably respond by believing that such comments reflect more of a student disposition toward lotus-eating than toward responsible judgment. But if the machinery of evaluation is based on and stimulates analytic ideas about the teaching act, its various aims, and the multiple styles by which it can be effectively performed, then his interest may be caught; he may begin to talk seriously and analytically with colleagues about the mysterious enterprise in which they are together engaged, and teaching may become a "thought about" and intellectually respectable aspect of university life. Until it is, it seems improbable that a busy scholar will invest much of his energy in improving it—whatever "improving it" may mean.

Obviously, there are many other considerations that must be taken into account here, and the three points italicized in this brief discussion have been brushed over far too lightly. Nevertheless, there may be some utility in opening the large box of questions associated with this trio of somewhat tendentious propositions: (1) The lack of any significant conceptual framework within which to set the problem of teaching makes teaching hard to evaluate, difficult to improve, and a little dull to discuss. The encouragement of some analytic thought may be quite valuable on this score as precursor, concomitant, and consequence of assessment efforts. (2) While psychometric elegance never demands apologies, there are some times when it is more cogent than at others. With respect to the evaluation of teaching performance, the warning implied by the computer-argot word *GIGO* is well worth heeding. (3) Conceivably, our goals of improved teaching may, perhaps, be attained more readily if they are sought as by-products of an effort to reformulate teaching as an intellectually interesting problem, worth the time of men who devote themselves professionally to difficult but significant conceptual affairs.

Current Practices in the Evaluation and Training of College Teachers

ALEXANDER W. ASTIN AND CALVIN B. T. LEE

THE CURRENT NEGLECT of undergraduate teaching has frequently been blamed on the professor's growing need to achieve professional visibility through publication. The increased pressures to publish, however, have also served to exacerbate a more fundamental problem: the lack of appropriate techniques for evaluating the professor's teaching ability. Although it is generally agreed that better evaluative techniques are needed, very little is known about just what techniques are now being used and to what extent. Until we learn more about the current state of the art, it is unlikely that we can significantly improve it.

In the spring of 1966, the American Council on Education initiated a survey to ascertain current techniques for the evaluation of undergraduate instruction. Its major purposes were, first, to provide an empirical basis for a critical appraisal of current practices, and, second, to serve as a point of departure from which proposals for improving existing techniques could be developed. In this report we shall present a detailed analysis of the major results of this survey.

METHOD

Sample of institutions

In order to ensure the widest possible coverage, the entire population of higher educational institutions, as listed in Part 3 of the U.S. Office of Education *Directory*,[1] was selected for study. At the two-year and four-year undergraduate colleges, the academic dean (or his equivalent) was selected to receive the survey. At the universities, the survey was sent to the dean of each of the following undergraduate col-

---

[1] Washington: Government Printing Office, 1965.

leges or schools: arts and sciences, education, engineering, business, and agriculture.

The questionnaire

The questionnaire was designed to obtain information in three general areas: the frequency with which various sources of information are used in judging a professor's teaching ability; techniques used for training new college teachers; and the importance of classroom teaching relative to other factors (such as publication, committee work, community service, and so forth) in the over-all evaluation of faculty members for promotions, salary increases, or tenure. Each respondent was also asked to enclose copies of rating forms or other instruments routinely used to obtain information about teaching ability, and copies of any studies, published or unpublished, that investigated the validity of these instruments. Each item concerning techniques for evaluation of teaching performance or for training college teachers was answered on a four-point scale: "used in all or most departments" (4), "used in some departments" (3), "used in a few departments" (2), or "not used" (1). Items dealing with criteria for decisions on salary, promotion, and tenure were answered on a three-point scale: "a major factor" (3), "a minor factor" (2), or "not used" (1). Respondents could also check a "not applicable" alternative for each item on this list.

Approximately 1,250 completed questionnaires had been returned to the Council by the time the analysis was begun in late May 1966. Of these, some 140 were eliminated from the analysis primarily because the respondent had not given sufficient information to identify which particular institution or school within the university was involved. The number of usable questionnaires from each type of college or school was as follows: junior colleges (128), teachers colleges (133), liberal arts colleges (484); and, within the complex universities, colleges of arts and sciences (110), of education (48), of engineering (109), of business (65), and of agriculture (33).

In this report we shall be concerned primarily with analyzing the data on current methods for training college teachers and for evaluating their classroom performance. A separate analysis of devices used by students to rate the effectiveness of college teachers has also been made.[2]

EVALUATION OF TEACHING EFFECTIVENESS

Most institutions claim that teaching effectiveness is a major factor in determining a faculty member's value to the institution: just what kind of information is being used to assess this effectiveness? As shown

---

[2] See companion article in this volume, Laura Kent, "Student Evaluation of Teaching," pp. 312–43.

in Table 1, the most frequently used of 15 sources of information are evaluations by the dean and the department chairman. Next in order, though used much less frequently, come the opinions of colleagues, the teacher's scholarly research and publications, and the informal opinions of students. These various sources of information are not

TABLE 1: *Frequency of Use of Various Sources of Information in the Evaluation of Teaching Effectiveness*

Source of Information	Used in All or Most Departments (%)	Not Used (%)
Chairman evaluation	85.1	3.4
Dean evaluation	82.3	5.8
Colleagues' opinions	48.9	8.7
Scholarly research and publications	43.8	21.6
Informal student opinions	41.2	9.6
Grade distributions	28.0	37.4
Course syllabi and examinations	26.4	28.0
Committee evaluation	25.1	52.4
Student examination performance	19.6	35.8
Self-evaluation or report	16.3	57.2
Classroom visits	14.0	39.5
Systematic student ratings	12.4	47.6
Enrollment in elective courses	11.0	49.9
Long-term follow-up of students	10.2	47.1
Alumni opinions	9.9	46.8

Source: Completed questionnaires from 1,110 academic deans.

independent, however. Since classroom visits are used very infrequently —are, indeed, taboo at 39.5 percent of the institutions, apparently—it follows that, even though the dean, the department chairman, and professional colleagues have the final say about a professor's teaching ability, their evaluations must be based on the opinions of others. Thus these final judgments must depend on hearsay evidence—informal student opinions. Of the institutions polled, only 9.6 percent said that informal student opinions were not used, whereas 47.6 percent indicated that they did not use *systematic* student ratings.

It is clear from the data in Table 1 that the professor's scholarly research and publication—not information based on classroom visits, systematic student ratings, student performance on examinations, and similar sources—are currently the primary considerations in evaluating his *teaching* ability. Although teaching effectiveness is talked about as though it were assessed independently of other factors, the heavy reliance on scholarly productivity as an indication of teaching ability greatly confuses the distinction between teaching and research and exaggerates the importance of research and publication. Given the interdiction against classroom visits, it may be justifiable to judge a professor's teaching on the basis of his publications, if they actually offer insights into his teaching ability. His presentation of new ideas and new research may manifest a vital concern with his subject matter and an ability to transmit his enthusiasm to a class. A clear, intelligent, and graceful literary style may reflect a similar style in the classroom. But it should be emphasized that this reliance on writing and research in judging teaching ability has an obfuscating effect: the evaluation of research overflows into the assessment of teaching, thus muddling the criteria for the latter. And it is obvious that not all textbooks, monographs, journal articles, books, and book reviews do provide trustworthy clues about teaching ability.

If the ultimate measure of the teacher's effectiveness is his impact on the student—a view which few educators would dispute—it is unfortunate that those sources of information most likely to yield information about this influence are least likely to be used. Carefully planned systematic student questionnaires offer an insight into the impact on the learner. Grade distributions can be significant in multisection courses with departmental examinations, if the instructor is made aware of the specific educational objectives of the course and if student performance is matched with indices of ability.

Results by type of college

Table 2 shows how frequently each source of information was used by each of the eight different types of undergraduate schools. One striking similarity is that all eight types rank chairman evaluation and dean evaluation as being either first or second, although junior colleges use chairman evaluation much less frequently than do other types. Junior colleges in other respects too are atypical in the methods they use for obtaining information about teaching effectiveness. Compared to the other seven types of undergraduate institutions, they rely more heavily on classroom visits, grade distributions, and long-term follow-up of students. (The latter emphasis may reflect the concern of the junior colleges with the transfer problem.) Although research ranks no lower than fifth in frequency of use at the other seven types of colleges, it ranks fifteenth (last) in the junior colleges.

With few exceptions, the five undergraduate colleges within the university show similar patterns of reliance on the various sources of information. Scholarly research and publication are a close third in order of importance (behind evaluations by chairmen and deans) for all five types, followed by the opinions of colleagues and informal student opinions. Classroom visits and long-term follow-up of students are uniformly low in order of importance.

Comparing the liberal arts colleges with the arts and sciences colleges of the universities, we find that the rank order patterns are fairly similar, but differences in the frequency of use of certain methods are apparent. It is significant, for instance, that while only 36.6 percent of

TABLE 2: *Frequency with Which Various Sources of Evaluative Information Are Used in Different Types of Institutions*

| | | | | Percent Reporting Use in All or Most Departments | | | | |
| | | | | University Colleges | | | | |
Source of Information	Junior Colleges (N=128)	Teachers Colleges (N=133)	Liberal Arts Colleges (N=484)	Arts and Sciences (N=110)	Education (N=48)	Engineering (N=109)	Business (N=65)	Agriculture (N=33)
Grade distributions	30.6	27.7	36.0	15.5	9.3	18.5	19.4	15.3
Classroom visits	42.2	25.8	9.8	2.0	4.4	8.7	5.2	3.0
Long-term follow-up of students	26.1	6.2	9.9	1.0	9.1	13.5	1.6	9.4
Scholarly research and publication	4.2	34.1	36.6	70.0	63.8	72.9	75.0	56.3
Chairman evaluation	65.8	89.6	82.2	98.2	91.3	92.7	88.7	93.9
Dean evaluation	82.7	80.5	83.5	71.8	91.7	80.4	89.1	84.4
Colleagues' opinions	29.2	34.9	50.6	62.0	48.9	53.8	71.9	46.9
Committee evaluation	15.7	17.3	28.9	30.8	28.9	23.3	30.0	6.3
Student examination performance	21.6	16.2	24.7	12.9	4.6	15.5	20.0	9.4
Systematic student ratings	16.1	4.9	11.2	11.3	13.0	14.0	20.6	26.5
Informal student opinions	33.6	28.0	47.2	35.0	48.9	42.5	47.6	28.1
Course syllabi and examinations	37.0	28.6	29.4	5.9	11.1	22.8	22.6	39.4
Enrollment in elective courses	6.8	7.8	14.0	11.5	2.3	8.8	14.8	3.2
Alumni opinions	8.2	8.7	11.2	2.9	2.3	13.3	16.7	9.4
Self-evaluation or report	22.3	14.8	15.4	11.0	27.3	11.9	26.3	12.9

300

the liberal arts colleges report that all or most departments use research and publication as an indicator of teaching effectiveness, 70 percent of the arts and sciences colleges regularly utilize such data. This emphasis at the arts and sciences colleges is even more striking when one realizes that no other source of information, except for opinions of the department chairman and of the dean, is used more frequently there. In the liberal arts colleges, informal student opinion is used to evaluate classroom teaching more frequently than is research and publication (47.2 versus 36.6 respectively), whereas university colleges of arts and sciences use informal student opinion only half as frequently as they use research and publication.

It is apparent that liberal arts colleges make a greater attempt to obtain information which will help them assess teaching, as is evidenced by the more even spread of the various lower-ranked sources of information used. They draw on grade distributions, classroom visits, student examination performance, course syllabi and examinations, and alumni opinions two to five times more frequently than do arts and sciences colleges.

Some surprising differences between the teachers colleges and the schools of education of the universities were discovered. Information from informal student opinions, self-evaluation, and committee evaluation is relied on more heavily at the university schools of education than at the teachers colleges; this finding is directly opposed to the results obtained in comparing arts and sciences colleges with liberal arts colleges. On the other hand, data on grade distributions, classroom visits, student examination performance, and course syllabi and examinations are used more at the teachers colleges. The pattern of use of scholarly research and publication in judging teaching effectiveness is comparable to that found in the comparison between the liberal arts college and the arts and sciences colleges, the university using this criterion much more frequently.

It is interesting to speculate on why the instructional staffs in the junior college and the teachers college tend to be more receptive than the staffs of other types of institutions to direct observation. Perhaps these institutions reflect a different kind of administrative philosophy or a different relationship between the administration and the teaching staff; whatever its cause, this characteristic raises questions worth exploring.

Other institutional characteristics

An additional series of analyses were performed to identify other institutional characteristics which might be correlated with various techniques used to evaluate teaching effectiveness. The institutional characteristics considered were selectivity, size, per-student expenditures, and certain categorical variables such as type of control and geographic region.[3] In order to control for the differences among institutional types reported in Table 2, this analysis was limited to liberal arts colleges and university colleges of arts and sciences. The institution's score (1–4) on each item concerning sources of information used in evaluating teaching was then correlated with each institutional characteristic.

Although many of the obtained correlations were statistically significant, the coefficients were uniformly small. (In view of the large amount of error usually associated with having only one person at an institution respond to single judgmental items of the kind used in the questionnaire, this result was to be expected.) The most consistent pattern of relationships was obtained with measures of institutional prestige or affluence: selectivity, per-student expenditures, and the intelligence and socioeconomic status of the entering students. The results for one of these measures, institutional selectivity, are shown in Table 3.

TABLE 3: *Correlations between Institutional Selectivity and the Use of Different Sources of Information for Evaluating Teaching Effectiveness*

Source of Information	Correlations between Selectivity and Use of Source	
	Liberal Arts Colleges (N = 414)	University Colleges of Arts and Sciences (N = 109)
Enrollment in elective courses	.17[a]	.23[b]
Colleagues' opinions	.28[a]	.13
Committee evaluation	.24[a]	.08
Scholarly research	.32[a]	−.03
Grade distributions	−.26[a]	−.17
Student examination performance	−.21[a]	−.18
Course syllabi	−.17[a]	−.17
Student follow-up	−.11[b]	−.18
Self-evaluation	−.07	−.23[b]

Note: Positive correlation coefficients indicate that the more selective institutions tend to use the source more often than do the less selective institutions. Negative correlation coefficients indicate that the less selective institutions tend to use the source more often. Data on selectivity were not available for 70 liberal arts colleges and one university college of arts and sciences.
[a] $p < .05$.
[b] $p < .01$.

The patterns of relationships within the two groups of colleges are very similar, although the correlations within the liberal arts colleges more frequently reach statistical significance because of the larger number of institutions involved. These correlations indicate that, in evaluating the teaching ability of its faculty, the highly selective college is more

[3] For a fuller discussion of these variables and of how data on them were obtained for institutions, see Alexander W. Astin, *Who Goes Where to College* (Chicago: Science Research Associates, 1965), particularly pp. 21–26.

likely than the less selective college to rely on scholarly research and publication, colleagues' opinions, committee evaluation, and enrollment in elective courses. The less selective college, on the other hand, is more likely to rely on student examination performance, student follow-ups, grade distributions, course syllabi, and self-evaluation. In many respects the differences in practices between the most and the least selective colleges resemble the differences found earlier between colleges and universities (see Table 2). A major exception is the use of classroom observation, which was not significantly related to selectivity within either the liberal arts colleges or the university colleges of arts and sciences.

Several other results from these correlational analyses should be mentioned. For instance, institutional size was positively related to the use both of the chairman's evaluation and of committee evaluations; it was negatively related to the use of the dean's evaluation. Thus, the larger the institution, the greater the reliance placed on the judgment of department chairman and of committees in assessing teaching effectiveness. These results are consistent with the differences noted earlier (Table 2) between the colleges and the (presumably larger) universities. Somewhat surprisingly, institutional size was also found to be positively related to the use of classroom visits within both the liberal arts colleges and the university colleges of arts and sciences. This finding is not consistent with the data in Table 2, which suggests a negative relationship between size and the use of classroom visits within the entire sample of institutions.

Criteria for salary, promotion, and tenure

In considering a faculty member for promotion in rank, salary increase, or tenure, institutions take a number of elements into account, of course. The respondents to the survey were asked to check whether each of 13 criteria was "a major factor," "a minor factor," "not a factor," or "not applicable." Table 4 summarizes the relative importance of these criteria. It would seem that classroom teaching is the most important since it was considered to be a "major factor" by over 90 percent of the respondents in all eight types of schools and ranked highest of the 13 factors. Yet, a more careful analysis of the university colleges, particularly those of arts and sciences and agriculture, indicates that the consideration of research is practically equal to that of teaching. Indeed, the difference between classroom teaching and research as major factors in the case of the arts and sciences colleges is only .9 percentage points as compared to the liberal arts colleges where the gap between the significance of classroom teaching and the second-ranking major factor—personal attributes—is greater than 30 percentage

TABLE 4: *Importance of Various Factors in Evaluating Faculty for Promotion, Salary, or Tenure*

Source of Information	All Colleges (N=1,110)	Junior Colleges (N=128)	Teachers Colleges (N=133)	Liberal Arts Colleges (N=484)	Percentage of Deans Checking Item as a "Major Factor" University Colleges				
					Arts and Sciences (N=110)	Education (N=48)	Engineering (N=109)	Business (N=65)	Agriculture (N=33)
Classroom teaching	95.9	98.2	94.0	97.6	93.6	91.7	93.7	95.3	93.8
Personal attributes	56.8	69.2	53.8	61.3	33.7	46.8	53.9	50.0	70.0
Length of service in rank	47.4	63.3	47.4	59.9	21.3	33.3	24.3	18.8	46.9
Research	46.6	1.0	27.1	31.7	92.7	79.2	82.0	84.4	87.5
Supervision of graduate study[a]	40.8	—	16.0	17.8	55.2	52.2	59.6	38.7	61.3
Publication	39.9	1.0	22.0	24.5	83.3	70.8	70.9	82.8	80.7
Student advising	39.5	42.5	37.7	46.8	20.2	38.3	29.6	22.2	62.5
Campus committee work	29.2	41.5	35.6	32.6	15.7	21.3	13.9	21.9	34.4
Activity in professional societies	25.3	18.3	28.2	23.9	19.8	33.3	28.4	35.9	31.3
Public service	20.5	15.7	22.0	16.1	23.2	48.9	14.8	29.7	43.8
Competing job offers	13.2	3.1	10.9	9.8	31.1	10.4	16.8	15.6	31.3
Supervision of honors program[a]	12.4	4.3	2.5	14.3	21.7	3.2	11.5	10.3	12.5
Outside consulting	5.3	4.0	12.3	2.4	2.8	17.4	5.7	6.4	9.4

[a] Percentages are actually based on considerably smaller N's because of the relatively high number of deans who checked "not applicable."

points. Thus classroom teaching looms over all other criteria at the colleges, but its relative weight is more subject to counterbalancing factors at the university colleges.

As would be expected, the two items, research and publication, produced by far the largest differences between the colleges and the universities. For each of the five university colleges, research and publication rank second and third, respectively, in importance behind classroom teaching. They rank much lower in order of importance in the colleges, particularly in the junior colleges, where they are ranked lowest of all the factors. The second- and third-ranking order of major factors for junior colleges, teachers colleges, and liberal arts colleges are personal attributes and length of service. Other factors which seem to be more important in the colleges than in the universities include student advising and campus committee work.

A series of correlational analyses were performed to discover relationships between the criteria listed in Table 4 and measures of some of the college characteristics mentioned previously. Again, these correlations were computed only for the liberal arts colleges and the university colleges of arts and sciences. The results of these analyses revealed a pattern of relationships similar to those found in the previous correlational analysis, involving various measures of institutional affluence and prestige. Specifically, the more selective and wealthier colleges are more likely to use the professor's research and publications as a basis for deciding questions of salary, promotion, and tenure. Conversely, the less affluent university colleges (but not the liberal arts colleges) depend more on outside consulting, membership in professional societies, and student advising. The wealthier institutions also tend to place a relatively high value on supervision of graduate students, although the relationships were not consistent for all measures of affluence.

A similar pattern of relationships was found in the case of institutional size, with the larger institutions valuing research, publications, and supervision of graduate students more than the smaller institutions. Protestant-affiliated institutions (colleges and universities alike) do not tend to emphasize these activities, although it should be noted that the institutions in this category tend to be somewhat smaller and less affluent than Catholic and nonsectarian institutions.

Formal methods for training newly hired faculty members

Little attention seems to be paid to training new faculty for classroom teaching. Most institutions have preregistration orientation sessions, but other methods for supervising or training new faculty are little used (Table 5).

TABLE 5: *Formal Methods for Training Newly Hired Faculty Members*

| | | | | | Percentage Reporting Use of Method in All or Most Departments | | | | |
| | | | | | University Colleges | | | | |
Method	All Colleges (N=1,110)	Junior Colleges (N=128)	Teachers Colleges (N=133)	Liberal Arts Colleges (N=484)	Arts and Sciences (N=110)	Education (N=48)	Engineering (N=109)	Business (N=65)	Agriculture (N=33)
Preregistration orientation sessions.	68.2	90.4	79.8	74.8	45.2	51.1	43.6	49.2	53.1
Seminars for new college teachers given by the institution.	32.2	48.7	44.4	40.0	19.6	15.9	20.6	27.1	33.3
Supervision of new college teachers by an assigned or designated member of the faculty.	26.0	44.4	30.9	25.9	10.6	8.7	27.2	23.0	19.4
Seminars for new college teachers given by the department.	13.4	29.1	22.1	10.6	6.9	12.8	10.9	6.9	3.0
Summer institutes or other such intensive programs for new college teachers.	1.3	1.9	1.6	1.2	2.1	0.0	1.0	0.0	3.0

Supervision of new college teachers by a designated member of the faculty is a method used only by 10.6 percent of the arts and sciences colleges as compared to 25.9 percent of the liberal arts colleges. Within the university colleges, the schools of engineering and business use this method twice as much as do arts and sciences colleges. At all types of institutions, departments do little about giving seminars for new teachers, and, similarly, summer institutes and other such intensive programs are very rare.

CONCLUSION

The uniformly high importance assigned to classroom teaching by some 1,110 deans in junior colleges, teachers colleges, liberal arts colleges, and universities could be interpreted to mean that the so-called neglect of undergraduate teaching is more a myth than a reality. However, in light of the data about how teaching effectiveness is actually evaluated, the apparent over-all importance assigned to classroom teaching is not as reassuring as it at first appears to be. Citing "classroom teaching" as a "major factor" in personnel decisions does not encourage improved teaching as long as teaching ability is more likely to be evaluated on the basis of scholarly research and publication rather than information more directly relevant to effective performance in the classroom. It is clear from this survey that deans and chairmen are overwhelmingly important as the sources of information about teaching effectiveness. If they wish to strike a balance between classroom teaching and scholarly research and publication, they must find ways to avoid using the latter to prove the former.

It is not our purpose to advocate one set of criteria for promotion over another. Rather, we would simply point out what the survey makes clear: that currently most institutions, unwittingly perhaps, engage in evaluation practices which, because they emphasize other academic activities, stand in the way of improving undergraduate teaching. It is obvious that institutions suffer from an inability to evaluate classroom effectiveness. Undergraduate teaching will continue to be neglected until those who evaluate, recognize, and reward the faculty find methods of accurately assessing teaching effectiveness. Only then will the high importance assigned to undergraduate teaching be more than a matter of lip service.

Appendix: Outstanding Teacher Awards

A total of 36.1 percent of the respondents to the survey replied that their institutions gave an outstanding teacher award. The university colleges tended to use this form of recognition much more than did the teachers colleges or liberal arts colleges, and the junior colleges ranked last (see Table 6).

TABLE 6: *Percentage of Schools Having Outstanding Teacher Awards* [a]

Junior colleges	13.3
Teachers colleges	26.3
Liberal arts colleges	29.8
Universities:	
1. Arts and sciences	62.3
2. Education	52.1
3. Engineering	55.1
4. Business	61.9
5. Agriculture	72.7
Total	36.1

[a] Based on completed questionnaires from 1,110 academic deans.

Types of awards

The nature of the awards varied greatly. Cash prizes ranged from $100 to $4,000, with a sizable number giving $1,000. The most generous award was a year's leave with pay. Gold watches, plaques, scrolls, and medals were sometimes given along with the cash prizes. One institution reported that it gave its annual recipient a plaque and, through a special fund, his choice of $200 worth of books for the college library, each containing the note that they were purchased in his honor as professor of the year. Student recognition usually took the form of designating, through a student poll, the "Best Teacher," "Man of the Year," "Professor of Greatest Influence on Students," "Outstanding Teacher," "Professor of the Year," and "Top Prof." Several schools recognized their outstanding teachers by naming them as university lecturer of the year, by asking them to speak at convocation or some other occasion, or by honoring them at commencement.

The manner of selection varied so much that it is not possible to make any generalization except that most of the respondents indicated that students were involved in the process; selection by faculty ranked next, then selection by administration, and finally selection by alumni. The following indicates the many methods used.

Selection procedures primarily involving students

STUDENT POLLS

1. Student poll of the entire college, the senior class, or upper classmen (sometimes including recent graduates).

2. Student poll for top group from which the president, deans, or a faculty committee (with or without students) select one.

3. Nominations by students or students and alumni, and selection of recipient by members of faculty.

STUDENT GROUPS

1. Election by student government, student national education association, members of honorary scholastic society, and interfraternity council.

2. Selection by student leaders in consultation with deans.

3. Nominations by student group, screened by special faculty committee, and final choice by president or university council.

4. Nomination of a group by the faculty, and final selection by student government.

SPECIAL COMMITTEE

1. Nominations of three teachers by all faculty members and two or three students from each major curricular area. Final selection made by the college administration.

2. Nominations of three or more faculty members by a select student group; review of nominations by the administrative staff. Final selection made by a visitor from another institution who observes the nominees in the classroom.

3. Secret committee that solicits opinions of graduating seniors and of faculty.

Selection by special student-faculty-administration committees

STUDENT-FACULTY

1. Selection by student-faculty committee sometimes acting on nominations from alumni, students, or faculty.

2. Nominations by faculty, students, or alumni. Final selection by committee appointed by the faculty senate.

3. Questionnaire ballot to three groups: (a) faculty, (b) dean's list students, and (c) equal number of random sample of students.

4. Nomination by faculty or students, accompanied by explanations, student evaluations, or other evidence on which a committee of faculty members bases final selection.

STUDENT-FACULTY-ADMINISTRATION

1. Committee of students, faculty, and administrators.

2. Screening by committee of faculty and students, and final selection by committee of administrators.

3. Nomination of three candidates by a committee of deans, former recipients of the award, plus an equivalent number of seniors. An outside dean visits each nominee and reports his selection of the one to receive the award.

4. Recipients chosen based on recommendations by alumni, students, department heads, and faculty colleagues. Final decision made by a committee composed of representatives of administration, alumni association, or faculty.

5. Nominations by seniors, faculty, or trustees. Selection by committee composed of three trustees, two senior students, dean of faculty, and one recent recipient of award. College president and chairman of the board serve as *ex officio* members.

6. Nominations by department, student clubs, and/or department chairman, with chairman contributing documentation supplemented by the dean from his files on student evaluation of instruction. Nominations evaluated and recipient named by a committee composed of dean, honor society representative, a senior, a faculty member, and last year's award recipient.

7. Nominations from faculty, students, and alumni evaluated by a student senate committee of undergraduate and graduate students. Names of twenty

or thirty nominees sent to a president-appointed five-member faculty committee which makes the final selection of recipients of the awards.

8. Three nominations made by each of four undergraduate student councils; two nominations from each of four executive committees of the undergraduate colleges; one nomination each from the dean of instruction and the dean of graduate studies. Selection made by a nine-man committee composed of a chairman appointed by the president, one member appointed by each of six deans, and two members appointed by the president of the alumni association.

Procedures primarily involving faculty

1. Vote of academic senate, faculty committee, or a special faculty committee composed of former winners.

2. Nomination by faculty personnel committee on basis of information from student evaluations, department chairmen evaluations, self-evaluations, and so forth. Selection is based on recommendation of dean and approval of president.

3. Nominations by entire faculty; president chooses one from top three.

4. Recommendation by self or other member of staff. Selection by committee of seven: president, dean, and five faculty members who are selected to serve on committee by the faculty senate.

Procedures primarily involving administrators

1. Selection by president on basis of conference with the dean, suggestions from faculty, and consultation with a representative cross section of students.

2. Selection by faculty committee appointed by dean or president.

3. Recommendations submitted by the heads of departments to the dean, who, on the basis of the nominations by heads of departments, makes recommendations to the president.

4. Selection by a committee of past recipients, dean, president, and departmental chairmen.

5. Selection by anonymous president-appointed committee of (a) regular faculty member and (b) outstanding graduate assistant for teacher awards. Committee may use any source of information it wishes to: evaluations and recommendations by dean or department chairmen, classroom observation, student polls, student performance in advanced courses, and so forth.

6. Selection by committee of the board of directors in consultation with the president.

Selection procedures primarily involving alumni

1. Alumni survey: coupon sent in from alumni magazine annually. Sometimes candidates nominated by a committee of faculty and alumni.

2. Selection by a committee of alumni, with the assistance of the dean or president.

3. Nomination by any faculty member or alumnus; selection by a secret committee composed of faculty and alumni.

4. Selection by committee appointed by the alumni association; committee bases its choice on nominating letters which it has appealed for from students and alumni.

5. Selection by administration-faculty-alumni committee based on nominations from department heads, faculty members, or students.

6. Nominations from departments and from student organizations and selection by a special alumni committee which may include faculty or student members.

Student Evaluation
of Teaching

LAURA KENT

O~N~ June 15, 1965, an *ad hoc* faculty committee transmitted to the Executive Committee of the Faculty of Arts and Sciences of Yale University a report on the subject of policies and procedures on tenure appointments, emphasizing in particular the role of teaching in tenure decisions and, with the reproductive instinct that committees share with lesser forms of life, recommending that another faculty committee be appointed to study the question of how to evaluate teaching. Although not opposed to the idea of having the individual teacher use student evaluations for his own self-improvement, the *ad hoc* committee felt that using such evaluations as a basis for tenure and promotion decisions "almost certainly would be useless or even vicious." In its reply, the Executive Committee turned down the suggestion of appointing yet another committee to study the evaluation of teaching (that had been done often enough, it implied), and instead made the following proposal:

> . . . upon completion of his course of study at Yale each student receiving departmental honors in Yale College and each recipient of a terminal degree in the Graduate School shall be invited to submit to the Chairman of the Department or Program in which he concentrated and to the appropriate Dean a written appraisal of the strengths and weaknesses of his educational experience, including the quality of instruction in lecture courses, discussion courses, and seminars.

The Yale report represents an attempt to solve the knotty problem of preserving the institution's reputation as a university and at the same time maintaining its integrity as a teacher of undergraduates. More immediately, the report is a direct response to widespread student protest over the university's failure to promote a popular teacher to tenure position and over the supposed poor quality of undergraduate instruction in general, an allegation being made more and more often by students in this country's institutions of higher learning.

In October 1965, another committee at another university made another proposal which addresses itself to the same problem. The Kahn Committee, appointed by the faculty council of Cornell University, suggested that the student government be given technical and financial aid in formulating questionnaires, analyzing results, and preparing and publishing a campuswide evaluation of courses.

These two approaches to correcting the presumed deficiency in the quality of undergraduate instruction are being tried, or at least considered, at other colleges around the country. An editorial in *The Harvard Crimson* expressed approval of the student government's move to review the whole question of tenure decisions and suggested that Harvard need not slavishly copy the "cautious" Yale plan.[1] *The Daily Princetonian* too commended the Yale proposal and suggested that Princeton might try something similar.[2] At Columbia, President Kirk came out in favor of using "responsible student opinion" as one guide in tenure decisions, a position opposed by his fellow administrators. At the City College of New York, it was the faculty rather than the students or the administration who proposed that the evaluations of a select group of students be considered in tenure decisions; later, they went so far as to approve a plan for involving *all* students, not just the outstanding graduating seniors, in such decisions.

At campuses around the country, course and teacher evaluation booklets are proliferating, sometimes with the approval of the administration and the faculty, but often without it. In the Washington area alone, student groups at Georgetown University, American University, George Washington University, the University of Maryland, Catholic University, and Howard University have published or are in the stages of planning to publish course evaluations. At C.C.N.Y., the University of Washington, the University of Michigan, and the University of Wisconsin, published guides have appeared during the past year.

This spate of "report cards" from students to teachers has been attended by a considerable amount of fanfare in the newspapers: "A NEW STUDENT REVOLT"; "FALLOUT FROM BERKELEY"; "THE BOOKWORM TURNS"; "SHAPE UP, PROF!" But in spite of the bemusement of the headline writers, the notion of having students rate the effectiveness of their instructors is not all that new. The University of Washington has conducted campuswide course evaluations since 1925. The University of Texas and Purdue University were experimenting with such evaluations, though on a more limited scale, at about the same period. Bennington, Georgia Institute of Technology, Michigan State University, and the University of Missouri—to name just a few—have long conducted such programs.

[1] Oct. 25, 1965.
[2] Nov. 8, 1965.

Why, then, this sudden furor about students grading their teachers?

Part of the answer probably lies in the sudden visibility of the American student today and the wide public attention given to his restlessness, his discontent with the *status quo*, his rebelliousness against the multiversity, and his awakened social consciousness and concern for "relevance" of the curriculum. In this context, the renewed interest in student evaluation of teaching can be viewed as one aspect of the new student revolt, one expression of the student's desire to have a voice in his own education and in the academic policies related to it.

More than that, the student evaluations now receiving coverage in the newspapers are different in nature from most of the evaluation programs which preceded them. For in the past (and the practice is still widespread), evaluations of the teacher's effectiveness were usually a private matter. Typically, use of formal evaluation devices was left to the discretion of the individual instructor. If he felt that such evaluations would be worthwhile to him, he asked the dean's office or the department chairman or the student government to provide him with the necessary number of rating forms, he administered the evaluations at his convenience, and he did not have to show the results to anyone. Nor was he under any pressure to change his ways in light of the student ratings. He could profit from or ignore suggestions as he saw fit. Even when the evaluation programs were compulsory rather than voluntary, the results were usually seen only by the instructor or, at most, by the instructor and his department chairman or the director of the evaluation program.

What is so "revolutionary" and newsworthy about the student rating programs being initiated or proposed today is that the results are no longer the private affair of the instructor in most cases. Now anyone with the money to buy a course evaluation guide can see what students think of a particular teacher. Now the teacher's classroom behavior is being subjected to the scrutiny of faculty committees on promotion and tenure, and student ratings are being used "for administrative purposes." Little wonder that some faculty members are alarmed at the prospect. Some are no doubt motivated by an honest distrust of the student's judgment or of the reliability of the rating device. Others feel that the classroom is sanctified territory and that to make the results of ratings available to the student body at large or to a tenure committee constitutes a violation of academic freedom. But there are probably many faculty members who fear such public exposure for the very good reason that they are poor teachers. And there are perhaps some institutions who back them in their opposition to student ratings out of a fear that their reputation as good undergraduate institutions will be revealed as a myth and their declared concern with the faculty member's teaching skill will be proved a matter of lip service only.

Turning first to the question of using student evaluations as a guideline in making a decision about promotion and tenure, one would hardly think that the notion were so radical and extreme. To put the matter simply: most, indeed probably *all*, colleges acknowledge that one of their main purposes is to educate undergraduates, and therefore that the faculty member's effectiveness in the classroom is a primary consideration in his retention, promotion, or advancement to tenure. Over 95 percent of the college deans responding to a recent survey report that they regard classroom teaching as "a major factor" when making decisions about promotion, salary, and tenure.[3] But how do they form opinions about the instructor's effectiveness in the classroom? Logically, it would seem that the opinions of the students who are directly involved in the learning situation might be one of their primary sources of information. And it would seem to follow, too, that these opinions will be more trustworthy if they are collected in a consistent and systematic way rather than if they drift haphazardly, in the form of gossip, commendation, or complaint, to the ear of the department chairman or the dean. How many colleges do indeed rely on some kind of formal method for gathering that information? How many take student opinion into account when arriving at decisions about the faculty member's future? On how many campuses is there any sort of student evaluation of teaching effectiveness, whether used in tenure decisions or not?

Report on the survey

To answer these and other questions relating to the methods which colleges are currently using to judge teachers and to encourage better teaching, in the spring of 1966 the American Council on Education sent a survey to administrators (usually the academic dean or dean of the college) at a large sample of junior colleges, teachers colleges, liberal arts colleges, and, at universities, the undergraduate schools or colleges of arts and sciences, business, engineering, agriculture, and education. The first part of the survey questionnaire, designed to discover how teacher effectiveness is now assessed, asked the dean to indicate on a four-point scale ("All or most departments," "some departments," "a few departments," and "not used") how widely a particular source of information is drawn upon "in judging the faculty member's teaching ability or teaching effectiveness."[4] Included in the list of possible sources was the item "systematic student evaluations." Table 1 shows the percentage of institutions, by type, which report that such evaluations are used in all

---

[3] See Alexander W. Astin and Calvin B. T. Lee, "Current Practices in the Evaluation and Training of College Teachers," pp. 303–5 of the present volume.

[4] For details about the sample and the questionnaire, see *ibid.*, pp. 296–97.

Source: Tables 1 and 2 in "Current Practices in the Evaluation and Training of Teachers," by Alexander W. Astin and Calvin B. T. Lee (see pp. 298, 300 of the present volume).

TABLE 1: *Frequency of Use of Systematic Student Ratings to Judge Teaching Effectiveness, Compared to Six Other Sources of Information*

Source of Information					Percent Reporting Use of Source in All or Most Departments				
						University Colleges			
	All Institutions (N=1,110)	Junior Colleges (N=128)	Teachers Colleges (N=133)	Liberal Arts Colleges (N=484)	Arts and Sciences (N=110)	Education (N=48)	Engineering (N=109)	Business (N=65)	Agriculture (N=33)
Systematic student ratings	12.4	16.1	4.9	11.2	11.3	13.0	14.0	20.6	26.5
Informal student opinions	41.2	33.6	28.0	47.2	35.0	48.9	42.5	47.6	28.1
Chairman evaluation	85.1	65.8	89.6	82.2	98.2	91.3	92.7	88.7	93.9
Dean evaluation	82.3	82.7	80.5	83.5	71.8	91.7	80.4	89.1	84.4
Colleagues' opinions	48.9	29.2	34.9	50.6	62.0	48.9	53.8	71.9	46.9
Research and publication	43.8	4.2	34.1	36.6	70.0	63.8	72.9	75.0	56.3
Classroom visits	14.0	42.2	25.8	9.8	2.0	4.4	8.7	5.2	3.0

or most departments. For purposes of comparison, the percentages for six other sources of information—informal student opinions, chairman evaluation, dean evaluation, colleagues' opinions, scholarly research and publication, and classroom visits—are given.

As Table 1 indicates, systematic student ratings are not widely used as a source of information about teaching effectiveness: only about one in ten institutions says that they are used in all or most departments. (Indeed, 47.6 percent say that they are not used at all.) University colleges of agriculture and of business make the most use of such ratings, a surprising finding and one not entirely to be trusted because of the small number of these types of institution in the total sample. Ranking next in frequency of use are junior colleges, which—because of their relative unconcern with the faculty member's scholarly research and publication, their emphasis on teaching, and their student-centeredness—might be expected to rely fairly heavily on systematic ratings. Liberal arts colleges and colleges of arts and sciences within the university make about equal use of systematic student ratings.

In view of recent clamor about students grading teachers, it should be pointed out that student ratings are actually used less now as a source of information than they were back in 1961. In university colleges, for instance, they dropped from fourth place in 1961 to tenth place in 1966 in a rank ordering of various sources of information; at liberal arts colleges, they dropped from fifth to twelfth position.[5]

Deans were also asked whether any research had been done on the instruments used to rate teaching effectiveness (whether that rating is done by students, faculty, or administrators). The proportion who said that research had been done was uniformly low, the two highest figures being 5.0 percent at university schools of education and 4.8 percent at university arts and sciences colleges. The figure for all types of institution was 1.7 percent.

The survey also asked: "Is teaching effectiveness evaluated by informal student polls or other devices based on student opinions?" The percentage answering "yes" at each type of institution was:

Type of Institution	Percent
Junior colleges	24.8
Teachers colleges	28.2
Liberal arts colleges	23.3
University colleges:	
Arts and sciences	43.4
Education	40.5
Engineering	39.4
Business	40.4
Agriculture	29.0
All institutions	31.0

[5] A comparison of results of the 1961 and 1966 surveys about evaluation of teaching is given in John W. Gustad's "Evaluation of Teaching Performance: Issues and Possibilities," pp. 265–81 of the present volume.

It should be pointed out that the informal student polls or other devices based on student opinions differ in two ways from the systematic student ratings discussed previously. First, they are more likely to be student-initiated and student-administered. Second, except on campuses where the results are published in the form of a course critique, these devices are usually seen only by the faculty member involved; administrators and other faculty members do not see them and so, of course, cannot use them as a source of information for judging the faculty member's teaching effectiveness. It is interesting to see that, except in the case of colleges of agriculture (and again, the small number of institutions of this type included in the survey forbids our setting any great store by the percentage figure), the percentages for university colleges are consistently higher than those for the two- and four-year colleges: there is a difference of slightly over ten percentage points between the type of university college reporting least use of these devices (engineering, 39.4 percent) and the nonuniversity college reporting most use (teachers colleges, 28.2 percent). This difference probably reflects the greater amount of discontent over teaching at the universities (particularly large public ones) and the greater activism of their student bodies.

Additional correlational analyses were performed to discover possible relationships between certain institutional characteristics and the various techniques used in evaluating teaching effectiveness.[6] They revealed that at university colleges of arts and sciences, the percentage of males in the student body was negatively correlated with a "yes" answer to the item. (The coefficient, $-.21$, was significant at the .05 level.) In other words, informal student polls and similar devices are less likely to be found at university arts and sciences colleges which have a relatively high proportion of men in the student body. For liberal arts colleges, a correlation coefficient of .10 (also significant at the .05 level) was found between the selectivity of the institution and use of informal student polls. Taken in conjunction with the relatively small percentage of liberal arts colleges which report the existence of such devices (23.3, as compared with 31.0 for all types of institution), this correlation suggests that at the relatively unselective institutions of this type, informal devices for rating teaching effectiveness are not much used.

Although it is not always possible to offer explanations or suggest interpretations for all these findings, the general implications of the survey are clear enough. In making judgments about an instructor's ability, administrators use systematic student ratings very infrequently. As Table 1 shows, they rely chiefly on evaluations by chairmen and by deans. And

---

[6] These analyses were limited to two types of institutions: liberal arts colleges and university colleges of arts and sciences. For a fuller explanation, see Astin and Lee. "Current Practices in the Evaluation and Training of College Teachers," pp. 301–3.

where do chairmen and deans get their information? Not, it would seem, in the classroom itself, for only at junior colleges and teachers colleges is classroom visitation practiced to any great extent: percentages reporting use of this method for judging teaching are uniformly (and appallingly) low at liberal arts colleges and university colleges of all types; 39.5 percent of all institutions report that classroom visits are not used even in a few departments. As is the case with systematic student ratings, the practice of having colleagues visit classrooms has declined substantially since 1961.[7]

Table 1 suggests one possible firsthand source of information which deans and chairmen draw on in forming their opinions about the instructor's teaching ability: informal student opinions serve as a basis for evaluation at 41.2 percent of all institutions. Use of this source ranks relatively high; at university colleges it ranks fifth after chairman evaluation, dean evaluation, scholarly research and publication, and colleagues' opinions.[8] (Given the decline in classroom visitation, this last item, colleagues' opinions, is probably subject to the same strictures as deans' and department chairmen's evaluations. And using research and publication as a measure of teaching effectiveness seems at best a dubious practice.)

Many educators argue against the use of systematic student ratings on the grounds that students cannot accurately assess teaching effectiveness. It seems curious, then, that so many of them do use "informal student opinion" as a basis for judging an instructor's performance. Yet informal opinion is, plainly, the only direct evidence that they do use to any great extent—that, and perhaps any impressions they pick up in their personal contacts with faculty members outside the classroom, airy substance indeed.

Nor is it clear why they should prefer informal student opinions to systematic ratings. By definition the informal opinions come to them at random, in conference with a few students (who are probably an unrepresentative sample), in casual social conversations that take place outside their offices, from overheard conversations among students. The value of comments made in such situations can be questioned.

A second reason commonly given for failure to use systematic student ratings is distrust of the validity and reliability of the devices used. But the survey makes it clear that institutions are not involved in doing research on whatever rating forms they do use (whether completed by students or not), and obviously the situation is not going to get any better until such research is done. (Also, because of the diversity of institutions and their differing goals and purposes, it seems likely that one instru-

[7] Gustad, "Evaluation of Teaching Performance," pp. 269–71.
[8] *Ibid.*

ment will not be suitable to all needs and that the individual institution might best explore for itself the possibilities of student ratings.)

Systematic ratings and informal student polls are not, of course, the only means for measuring more directly the teacher's success or failure in the classroom. Other approaches to the problem have been suggested and may, in the long run, be more trustworthy than student opinion. At the present time, we simply do not know. But certainly student evaluations tell something about the impact that a teacher has on his students. In any event, they would certainly seem more trustworthy than the sources now drawn upon most heavily to evaluate teaching effectiveness.

KINDS OF RATING FORMS USED

In its survey, the Council requested that the dean send, along with the completed questionnaire, copies of any devices which were routinely used for teacher evaluation. The result of this request was a flood of rating forms, student "opinionnaires," recent graduate questionnaires, and so forth. About the safest generalization that can be made about these instruments is that they are diverse, ranging from a single page to six pages, from four to over fifty items (the majority containing from eleven to thirty).

The form that the items take varies too, although most questionnaires make use of items which can be scored fairly easily. Items may be of the multiple-choice descriptive type:

> Your opinion of the amount of homework for the course is:
> 1. Superior, proper in amount and emphasis
> 2. Good, generally supplements work
> 3. Fair
> 4. Somewhat inadequate in value and proportion
> 5. Poor in most respects

A more elaborate example of this type of item is:

> How does this instructor respond to questions from students in the class?
> a) actively solicits questions and responds in an appreciative manner
> b) usually responds in a positive manner, but sometimes seems to wish questions weren't asked
> c) does not encourage student to question or to take part in discussion, but now and then seems more positive
> d) usually seems resentful and hostile when students either question or offer a slightly different point of view; often tries to "cut the student down in class."

Graphic items require the rater to check along a horizontal continuum. Sometimes the intervals are carefully labeled:

RANGE OF INTERESTS AND CULTURE

10	9	8	7	6	5	4	3	2	1	0

Instructor has very broad interests and culture; frequently relates course to other fields and to present-day problems.	Instructor has fair breadth of interests and culture; occasionally relates subject to other fields and to present-day problems.	Instructor is narrow in his interests and culture; seldom relates subject to other fields or to present-day problems.

In other cases they are left vague:

Does he appear sensitive to students' feelings and problems?

Unaware   Responsive

The rater may be asked to circle a number or a letter grade or to put a check mark in a box: frequently a five-point scale is used (with "5" representing "superior" and "1" representing "poor" or "needs improvement"):

Clarity of Speech.   5   4   3   2   1   N (not applicable)

Some items require him to write in a number or a letter grade; for the following item, the rater was told to put a "5" for "Strong Agreement," and so forth down to "1" for "Strong Disagreement":

Course as a whole well organized. _____
Teacher handles class effectively. _____

Most items allow for at least five gradations in response, thus permitting fairly subtle distinctions, but some allow for only a two-valued response: "Agree-Disagree" or "Yes-No." And finally, a few rating forms are entirely open-end, calling for short comments on such matters as "Instructor's attitude toward his subject," "His attitude toward the students," "Attitude of students toward him," and so forth. One "evaluation opinionnaire," representing an extreme in "open-endedness" to the point of being more like a projective test than a rating form, asks the student to "complete the sentences to express your real feelings," and contains such items as:

1. This course
2. What I liked
3. I feel that the instructor
4. If I were teaching this course I would
5. The class discussions

Sometimes items are phrased in an elaborately explanatory and discursive manner:

The student should receive 50 minutes of instruction during each class period. An appropriate story, personal experience, or joke may illustrate or emphasize a point while irrelevant stories and discussion unrelated to the subject waste time. How does effective use of the period in this subject rank?

At the other extreme, items may be terse, simply mentioning the general quality or characteristic being rated: "Organization of lectures," "Ability to communicate subject matter," and so forth.

Almost without exception, the forms are to be filled out anonymously. In the directions, the student is assured that his identity will be concealed and that he may therefore comment freely. He is urged to print any long answers so that his handwriting will not be recognized. To further protect the student from any vengeful tendencies on the part of the instructor, the completed questionnaires are frequently put in an envelope which is sealed in view of the class, carried to the dean's office, and not given to the instructor until after the final grades are posted. In some cases, the instructor is required to absent himself from the room while the rating forms are filled out.

Although the American Council questionnaire did not explicitly request the dean to specify in what way and by whom the rating forms are used, it is clear, from examining the forms and from reading any comments that were made, that in most cases their use is not mandatory: the instructor requests the rating forms for his own enlightenment and improvement. Often the directions to the rater mention this voluntary aspect, emphasizing that the instructor is eager to get "a frank and honest statement from the members of his class as an aid to growth in effectiveness as a teacher." Most of the rating forms are obviously intended for the instructor's eyes only. Very occasionally, the directions indicate that the dean or department chairman will see the ratings, but in these cases the implication is that they will be used merely to advise the instructor about his teaching, to talk things over with him in a friendly and constructive way. Never is there a hint that the ratings will make a difference in his retention or promotion.

With the present focus on student evaluation of teaching, it seems likely that in the future more and more faculty members will be under pressure to participate in these programs. One section of the Muscatine Report is probably a good sign of things to come: commenting that some of the committee members were reluctant to impose student ratings on all instructors, willing or not, the committee nonetheless agreed that "at least one large-scale campus-wide experiment with student ratings would be worthwhile," since too many instructors get no feedback from their classes, and even those who use the rating forms do not necessarily use them wisely.[9]

[9] *Education at Berkeley: Report of the Select Committee on Education* (Berkeley: Academic Senate, University of California, March 1966), p. 58.

Or perhaps institutions will adopt something like the procedure currently followed at Montana State College. There, student ratings are kept on a voluntary basis and are seen by the instructor only, although names of instructors requesting ratings are listed in the dean's office and are available to the Curricula and Instruction Committee. Moreover, "any instructor who does not voluntarily submit himself to appraisal may be asked to do so by the students of his class"; if at least 20 percent of the class petitions the student section of the Curricula and Instruction Committee, and if the claim is determined to be valid, the chairman of the student section notifies "both the instructor and his department head of the class request." [10] Although these provisions do not say that the faculty member must submit himself to evaluation, he is obviously under considerable pressure to do so.

Rating forms use various means of controlling for possible bias. Commonly they contain an "identification" section which asks for the student's major, class standing, and grade-point average; frequently the student is asked to indicate whether the course is required or elective and what grade he expects to receive in it. This information obviously helps the instructor interpret the results. More elaborate procedures may be used. For instance, one form contains a section in which the student is asked to check from a list of ten the three qualities which he thinks are most important in good teaching: systematic organization of subject matter, good speaking ability, ability to explain clearly, ability to encourage thought, sympathetic attitude toward students, expert knowledge of subject, enthusiastic attitude toward subject, fairness in making and grading tests, tolerance toward student disagreement, and pleasing personality. Thus the instructor is given some notion of the student's values and can interpret responses accordingly.

Rating forms usually contain a few items which call for an over-all evaluation of the course or the teacher. For instance, the student may be asked to give his general estimate of the instructor as a teacher, using a five-point scale, or to rank the course or the instructor in comparison with other courses or instructors. Or he may simply be asked: "Would you recommend this course to a friend?"

Two or three open-end questions are found on most rating forms; they may specifically ask the student to name three things that he liked and three that he disliked about the course, to "describe the course as it should be described in the college catalogue," to list a few ways in which he thinks the course could be made more worthwhile, or to indicate what he would change in the course if he were teaching it. Or they may simply call for "additional comments." Forcing the student to specify a given

[10] "Montana State College Faculty Rating System Approved by the Instructional Faculty, March 2, 1950" (Mimeographed).

number of strengths and weaknesses of the course or the instructor probably elicits more helpful information than can be obtained by simply leaving it to the student to decide whether he has any general remarks to make. Moreover, items which ask him to name positive as well as negative qualities underscore the constructive purpose of the rating form and, perhaps, are one means of overcoming a student's reluctance to criticize.

Although a few rating forms manage to pare down the areas covered to three or four (for instance, one simply asks for a rating on a four-point scale of the teacher's ability, conscientiousness, fairness, and over-all effectiveness), most forms tend to be rather detailed and to cover more areas. Typically, they ask questions about course goals and purposes ("Were the aims and objectives of the class made clear to you?"), the content ("Is the content of this course kept up to date?" "Does the teacher relate the subject matter of the course to contemporary life?"), materials such as textbooks and audio-visual aids, assignments (amount of time required each week to prepare for the course, relevance of papers written, number of examinations, and so forth), and teacher behavior.

Most forms contain some kind of question about the teacher's mastery of the subject matter, although critics have pointed out that the student may not be able to make a very accurate judgment about this. Certainly a flat question such as "Does the teacher seem to know the subject matter?" is suspect. Some questionnaires try to circumvent the difficulty by asking about specific behavior which may be taken to indicate a grasp of the subject matter. For instance, one calls for a rating of the following statements: "His explanations were lucid and accurate"; "He answered questions in an expert and authoritative manner"; "His analysis of the course material showed depth and insight"; "He had an adequate grasp of the broad, general concepts of his course as well as an understanding of particular details." Almost inevitably, there are items about the instructor's being well prepared for class, organizing his lectures well, grading fairly, lecturing enthusiastically, encouraging questions, and stimulating classroom discussion. (It is apparently assumed that all classroom discussion is fruitful so long as everyone participates and no one monopolizes.)

The teacher's personal traits and relations with his students are also touched upon, and by looking at the sort of questions asked, one gets a rather amusing picture of the ideal teacher as he is conceived by the constructors of rating forms. He must be friendly, sympathetic, *never* sarcastic. He must encourage students to see him during his office hours. But he must not be so friendly as to lose dignity and authority; he must maintain order and discipline in the classroom. (Two of the more unusual items which I came across, and which bear on the instructor's relations with his students, were: "Did he treat you in a democratic spirit?" and

"Is he or she overly partial to the opposite sex?") In appearance, the instructor should be neat and well groomed. He should not have a flat monotonous voice or any "annoying mannerisms," nor should he stand in such a way as to obscure the blackboard. And above all, he must have a sense of humor. (It is startling to discover how many forms contain a "sense of humor" item; only once did I find a counterbalance to this demand for wit and jollity: "Does the instructor try to be funny to the extent that his humor becomes a source of annoyance?") Although many of these items—and others such as "Is the room well ventilated?" and "Is there sufficient light?"— seem trivial, perhaps when the forms are used wholly for the edification of the teacher they are helpful. An instructor may profit from being told that he says "uh" and "ah" too much, that he addresses remarks to the blackboard rather than to the class, or that his habit of cracking his knuckles is irritating to the students. But occasionally one comes across items which seem to have only tangential bearing on the purposes of education: "The teacher manifests a real interest in the entire college program by willingness to cooperate (including student activities)," or "Classes always start and end on time."

Sometimes items on a rating form indicate the objectives and emphasis of particular types of institutions. For instance, church-related colleges frequently ask such questions as: "How well does your instructor relate the work of this course to a basic Christian philosophy?"; "Do you feel that this teacher is a positive influence on your Christian faith?" Professional schools may ask, "Do you think the subject matter covered will be of practical importance in your actual work?" or "Was the technical content of the course too advanced?" Even though many instructors complain that standardized rating forms are not suited to their particular courses, very few of the professional schools which sent material seem to have devised their own special forms. Junior colleges seem to ask a lot of questions about the teacher's having friendly relations with students and maintaining order in the classroom.

In general, many of the rating forms that I examined seem to suffer from either a lack of organization and a tendency to ask too many questions or from overgenerality in the phrasing of items. It is interesting to look at the University of Washington's "Survey of Student Opinion of Teaching," a rating form developed out of experience with student evaluations of teaching, and out of continued research with the instruments used, over a period of some 41 years. This rating form (reproduced here) consists of ten items (each to be rated on a five-point numerical scale) which show the highest relationship with over-all judgments of teaching effectiveness, two open-end items, some identification questions, and a rating of the subject matter of the course. Research shows that "there was a direct statistical relationship (correlation range: .70 to .84)

UNIVERSITY OF WASHINGTON

Survey of Student Opinion of Teaching

Instructor's Name_____Course and Number_____

My major is_____

This course is required_____elective_____(check one)

My cumulative GPA is below 2.5_____2.5 to 3.0_____3.0 to 3.5_____
above 3.5_____

I previously attended junior college_____another 4-year college_____

only UW_____

This survey is made at the request of your instructor in this class. The information the instructor receives will not identify any student individually. He will receive a summary of class ratings and comments only after the quarter is over. At that time the individual instructor alone determines whether this information is to be destroyed or whether it is to be made available to any other person for reference.

Listed below are several qualities which describe aspects of instructor behavior. Rate your instructor on each of these items by drawing a circle around the number that best indicates his position in comparison with other teachers you have had. Rate each item as thoughtfully and carefully as possible. Do *not* omit items. Of course, it will be the very unusual case when the number you circle is the same for all items.

	Outstanding	*Superior*	*Competent*	*Only Fair*	*Of Less Value*
1. Interprets abstract ideas and theories clearly..........	1	2	3	4	5
2. Gets me interested in his subject....................	1	2	3	4	5
3. Has increased my skills in thinking.................	1	2	3	4	5
4. Has helped broaden my interests....................	1	2	3	4	5
5. Stresses important material........................	1	2	3	4	5
6. Makes good use of examples and illustrations.........	1	2	3	4	5
7. Has motivated me to do my best work...............	1	2	3	4	5
8. Inspires class confidence in his knowledge of subject...	1	2	3	4	5
9. Has given me new viewpoints or appreciations........	1	2	3	4	5
10. Is clear and understandable in his explanations........	1	2	3	4	5

Your instructor would like to know if there is something you believe he has done especially well in his teaching of this course_____

_____

_____

_____

Your instructor would also like to know what specific things you believe might be done to improve his teaching in this course_____

_____

_____

_____

Thus far your judgments have been restricted to characteristics of the *teacher* himself. For the item below indicate your feeling for the *subject matter* of the course by checking (√) the appropriate entry.

The subject matter or content of the course is:

    Highly interesting_____

    Moderately interesting_____

    Not very interesting_____

Circle the final grade you expect to receive in this course:

    A   B   C   D   E

between the ratings on the ten items and the students' perception of the degree of help in understanding received from the instructor. . . . Correlations between the scores on the ten items and the question by which the students' increased interest was assessed varied from .54 to .86." [11] In other words, the ten items are closely related to students' reports that their understanding and interest in a subject matter has been increased by the teacher. Both the content and the phrasing of these items should be noted: they deal chiefly with the instructor's lucidity and his ability to broaden the student's knowledge and interest, and most of them are phrased in such a way as to bring the student into the evaluation.

Some of the other rating forms I looked at were similar to the University of Washington survey in that they treat the student as involved in and at least partly responsible for the learning situation rather than as a passive recipient, a consumer (to use the all-too-current and revealing metaphor) who must be sold a product by the skillful manipulations of the instructor-salesman. Some items of this type from other rating forms are: "This course has stimulated me to careful and consistent preparation"; "I have a clear idea of the value of my work in this class and would know how to make it better"; or "How well have you assumed your responsibility in the learning and progress of the class?" "What has been your attitude in this class?" Other items which seem well conceived are those which ask the student to report on specific behaviors rather than on elusive and abstract qualities such as "mastery of subject matter," "instructor as a human being," and so forth.

Judging from most of the rating forms which I looked at, I must conclude that too often there are good grounds for the faculty member's distrust of devices now used for student evaluations. But this is not to say that no kind of evaluation should be attempted. If present instruments are poor, they must be improved. To accomplish this will require considerably more effort, careful thought, and courage to experiment and to follow through by doing research, than is presently being manifested by colleges.

PUBLISHED EVALUATIONS

"Institutionalizing the grapevine" [12] by means of some kind of published course and teacher evaluation booklet is not a new idea. A *Confidential Guide to Courses* was initiated at Harvard in 1924. The Third National Student Congress in 1949 gave its backing to the notion of having students rate faculty members. Not until the last few years, however,

[11] Thomas D. F. Langen, "Student Assessment of Teaching Effectiveness," *Improving College and University Teaching*, Winter 1966, p. 23.
[12] *University of Minnesota Daily*, Oct. 16, 1965.

has the practice of making the results of such ratings available to the student body at large (and to anyone else who cares to buy the guide) become widespread. Now more and more students are publishing such evaluations or expressing an interest in doing so: "student-initiated course and teacher evaluation is spreading on American campuses like a new fad; unlike piano-wrecking and stuffing telephone booths, the idea . . . has stuck and is growing in influence and sophistication." [13]

The published evaluations now in existence range from the sophisticated *Confidential Guide* of Harvard to the University of Michigan's matter-of-fact special issue of *The Michigan Daily* to the California State College at Los Angeles *PROFile*, which reports in numerical form the "score" that each professor received from each rater on some eight items, plus two or three sentences of comment. In general, course evaluation booklets serve one or more of three purposes: (1) they give course descriptions, (2) they evaluate teaching, or (3) they evaluate the total curriculum of a department or of an entire institution.[14]

The first purpose has been described by one Canadian editor as "anticalendar" since it removes the sugar-coating from the university calendar's description of courses.[15] The typical college catalogue is notoriously inadequate in its description of courses, not willfully but because the compilers of such catalogues really have no way of knowing exactly what a particular class as taught by a particular teacher is really like. Published course evaluations remedy this deficiency by reporting, for instance, on the content of the course, the textbooks used, the amount of lecture as compared to discussion, the number and type of examinations given, the number of papers required, and the stress which the instructor puts on class attendance. For some student-directed course evaluations, those at Oberlin and Brandeis, for instance, the instructor himself is asked to write the course description—one device for involving the faculty member in such published evaluations and, perhaps, making him more amenable to them. At many institutions, including the University of Wisconsin and Bryn Mawr, such course evaluations are intended chiefly for freshmen. At large universities, they are designed to give all students—and particularly commuters—information which they would otherwise have little chance of learning. The booklet may obligingly label the easy courses—"gut," "mickey," or "crip," depending on which part of the country they come from.

Usually the published evaluations are more than just descriptions of various courses. They have the consciously missionary purpose of improv-

[13] Philip Werdell, *Course and Teacher Evaluation: A Student's Confidential Guide* (Washington: United States National Student Association, 1966), p. 1.

[14] *Ibid.*, pp. 17–22.

[15] Quoted by *The Collegiate Press Service*, Oct. 4, 1965.

ing teaching and thus contain comments, enthusiastic or gently critical or sharply acid, about the teacher's effectiveness as teacher. The *SLATE Supplement to the General Catalogue* is especially articulate about its corrective purpose:

While we praise and blame individual instructors, we recognize that many professors, particularly among the non-tenured, would like to be more conscientious teachers. . . .

. . . the student must help the University to recognize that "publish or perish" is not the only possible path upward in the academic world; that "A good researcher is a good teacher" is a myth perpetrated on the legislature, the students, and the citizenry by good researchers who are all too aware of their deficiencies as teachers; that teaching ability is neither inborn, nor automatically bestowed with the Ph.D., nor so esoteric an art that it cannot be learned. By encouraging students to desert bad teachers for better ones we hope to help administration and faculty policy makers recognize that teaching is a learnable skill, distinct from research, still important in the University.[16]

What kinds of information do these published evaluations give about teachers? They rarely comment on his personal appearance or nervous mannerisms. The content of comments varies from one institution to another, of course—and a very informative notion about the values of students at different institutions can be gained from reading evaluation booklets—but in most cases they seem to mention the instructor's enthusiasm for his subject, the organization of the lectures (instructors who ramble or indulge in irrelevancies come in for sharp criticism), his manner of presentation (and, again, enthusiasm is highly rated), his fairness in grading (instructors who grade too easily are not admired), and his personal traits (warmth and friendliness being particularly valued). Frequently, and particularly at the larger universities, personal traits are not considered at all; emphasis is entirely upon the teacher's grasp of and ability to communicate the subject matter in an organized fashion. A past vice-president of the National Student Association comments: ". . . the primary objectives of the student in a given course and the attributes he seeks in an instructor are most directly concerned with impersonal factors." [17]

Critics who charge that students are simply not able to judge effective teaching might be surprised at the sophistication and perspicacity of some of the comments. Students seem to have little respect for the "easy" teacher and no objection to working hard in worthwhile courses: "Work load heavy but worth the effort"; "the teacher was too lenient with stu-

[16] Berkeley, Calif.: SLATE, 1964, p. 47. (SLATE is a campus political organization.)

[17] Richard J. Medalie, "The Student Looks at College Teaching," *The Preparation of College Teachers*, ed. Theodore C. Blegen and Russell M. Cooper (Washington: American Council on Education, 1950), p. 51.

dents who were unprepared"; "the serious student in this field should look for more challenging work." Contrary to the apparent assumptions of many of the rating forms discussed previously, a sense of humor is not always regarded as a saving grace: "Most students 'had a lot of chuckles' . . . but many complained that they 'didn't learn very much chemistry' [because of the instructor's] antics." Sarcasm is not universally feared and despised: "They call him clever and able, and appreciate the sarcasm which he serves up in heavy doses." Showmanship is not always confounded with effective teaching: "[The instructor is rated] entertaining, fun, not terribly challenging, and not at all profound"; "I expected more detail and [fewer] pyrotechnics"; "[The instructor] likes to strut and fret his hour upon the stage." Nor does the instructor's being a good guy save him from criticism: "Personally a charming man, [the instructor] is perhaps the most inept lecturer you will meet at [this institution]."

Perhaps on the principle of "If you can't say something nice, don't say anything at all," many of the commentaries seem to go out of their way to make some kind of positive statement about even poor teachers: "Very logical if somewhat dry. Appears a bit dogmatic but open to questions"; "A slight communication problem due to accent and rapid speech. However, he is very patient and gives clear examples to illustrate material. His knowledge of subject is excellent"; "When he was not reading from papers or manuscripts, his lectures were very stimulating and provocative." Though most criticisms show an attempt to be matter-of-fact and even, sometimes, gentle, others obviously take delight in a certain amount of acerbic wit: "He is like a used car salesman selling Tolstoy to a customer who he is sure won't buy"; "[The instructor] drew no favorable comments and several obscene ones." But on the whole those who write up the evaluations from the data collected apparently try to give a fair and balanced picture.

The third purpose, that of evaluating the total curriculum of a department or an institution, is a little too ambitious for most published evaluations. Those that are concerned with over-all curriculum reform usually base their judgments on some sort of senior questionnaire in which the graduating student assesses his total college experience, including often a list of the best and worst courses and teachers he has had and a general critique of his major department or of the total curriculum. The SLATE Supplement regularly includes essays, some written by students and others by faculty members, dealing with particular problems in higher education and, often, suggesting reforms. The evaluation booklets of the University of Massachusetts and the University of Pennsylvania also include feature articles. The student government of the City College of New York devoted considerable energy to spreading the word that the science sequence of courses designed for nonscience majors did not live up to the catalogue description—that it gave the student "a superficial acquaintance of a specific science rather than a broadly based conception of the purpose, methods and philosophy of all science"—and suggested specific reforms. Eventually their suggestions were adopted and the sequence changed.[18]

Other features of course evaluations which seem to be widespread are an introduction outlining the purposes of the booklet, a fairly detailed description of the methods used to collect the data and formulate the general comments, and a disclaimer of the following type:

> We wish to emphasize to students that the opinions expressed in this Evaluation are precisely that, and do not necessarily represent facts. While every precaution was taken to ensure the accurate representation of the opinion expressed in the responses to our questionnaire, in the final analysis each individual must judge for himself the validity of these opinions. This Evaluation is intended as a supplement to, and not a substitute for, the various other criteria available for judging courses. . . . It should also be emphasized that courses and teachers often, although not always, do change, and that this Evaluation is therefore historical and not necessarily predictive.[19]

Another course evaluation points out that its survey is "not statistically valid" because it is based on opinion rather than fact and because only one or two classes of each faculty member were polled. Another admits to an error in its previous evaluation of two professors who were rated "low" in teaching effectiveness but revealed by later evaluations to have many admirers among the students; the publication takes the opportunity to point out that it is "quite common for a professor to draw contradictory reactions from students in the same class" and that ultimately the individual student must rely on his own judgment rather than regarding the evaluation as "gospel truth." In short, student evaluations are careful to point out their own weaknesses and to disclaim infallibility.

As an aid in interpreting results, some booklets indicate the total enrollment of the class, the percentage of that class who filled out the rating form, and even (in the case of the University of Michigan's *Review of 53 Key University Courses*) the grade distributions of the respondents.

The group within the student body responsible for conducting the student evaluation may be the student newspaper (as in the case of Harvard), a campus political organization (SLATE at Berkeley), or a group within the student government itself. (The first two groups were more or less the pioneers, but at the present time the last group is probably the more frequently involved.) Werdell, whose *Course and Teacher Evaluation* is, among other things, a how-to-do-it manual for students planning

---

[18] Werdell, *Course and Teacher Evaluation*, p. 8.
[19] *Student Course Evaluation*, Educational Policies Committee, Brandeis University Student Council, May 1966, p. 1.

to initiate evaluation programs, points out that in those cases where impetus does not come from the student government, one of the first requisite steps is to get its official support in the form of "thorough and mature" legislation.[20] When selecting or constructing the rating form to be used, students should involve as many interested parties as possible: "One of the best ways . . . is by a brainstorming session in which every student lists what he or she feels the problems of education are." [21] Faculty members too may be asked what sorts of information they would like to get from student evaluations or how particular items should be phrased. The prefaces of most course evaluations make it clear that in preparing the questionnaires students asked for expert guidance from members of the psychology departments or other nonstudents knowledgeable in the ways of constructing such instruments. Usually considerable care is taken to involve the faculty by discussing the project with them, either face to face or at departmental or senate meetings, and by asking for criticisms and suggestions after the evaluation has been published.

The procedure for collecting data is usually as follows: rating forms are distributed on a campuswide basis. They are handed out in residence groups, left at strategic points on campus where commuters may pick them up, and so forth. The greatest drawback to this method of distribution is, of course, that the return may be small, and perhaps more evaluation programs have faltered because of student apathy rather than faculty opposition. A return from one-third of the total enrollment of a class is considered very high. In one course evaluation program, the student committee requested faculty members to participate and asked those who agreed (less than one-third) which classes they wanted to have evaluated; then a survey worker administered the form itself. Obviously, such a procedure means that a much higher proportion of students in a given class participate and that therefore results are more representative, but the bias involved in making faculty participation voluntary would seem to vitiate this advantage.

Some institutions use only multiple-choice or other easily coded items and punch the responses onto IBM cards, but in most cases the published evaluations do not claim to be "scientific" or representative of student opinion. (An exception is the University of Washington's *Course Critique*, whose comments are supported statistically.) Some typical procedures used in writing the commentaries on each course are as follows:

The course evaluations themselves are written entirely by members of the *Crimson* staff. An effort is made to enlist writers who have taken the particular course, but in some cases the course is reviewed solely from information

[20] P. 27.
[21] *Ibid.*, p. 28.

gleaned from the polls. . . . Each writer usually reviews about three or four courses, writing these up from the polls and from his own impressions. . . .[22]

After a sub-committee of the Academic Affairs Committee [of the student government] distributed and then collected these questionnaires, they evaluated the courses from the information which was available to them. When they were not satisfied by the information they obtained in this manner, they held personal interviews with students. Naturally all students did not agree on their evaluations of a course so we chose that information that reflected a general consensus. . . .[23]

The answers to the questionnaires were compiled by approximately thirty volunteers, and these results were then put into written form by students who objectively reported the opinions expressed. The writers had not, for the most part, taken the course or courses with which they dealt—a policy whose possible cost in lowered comprehension and clarity was, we feel, more than offset by the gain in objectivity.[24]

The course evaluations in this issue are based on questionnaires we distribute on campus each semester. After collection, they are evaluated by upper division or graduate students in the respective departments. . . . The departmental editors also draw on their own knowledge of the subject matter and the department. They frequently discuss courses and professors with friends and acquaintances.[25]

Obviously most of these methods leave considerable room for subjectivity and impressionism. But as long as this possibility is made clear to the readers, this method of "writing up" the results need not be considered a defect; it may be considerably more helpful and meaningful than those course evaluations in which the rating given by each student on each item in the survey is listed.

Costs of course evaluation programs will depend, of course, on the amount of data collected, the process by which the data are analyzed, and the elaborateness—insofar as format and printing are concerned—of the booklet produced. Some course evaluations pay their own way through advertising or sales; others are supported by funds from the student government (which may come from the administration), or directly by the administration itself.[26]

The United States National Student Association has set forth certain guidelines and helpful hints to those students interested in starting programs. First, evaluations should be published annually at least: "Not only does this allow for changes from year to year; it can also help bring about needed innovations and reforms at a faster pace." [27] Second, "it is advisa-

[22] Richard Cotton, "Course Evaluation at Harvard" (Mimeographed).
[23] Course Evaluation, Student Government of the University of North Carolina at Chapel Hill (1965), p. 2.
[24] Brandeis, Student Course Evaluation, p. 1.
[25] SLATE Supplement to the General Catalogue, p. 3.
[26] Werdell, Course and Teacher Evaluation, pp. 31–32.
[27] Ibid., p. 25.

ble to start on a small scale," evaluating just a few courses, involving just a few students in the evaluation, or using a brief rating form, and to emphasize that the program is experimental in nature; by not attempting too much at first go, a course evaluation program can more easily establish a good reputation.[28] If the program is to be successful, it should try to involve all constituencies in the academic community: the administration, the faculty, and of course the students themselves, since unless a reasonable proportion participate and unless they are frank without being acrimonious, the program will have little value. To all these interested parties, then, the students responsible for the program must present their case from the beginning, stressing the constructive nature of the evaluation and the necessity for serious participation. Good public relations and some show of an effort to listen to and consider suggestions are essential. And finally, some attempt should be made to evaluate the evaluations, to discover responses of the administration, the faculty, and the students after the booklet is published, and to try to find out what changes, if any, occur because of the program.[29]

In the absence of a large and systematic body of evidence—and even of an appropriate set of criteria by which to determine effectiveness—it is difficult to reach any conclusions about just what changes, desirable or undesirable, course evaluations bring about. According to the editor of the Harvard *Crimson*, the *Confidential Guide* "has had a rather strong influence upon [students'] choice of courses and instructors. One enthusiastic review usually produces at least a 25% rise in a course's enrollment —and vice versa. In at least two cases in the past two years, enrollment in two freshman courses fell so drastically after two pans that they were discontinued." [30] Mention has already been made of the change in the science sequence at C.C.N.Y. And it is fairly safe to speculate that many published evaluations fulfill their function as supplements and correctives to the official description of courses, giving the student a fairly accurate idea of the nature of a particular course. But do they bring about any improvement in teaching? The most important consideration here is the individual faculty member's acceptance of this purpose of the program and his willingness (and ability) to learn from what is said (always granting that he feels it is valid). Typically, faculty reaction to published evaluations is mixed: at some institutions—Northwestern University and Brooklyn College, for instance—they are well received, at others, rejected completely (the chief grounds for this rejection usually have to do with the reliability of the rating form used, the methodology of the study, or the acidity of the commentary). At C.C.N.Y.'s Bernard Baruch School

[28] *Ibid.*
[29] *Ibid.*, pp. 28–35.
[30] Cotton, "Course Evaluation at Harvard."

of Business and Public Administration last January, a special issue of the student newspaper which published "a two-page list of the editors' opinions on the competence of 51 faculty members," was withdrawn from circulation by the dean on the grounds that "several opinions might be libelous." [31] At the University of Washington, faculty reaction to the student-initiated *Course Critique* was described as "lukewarm," perhaps because the university's own evaluation program, conducted for over thirty-five years, seems sufficient. Even the best-conducted course evaluation can be effective only if the faculty is indeed concerned with improving the quality of instruction, and at all too many institutions they are probably not. As Werdell puts it:

> When an instructor has higher priorities than teaching, when he feels he has nothing more to learn from students, when he is not bothered by students' falling asleep and reading the paper in his class, when, in short, he is simply not a good teacher, it would be quite surprising if he were to be changed by simply receiving student opinion—either published or unpublished.[32]

But at the very least, a program of course evaluations can be regarded as one way of giving students a voice in their own education, of allowing them an opportunity for constructive participation in the academic community, of providing them with "a prime channel of communication of substantive information about educational policy . . . to the faculty, to the administration, and to the students themselves." [33]

Pros and cons

To the question "Can the Student Evaluate His Teacher?" the simple answer is, of course, no. Partly because he has not the ability, partly because he has not a real opportunity, partly because no scheme for recording his evaluation can be both fair to him and intelligible to any one else. Going further, I may add that he has no right to even try, and that encouraging him to do so is simply to aggravate his already considerable power of mischief.[34]

Most opponents of the notion that students should have some voice in evaluating the effectiveness of their instructors are not so outspoken as the anonymous author of this statement. But though immoderately expressed, his views are representative of the objections usually raised against student evaluations. Some of the pros and cons have been touched on in the preceding discussion of survey results, rating forms, and published evaluations. It remains to make more explicit both the arguments against student ratings and some of the answers that have been made to these arguments.

[31] *New York Times*, Jan. 29, 1966.
[32] Werdell, *Course and Teacher Evaluation*, p. 26.
[33] *Ibid.*, p. 17.
[34] Quoted by Werdell, *Course and Teacher Evaluation*, p. 7.

First, much of the opposition to student ratings seems to be motivated by a deep-seated and pervasive distrust of the student. He is seen as an incompetent judge, biased, immature, and arbitrary. He is charged with confusing good teaching with showmanship and with construing evaluations as an open invitation to exact retribution, to get back at the instructor for the grade he has received.

These criticisms may be justified by the attitudes and responses of some students. But to jump to the conclusion that all, or even most, students are incompetent, gullible, or vicious is to fall wide of the mark. Those who have seriously examined the question of student ratings seem to agree that they have some value. Irvin Lehmann states: "Students are perceptive, and they become more so when they realize that their opinions are seriously regarded . . . Even if one accepts the often reiterated comment that 'student judgments must be discounted,' the evidence is that they should not be completely ignored." [35] Gustad points out that at present students "are virtually the *only* direct observers," and that they are reasonably competent if they are asked the right questions.[36] Gustad shares the widespread opinion that students, particularly freshmen and sophomores, are probably not good judges of an instructor's knowledge of his field: his "professional maturity," to use the term which Smalzried and Remmers apply to one of two factors which they found to make up teaching effectiveness.[37] But as Medalie argues, this "absence of professorial qualification . . . is not sufficient reason for labeling student evaluation of instruction . . . useless, as many of the skeptics would do." [38] For even if it is true that students cannot accurately assess an instructor's mastery of his subject matter (a factor which can be rated with a fair degree of accuracy by other faculty members), they are perfectly capable of saying whether the instructor has presented the subject in an organized manner, whether he communicated it to them, and whether he seemed interested in it. Students can also report their own responses: they can tell if their understanding has been increased, their interest aroused, their curiosity stimulated. These responses in themselves are not proof of a deep and lasting learning experience, but it seems safe to say that in the absence of understanding and interest, nothing meaningful can take place.

Students have, to be sure, certain vested interests in what goes on in the classroom. They prefer exciting lecturers to dull ones, teachers enthusiastic about their subject to those who seem bored by it, instruc-

[35] Lehmann, "Evaluation of Instruction," *Evaluation in Higher Education*, ed. Paul Dressel and Associates, Office of Institutional Research (Boston: Houghton Mifflin Co., 1961), p. 353.
[36] Gustad, "Evaluation of Teaching Performance," p. 276.
[37] Lehmann, "Evaluation of Instruction," p. 349.
[38] Medalie, "The Student Looks at College Teaching," p. 52.

tors involved in teaching to those who obviously couldn't care less. In this sense they are indeed biased. But, as an editorial in the *Columbia Daily Spectator* points out, so is the other group—composed of faculty members and administrators—that is called upon to judge teaching effectiveness: "Neither group is impartial, but the interaction of their different interests may well lead to fairer and more accurate evaluation . . ." [39]

It is frequently maintained that, because many students would rather be entertained than educated, the use of student ratings will lead the teacher to become a popularity-seeker. As Max Lerner puts it: "If the teacher gets too self-conscious, if he strives for approval, then he is running after strange gods. The poor devil is always tempted to over-dramatize his subject, oversimplify it, make things 'clear' . . ." [40] Certainly these dangers exist. But research indicates that the instructor's "popularity in extraclass activities . . . is probably not appreciably related to student ratings of that teacher." [41] Moreover, one should not assume that the entertaining or popular teacher is necessarily compromising himself or his subject matter (though intradepartmental jealousies may declare this to be the case) or that the student cannot learn by being delighted as well as by being explicitly instructed.

The anonymous critic's charge that the student "has no right to even try" to evaluate his teachers touches on another common view: that whatever the student's competence or incompetence, it is simply not his proper role to judge his instructors. In this view, student ratings (except when they are seen only by the faculty member concerned) can only create an atmosphere of ill feeling and suspicion; they represent a dislocation in the ideal instructor-student relationship.

Yet the violation of this ideal seems not so much the fault of the students as of the institution, which—if the more vocal student groups are to be believed—has too often failed to involve students as apprentices in the adventures of scholarship, "learning from the teacher by watching his mind at work and helping where he can." [42] Had this ideal governed relationships between faculty members and students in the recent past, the present outcry against poor teaching might not be so vociferous.

Jacques Barzun expresses one variation of this view when he protests against the use of student ratings in making tenure decisions on the grounds that it would be too much "to have yet another constituency

[39] "Students and Tenure," *Columbia Daily Spectator*, Dec. 17, 1965.

[40] Lerner, "Should College Students Grade Professors?" *Washington Star*, Oct. 31, 1965.

[41] H. H. Remmers, "Rating Methods in Research on Teaching," *Handbook of Research on Teaching*, ed. N. L. Gage (Chicago: Rand McNally & Co., 1963), p. 368.

[42] Lerner, "Should College Students Grade Professors?"

exercising influence over professors." [43] Surely this is a strange position for an educator to take: one would think that students are the instructor's primary constituency, and that most of his actions should be influenced, whether through student ratings or in less direct ways, by them.

The view that students have no right to judge is rapidly losing ground as the concept of academic freedom is extended to include students. More and more, educators are coming to feel that "students have the right to bring their interests and opinions to the attention of the college," and that to acknowledge this right is to recognize a legitimate claim. [44]

A third frequently voiced argument is directed not against the student but against the rating devices themselves. For instance, the Muscatine Report says that such instruments are "subject to bias and unreliability and may reflect other aspects of teacher performance than those most central to basic educational purposes." [45] Unquestionably, most rating forms could be improved, but it should be recognized that the element of bias can never be completely removed: such devices are by their very nature "biased" in that they depend upon the judgments of human beings who are necessarily subjective in their judgments. Thus they are limited by "the characteristics of the human rater—his inevitably selective perception, memory, and forgetting, his lack of sensitivity to what may be psychologically and socially important, his inaccuracies of observation . . ." [46] But because teaching is too complex a kind of behavior to be amenable to objective tests and measuring devices (at least at the present time), rating forms have been, and will probably continue to be, the type of instrument most widely used to evaluate teaching. Moreover, researchers are not entirely ignorant of the ways of these rating instruments, or of student raters. Over the year, a few useful findings have emerged.

For instance, ratings do not seem to be much affected by such factors as class size, rater's sex, rater's grade-point average, or teacher's sex. Required classes are not rated more severely than elective ones nor are nonmajors harsher in their ratings than majors. [47] Most studies indicate that the grade which a student expects to receive in a course is not related to his rating. (One exception to this finding occurred in the evaluation program conducted at the City College of New York in December 1965: in

[43] Quoted in "Men of Little Faith," editorial in the *Columbia Daily Spectator*, Dec. 7, 1965.

[44] Charles Frankel, "Rights and Responsibilities in the Student-College Relationship," *The College and the Student*, ed. Lawrence E. Dennis and Joseph F. Kauffman (Washington: American Council on Education, 1965), p. 246.

[45] *Education at Berkeley*, p. 57.

[46] Remmers, "Rating Methods in Research on Teaching," p. 329.

[47] Lehmann, "Evaluation of Instruction," p. 352. See also E. R. Guthrie, *The Evaluation of Teaching: A Progress Report* (Seattle: University of Washington, 1954), pp. 6–7.

this instance, it was found that students who expected to get A's and B's in a course tended to rate it higher than did other students.)[48] The larger the number of raters, the greater the reliability of the ratings: "If 25 or more student ratings are averaged, they are as reliable as the better educational and mental tests at present available." [49] A study at the University of Michigan indicated that there tends to be a consensus among students in their ratings of very good or very bad teachers, but less agreement about those in the middle range.[50]

Indeed, there seem to be only two factors that do have significant bearing on student ratings: the rater's class (graduate students tend to give higher ratings than do undergraduates; there are no significant differences in the ratings given by underclassmen and those given by upperclassmen, however) and the teacher's rank (instructors are rated lower than other ranks; however, among the other ranks, there are no significant differences).[51]

Finally, it has been found that students tend to be overly lenient in their ratings, particularly in cases where the administration conducts the program and requires evaluation of all faculty members and in cases where the faculty member himself requests evaluation and rating forms are filled out during the class period, thus making student participation more or less mandatory. At the University of Washington, for example, where evaluations are conducted by an office of student ratings and returns may be seen by its director (though the faculty member is left free to decide for himself if he wants such evaluations conducted in his class and if he wants the results forwarded to his department chairman), this tendency to rate high constitutes a major shortcoming in the program. Langen reports:

the median associate professor and the median assistant professor are more "superior" than "competent" and the median instructor is "competent plus." Even the bottom 10% of associate and assistant professors are "competent plus" and the bottom 10% of instructors seldom go below "competent minus." [52]

Most of these findings are based on studies limited to one rating instrument and one institution, so it is not possible to generalize from them too much. On the points mentioned, however, findings from different studies have been consistent with one another.

[48] *New York Times*, May 21, 1966.
[49] Remmers, "Rating Methods in Research on Teaching," p. 367.
[50] L. S. Woodburne, "Guidelines for Student Ratings of Teachers," Paper delivered at the Twenty-First National Conference on Higher Education in Chicago, Ill., March 15, 1966.
[51] Lehmann, "Evaluation of Instruction," p. 352.
[52] Thomas D. F. Langen, "Student Assessment of Teaching Effectiveness," p. 25.

Conclusions

It is foolhardy to regard student evaluations as a cure-all for the ills of higher education, but it is equally rash to dismiss them out-of-hand because their worth is not yet proven. Neither blind acceptance nor mulish rejection is an appropriate response at the present time. Granting at least that student evaluations offer a hopeful possibility for solving some of the current problems connected with evaluating teaching effectiveness and improving the quality of undergraduate instruction, we can delineate a few of the basic issues connected with their use.

First, and most immediately pressing, for what purposes should student evaluations be used? Should they remain unpublished and private to the teacher? One advantage to this practice is that it gives the instructor being rated a chance to read all the questionnaires, whereas in the case of published evaluations or evaluations that go to a chairman or a dean, he usually sees only a summary statement.[53] On the other hand, if only the instructor sees the ratings, he is under much less pressure to take their suggestions. And in cases where faculty participation in the rating program is voluntary, it is likely that those instructors who most need improvement will not even use the forms.

Should student evaluations be published in course and teacher critiques? How valuable are such critiques in helping students select classes? Do they give a reasonable and balanced picture, or do editors tend to sacrifice fairness to a desire to be clever? Are published evaluations specific enough in their comments to be helpful to teachers?

Should student evaluations be used as a basis for tenure and promotion decisions? Both the Yale faculty committee and the Muscatine committee answer this question in the negative, emphasizing the unhealthy atmosphere and ill feelings that may result from such use. In general, faculty feeling until fairly recently is summed up by Lehmann's statement that "the use of rating scales as a 'stick' by department heads and deans can only be injurious to faculty morale. It also encourages in students a false sense of their own capability and importance in passing judgments on professors." [54] Obviously, the tide of opinion on this point is turning: though some educators still deplore their use, many others recognize that systematic student ratings may be a useful addition to current methods of evaluating teaching effectiveness.

Granting that student evaluations should be used in promotion and tenure decisions, should all students or just a select group rate the instructors? In most cases, the answer so far has been that only the opinions of superior students should be considered. An exception is the City

[53] Werdell, *Course and Teacher Evaluation*, p. 24.
[54] Lehmann, "Evaluation of Instruction," p. 349.

College of New York, where the chairman of the faculty council of the liberal arts school made the following statement: "We thought that the relevance in evaluating a man as a teacher is by asking not just the superior student but the adequate and even mediocre one." [55]

What bearing do the characteristics of the institution have on the use of student ratings? For instance, it has been suggested that published course and teacher evaluations are particularly needed at the multiversity and at commuter colleges, where size or the absence of a resident student community results in inadequate communication among students about courses and teachers; on such campuses, published critiques make it possible for the student to get information not otherwise available to him.[56] Similarly, student ratings might best be used "for administrative purposes" at large universities, where emphasis on research may be an impediment to adequate concern with teaching and where size prevents faculty members from knowing one another even by reputation. At smaller institutions, and particularly at residential colleges, where the grapevine is likely to be in better working order, published guides and systematic student ratings for administrative purposes may be superfluous (as a professor at Amherst puts it, that college is small enough "for student opinion to be easily felt" [57]) and may even be injurious if close faculty-student relationships exist.

If campuswide evaluation programs are instituted, how can the full cooperation of the student body be enlisted? Many student evaluation programs are unsuccessful simply because not enough students take part. Even at Harvard, with its long history of published course evaluations, student participation is described as "too slow and tentative." If only one out of five students in a given course chooses to participate in evaluating the course, there is always some suspicion that the sample is biased—made up, perhaps, of the enthusiasts and the disgruntled—and the comments therefore unrepresentative of student opinion. (It could also be argued that the respondents are the serious students, the ones most vitally involved in the educational experience, and that therefore their ratings are likely to represent the most thoughtful and responsible student opinion. In voluntary programs where participation is low, the direction of the bias is a matter of conjecture.)

In cases where the student is under pressure to participate, as when the instructor himself administers the rating form during class time, this failure to cooperate may take two forms: students may not answer open-end questions fully enough to be helpful to the instructor, and students may

[55] Quoted in New York Times, May 14, 1966.
[56] Werdell, Course and Teacher Evaluation, p. 12.
[57] Quoted in Collegiate Press Service, Oct. 27, 1965.

not be honest enough in their responses. (Their tendency in such cases is to be too lenient.)

Finally, there are a number of considerations connected with the rating devices themselves. What questions should students be asked? Should the same rating form be used for all courses in all departments and at all levels? Which is preferable: a rating form composed of open-end items, which permit freer and more detailed responses, or one made up of easily coded items, which are more amenable to statistical analysis? How reliable is the device being used? How valid is it? Does it measure what it should be measuring if it is to provide an accurate and meaningful estimate of a teacher's effectiveness?

As Gustad points out, we are still patently ignorant of just "what contribution the teacher makes to what the student learns." [58] We make certain assumptions about what characteristics and behaviors of the instructor constitute effectiveness in teaching, but these assumptions are for the most part untested. However reliable the instruments we use, and however responsible, perceptive, and honest the student raters, the value of student evaluations must remain uncertain until we know that the qualities they are asked to assess are indeed related to the ultimate goals of education. And all too frequently, educators are even uncertain about what those goals should be.

This is not to say that we should delay action until we have come up with clear-cut answers to all these questions. That something is very wrong with undergraduate instruction at some of our institutions seems indisputable. The immediate situation requires that we proceed on our assumptions; the ultimate health of higher education will depend on our willingness to test these assumptions: to reject them if they prove false, to explore new possibilities. The new student involvement in the educational process—of which student evaluation is just one aspect— offers us an opportunity to come to grips with both matters of fact and matters of value in education.

[58] Gustad, "Evaluation of Teaching Performance," p. 280.

PART SIX

Curriculum Reform and Re-Formation

Reforming
General Education*

DANIEL BELL

It has been suggested that a liberal arts education has lost its force; that because of the recent curricular reforms the secondary school already covers, or will soon do so, the "general education" features of the college are mere repetition; and that the requirements of early specialization are in the process of transforming the college into a pre-professional school. In short, it has been stated that because the college is no longer the terminal educational experience, it has lost its distinctive function and is becoming simply a corridor between the secondary and the graduate schools. . . .

Let me begin by stating my commitment to general education within the framework of a liberal arts program in a college. By a liberal arts program, I mean an emphasis on the imagination of the humanities and history and the treatment of the conceptual grounds of knowledge in the sciences and social sciences, as the central core of the college's concern. By general education, I mean the focusing of this concern on courses which cut across disciplinary lines (as in the case of contemporary civilization and humanities programs) to deal with the history, tradition, and great works of Western civilization, and on courses which deal with the integrative problems or common subject matters of several disciplines. By a college, I mean a four-year school, standing between the secondary school and the graduate institution, which performs a function that differs from the other two. . . .

There is not, I believe, in education—and perhaps not in life—a quota of eternal verities, a set of invariant truths, a single quadrivium and

* Copyright © 1966 Columbia University Press. This paper is a rearrangement and adaptation of materials in chapters 4, 5, and 6 of *The Reforming of General Education: The Columbia College Experience in Its National Setting*, by Daniel Bell. The American Council on Education gratefully acknowledges the cooperation and permission of the Columbia University Press to publish extracts of this important book.

trivium that must be taught to a young man lest he be charged with the failure to be civilized or humane. There are tasks—tasks appropriate to the elucidation of tradition, the identification of societal values (which can be rejected as well as accepted), and the testing of knowledge—which have to be met by a college. . . .

But one has to locate the arenas of change if one seeks to determine what is in need of change. Society, the system of social arrangements to meet needs and solve tasks, is today changing rapidly, especially as technology, the instrument of change, becomes more amenable to definition and direction. Culture—the deposit of experience, the realm of judgment, and the arbiter of standards—changes more slowly, for in the domain of mind many truths and values coexist and there are no simple tests, such as functional rationality in economics, to determine the better mode. Human nature, that stubborn compound of passion and intelligence, unlimited appetite, and parochial upbringing, changes more slowly still. The educational process has to take all these dimensions into account in shaping the balance of experience and imagination that becomes for the individual a working principle in ordering his life.

Each generation—such is the nature of modernity—seeks to discover its own entelechy and, in so doing, to renew history as the present and to reshape the past, to assimilate the received ideas and to choose those relevant to its concerns. In this regard, the university with respect to its traditional function is in an anomalous position: it is called upon not only to conserve the past and reinterpret the present, but also to test the new. In fact, the confrontation of the "new"—the new not of sociology or the sciences, for these are part of a continuing tradition, but the new of sensibility and of that which calls itself post-modern— is the most perplexing challenge to the university today. It is first and foremost the problem of the humanities, since these are the bearers of tradition.

Whatever else may be said in criticism of American colleges (at least of the best of them), they cannot, as Lionel Trilling has pointed out, be called "indifferent to the modern." In fact, the tide—the literature of Yeats, Eliot, Lawrence, Joyce, Proust, and Kafka, and of such forebears as Rimbaud, Baudelaire, and Dostoevski—runs so strong as to swamp us all. This is a literature whose force, as Trilling puts it, "may be said to derive from its preoccupation with spiritual salvation. It is a literature which has taken to itself the dark power which certain aspects of religion once exercised over the human mind." [1] . . .

Is it the task of the university to be a clerisy, self-consciously guarding

---

[1] Lionel Trilling, "Commitment to the Modern," A commencement address at Harvard University, July 1962, reprinted in the *Harvard Alumni Bulletin*, July 7, 1962, pp. 739–42.

the past and seeking assertively to challenge the new? Or is it just a bazaar, offering Coleridge and Blake, Burckhardt and Nietzsche, Weber and Marx as antiphonal prophets, each with his own call? No consensual answer is possible, perhaps, because the university is no longer the citadel of the traditional mode—only the simple-minded can believe it is—but an arena in which the critics once outside the Academy have, like the tiger (or Tyger) once outside the gates of society, found a place—deservedly—within. And the tension between past and future, mind and sensibility, tradition and experience, for all its strains and discomfitures, is the only source for maintaining the independence of inquiry itself.

If the confrontation of modernity with tradition and of rational intellect with modernity is one of the tasks of a college in responding to the sentient few, the humanizing of the educable many is, perhaps, the great task of liberal education today. The question is not "who is this new man, the American?" but "who is the generic man that stalks the world today?"

All of ancient wisdom recognized the double nature of man; as *behema* (wild animal) or *halachic* (law-abiding); Apollonian and Dionysian; Caligulaic and Stoic; sinner and redeemed; instinct and reason; impulse and intelligence. But each age has also seen man through a special prism fashioned to its controlling view of man's centrality. For the Greeks, virtue and reason constituted man's essential nature, and man realized his potential through the rule of measure and the life of the mind. The Christians saw man as struggling against powerful sinful impulses, hopefully transfigured by the healing power of love. The bourgeois world-view, concentrating on things—property and money—introduced a test of functional rationality for the efficient allocation of labor power and the maximal use of resources. The "reactive" philosophies of the late nineteenth century—Nietzschean, Sorelian, Paretian, and Freudian—showed us the irrational forces that are dammed up and spill over when the "self," divided by functions and curbed by social repression, breaks loose.

Modern social science, reflecting on man in a complex, interrelated, differentiated world, has given us a still different picture—that of behavioral man. Behavioral man is a learner, capable of great feats. Far removed from his animal origins on this evolutionary scale, he has created many tools for shaping and even transforming his environment. But in his relations with other men, behavioral man is a seeker not of truth but of deceptions, about himself as well as others. . . .

So, behavioral man is social man—social product, social producer, and social seeker—to a greater degree than he is philosophical man, or religious man, or political man, or the great man held up as avatar by common folk. The traditional images of man have stressed motives like reason or faith, impulse or self-interest; the behavioral science image stresses the "social-adjusting" definition of all these. Is this then the whole truth or even just an added truth?

But what, then, is reality? It was Zeuxis, the Ionic iconographer, who painted grapes so naturally that, as Pliny tells us, the birds flew up to peck at them. But who was the deceiver, and who the deceived?

What are we to say of a world where man has become a searcher of deceptions, about himself as well as others, without seeking for truth? Can one accept behavioral man on his own terms? Or does the university have a responsibility to change this man—for the portrait of modern man as portrayed by Berelson and Steiner [2] is an indictment of contemporary society, an indictment that brings the university before the bar of humanitas? If nothing else, the nature of behavioral man is a justification for strengthening the humanities in liberal education.

In elliptical fashion, I have begun with two realms, that of sensibility (and the demonic) and that of social man (and his self-deceptions), and posed perhaps extreme formulations about each. Yet this was not done for rhetorical or paradoxical purposes, but to define two aspects of the culture as these present themselves in the form of tasks for the university. For the lure of sensibility attracts those sentient and talented individuals (as well as their modish camp followers) who, in exploring the limits of esthetic and moral radicalism, fall at times into a dandyism, a beat or nihilistic mood which subverts not only the existing order but tradition itself. The self-deceptions—and often the single-minded careerism—of behavioral man (the mass-man foreshadowed by Ortega y Gasset) muffle a social conscience and a spirit of critical inquiry which are the necessary attributes of a civilized man. In what way, then, can or should the university confront both challenges?

The university cannot remake a world (though in upholding standards it plays some part in such attempts). It cannot even remake men. But it can liberate young people by making them aware of the forces that impel them from within and constrict them from without. It is in this sense, the creation of self-consciousness in relation to tradition, that the task of education is metaphysics, metasociology, metapsychology, and, in exploring the nature of its own communications, metaphilosophy and metalanguage. This, in itself, is the enduring rationale of a liberal education and the function of the college years. . . .

In contrasting general education with specialism, the Harvard report of 1945 defined the first as "that education which looks first of all to

[2] Bernard Berelson and George A. Steiner, *Human Behavior: An Inventory of Scientific Findings* (New York: Harcourt, Brace & World, 1964).

[the student's] life as a responsible human being and citizen" and the second as occupational training through the acquisition of an art or a technique. On reflection, both definitions seem wide of the mark. One cannot civilize a man "in general," for it is only by confronting him with problems that are meaningful to him, most directly by the moral choices that may occur in the pursuit of his own profession, that one can tell whether or not he has learned to apply the humane arts. As for the second: to acquire a technique without at the same time becoming aware of the intellectual context of the art, is to quickly outmode that training itself.

In fact, I do not think that the distinction between general education and specialism really holds. One must embody and exemplify general education through disciplines; and one must extend the context of specialism so that the ground of knowledge is explicit. The common bond of the two is the emphasis on conceptual inquiry. To this extent, in the reconciliation of liberal education and specialism, training cannot deal with techniques in the narrow sense, but with the foundations of knowledge itself: i.e., how a particular discipline establishes its con cepts; how these concepts, seen as fluid inquiry, need to be revised to meet new problems; how one establishes the criteria of choice for one, rather than another, alternative patterns of inquiry. In effect, general education is education in the conduct and strategy of inquiry itself.[3]

There are three rationales for establishing the centrality of method, or of conceptual inquiry, as the foundation for college education—cutting across general background as well as the specialized courses. One is that in the present phase of the organization of knowledge, one can no longer train people for specific intellectual tasks or provide a purely vocational training. In effect, obsolescence of specializations indicates that one cannot any longer educate a person for a "job." One has to provide the means for intellectual mobility, for continuing education, for mid-career refreshment; and this can be done only by a grounding in the modes of conceptual inquiry.

Beyond this sociological fact is the second of the rationales—the overturn in the structure of scientific thought that was initiated by the conceptual revolution in physics in the mid-1920s.[4] For a short time during the late nineteenth century, a number of leading scientists—Karl Pearson, W. K. Clifford, and Lord Kelvin, among others—held

---

[3] For an illustrative "paradigm" of this organization of inquiry, see Joseph J. Schwab, "What Do Scientists Do?" *Behavioral Science*, January 1960.

[4] I follow the line of reasoning used by Thomas Kuhn in his *The Structure of Scientific Revolutions* (Chicago: University of Chicago Press, 1962), and I borrow some specific examples from Joseph Schwab's *The Teaching of Science as Enquiry* (Cambridge, Mass.: Harvard University Press, 1964), pp. 9–14.

the view that science was a matter of uncovering the "facts of nature" and reporting on what was immediately observable and measurable. . . .

The nature of scientific inquiry today implies the disappearance of the "self-evident giveness" of fixed dimensions, or the idea that facts can be treated as self-existing givens. In one sense it is a return to the original Kantian proposition that knowledge is contingent on the knower and on the questions he asks to organize and guide his operations. But contrary to Kant, the new scientific conceptions do not arise out of some fixed *a priori*, for the selection of facts depends in each case upon conceptual principles of the inquiry, and these are not fixed but subject to change.

This conceptual revolution is not restricted to physics alone. As a mode of inquiry it has changed the character of all the sciences. . . . The consequence of these revolutions in conceptual inquiry—the third rationale for establishing the centrality of method as a keystone of general education—is that the duration of a revisionary cycle in scientific knowledge has been drastically shortened. . . . Almost every field today is in a state of fluid, rather than stable, inquiry; one can no longer assume a fixed body of received knowledge as the guide to further problems. The result is that the biology or chemistry or physics or sociology or economics that one learned thirty years ago is wholly inadequate to the newer conceptual structures that guide inquiry at the frontiers of these fields today. . . .

The responsibility of educators is a heavy one. It requires a consistent self-consciousness in science and social science education. . . . What is required is a radically new approach to science teaching as conceptual innovation, conceptions that involve scrutiny of the organizing principles of each discipline as an integral part of the imparting of the discipline itself. It is in this sense, perhaps, that one joins hands with the old notion of the quadrivium (arithmetic and music as the exemplars of proportion and harmony; geometry and astronomy representing the structure of things) and the trivium (grammar, rhetoric, logic representing the structure in words). In that ancient formulation an "art" was a technique, and the seven liberal arts that constituted the core of education were not so much areas of knowledge as tools for getting and dispensing knowledge. But the purpose of such techniques was also, at least for the creative few, to lead them to *scientia*, or the structure of ideas itself. It is in this sense that the centrality of method has a focus, and a goal—the idea of the creative formulation of change, of *scientia*.[5]

In this emphasis on the centrality of method, there is a positive new role for the college as an institution standing between the secondary

[5] See James S. Ackerman, "On Scientia," *Daedalus*, Winter 1965.

school and graduate research work. One of its fundamental purposes must be to deal with the modes of conceptualization, the principles of explanation, and the nature of verification. The world is always double-storied: the factual order, and the logical order imposed upon it. The emphasis in the college must be less on what one knows and more on the self-conscious ground of knowledge; how one knows what one knows, and the principle of the relevant selection of facts.

In this emphasis on method, one risks that sterile debate—whether you can teach method apart from subject matter. The answer, of course, is that one cannot. But the shoe is really on the other foot: can one teach a subject without an awareness of method? In this respect, the distinctions, for pedagogical purposes, between conceptualization, discipline, and subject matter should be clear. A *concept*, in this specific usage, is a term that allows us to group together different phenomena, or selected aspects of phenomena, under a common rubric. The grouping we make is a function of whatever different purpose of analysis we may have in mind. A *discipline*, then, consists of a coherent group of interrelated concepts that can be applied to kindred phenomena and that allow one to make theoretical or explanatory statements about the relationships of these phenomena. A *subject matter* is a related class of phenomena that can be analyzed by a particular discipline. (Thus sociology is a discipline and ethnic-group relations a subject matter; economics is a discipline and international trade a subject matter.)

All of this leads to the preliminary proposition—a point I shall emphatically come back to in the discussion of curriculum—that the nature of college education can now be envisaged as a series of logical steps in which first comes the acquisition of a general background, second the training in a discipline, third the application of this discipline to a number of relevant subjects, and fourth the effort to link disciplines in dealing with common problems. It is this progression, involving at each step of the way an awareness of conceptual innovation and method, that is the heart of the ordering of a curriculum. . . .

The pattern of knowledge is fundamentally triadic, and different principles govern the acquisition of knowledge in the sciences, the social sciences, and the humanities, with important consequences for the theory and practice of pedagogy. In the sciences (and in mathematics), the learning is *sequential*: within any science, stipulated levels of prerequisites define the kinds of knowledge necessary before one can proceed to the next level. In the social sciences, the pattern is one of *linkages* between fields. Elements of economic policy, for example, are understandable only in a political context, and this in turn is dependent upon some conception of the social community. In the humanities, knowledge is *concentric*; one moves within many different circles of meaning in the effort to attain, if ever, an understanding of a text and an experience. . . .

If this triadic division has any validity, then a number of pedagogical consequences may follow, particularly for the relation of specialized work in college to graduate school, on the one hand, and of the colleges to the secondary schools, on the other. In the social sciences, for example, it suggests that a crosshatching arrangement may be necessary, wherein a student who wanted to study sociology in graduate school would as an undergraduate major not in sociology but in history and economics, or psychology and anthropology. This is not to argue for interdisciplinary courses in the early college years, but quite the contrary. Where interdisciplinary courses have failed, it has been because they have taken up "cross-hatch" topics before a student had any knowledge of the disciplines required. In those courses, a student was introduced to the social sciences through the topic of "culture and personality" before knowing any anthropology or psychology; or to the topic of "planning and the market" before knowing any economics or political science. This is not meant to derogate such topics. But if they are to be valid as social science subjects, students should have some knowledge of the disciplines first, rather than pick them up, *ad hoc*, along the way, in the general social science course. The argument here is that a grounding in a discipline, in its conceptual frameworks and analytical techniques, should be the prerequisite for interdisciplinary work. Students who seek to pursue one or another social science field in graduate school would do well not to specialize in that subject in college but to concentrate on disciplines that would provide the contextual basis and the linkages for a better understanding of his own subsequent graduate specialization. . . .

The very conception of an intellectual discipline implies a method of analysis and a logical framework of concepts at high levels of generality and, indeed, of abstraction. The heart of a college education today is mastering a discipline (not acquiring a specialization which is a fixed knowledge of a small piece of subject matter through the use of a discipline). But within a liberal arts framework, mastering a discipline gains a significant dimension only if that mastery is placed within a proper sequence of understanding. What I have been proposing is such an orderly sequence. The idea of a "third tier," which I propose, is that it would apply for each field, or set into appropriate context, the knowledge previously acquired. The Columbia College curriculum would thus be organized on these four "steps":

1. History and Tradition. The first step is a detailed discovery, through the Contemporary Civilization and Humanities program, of

the history and traditions of Western civilization, the awareness of the great works of moral imagination and science, the basic processes of social change, the great intellectual movements of self-conscious reflection and ideas on the events of change.

2. Introduction to a Discipline. The second step is the introduction to a discipline. Through the proposed "math-science" courses, the nonscientist will have a detailed sense of how a specific science acquires, utilizes, and revises its basic concepts. Through the proposed social science options, all students will have the opportunity of learning how at least one social science organizes its perspective on society; and in the case of the social science major, he will have an introduction to a discipline other than his own.

3. The Extension of the Discipline to Subjects. The organization of the major program is essentially the application of the discipline to different subject matters in the field, and this would be the heart of the third year and the upper-college courses.

4. The Third Tier. The third tier is a synoptic program, at the senior level, whose purpose is twofold: to deal with the methodological and philosophical (and, in the case of the social sciences, historical) presuppositions of a field, to show the application of the discipline to general problems, or to issues requiring a multidisciplinary approach, in order to test the operation of the discipline in a wider context. These contexts, almost invariably in the social sciences, and increasingly in the biological sciences, involve issues of value or of moral choice; and the explication of the value problems involved would be an added purpose of these courses.

So defined, the third-tier courses become a distinctive contribution to general education. They seek to explore interrelated issues between disciplines, to try to create a philosophical sophistication about the foundations of the fields, and to raise, where possible, value problems in the application of the discipline. These third-tier courses differ from earlier kinds of general education courses—such as Contemporary Civilization B at Columbia or Social Science 2 at Chicago—which were either introductory courses implying the existence of an interdisciplinary set of logically related concepts (as at Chicago), or courses focused mainly on great historical topics (such as industrialization) or large-scale policy choices (such as planning versus laissez-faire) to which the student brought no previous work in at least one discipline in order to appreciate either method or materials. The present proposal differs further in that the same third-tier, or synoptic, courses would not be required of *all* students in the College: each division—the social sciences, the humanities, and the sciences—would have third-tier courses appropriate to the particular problems of each field, and each student within a divisional area would be required, in his senior year, to take a specified number of these third-tier courses.[6]

In principle, there would be *four* kinds of courses in the third tier. These would be courses in:

1. The historical foundations of the intellectual disciplines in the field;
2. The methodological and philosophical presuppositions of the disciplines;
3. The extension of the various disciplines to applied problems;
4. Comparative studies, particularly of non-Western cultures. . . .

General education, in the main, had three broad aims:

1. To provide a "common learning";
2. To give the student a comprehensive understanding of the Western tradition;
3. To combat intellectual fragmentation with interdisciplinary courses.

The idea of a common learning was an attempt to recapture the humanist ideal of an age when, as Douglas Bush put it, all educated men had more or less the same kind of classical education and read, spoke, and wrote the same language, literarily or metaphorically or both. But the effort to create a common language froze into one dogma that a common learning had to be a specific number of "great books." Or it settled on the notion that isolated masterpieces could be approached, apart from their time and context, as works that spoke so directly to the individual that the common reading of such works would provide a common experience. Or the humanist goal was obscured by the claim that a tradition consisted only in the reading of the works of the past.

The trouble with these approaches lies in the idea that a few works can define the central range of human issues and experiences, and that if individuals are exploring great emotional and imaginative themes in order to achieve a common ground of discourse, they all have to read the same works. What may be more important than a single tradition and a single past (for there are many traditions and many different pasts) is to have the student accept *the idea* of tradition (and become part of its continuity) and *the idea* of the past (and relate himself to it). Nor can the humanities assume that there exists only an "eternal present" in which sensibilities are awakened anew with each encounter; without history the humanities are only myth and commentary. An intellectual community is not necessarily defined by similar readings and a common fund of allusions (though this makes discourse easier) but rather by common standards and values that permit the

---

[6] While these would be required for students within each division, there is no reason why they should not be open to qualified students who would want to take some third-tier courses in fields other than their own.

interchange of judgments and opinions on diverse matters of experience.

The second purpose of general education, a comprehensive understanding of the Western tradition, has, particularly in the last ten years, come to seem parochial. The study of other civilizations as rich and complex as Western culture has contributed to this parochialism, along with the growing syncretism (particularly in the arts and to some extent in religion) that tends to mingle diverse traditions into a *musée imaginaire*. As a result, a number of schools have been perplexed by the question whether the Western tradition means the study of "Western civilization" (e.g., an effort to combine ideas, arts, and religions into a succession of "periods" or "styles"—Gothic, Renaissance, Baroque, etc.), or, more simply, the study of "Western history," in which the chronology of events and "islands of ideas" build up a loosely patterned background to the present. The question has been unresolved.

The interdisciplinary aim has suffered the most and has indeed all but disappeared from many general education curriculums. Institutional factors in part account for this failure: in many colleges the departments preferred to concentrate on the disciplinary sequences and directed their students to the specific research problems of their subject, instead of attempting the more difficult task of searching out a conceptual language common to several fields (there is still no agreement between anthropologists and sociologists on the scope of the term "culture"). Even more telling were the intellectual difficulties inherent in interdisciplinary studies. To some scholars such studies meant a new holistic approach that would fuse diverse disciplines (e.g., the study of "culture and personality" or of "national character" would combine anthropology and psychology, or psychology and history), but this early enthusiasm did not materialize into a continuing body of work. To others it meant the study of policy problems, bringing the resources of different disciplines to bear on specific issues. (A favorite chestnut has been Planning versus the Market.) But students were often asked to consider complicated topics when they had no training in any of the disciplines necessary for intelligent judgments about the dispute. Criticism of such topics was airily dismissed with the argument that these topics were primarily "value problems" or "moral issues," as if a discussion of goals required no technical knowledge at all.

My objection to interdisciplinary courses is not to the idea itself, but to the place they occupied in the general education sequences.

The disenchantment of many colleges—I do not mean Columbia, Chicago, or Harvard—with the idea of general education, and their difficulties in recruiting teachers for the courses, have led a number of them simply to substitute "distribution" requirements for the general education sequences; and this has brought them back to the very disorder that had prompted the widespread adoption of general education in the mid-1940s and the 1950s.

A "distribution" requirement means that a student has a free option in the number of courses outside his major subject or concentration. Thus a science major might be required to take at least two social science and two humanities courses. No specific courses are stipulated or prescribed. Nor is there any ordered sequence or arrangement of courses. It is simply assumed that a student's education is broadened by some courses in other fields than his own. Ironically, a number of educational "radicals," once fiercely opposed to what they called the "cafeteria system," are now enthusiastically in favor of this laissez-faire arrangement on the grounds that students should be encouraged to prowl around on their own, taking any courses that intrigue them, and that a distribution requirement is as good a way as any of shaking up the creaking system because it shows the faculty what the students really want.

The return to a distribution requirement is, I believe, an admission of intellectual defeat. At worst, it serves up a mishmash of courses that are only superficially connected. At the very worst, it stimulates a modishness that caters to the immediate and the sensational, or that looks for esoteric or gnostic links because the ordinary canons of intellectual order are too repressive. Pascal once said that law without power is anarchy (and power without law is tyranny). One may extend the apothegm by saying that anarchy without intellectual order is perversity (and intellectual order without freedom is dogmatism). . . .

If the task of the college is to broaden the context of specialism, it will not be accomplished by literary poultices. It *can* be achieved, perhaps, by making the intellectual specialist knowledgeable about the logic of inquiry and the philosophical presuppositions of a subject. "The intellectual life of man," William James once wrote, "consists almost wholly in his substitution of a conceptual order for the perceptual order in which his experiences originally come." [7] The effort of sophistication, the beginning (but not the end) of self-consciousness, is the effort to uncover the underlying intellectual structure in which one's work is embedded. In this way, the context of specialism can be enlarged, and becomes an aspect of the liberal education itself.

But to deal with concepts alone would mean choosing an arid intellectualism that would dry up our senses and leave us only with the shadows in the cave. Concepts are "maps of relations," but by their nature they are "forever inadequate to the fullness of the reality to be

[7] William James, *Some Problems of Philosophy* (New York: Longmans, Green & Co., 1940), p. 51.

shown." Reality, James insisted, "consists of existential particulars" of which "we become aware only in the perceptual flux." [8] . . .

An ordered curriculum, it is argued, must have a set of substantive ends rooted in some moral definition of man or some ultimate picture of nature. But those who posit virtue or reason as the ends of education, or of society, put too much faith in their resounding abstractions. To say that the purpose of education is the rational pursuit of knowledge, or a love of truth, is not to state an end, for these are the necessary conditions of any intellectual life.[9] Those who speak of the need for fixed ends usually mean a fixed set of books or a fixed set of ideas that for them exemplifies truth or a specific notion of obligation. But such a conception would lead only to the circumscription of truth and the creation of a closed system of dogmatic and even tyrannical knowledge (even though the tyrant may have a philosopher as his adviser). . . .

The ends of education are many: to instill an awareness of the diversity of human societies and desires; to be responsive to great philosophers and imaginative writers who have given thought to the predicaments that have tried and tested men; to acquaint a student with the limits of ambition and the reaches of humility; to realize that no general principle or moral absolute, however strongly it may be rooted in a philosophical tradition, can give an infallible answer to any particular dilemma.

Writing a curriculum, like cooking, can be the prototype of the complete moral act. There is perfect free will. One can put in whatever one wishes, in whatever combination. Yet in order to know what one has, one has to taste the consequences. And as in all such acts, there is an ambiguity for evil, in that others who did not share in the original pleasures may have to taste the consequences. In sum, it is the moral of a cautionary tale.

[8] *Ibid.*, p. 78.

[9] "Truths are as plentiful as falsehoods, since each falsehood admits of a negation which is true. But scientific activity is not the indiscriminate amassing of truths; science is selective and seeks the truths that count for most, either in point of intrinsic interest or as instruments for coping with the world," Willard Van Quine, *Methods of Logic* (New York: Henry Holt & Co., 1950).

Commentaries on

Reforming
General Education

CHARLES MUSCATINE, M. MARGARET BALL,
RICHARD H. SULLIVAN

Re-Forming—Not Simply Reforming—
General Education

CHARLES MUSCATINE

So much of Professor Bell's book *The Reforming of General Education* has been compressed into the abridged paper [1] that I hope to be forgiven for making generous reference to the book itself and at many points commenting on it rather than on the paper. Recourse to the book is also helpful in making clear that Professor Bell is well aware of the issues and possible criticisms surrounding his views. What a commentator can contribute, then, is mostly in the way of elaborating and emphasizing, and not in bringing forth ideas that Professor Bell may have overlooked.

In his thoroughly laudable attempt to protect the identity of the liberal arts college, Professor Bell seems to me to conserve too much of its traditional machinery. Rather, curricular reform should start with re-examination of the idea of "curriculum" itself. More than invention and reshuffling of courses, we need to examine the "course" as an institution. While Professor Bell beautifully disposes of "the old debate" between the teaching of method and the teaching of subject matter, he does not re-examine—he tacitly conserves—the conventional concept of college teaching itself. (If the example of literature teaching cited in the book on page 226 is any indication, he favors a kind of teaching in which the teacher may be doing too much of the work.)

[1] See footnote on p. 347 of the present volume.

What I am suggesting, of course, is that the problem of general education in college may be related more closely to the problems of college education in general than Professor Bell has it. It may be less related to the presumed enemies without—the graduate schools, with their cry for specialization; the high schools, with their various encroachments—less related to these than to the enemy within: namely, the intrinsic badness of college courses themselves in answering the legitimate needs and desires of today's students. It is a pity that an account of the nature of our students had to be excluded from this study. Judging by his brief analysis of the condition of professors, Professor Bell on students would have been highly illuminating.

Concerned to reform the "intellectual structure" of college education, Professor Bell makes some unchallengeable observations on the accelerating obsolescence of factual knowledge; his proposal to emphasize something less perishable than "subject matter" is surely in the right direction. As the informing idea of the curriculum, he would replace subject matter with "the modes of conceptual inquiry" of each of the major disciplines.

Accepting the rightness of this general direction, we may wish to object that the study of "modes of conceptualization" is not equally satisfying as an informing concept in all parts of the college nor at all times in the undergraduate's career. It seems to be most formulable and discussable for the natural sciences, though even here it sounds more like a high-level (graduate?) philosophical inquiry than a study continuously and informingly present. In humanities it sounds even less satisfactory. Professor Bell's distinction of three characteristic patterns of learning—science as *sequential,* social science as *linked,* humanities as *concentric*—clarifies the problem but does not quite solve it. *Sequence* and *linkage* suggest controllable and describable "modes of conceptual inquiry" much more promisingly than does *concentricity.* I am not saying that a general methodology of the humanities is impossible; but I *am* saying that we are far from having one, or even of having enough pieces to organize a curriculum on.

Some indication of the difficulties here are expressed by Richard Sullivan in his comments on the proposed "third tier" senior courses.[2] The difficulty in the humanities "third tier" is well illustrated in Professor Bell's recommendations (pp. 266-67) of a course in the history of criticism; a course in modern literature; a course in the nature of language; and a literature course in a foreign language. All of these are, of course, perfectly solid subjects widely offered at present. None, however, suggests a *coherent* account of the "methodological and philosophical presuppositions of the discipline" (p. 258), if indeed the humanities is a "discipline" in quite the same sense that science is. The

[2] See Sullivan, "Perplexities and Realities," pp. 336–69 of the present volume.

history of criticism is far from coherent, and the coherent discipline of linguistics is hardly characteristic of the humanities.

Another source of discomfort in the proposal is its apparent deferment, to the fourth year, of questions which insistently thrust themselves on even the youngest student: "how his major subject can be applied to a problem area" (p. 209); and "the issues of value and moral choice; . . . the explication of the value problems involved" (p. 257).

An excellent guidepost to constructive modification of his proposals can be found in Professor Bell's own wise observation that "One cannot civilize a man 'in general,' for it is only by confronting him with problems that are meaningful to him, most directly by the moral choices that may occur in the pursuit of his own profession, that one can tell whether or not he has learned to apply the humane arts" (p. 157). Suppose we pursue for a moment the notion that general education may not be something different from specialized education, but can, rather, be thought of as specialized education taught in a certain spirit. What spirit? Again one can hear the satisfying note here and there in Professor Bell's language [emphasis mine]:

The discussion has to be put in a context wherein the student understands the nature of evidence, the reason *why a scholar chose* some facts rather than others. . . . (p. 172)

[The old history of sciences course] did not give the student the sense of what *science as an enterprise* did. . . . (pp. 237–38)

. . . one must study how a particular discipline *goes about its business.* . . . (p. 238)

The phrases emphasized are satisfying for their fleeting suggestion of the wholeness of scholarship. They suggest the integration of the theoretical, the methodological, even the factual, with such matters as interest, motivation, values, and moral choices. Science "as an enterprise" is what scientists as men *do*; it is a complex of skills and attitudes, a characteristic stance, a style of life. The same can be said of the enterprises of the social scientist, the historian, the critic, and the artist. It is a creative person's whole stance, his life style, that will survive the obsolescence of knowledge, and might provide an even more pervasive and secure basis for education than Professor Bell's "modes of conceptualization."

An education centered on this idea might work well with the beginning students in many places who do not seem to have the prefabricated motivation and natural intellectual bent that Professor Bell assumes in his Columbia freshmen. One would *begin* with real scientific, social, and ethical problems in all their lifelike difficulty and urgency—and let the student derive from them the energy to go on to the specialized disciplines and learn how scholarship can be brought to bear on these problems. Early specialization would not be frowned on; generalization—putting the specialty in its proper perspective—could safely come later. Indeed, genuine enthusiasm and motivation in one special field can be harnessed to the service of the others. If you want to reach a dedicatedly anti-aesthetic engineer with a course in baroque painting, first lure him into a discussion of the beauty and ugliness of roads, bridges, and buildings.

A courageous reforming of general education in the colleges should not at the same time limit our secondary schools to "emphasis on primary skills and factual data"; high school factual data become obsolete, too. Neither should it be afraid of the graduate school. Indeed, it should expose the student to real scientists, real historians, real critics, and real artists as early and as often as possible, so that they can convey to him (not a group of survey courses!) a sense of what different kinds of creative persons solving different kinds of problems are like.

Reforming general education should have a salutary effect on professors themselves, on their teaching and their scholarship. The young are embarrassingly but constructively candid in their current demands for relevance in the college experience. To answer them candidly would not necessarily be to abandon the intellect or to give up tradition for ephemeral concerns. It would, however, lead to a revival of true dialogue in teaching and to some redefining of tradition. We would have to reshuffle the great masterpieces and reinterpret some of them. We would have to rewrite a lot of history, and possibly put the histories of science and technology in a more prominent place. We would have to re-examine what we mean by "Western Civilization" and whether the concept is still useful. (Are we ready to rethink it as "Human Civilization"?) We would certainly have to give more concerned attention to what Professor Bell calls "non-Western Civilization."

Toward Open-end College Education

M. MARGARET BALL

MY FIRST COMMENT is that I heartily concur in much that Professor Bell has said both in his paper and in the excellent book from which it was distilled.

On the ends suggested by Dr. Bell, most of us would agree that a major task of liberal education is "the humanizing of the educable many." We might also agree that in so doing, within the framework of our educational patterns, the humanizing process—viewed as a widening of horizons on both human societies and great ideas—must somehow be combined with the study of disciplines so as to lead eventually, whether directly or indirectly, to earning a livelihood. I would, perhaps, go further than Dr. Bell in emphasizing the desirability that the student develop a system of values by which he can live by the time he graduates.

I certainly agree that "one has to provide the means for intellectual mobility, for continuing education, for mid-career refreshment" both for a furthering of the humanization process and for more practical reasons. That it is important to learn how to learn in the course of a liberal education goes without saying, as does the desirability of learning how to apply the mind to subject matter in such a way as to be able to use one's discipline, with or without retooling, at any given future point in time.

Since I have been asked to comment on Professor Bell's proposals from the standpoint of the education of women—at least in part—I may say that an approach which stresses these goals should have great utility for *all* students in this period of rapid change. It may be particularly promising for women, since many of them expect to be in and out of their disciplines from time to time as they seek to fit careers or jobs into patterns of marriage and child-rearing. Women know from the moment of graduation, if not before, that they are likely to have difficulty in keeping up with their fields. Men, too, are probably becoming aware that they may have a problem, although for most of them the problem may well derive from changes within their discipline rather than from outside pressures or commitments.

Dr. Bell's approach would appear to have other virtues for women students. Women who are married, whether or not they are employed outside the home, are necessarily concerned with home and husband (if they would *stay* married), children, community, and self—probably in that order. We will not go into the matters of home and husband at this point, or how to remain happy though house-keeping. As mothers, however, women have the job of both helping and understanding their offspring. The emphasis on methodology in Dr. Bell's plan should help them cope with such study problems as the new math, on the "helping" front. The emphasis upon the need to be familiar with and able to relate to tradition, to be aware of "the great works of moral imagination and science, the basic processes of social change, the great intellectual movements of self-conscious reflection and ideas on the events of change" should offer considerable assistance not only in helping to mold character but also in understanding the changing behavior patterns that seem to accompany each new teen-age generation.

To state the matter on a broader basis: In American society, women largely seem to have inherited the chief responsibility for perpetuating our cultural heritage, not only in transmitting it to their own children but also in supporting various community projects related to that heritage—its general transmission and enjoyment. The breadth of approach suggested by Dr. Bell would obviously help women educated under it to sustain at least some of the roles that most of them find themselves assuming in home and community. From the standpoint of self, the vast majority of women graduates soon discover that if they would continue to grow—either for their own benefit or to keep up with their husbands and children—they must themselves take the initiative for their continuing education. Any approach that provides a broad base for this process, as does Dr. Bell's, has much to recommend it.

But let us not assess the proposals purely on the basis of sex. Dr. Bell has not recommended them as an academic palliative for the ills of women, but rather as a possible cure for the ills of undergraduate educational programs, and properly so.

Dr. Bell's central theme is that the desired goals of undergraduate liberal education can be achieved only by concentrating on method—by teaching "modes of conceptual inquiry," "principles of explanation, and the nature of verification" rather than facts—within the context of the several disciplines. With his repudiation of the teaching of method in a vacuum, no right-thinking person can disagree. The teaching of facts *per se* has long been suspect, at least in the better educational circles. In general, the liberal arts institutions have claimed that their central function was to teach people "how to think." Granted that Dr. Bell's formulation of primary function is more precise than that of many of his predecessors, and recognizing that facts, long unstable, are now notoriously so, we may ask the question: Is method likely to be sufficiently more stable than information to warrant giving it the central educational role that Dr. Bell has assigned to it? Is there, in short, any reason to believe that method will be immune from change in a cosmos that is spinning as rapidly as this one? The only answer, I suspect, rests on the point that method is apt to change to a lesser degree, and at a slower pace, than information. And this probably is sufficient to support Dr. Bell's main contention. Certainly one must try to find something of at least relatively enduring value in the educational process—ideas, values, methods—or give up the notion that there is any point whatever to attempts to "educate" the young in a period of rapid change.

Dr. Bell's proposals for a progression from "acquisition of a general background" to "training in a discipline," the application of one's own discipline to relevant subjects, and "the effort to link disciplines in dealing with common problems," cause me a few difficulties that are probably not insuperable. The first—general background—appears on its face to take us back to the existing general education courses from which the scheme as a whole purports to release us, although admittedly the impact of such courses would be materially affected by the rest of Dr. Bell's proposals. If, however, instead of the approaches to be found in some Contemporary Civilization courses—the interdisciplinary approach, which he deplores at this level—one should incorporate selected courses in history, literature, philosophy, and perhaps religion into the freshman and perhaps sophomore programs, this difficulty might be largely overcome. Together with his "third tier" concept—which rightly places the interdisciplinary approach at the advanced, rather than the elementary, level—we might come closer to our goal than most of us now succeed in doing.

The introduction of the student to modes of inquiry in the sciences, social sciences, and humanities might well go on concurrently with some of the acquisition of general background envisaged in the first step. Certainly, the student's introduction to his discipline should come no later than the sophomore year, if he is to be able to contribute from his own study to the interdisciplinary approach to problems envisaged at the advanced undergraduate level. This view seems not inconsistent with what Professor Bell is proposing.

It is important, I think, that Dr. Bell envisages a consideration of "issues of value or of moral choice," and "the explication of the value problems involved" in the third tier. To this extent he goes a certain distance along the road I mentioned earlier in urging the desirability of the student's developing by graduation a system of values by which he can live. Dr. Bell, however, relates the matter of values and moral choices explicitly to the discipline at this stage, and it is unclear how much further he would be prepared to go.

This leaves me, I suspect, agreeing with Dr. Bell on the ends of liberal education and on a fair share of the means that he has so ably outlined. If the discussion of means is pursued in our institutions, we may find the new approaches to the agreed-on ends that are so badly needed if our graduates are to ground their specialties in the total culture.

Perplexities and Realities

RICHARD H. SULLIVAN

PROFESSOR BELL'S STIMULATING AND PROVOCATIVE PAPER, like his book, refers essentially to three noted investments in general education, by Columbia, Harvard, and Chicago. They were undertaken at different points, for different lengths of time, and with different rationales and institutional arrangements. One might argue that this variance is eloquent testimony to the great diversity that confronts any analyst or examiner, for these three varying efforts have been attempted by faculties of institutions that, by many objective criteria, are very close to each other on any total "map" of higher education.

That his inquiry has been thus restricted is a matter, to me, not for criticism but for regret. All three undergraduate colleges of reference exist within major private universities of exceptional financial resources, of outstanding scholarly competence, of restricted student enrollments, and of unusual selectivity in admissions. It is difficult and perhaps risky to transfer to a larger spectrum of colleges his particular formulations of new kinds of—or a new basis for—general education. This seems to me to be the case, not only because of the different characteristics, controls, and resources, but also because some of his suggestions could be implemented, in my view, in the near future almost solely by a faculty of real scholarly distinction.

I refer particularly to the "third tier" courses, which seem to me the most novel and important of his many useful formulations. In many of the now rapidly changing fields of study in the natural and behavioral sciences, I do not feel confident—perhaps from lack of knowledge, to be sure—that any high proportions of the teachers and researchers there engaged could find substantial agreement among themselves on "the methodological and philosophical (and, in the case of the social sciences, historical) presuppositions of a field" or could readily and with high priority "show the application of the discipline to general problems or to issues requiring a multidisciplinary approach, in order to test the operation of the discipline in a wider context."

Moreover, in this discussion Professor Bell continues: "These contexts, almost invariably in the social sciences, and increasingly in the biological sciences, involve issues of value or of moral choice; and the explication of the value problems involved would be an added purpose of these courses." The long sweep of practice to rule such questions out of the "legitimate" boundaries of many subject matters will not be easily overcome.

Much as I admire what might likely result from such a "distinctive contribution to general education," I fear that this would require (1) a major shift of attention even of those highly competent scholars who are willing or anxious to teach undergraduates at the expense of their research time; (2) a new kind of moral as well as professional decision to explicate value problems residing in their disciplines; and (3) in the longer run, a substantially altered preparation of future college teachers. I find, curiously perhaps, analogies between Professor Bell's intriguing vision, with its accompanying, implicit tasks, and the efforts of many of the groups that have been revising secondary school curricula in mathematics, physics, biology, etc., with their realization that the schoolteachers had to be educated anew to understand and to cope with the revised materials and techniques. The latter accomplishment has been far from perfect, despite relatively large and very expensive attempts.

I feel, then, it would be easy but fallacious to underestimate the radical nature of Professor Bell's enticing proposals and the magnitude of the effort to bring into being the full sweep of his suggested curriculum. His suggestions may be more of a challenge to university faculties, wearing at least three of their hats, than at present to college faculties *per se*. Are they, as scholars, willing to undertake the particular examination of their own and related disciplines that would, I think, be required for the creation of such courses? Will they devote enough attention to their roles as, in part, teachers of undergraduates to pitch such courses at the levels of the undergraduates *and* to teach them? (For in some fields, I suspect, Professor Bell's language might aptly describe the topics for quite advanced seminars.) Finally, as teachers of the graduate students who will be the future mentors in such courses, will they prepare and encourage the latter to go in these directions?

I must confess also to some perplexity in trying to visualize an even or equal application of Professor Bell's analysis and suggestions to the range of "major" fields now typically represented in an undergraduate college. He argues against the interdisciplinary course that, particularly in the social sciences, comes too early, before the student "has a grounding in a discipline, in its conceptual frameworks and analytical techniques" which "should be the prerequisite for interdisciplinary work." Yet he then organizes (or, at Columbia, continues with modifications) the Contemporary Civilization and humanities program as the first "step" in the general education curriculum. These are interdisciplinary, involving history, literature, philosophy, and potentially others. Does one infer that these are not disciplines or, if so, that the argument against too early generalization does not here apply?

This is, as I see it, a central issue for debate, both in theoretical and intellectual contexts and as practical questions, such as staffing of courses. And it may be of particular importance because such endeavors—by whatever institutionalized name—in "Humanities" or "Western Civilization," or the like, have been the most visible and widely used approach to "general education." Yet they do not meet with uniform acceptance. Within a particular college faculty the argument may indeed rage between those who have become committed to a humanities course or sequence and those from the same and related departments who espouse a (claimed) tighter and more controlled study of single disciplines and oppose the (alleged) deluding generalizations of freshmen and sophomore students in humanities. And the argument comes not, or not only, from the teachers of advanced specialties but from men dedicated to teaching undergraduates, including freshmen.

A related question concerns the advisability and the possibility of including scientists in the efforts to introduce students to the history of Western civilization. The attempts to do so have been, so far as I can guess, sporadic, limited, and largely unsuccessful. In the array of seminal ideas presented in such courses, those of science are mostly omitted; the enormous impact of science and technology is understated or presented—if at all—by some faculty members who in private may boast to colleagues of their scientific incompetence or confess their hostility to the consequences of science as "inhumane." The present growth of history of science as a recognized discipline in the graduate schools promises relief from the dilemma, perhaps, but practical effects for all but a handful of colleges are very distant.

Finally, of all the efforts to provide general education encompassing the three main groupings of science, social science, and humanities, those in science have seemed to me the most difficult and perplexing. Yet they may be the most urgent, if one accepts my own loose observation that, among well-educated adults, the scientists are more literate in the other fields than the nonscientists are in science. The most common pattern has perhaps been the combination of a distribution requirement of one or two courses in science with the use of a multi-track system in one or several departments, so that the nonscientist may be exposed to some sampling of science without foundering. The mathematics-physics and mathematics-biology sequences proposed by Professor Bell seem to me logical and appealing, but one must await the reactions of scientists individually and departmentally. For the most part, I think, the institutional or educational obligation to teach science to the nonscientist has met with less enthusiasm from the science faculties than the apparently parallel obligation to teach humanities or social science to the science students has been received by the nonscience faculties. The explanation, which I am still seeking, may possibly be twofold. It may lie in the sequential nature of learning in the sciences and in the difficulties (and distaste) of compromising the sequential dependency. And it may lie also in the fact, or likelihood, that a terminal, formal experience in a science course is indeed more final for the nonscientist than a similarly terminal experience with other subject matter is for the scientist.

Practicalities in Curriculum Reform: Additional Views

WHILE ONE CAN ONLY ADMIRE and find much nourishment for reflection in both the brilliance and the reach of Professor Bell's formulations, one can still be troubled by at least four serious considerations. All four derive significant force from the present climate in which serious attempts at curricular reform occur. Indeed, it is the nature of this climate that, in large part, stimulates such attempts and defines the urgent need for them. Too briefly, the components of this atmosphere include the better qualifications of the students entering college, the pace and tempo of social change (including the rapid advancement of knowledge and its impact on the concept of the disciplines), the demands and incentives from the larger society for increasingly specialized technical competence, and the harrowingly familiar rise in enrollments, an entailment of the vaunted population explosion, which brings not only *more* students to the campus, but also more *kinds* of students. Against these grounds of circumstance, there is some merit in heeding the four issues to which Professor Bell's presentation gives rise.

First, there is considerable doubt that the fit is optimum between the logical ordering of the curriculum that Bell proposes and the psychological conditions under which students most effectively learn. For example, Bell's first year, despite its attractiveness to relatively mature intellectuals, smacks of the enforced acquisition of culturally important background information whether or not it is perceived as relevant or vital by the freshmen themselves. The lack of attention to student motivation, so characteristic of college curricula for so long, may have been viable with more docile and less demanding generations; it seems unlikely to remain feasible in relation to today's students. To the extent that students are doubtful about the quality of the world passed on to them by their elders and are a bit anxious about its dangers and sources of frustration, will they respond with enthusiasm and involvement to what amounts to old wine in new bottles? Neither the first year of Bell's curriculum nor the essentially conventional "training in a discipline" may have a meaningful appeal to informed youth whose strongest orientations are toward pressing contemporary social problems, questions associated with their own identity and role in a context of radical cultural shift, and the issues bound up with values in a technological world where Whirl often appears to be king. Like the business of the increasing range of individual differences among students, this matter is one that can be brushed aside only at the risk of reducing the relevance and centrality of the college as a device for delivering broadly educated and responsible citizens to a needful society.

Second, one must ask whether and how soon a faculty can be developed to implement a curriculum like Bell's, especially at his level of third-tier courses. Parenthetically, this question raises again the query—the third-tier offerings aside—of how conventional Bell's reformation may at bottom be. Nevertheless, his ideas do demand a professoriate with wider intellectual interests than seems presently modal. Ours is a time in the history of the academy when the pay-off for professors lies in research and professional consulting services based on deeply cultivated but narrow expertise. Where is the leverage in our system of rewards that could move a faculty not only to a stronger and more generalized commitment to teaching, but also to teaching in situations that reach across traditional disciplinary boundaries, demand the exploration with students of the assumptions and implications of the very fields of scholarship in which professorial roots are deeply planted, and require a sufficient range (as opposed to specialized depth) of knowledge to enable faculty members in one discipline to communicate effectively with both students and fellow professors of very different disciplinary persuasions? Applauding the happily imagined outcome of such an arrangement, one still must face up to the question of how to achieve it in the face of a powerful reward system that currently seems to work directly against it.

Third, a good bit of lip service is paid to the importance of the professor in the educative process because of the ways in which he serves as a model of adulthood for students to emulate critically or to use profitably as a point of departure in the shaping of their own character. In Bell's proposals, the faculty of the college does indeed serve this modeling function, but only in one respect: as reflections of men devoted to serious intellectual inquiry. To Dr. Bell's credit, he is insistent on displaying for students the messiness, the differences among innovative scholars, and the ambiguities and difficulties in the process of inquiry, as well as exhibiting for them the cleaned-up and polished products of research and the intellectual quest. But although the college may properly be concerned above all with the minds and intellects of students, it must realize that minds and intellects do not come to them in disembodied forms. Many of our students search not only for models of intellectual dedication but for examples of the informed and responsibly committed man, models of the man of long perspective who still is profoundly and actively involved in the affairs of his own time. Where in Bell's curriculum is provision made for this kind of educative exposure, for the meeting of this kind of urgent need among young people? We are brought back here to the passage from Professor Willard Van Quine, which Bell quotes with considerable approval. By adding italics to two small words, that passage gives weight to a recurrent source of concern in the issues raised here. Quine speaks of the "truths that count for most, *either* in point of intrinsic interest *or* as instruments for coping with the world." Bell's curriculum seems heavily slanted toward truth of the first kind and the kind of human models associated with them. Students may have a strong disposition toward truths of the second variety and the models of men that they most centrally entail. Without urging an option for either side, one may find profit in keeping a wary eye peeled for too severe a tipping toward what probably appeals far more to what is most professorial in professors rather than toward what is most immediate in intelligent and questing youngsters.

Finally, Bell assigns the central place in his curriculum to modes of conceptual inquiry, rationalizing this primacy of method on the ground that it provides the link between the embodiment of general education in the disciplines and the fundamental bases of specialized knowledge. The argument is, in many ways, a compelling one. Yet, as is made clear in *The Reforming of General Education* itself, the traditional divisions of the seamless garment of knowledge into the disciplines and the nature of scholarly inquiry as we presently conceive it are themselves reflections of our particular time and are subject to change. Because the life of an intellectual method has been markedly shortened as knowledge generally has expanded, and because the boundaries of the disciplines have proved at most to be only semipermeable, a curricular structure erected on such a base is almost certain to be particularly vulnerable to new developments in science and the humanistic forms of inquiry. What provision is available to minimize the lag between professional discovery and appropriate curricular adjustments? Is there danger of freezing a somewhat different curricular pattern into an even more hardened mold than the structures with which we now work so uneasily? More important, in a rational devotion to methods that may be as evanescent as "facts," is there a danger of missing both kinds of truths that Quine mentions; and in some domains of educational concern—the world's literatures, for example—is there a possibility that, because the canons of scholarship are so far removed from the immediacies of educationally meaningful experience, Bell's curriculum will prove caviar to a far-too-large general?

That such problems as these can be raised is a tribute to the provocative values in Professor Bell's wide-ranging and eloquently phrased ideas. It would be a tribute gracelessly paid if, for whatever reason, insufficient attention and brainpower are invested in unraveling the issues that his systematic thought has generated into articulateness for us.

The Colleges' Crisis
of Integrity:
A Headmaster's View

DONALD BARR

As a dignified public rumination on Columbia University's problems in assembling a curriculum for young college students—one which will satisfy the polymaths as to breadth and the scholiasts as to depth, restore excitement to the freshman year, assimilate the huge but inchoate revolutions now going on in all our knowledges and schemata, be neither ethnocentric nor befuddling, and protect the liberal arts college from the Catherines of the high schools and the Fredericks of the graduate schools—and, having assembled this Great Curriculum, in deploying its learned grantsmen and cubicle-dwellers to *teach*, Daniel Bell's report, *The Reforming of General Education*,[1] could hardly be expected to deal with all the real problems in all their vital and embarrassing particularity. But this makes the book more useful. Parish bickerings have a way of looping up into theology, and that makes them interesting: it reminds us how important we are. In one of G. K. Chesterton's fantasies, a wild don writes:

What . . . is a puddle? A puddle repeats infinity and is full of light; nevertheless, if analyzed objectively, a puddle is a piece of dirty water spread very thin on mud. The two great historic universities of England have all this large and level and reflective brilliance. They repeat infinity. They are full of light. Nevertheless, or rather on the other hand, they are puddles. Puddles, puddles, puddles, puddles.

The most interesting thing about Professor Bell's book is that, though he is clearly uneasy about both the ecology and the optics of his puddle, in the end he has surprisingly little to say about either. He tells us, so to speak, a great deal about the cloud formations overhead, the stars at

[1] New York: Columbia University Press, 1966.

373

night, the diastrophism below, passing cats, and the principles of hydro-dynamics. But his picture of the puddle is not *of mud* but *muddy*. And this tells us something about puddles. If this paper singles out the Bell report for overinsistent rebuttal, and if once in a while an *ad hominem* argument creeps in, that is because I believe no one is better able to write on the reforming of general education than Professor Bell, one of those bold and gentle, worldly and scholarly men whose spirit can make a university great; and therefore his report is a better-than-fair sample of university thinking on curriculum. This paper is not really about Professor Bell; it is about survival behavior on the campus.

MANIFESTATIONS OF APATHY

The Bell report has three characteristics which are uncharacteristic of its author and therefore significant: its aura of dismay, its lack of empathy with students, and its parochial use of sources.

Professor Bell displays the obligatory tough-mindedness, confronting challenges and re-examining assumptions with the best of them, yet one feels—it cannot be documented, which is my point—that the students have at last succeeded in conveying a sense of failure to the faculty; that the etiology of the trouble must be traced back beyond curricula, back beyond polities, to something in the moral condition of university folk; that this professor cares deeply; that he is, in fact, hurt; and that he is too good a sociologist to believe that his explanations exculpate the institutions.

The phenomenology of failure is always fascinating. Professor Bell could have studied it with profit to his ontology and without the cost even of a subway token, although the data on Morningside Heights are not as bizarre as those on some other renowned campuses. The basic phenomena are *antimysticism, dysrelation, conspiracy, part-timing*, and *disappointment*.

1. Whether or not, after we have examined such things as Zen, we still accept the Christian definition of mystical experience as "experimental knowledge of the presence of God," we can probably describe the current antimysticism as a search for experimental knowledge of the *absence* of God. The widespread use of "pot" and LSD, and the appetitive reaching out for new modes of heightened "awareness" or "perception" seem to be not merely for the sake of the awareness but also (and ofter primarily) for the reassurance that such awareness can be obtained by chemical (material) or essentially masturbatory (self-granted, not God-granted) means; that is, the means are the real end. We cannot say, therefore, that antimysticism is produced by anticlimax, and that if the intellectual revelation of college were more satisfying students would not seek these other revelations. It is not that simple.

2. We can probably learn much from dysrelation, the compulsion to suspend, distort, or mock normal relations with other persons. The higher the prestige of a college, the more frequently its students seem to suffer from severe alienation—a paradox, since alienation is the classic malaise of the superfluous man, while its current victims are precisely those adolescents who have, after fierce competition, been chosen for lovingly subsidized, obviously pregnant opportunities for education. Kenneth Keniston has studied Ivy League alienation closely in *The Uncommitted*,[2] and though in the end he more or less blames it on that convenient devil, technology, his clinical material and psychiatric interpretation are immensely interesting. Further studies *may* suggest that alienation is less frequent in the vocationally oriented, lower-prestige institutions. Dysrelation seems to affect the father-son (and therefore teacher-student) relation the most, but apparently it invades even the newly explored relations of sex; one *hears* of babies conceived by strangers during parietals and aborted by friends on overnights. Some homosexuality may be dysrelational, a mockery of normal relations. The Ivy League public image now includes the Office of the University Pardoner (M.D., F.A.P.A.), crowded at all hours with undergraduate *tiqueurs* and isolates; but it would be helpful to know how much of this is anti-intellectual canard, how much is the result of ambitious self-diagnosis by youngsters who have lived a little too long on chocolate bars and cokes, and how much is genuine dysrelation. It is too simple just to say that if colleges occupied students' minds with the delights of objective mastery and mystery, the adolescents would have less self-conscious and more generous relations with their teachers, their fellows, and the world.

3. Conspiracy may be a form of dysrelation, too, insofar as it is the secretizing of commitment; or it may be fulfillment of the adolescent's wish for a new, substitute authority—in this case, The Secret—which will be both demanding and permissive, which will provide structure but relax certain childhood constraints. In any case, conspiracy is certainly The Style at some colleges; even Catholicism tends toward Opus Dei, and socialism (once the most joyous of student creeds) toward Maoist infiltration. It would be oversimplifying to say that students bind themselves to private truths because the open truths of culture have been allowed to look banal and technical.

4. When the present generation of sociology professors and headmasters was young, college was central to our experience. Some students had to work; but figuratively speaking, if a student worked in the campus laundry he resented the laundry's pulling him from the classroom, not the classroom's pulling him from the laundry. An extraordinary number of college students now regard college as just *one* of the things they do,

[2] New York: Harcourt, Brace & World, 1965.

along with the job, the picketing, the sex, and what not; and to some, college is even peripheral. One finds oneself next to a college girl at dinner: "Do you like it here at X?" "Oh yes, I love it, but I'm transferring next term." "Why?" "My boyfriend is graduating, and he'll be in medical school at the University of Y, so I'm going there." Poor little camp follower! This motive for movement is rather appealing, though the *possible* image of a sensitive and promising young girl only occasionally sitting up to study is not. But the increasingly casual acceptance of disruption in education, contrasted with the resistance to disruption or postponement of other activities, is an alarming fact. At some colleges, one would almost think that student leaves-of-absence were part of the honors curriculum; they may be chiefly therapeutic and maturational, but *how are they thought to work?* Neither the student nor the dean, it is certain, regards them as punitive any more, though the form letter may sometimes still be worded in probationary jargon. To suggest that the dean grants the leave because he cannot think of any way to engage the student except by letting him see that things are even worse in the outside world is unfairly simplistic.

5. But it is not an oversimplification to believe the significant number of college students who say simply that college has been oversold, that they are disappointed at the perfunctoriness of the teaching, that the level of class discussion is surprisingly low, that the curriculum is too prescriptive, and that they have been told to "hurry up and wait."

Beginnings of apathy

Professor Bell's consciousness of these phenomena is articulated only in abstracted observations that the liberal arts college "is no longer a 'transforming experience' for a youth coming into a wide world of humane learning"; that "the student comes to a college and expects to find a 'community.' Instead he finds a 'society'"; that curriculum-planning "must take into account . . . how the students' own needs and puzzlements affect them"; and that faculty members are "all aware of the dissatisfactions and disorientations of the students about the character of their educational experience." But how highly he values the excitement of the transition from high school to college is shown by his most far-reaching proposal for curriculum reform: There should be a "division of labor" between high school, college, and graduate school. High schools should concentrate on "facts and skills." In social studies, they should teach "large amounts of useful factual information in simple interpretative schemes [which] would serve as the foundation for later college studies." In the humanities, they should "concentrate on the original intentions of the trivium, to assume the discipline of the written and spoken word by dealing with the skills of composition . . . with knowl-

edge of genres and the more formal classificatory and instrumental elements," leaving subtle literary experience to the colleges and not "taking
the edge off" great books. Mathematics, physical science, and foreign
languages may, however, "extend back" into high schools as much as one
likes, apparently because the first several years of these "sequential" subjects are rather mechanical anyway. At the other end of the path, the
graduate school will emphasize "specialization and research." Safely in
between, the college—"one of the few places of broad intellectual adventure"—will "exercise a singular function—the training in conceptual analysis in the grounds of knowledge, the criteria of theory, and the standards
of judgment."

This is university thinking of a high order. We must not accuse Professor Bell of trying to make the high schools duller so that the colleges
may *seem* more interesting. His problem appears to be that the critical,
questing, and superbly impatient mind of the bright fifteen-year-old is
now lost to him. Once upon a time, it is said (but the tale may be
apocryphal), Daniel Bell taught youngsters of high school age under the
old Hutchins plan at Chicago; and he taught them—brilliantly, un-
stintingly, shockingly—Freud, Marx, the works that he now says "should
be confronted primarily in later years." *Dove sono i bei momenti . . .?*

Consider, for example, his prescription for English composition: "it is
entirely the responsibility" of the high schools "to assure the proficiency
of their students in English composition"; so "the colleges comprising
the Ivy League would, as a group, establish the regulation that any student seeking admission to these colleges must meet a standard of composition set forth in a common college-board type entrance examination."
(Would the standard permit sentences like that one? How many points
should come off the college-board type entrance examination score for
using "comprise" in that way?) As a sociologist, Professor Bell should
know that any such regulation would impose the old class patterns back
on the Ivy League, which has just courageously escaped from them, and
that tax-supported universities, growing in style and freedom, and already
able to attract many of the best students and professors from the "best"
private universities, would practically finish them off. What perhaps he
does not remember is how youngsters learn to write. They need, first,
technique—grammar, paragraph design, a small bag of rhetorical tricks
—and, second, something they *want* very badly to say very well. A teacher
may "cover" the technique thoroughly by assigning themes like "How
I Spent My Summer Vacation" and "Symbolism in *The Grapes of
Wrath*," but most of the students will not—they cannot—learn this way.
It is in grappling intellectually with the experiences that crowd in upon
them, trying to delineate big, pullulating ideas, that they gradually learn
graceful and responsible expression. Professor Bell notes that the required

freshman composition course is "extremely costly to the college, especially at a time when salaries are rising sharply and *teaching schedules
are being reduced*" (emphasis mine but incidental); he might have added
that the course is largely ineffective and that it contributes heavily to the
boredom and disenchantment of freshmen. A sensible college administration would put off separate formal instruction in composition until
the junior year, *after* the presumably idea-begetting General Education
has begun to work, and meanwhile would temporize by a little *ad hoc*
servicing of students' papers for various courses.

The Bell report says—and here we may have a paradigm of university
thinking on *any* subject—that three kinds of questions must be confronted before a curriculum can be decided upon. They are *sociological*
(social changes affect the role of the college), *intellectual* (knowledge
has its own organization and priorities), and *institutional* (the departmental, budgetary, and administrative structure of the university affects
the college). There is no mention of psychological questions, though
Professor Bell quotes with approval Dean Hawkes' statement (1922)
that "the student is the focus of the undergraduate college" and Professor Buchler's historical comment on "an outlook that stressed attention
to the individual student and the continuity of the educational process
with the living process," and himself asserts that "the College sought
primarily to be aware of the individual person whose capacities it was
trying to develop." With those phrases the matter ends.

THE DOMAIN OF A CURRICULUM

"What," asks the catalogue of a certain private school, "is the *domain*
of a curriculum?" And it answers that the domain of a curriculum is not
a nation, as many Europeans think; not a state, as some Americans think;
not a municipality or school district, as other Americans think; not a
school as most private school men think; not a classroom, as many teachers think. The domain of a curriculum is one student.

That is the first principle of curriculum reform. When we speak of the
curriculum of a college, we really mean a collection of curricula, the
curricula of individual students. How uniform or diverse is this collection
to be? That depends on how it is supposed to work, not collectively but
distributively. It would be well if university folk, before confronting
those sociological, intellectual, and institutional questions that precede
their decisions on curriculum, were to ask the question: "What is going
on in the student's mind?" *Training* can be prescriptive; *education* occurs by consent; is thy student a dog? (Actually, Professor Bell has done
a good deal of research on the content of Columbia students' minds, and
he intends to publish it some day in sociological journals. But whatever

he learned did not prevent his assuming, in almost every thought and phrase, the passivity and plasticity of the student.)

Good students, the kind of students colleges want, are not passive and not plastic. They have survived twelve years of the numbing, curiosity-quenching, mediocrity-rewarding processes of conventional elementary and secondary "education." Anyone who has watched bright-eyed first-graders bubbling with intuition in a science lesson, and then watched stolid high school sophomores in a biology class, knows how much intelligence is destroyed in our schools. Much, but not all: those many youngsters who retain their awe and love and intuition do so because they learn early to take control of their learning; they have ego strength; they *use* school, lovingly at times, contemptuously at times; and they will defend their autonomy.

Their patterns of development are wonderfully various. Some satisfy their need for mastery by passionate work in one field. Others bustle from subject to subject, eager about everything. Some are dunces at numbers and prodigies at words, or the reverse. Others have a bland competence in all academic pursuits. Some are fictive, some factual. Some work in belated spates, others with steady promptness. By the time they get to college, they are really *persons*, and a faculty committee which decides that first they must all study a common curriculum, anthologized from the best that has been thought and said, and designed to average them up a bit, and that then they must each pick a major, prescribing a sequence of experiences, articulated *a priori* (that is, as if students were incapable of any but *managed* discoveries), and designed to turn them all into specialists, is ignoring reality. No one is final: people do change: the engineer discovers history, the poet discovers logic, the dilettante discovers God; the specialist explores at last, the generalist begins to dig. But each has his distinctive *way* and *season* of changing. It is the proper wisdom of elders to encourage those changes, to suggest, to warn, to cajole, to reassure, to evaluate; but to enforce change on an arbitrary schedule is a violation of person.

That is the second great law of curriculum reform. The curriculum for each student should be a conversation, not a lecture.

Recognizing—in principle—that he is planning for persons, Professor Bell has investigated the high school backgrounds with which students come to college; the curiously parochial character of his investigation is revealing. He is able to discern in American high schools during the past ten years four developments which may affect the needs of college freshmen: national schemes of curriculum reform; the Advanced Placement program; teacher-improvement workshops and institutes; and "interdisciplinary" courses in the humanities and social studies. The first three have largely been conducted by college and university people, and the fourth was copied from the colleges. No one will deny the enormous and partly beneficial effect that UICSM, SMSG, PSSC, CBA, CHEMS, BSCS, and the rest have had on secondary schooling, though many critics have come to believe that if certain of these reforms had been less dominated by cliques of university folk—operating (it is said) in a *du haut en bas* manner; spending time and money on national-mission gestures and organizational embellishments designed to impress rather than convince public school people; duplicating costly facilities that were already underutilized, and passing up professional technical assistance that could not be duplicated, out of a desire to prove the practical virtuosity of theoreticians; and uncritically favoring purism—more appropriate and far less expensive changes might have been contrived in high school science. The Advanced Placement program has likewise had some interesting and beneficial effects, though it is questionable whether, in view of the boredom of so many bright freshmen in college, college freshmen courses should continue to serve as models for high school courses in certain subjects. It is questionable, too, whether the bribe of possible college credit need be offered any more to encourage high school seniors to take advanced courses. It is more difficult to assess teacher-training programs; but many of the in-service institutes are mere adjuncts—in military jargon, "penetration aids"—to the new national curricula; and many others leave to the teacher trainees the crucial task of translating material into high school terms; while some of the preservice programs are little more than ingenious schemes for using liberal arts colleges to circumvent rather than reform the teachers colleges, which in general have a tight grip on the certification authorities and a flaccid grip on substantive knowledge.

Let us concede it at once: the high schools of the country are, in general, awful. They are not awful in the way that many university critics (like Dr. Conant) with a passion for coverage and a disregard for the *visibility* of the child think them to be. Nor are they so awful that colleges even now cannot learn much from them: in fact, multi-tracking, an administrative device which permits departments to recognize gross differences in students' interests and abilities without abating the prescriptive approach, and which Professor Bell refers to almost as if it were a major new Columbia discovery, has been a standard practice (under that name) in American high schools for many years. In spite of the wretched state of their establishments, high school administrators and teachers have developed a good deal of empirical wisdom about curriculum construction. One might state a few rules of thumb, school proverbs, and the like:

1. Students should know what rigor is, and should practice it *once in a while*, as a reminder. They should esteem the perfect, but still respect

the imperfect. Every student must encounter every idea for the first time but need never encounter it for the last time. "Once and for all" exposition kills the subject once and for all. The definitive does not exist, but the boring certainly does. If ever the last word on a subject were said, *all* the words would be wasted. A student can never know everything, but he can eventually know almost anything; he feels the first, and must be made to feel the second.

2. Some facts are toys and some are implements; students should enjoy both and know the difference. Whatever topic one can name, some great man knew nothing about it, and some student will find out about him. A student can get good grades and a poor education, but if he gets poor grades, he will not be allowed to get a good education; this makes it possible to teach him a few things he does not like to learn; this trick must not be used too often; but it is.

3. Concept and drill can be separated: a child need not be perfectly proficient in the multiplication table before reasoning from the concept of multiplication to the concept of division; and he can do quite subtle arithmetic problems about Farmer Jones before mastering Peano's axioms. Concepts and precepts, however, should not be *completely* separated: there is no fixed rule as to which the student should experience first—as a matter of fact, there is no first.

4. There is a difference between maturity and readiness. If maturity determined readiness, teachers would learn faster than their students, whereas any wise teacher *feels* his students pursuing him, and devouring him, starting at his heels.

5. At different ages, we learn the same things in different orders. What is logically primitive may not be psychologically primitive. (The idea of a "set" in mathematics is logically primitive but psychologically complex, in spite of all the misleading simplifications that textbook writers have invented.) What is the "best" order? Best for whom?

If college administrators would take a pluralist view of the patterns of learning, restore the elective principle, and respect teaching as a high art; if professors would stop pretending that they were teaching undergraduates when they meet only with graduate-style seminars of the most carefully selected students, if they would stop regarding English composition and first-year calculus as camp, and if they would stop hiding in committee rooms; *then* something of the old adventure might be felt again on campuses, and our brave little liberal arts colleges would no longer have to fear partition between Catherine the Secondary and Frederick the Graduate.

Collegiate Education for
Modern Culture

R. J. HENLE, S.J.

IN THIS BRIEF PAPER I wish to present, in a blunt and forthright manner, a thesis concerning modern collegiate education. I will state the thesis, then explain and illustrate it, and, finally, point out some of the problems it entails.

For all the attention we have given the modern disciplines, for all the hundreds of faculty committees on curriculum, for all the studies conducted under foundation grants, for all the books, the essays, and the laudable experiments, we do not have anywhere in the United States a college curriculum which is truly modern and which at the same time does for the modern student what a "liberal" education was expected to do for the student in the Renaissance or in the nineteenth century.

I have deliberately avoided calling this a modern *liberal* education, because the term *liberal* is now so charged with the emotional residue of past strife and so loaded with historical connotations that it tends to block the radical rethinking of education which I am calling for. I can find no word which designates the kind of college curriculum I have in mind: a modern analogue to the literary education of the Roman gentleman, to the pre-university and the faculty of arts education of the medieval university, and to the Oxford-Cambridge education of pre-World War I England. We have not produced the modern equivalent to this sort of education, an education designed to bring a person to a maturity which is universally human and yet within his own time and culture. To be sure, we have tinkered with tradition; we have added and subtracted; but we have not been thorough enough nor radical enough nor ruthless enough in our approach to modern collegiate education.

Now when I say "modern," I do not mean "contemporary." There is a great deal of talk about being contemporary, being up-to-the-minute, using the latest materials. This is neither modern nor good. The one way to make sure that you are going to become obsolete so fast that you won't even have time to be obsolescent is to be 100 percent contemporary today. The curriculum built out of contemporary concerns, contemporary interests, contemporary art, contemporary literature, is inevitably third-rate and would be dated before the student had completed it. We must resist the specious lure of being contemporary.

We must likewise avoid the "fallacy of the immediate present." The "immediate present," if the term is taken literally, has no meaning for man at all. The present has human meaning only in the perspective of history, only through the past which enriches it and the future with which it is pregnant.

What I do mean is that this new collegiate education should be relevant to the contemporary world and to the emerging world, the future world. A page of Plato or a poem of Pindar may be far more relevant to the contemporary modern world than last night's television show or yesterday's magazine of opinions.

But if an insight of Confucius or a painting of the seventeenth century is more relevant to the modern world than 99 percent of current stuff, it is true on the other side that a collegiate education today must somehow be inspired by, filled with, formed of the basic ideas and viewpoints of the modern world and true to the totality of modern culture.

A SCIENTIFIC SOCIETY

The problem of creating a new collegiate curriculum has not arisen simply because of the emergence of modern science. All phases of modern culture and of modern life help to create and enlarge the problem. For example, the increasing urbanization of man's environment as well as changes in such ancient and traditional studies as Sacred Scripture and Dogmatic Theology, as well as many other factors, contribute to the complexity of the problem. Yet it is true that at every point the problem has been rendered modernly different and peculiarly difficult by the emergence of modern science and by its pervasive incorporation into our society. There may be, as Snow has argued, two reflective intellectual cultures, the scientific and the humanistic, but there are not two societies. Modern society *is* a scientific society. Science is installed, first, as a set of intellectual disciplines; second, as a social enterprise affecting all phases of our society; and third, as an instrument not only to understand but also to control our world, whether man-made or natural. Technology, the out-thrusting influence of science on all human activity, is revolutionizing the conditions of human life. One of the tasks of a modern collegiate education is to do justice to all these aspects of science as it now exists and operates.

Most discussions of curriculum in the United States focus on our alleged failure to provide an adequate scientific education for our nonscience majors. I believe that we have indeed failed to do so. The non-science major is scientifically both illiterate and ignorant. Moreover, his ignorance is not merely a lack of knowledge; it is given a positive character by his erroneous conceptions of the matters which science studies as well as of the nature of science itself. Dr. Bronowski illustrated this some years ago by stating: "If I were to say with enough solemnity that the stars must be very young because they are made up of neurons and enzymes, no statesman would wink at me." [1]

And what do we do about this failure? We tinker with the curriculum. We work out a new course designed specifically for those who do not intend to learn science. I am not saying that courses like this are useless or unintelligent. I do say, emphatically, that this is a superficial approach to an educational system and a totally inadequate solution to the problem. In fact, we have not really recognized the true problem. For not only are nonscience majors ignorant about science; science majors are ignorant as well. Very few people highly trained in a science really understand science. Certainly the chemistry major knows a great deal more about chemistry than does the student of Old English. But does he really understand his chemical knowledge as a science? Does he have any real understanding of the totality of modern science? Does he have any perspective, historical or cultural or other, within which to locate his own knowledge and his own scientific activity? The product of modern scientific education is a highly specialized mind—and to this I have no objection—but it is all too often a mind which is cabined, cribbed, and confined within what is, relatively speaking, a very parochial part of modern culture, and even of modern science.

The basic problem, then, is common to both science majors and non-science majors. To correct it, we must achieve a radical breakthrough at the fundamental levels of higher education. We must find a way to present the totality of science as well as its internal variety, to teach the nature of science, to convey the total cultural impact of science—its place in history, the change in the general view of the world and of man from sub-cell to super-society, from subatomic structure to stellar masses. This radical reflective understanding of modern science should be common to scientist and nonscientist. Just because a man is going to major in science is no reason for excluding him from a modern scientific education.

A little earlier I described the nonscience major as both illiterate and ignorant. I wish to turn my attention now to this illiteracy. A man may be ignorant of a field, but if he is literate in it, he can overcome his ignorance. Let me illustrate the main point here. When Gilbert published his classic treatise on the magnet in 1600, every educated man in

---

[1] Jacob Bronowski, "The Educated Man in 1984," *Science*, April 27, 1956, p. 711.

Western Europe was able to read it. Very recently I obtained a copy of Daniel C. Mattis's *Theory of Magnetism* (publication date, 1965),[2] which presents a complete summary of the current scientific understanding of magnetism. However, I found that I was unable to "read" this book. I believe that by any normal standard I would be classed among the educated part of our population and yet, to my disappointment, I was unable to read this book beyond page 12.

In medieval and Renaissance Europe every educated man possessed the *artes*—the instrumental skills and disciplines—which were the keys to the whole world of culture. He knew Latin, and in this language he could listen to lectures in Bologna, Paris, Oxford; he could read the astronomy of the Arabs, the medicine of the Greeks, the theology of the Fathers, as well as the latest treatise from the scriveners' shops of Paris, Munich, or Naples. He had been trained in the *Organon* of Aristotle; he knew the forms of reasoning, the types of argumentation; he had studied logical probability and demonstrative certitude. He could do basic grammatical analysis and he had a basic knowledge of mathematics. And so, French or German or English, surgeon or theologian or natural philosopher, this educated contemporary of Gilbert was able to read and understand the *De Magnete*. But I am trapped by my own ignorance and pride. To read physics I am unable; to go to school again I am ashamed.

But what have we done about identifying the *artes* which are instrumental to modern learning and which would make the educated man of today a full citizen in the modern city of culture? We can easily identify some of these *artes*: statistics, mathematics of a sort, modern linguistics, modern and traditional logic, perhaps an as yet uncreated logic of concept formation, an open-minded reflective general theory of methodology, now also perhaps Fortran and other computer languages and techniques. I am not talking about courses—I am not saying that, for example, we should add a course in statistics for everybody in the freshman year. But I do believe that we must identify these *artes* and see to it that all educated people possess them. It makes little difference whether we have 200 pages or 50 pages on electricity in our physics course. What is absolutely essential is that we teach people what they need to know in order to "read" physics. And note, this is not a problem that exists only in the sciences, though there it may be most striking; it exists in all areas of our culture. There are people who cannot "read" poetry, others who haven't the foggiest notion of how to "read" an abstract painting.

We try to solve the difficulty by taking scientific or artistic or philosophical matters out of their appropriate "languages" and methods and

[2] New York: Harper & Row.

expressing them in a vague sort of intellectual koine. These efforts are not worthless. On the contrary, they can be quite effective. But they are a makeshift; they do not face up to the basic problem which lies deep in our system of education and our culture. To overcome it, we must identify the intellectual instrumentalities of our total culture, and we must find an efficient and effective way of putting them in the active possession of every educated person.

THE DISCIPLINES IN THE MODERN CULTURE

There are several obstacles, real or alleged, which prevent the development of the sort of education I envision. For instance, it is frequently said that we cannot teach the modern disciplines adequately because of the vast accumulation of knowledge. The amount of knowledge in all fields has increased so tremendously, it is contended, that in four short years a student can barely sip and taste at the font of learning.

But this view implies a quantitative concept of understanding, a notion that the modern disciplines are "bodies" of knowledge which grow by material addition. In this conception, to learn one of these bodies of knowledge means to learn all the accumulated knowledge in it, and this in turn is taken as constituting an "understanding" of that body of knowledge.

It seems to me that this view distorts the nature both of intellectual disciplines and of education. It is true that a man must acquire a certain critical mass of knowledge in order to understand a given discipline, but there is really no correlation between the amount of knowledge he has and the degree and quality of his understanding. In any science a man can derive a very deep understanding of a theory or a law by reflection or by study of a few carefully selected examples of phenomena. The multiplication of instances and facts tends actually to prevent adequate study. Indeed, we generally try to teach our students too many things as it is now. We fill their minds with what Whitehead has called "inert ideas"; we flood them with verbalisms.

Moreover, modern disciplines have not grown by a sort of accumulation of pieces of knowledge. Human understanding grows chiefly by reducing the welter of discrete and chaotic facts of experience to unifying and organizing insights. As disciplines mature they also achieve a greater economy, a greater unity, and a greater simplicity. One of the highest intellectual beauties of modern disciplines is the way they bring under a single luminous concept or a single precise definition or law or a single elegant equation, a potentially infinite number and variety of facts or a multiplicity of concepts, principles, or theories. In a sense, then, at the point of the final development of a science, a man would need to learn much less than before in order to understand it as a science. What the educated person needs is not a vast catalogue of information, even though it be a catalogue of scientific laws and theories. Rather, what he needs is that kind of intellectual grasp of a discipline which enables him truly to understand it and to make it truly a part of his own being as an educated person, that kind of intellectual grasp which enables him to appreciate the internal meaning of a discipline and its place in the total world of culture. This sort of intellectual grasp does not depend upon the mastery of a vast amount of knowledge within a given discipline. This elegant simplification suggests a possible way of communicating to scientists and nonscientists alike an adequate understanding of the totality of modern science. So I don't believe that the proliferation of knowledge makes the kind of education I'm talking about impossible.

But there are genuine obstacles, and very great ones, to our taking a really creative and radical approach to a modern collegiate education.

First, because of our past inadequate education and because of the rapid changes which have gone on in our society, our culture, and our science, a large number of teachers—and I mean university faculties—are obsolescent or even obsolete in regard to knowledge outside their own particular disciplines. Of course, many faculty members in the United States are also somewhat obsolete in their own disciplines. But even the very large number who may be keen in their own field, up-to-the-minute, reading, studying, researching, are quite out of date even in cognate fields. This has several effects. For one thing, it means that the majority of our faculty who, after all, are the custodians of the liberal curriculum, cannot really think about the whole range of modern disciplines in a truly modern way. For another, it means that they have positive misconceptions about other disciplines, and consequently that they are transmitting to students erroneous views about the totality of modern culture. For while they may be primarily engaged in teaching history or English or physics, in which they are specialists, they are always indirectly teaching their own total personal education and culture. Finally, there is necessarily a great cross-usage in modern culture, so that people who are dealing, say, with psychology are also using theories and data from physiology, from sociology, from literature, even, perhaps, from philosophy. But unfortunately, because they are out of date in these fields, what they are teaching is often a worn-out theory, a discarded viewpoint, or a hoary old myth that once passed as fact or respectable theory in some discipline. Dr. Zirkel some years ago wrote an article in *Science* in which he talked about the "three biologies": the biology of the modern, up-to-date biologist who is excitingly in touch with the growth of his discipline; the ordinary biology that even most biologists keep teaching, particularly, say, in high school; and finally, the biology that is taught in other fields. For example, he said that he had examined a number of texts in the field of education and had found that he could derive from them this third, very antiquated and even falsified kind of biology.

The other side of this picture is, of course, the extreme specialization of the university professor. In a way his classroom is like Leibnitz's monad. Ensconced there in isolated authority, protected from the intrusion of deans, registrars, and other such, he closes himself and his students off from the rest of the world of learning. The monad classroom has no windows. Dr. Rabi has commented:

> Wisdom is, by its nature, an interdisciplinary quality, and not the product of a collection of specialists. Although the colleges do indeed try to mold the student toward a certain ideal of the educated man of the twentieth century, it is too often a broad education administered by specialists. The approximate counterpart to this ideal of this educated man, embodied in a real living person, is a rare being on any college faculty. Indeed, in most colleges and universities, the student is the only really active connecting link between the different departments. In a certain paradoxical sense, the students are the only broadly educated body in the university community, at least in principle. It might be equally as instructive and useful to have the faculty examined by the students from time to time, as to have the students examined by the faculty, according to immemorial custom.[3]

In this situation, it is extremely difficult to find faculty members who can address themselves to a total reorganization of the curriculum.

Finally, I want to advert to the difficulty of breaking through the established structures and framework. The sort of education I have been talking about is rendered almost impossible by the departmental structure of our universities. Though this structure serves many useful purposes, it also promotes cohesive cultural enclaves within which certain stereotypes of membership are developed. Programs tend to be organized along departmental lines. Interdepartmental programs are notoriously hard to manage, and the renovated collegiate program which I envision would be the most interdepartmental of all. The departmental structure, taken together with the reduction of the student's formal academic life to fairly uniform class units and course units, makes it almost impossible for us to think of a completely different reordering and interrelating of our educational disciplines.

I would indeed like to see a group of faculty from all the main disciplines work together to bring themselves up to the full light of modern culture and to purge themselves of all presuppositions about classes and courses and curriculum. Then they might be able to address themselves to a truly creative and radical revolution in college education.

[3] Isador Rabi, *My Life and Times as a Physicist* (Claremont, Calif.: Claremont Colleges, 1960), pp. 50–51.

Knowledge Structure and
Curriculum Development

CALVIN B. T. LEE

CURRICULUM REFORM FOR UNDERGRADUATE EDUCATION is, too often, merely the art of the possible. This is not to say that institutional realities should be ignored, but they do obscure the mission. By conforming to traditions on the campus, influences of powerful and weak chairmen and faculty members, and biases of deans and presidents, those in charge of curriculum development often push the fundamental questions of pedagogy to the background and leave decisions to compromise, neglect, or accommodation.

In the last several years a number of colleges have revisited, restudied, and reformed their curricula. More will do so in the very near future. The reasons are many: entering freshmen seem to be better prepared today than they have ever been; there is a movement toward more independent study and off-campus work; there is a questioning of the "relevance" of the present curriculum to the student's life; there is some feeling that a better teaching environment is possible, and that college tries to jam too much in at one time with too many courses, too many requirements, and not enough cohesion. There is, further, a feeling that student "alienation" can be coped with by a revision of the curriculum and a restructuring of classes. Finally, there is the fear that the demands of the graduate schools and the growing numbers of students going beyond the bachelor's degree have forced college students to overconcentrate in their majors.

These reasons for curriculum reform are, by and large, results of external factors and pressures. There are also internal factors at work, which often are not recognized until the need for curriculum reform has already been decided upon. The growth of knowledge forces college faculties to take account of the new insights into learning theory and the structure of knowledge—the ordering of the various intellectual

389

disciplines into some coherent hierarchy or pattern either by subject matter or by modes of inquiry. This may be a time for a major overhaul rather than simple readjustment in the curriculum—a time for reconstruction rather than reform.

There appears to be a more rational approach to curriculum planning, one which could take into account the function of the curriculum as a whole and in its separate parts. Whereas most aspects of pedagogy were formerly relegated to the educationists, recent attention has been given to these matters by some of the most distinguished scholars in the various disciplines. Two outstanding examples of this trend may be seen in the Physical Science Study Group, directed by Jerrold R. Zacharias at M.I.T., and the School Mathematics Study Group, directed by Edward G. Begle of Stanford. Moreover, some of the most distinguished psychologists and sociologists have in recent years turned their attention to the problems of education, long a neglected and even despised field of study. Some of the ideas in Jerome Bruner's *The Process of Education* [1] and *Toward a Theory of Instruction* [2] will have an impact on higher education. Daniel Bell's penetrating *The Reforming of General Education* [3] contributes to our understanding of the structure of knowledge and gives us an interpretation of what this means for the structure of a liberal arts curriculum. Furthermore, advances made in techniques of evaluation and assessment offer hope of finding evidence and proof of the productivity of undergraduate education hitherto undisclosed. It is clear that new ideas and new approaches are needed for curricular development.

The process of curriculum reform can be divided into three major steps: stating the objectives, formulating the pedagogical framework, and assessing the results. None of these steps is simple. The first is nebulous, the second raises some questions about validity, and acceptable techniques are lacking for the last. This paper touches on the first step, but is confined primarily to the second step and concentrates on the renewed interest in the structure of knowledge and its potential impact for formulating the pedagogical framework.

FORMULATING THE PEDAGOGICAL FRAMEWORK

Implicit in the formulation of a curriculum are not only suppositions about educational objectives, but also theories about the structure of knowledge, the nature of the learning process, and the methods appropriate to them. Educational objectives must relate to a pedagogical framework which is prescribed within the limitations of time, facilities,

---

[1] Cambridge, Mass.: Harvard University Press, 1961.
[2] Cambridge, Mass.: Harvard University Press, 1966.
[3] New York: Columbia University Press, 1966.

manpower, and abilities of students. The faculty must distinguish attainable goals from the unattainable and order the curriculum so that learning is maximized. Priorities must be stated and a hierarchy of educational objectives agreed upon so that academic outcomes can be realized.

Curricular decisions that must be made about knowledge objectives are, first, how much knowledge shall be required learning and, second, how knowledge is best organized for learning. To put it another way, the curriculum reformer should seek to avoid arbitrary choice of subjects to be taught, arbitrary ordering of the curriculum, incompleteness of the curriculum, and aspects of the curriculum that are uneconomical, both in time and expense.

EDUCATION AND STRUCTURE OF KNOWLEDGE

Interest in the structure and unity of knowledge, for centuries a concern primarily of philosophers, dates back at least to Plato's organization of the disciplines as seen in the imagery of the Divided Line. The current interest in the structure of knowledge is stimulated by two pedagogical concerns: (1) intellectual obsolescence, and (2) efficient teaching and learning. With regard to the problem of intellectual obsolescence, Daniel Bell has written:

. . . in the present phase of the organization of knowledge, one can no longer train people for specific intellectual tasks or provide a purely vocational training. In effect, obsolescence of specializations indicates that one cannot any longer educate a person for a job. One has to provide the means for intellectual mobility, for continuing education, for mid-career refreshment; and this can be done only by a grounding in the *modes of conceptual inquiry*.[4]

The use of the structure of knowledge as a device for organizing materials for more efficient learning was stimulated greatly by projects to improve the teaching of science and mathematics in elementary and high school. It has brought about the revolution of new math, new biology, new chemistry, and, recently, new English. Great scholars have been brought together into study groups to analyze various disciplines for the purpose of training youngsters and bridging the gaps between elementary, secondary, and higher education. The structures of various disciplines have been analyzed for the purpose of systematizing patterns of knowledge for optimal learning. The implications of this work for higher education are enormous, not only because students will come to the colleges better prepared, but also because the logical progression of education from elementary to secondary to higher

[4] Bell, *The Reforming of General Education*, p. 158.

education may well be broken unless the colleges reform their own methods.

Basically, the approach taken by these study groups is to view a "subject" as fundamentally a mode of inquiry about something. Bruner says:

. . . a theory of instruction seeks to take account of the fact that a curriculum reflects not only the nature of knowledge itself but also the nature of the knower and of the knowledge-getting process. . . . We teach a subject not to produce little living libraries on that subject, but rather to get a student to think mathematically for himself, to consider matters as an historian does, to take part in the process of knowledge-getting. Knowing is a process, not a product.[5]

If Bruner's thesis is an acceptable one, it means that the educational objectives should be matched with the structure of knowledge. In doing so, those in each field should be able to describe its mode of inquiry, skills, and rules for truth; identify the domain of the discipline and its unique contribution to knowledge; determine the key concepts of the discipline; and explain the instructive character of the discipline.

If the pursuit of truth is the goal of higher education, the emphasis is on the process of arriving at truth. As Joseph Schwab has said:

. . . truth is a complicated matter. The conceptual structure of a discipline determines what we shall seek the truth about and in what terms that truth shall be couched. The syntactical structure of a discipline is concerned with the operations that distinguish the true, the verified, and the warranted in that discipline from the unverified and unwarranted. Both of these—the conceptual and the syntactical—are different in different disciplines. The significance for education of these diverse structures lies precisely in the extent to which we want to teach what is true and have it understood.[6]

Furthermore, the knowledge structure approach, according to Bruner, promotes what the psychologists refer to as transfer:

In essence it [the transfer of principles and attitudes] consists of learning initially not a skill but a general idea, which can then be used as a basis for recognizing subsequent problems as special cases of the idea originally mastered. This type of transfer is at the heart of the educational process— the continual broadening and deepening of knowledge in terms of basic and general ideas.[7]

Thus the advantages of utilizing the structure of knowledge in curriculum planning are (1) analytical simplification, (2) promotion of mental transfer and coordination of patterns of knowledge, and (3)

---

[5] Bruner, *Toward a Theory of Instruction*, p. 72.
[6] Schwab, "The Concept of the Structure of a Discipline," *Educational Record*, July 1962, p. 205.
[7] Bruner, *The Process of Education*, p. 17.

dynamic learning that is capable of adjusting to new ideas in the disciplines. The emphasis of recent writings on the relationship of the structure of knowledge to education is on the *logical* order inherent in knowledge itself as distinguished from the classical curriculum pattern which was based on simple categorization rather than ordering and from the period of progressivism in American education when the emphasis was on the *practical* ordering of knowledge for the purpose of solving personal and social problems. The classical pattern, as espoused by the *Yale Report* of 1828, maintained that "The two great points to be gained in intellectual culture are the discipline and the furniture of the mind; expanding its powers, and storing it with knowledge." Its method—or philosophy—of learning, under the name of "mental discipline," was Aristotelian and had the premise that the "soul" as a self-active principle revealed itself in certain "faculties" and that a student could develop authentic mental power by being made to exercise these various "faculties." It was assumed that such power could be freely transferred from one field of study to another and from the general "culture" of college days to the future vocations of life. Thus the classical literature of Greece and Rome, pure mathematics, and other subjects of this nature which could not readily be mastered outside college comprised the curriculum;[8] it was an adaptation of the classical categorization of the trivium and quadrivium.

The new emphasis is on the modes of inquiry of scholars as contrasted to curricular content of factual and descriptive materials. There are two immediate difficulties with this conceptual approach. The first is the question of whether all disciplines are sufficiently structured for such logical ordering and analysis. If Schwab's syntactical structure refers to the underlying *form* or *arrangement* of elements, it suits most clearly those disciplines where a clear methodology or related methodologies have been posited, such as mathematics or physics. But does it suit all of the arts and social sciences? David B. Truman's presidential address to the American Political Science Association, "Disillusionment and Regeneration: The Quest for a Discipline"[9] is suggestive of the kind of thinking necessary. Does the notion of the paradigm—a common set of beliefs, constituting a kind of open-end model that more or less explicitly defines the legitimate problems and methods of a research field—apply to each and every discipline?

The second problem is to find a structure of knowledge which is sufficiently acceptable to scholars of different disciplines so that a curriculum can be organized in a more coherent, sequential manner. The

[8] Willis Rudy, *The Evolving Liberal Arts Curriculum: A Historical Review of Basic Themes* (New York: Bureau of Publications, Teachers College, Columbia University, 1960), p. 2.

[9] *American Political Science Review*, December 1965, p. 865.

physics and mathematics study groups, it should be remembered, had the definite objective of analyzing a particular subject matter for the purposes of teaching it more efficiently and effectively. As such the emphasis was not on the importance of one subject or one mode of inquiry against another, but on method in the particular discipline. In establishing the insight that the conceptual approach to the discipline is the most effective, they have made a major contribution, but this approach also implies that the content and sequence of the entire curriculum must be logically ordered within the framework of a unity of knowledge.

The present curriculum reflects the pluralistic state of the world of knowledge today, and one of the major difficulties in designing a curriculum is to pull together these many different knowledges, each with its own language and pursuing its own ends and goals. As reflected in human behavior, this means that faculty members are content if a new curriculum does not hurt their departments, and if they are left undisturbed, they may not have much respect for the disciplines of their colleagues, but be willing to tolerate them.

While pluralism is not to be deplored—for it has been highly productive in generating knowledge for mankind—it is, nevertheless, a serious problem for those who are concerned with ordering the precious four years for the maximum intellectual growth of students. The problem can be stated simply enough: How can the curriculum be structured so that the autonomy of the disciplines does not result in anarchy in the program as a whole? The answer—oversimplified—lies in finding similar patterns of inquiry among related disciplines.

King and Brownell, in seeking a unity of knowledge, conclude that:

With respect to the curriculum and the schools, only a pluralism of knowledge seems plausible. We have no consensus on the unity of knowledge amidst the scholars. . . . We would submit that the unity of knowledge is to be found in the end and direction of movement: the pursuit of truth and meaning. It is to be found in the adherence to discovery, penetrating inquiry, critical scrutiny. . . . It is to be found in a human focus for knowledge—the unity of persons as ends not means.[10]

For Daniel Bell, the pattern of knowledge is fundamentally triadic: knowledge is *sequential* in the sciences and mathematics, is one of *linkages* between fields in the social sciences, and is *concentric* in the humanities.[11] Any such formulation has important consequences for the theory and practice of pedagogy. This is the crucial point for the curriculum reformer. How one postulates the structure of knowledge could well determine certain pedagogical results on the relationship of high

---

[10] Arthur R. King and John A. Brownell, *The Curriculum and the Disciplines of Knowledge* (New York: John Wiley & Sons, Inc., 1966), pp. 61–62.
[11] Bell, *The Reforming of General Education*, p. 174.

school to college, the sequence of courses in college, and the relationship of undergraduate curriculum to graduate work.

There is not, as yet, and perhaps there never will be, a "right" classification of knowledge for pedagogical purposes because each may be right in its own way. Given the desire to organize knowledge in such a manner to make learning efficient and dynamic, the educator is nevertheless faced with the selection of one of the many approaches on which to build a curriculum. The important issue is which of the contrasting modes for classifying knowledge raises the proper educational problems and issues for the advancement of educational objectives.

THE STRUCTURE OF KNOWLEDGE AND LEARNING

It is difficult enough to have scholars of different fields delve into the problems of the structure of their disciplines and to interrelate them; but to have them delve into the sophisticated problems of the psychology of learning is perhaps asking too much. Psychology as a field is not one that is trusted by scholars (then again, which one is, except one's own), and the arguments, if they are to be successful, must be either logically coherent or demonstrable by empirical data. Nevertheless, some elementary notions about the relations between the structure of knowledge and the structure of learning are necessary before one moves on to the important subject of content of the curriculum.

The question is how instruction should be organized to take into account both the logical order of disciplined knowledge and the psychological order of development of the student's cognitive powers. There is a distinction between the formal organization of subject-matter content and the internalized representation of this knowledge in the memory structures of a particular individual. David Ausubel, for instance, compares the two structures of knowledge with respect to four of their principal attributes: (a) meaning, (b) process of organization, (c) arrangement of component elements, and (d) cognitive maturity of content.[12] He says that

. . . psychological meaning is always an idiosyncratic phenomenon.

. . . meaning depends not only on the learner's possession of the requisite intellectual capacities and ideational backgrounds, but also on his *particular* ideational content. When an individual learns logically meaningful propositions, therefore, he does not learn their logical meaning but the meaning they have for him.[13]

Meaning, therefore, depends also on the student's previous knowledge of specifics, facts, terminology, and conventions. Although an

[12] Ausubel, "Some Psychological Aspects of the Structure of Knowledge," *Education and the Structure of Knowledge*, ed. Stanley Elam (Chicago: Rand McNally & Co., 1964), p. 223.
[13] *Ibid.*

individual's psychological structure of knowledge of a discipline can correspond to the logical structure in that discipline, the degree of parallelism depends on the development of mature cognitive capacities and does not occur at the early stages of subject-matter sophistication.[14]

When does a student acquire the intellectual abilities and skills of application, analysis, synthesis, evaluation, and judgment? The important point which Ausubel makes is that:

Relative level of abstraction of subject matter content becomes an important pedagogic consideration in determining the order in which pupils should be introduced to the different scientific disciplines.[15]

Thus, logically, the phenomenologically more fundamental and simple laws of physics and chemistry should be studied before the more complex and variable data of biology; psychologically, however,

. . . the logically simple laws of physics and chemistry are more abstract and difficult than the logically complex laws of biology which are both more descriptive in nature and closer to everyday, concrete experience.[16]

An important pedagogical implication of the structure of knowledge is that the elemental facts, terminology, and conventions of a discipline must be taught at the same time that one is teaching the processes of the discipline.

Another implication is that

. . . the categorizing of knowledge makes possible the transfer of learning from one knowing situation to another of the same kind. From the classification of knowledge and characteristic ways of knowing the educator should be able greatly to economize the learning effort by making use of transfer from element to element within each way of knowing. He may thus concentrate on teaching the ways of knowing rather than multiplying particular elements in knowledge without reference to their membership in classes of similar elements.[17]

Thus efficient learning and teaching is facilitated if common features and structural similarities can be found so that duplication of learning can be eliminated and more emphasis placed on the inside-into relationships between one discipline and another. Phenix suggests, for instance, in his classification of knowledge into nine generic classes, that there are kinds of knowledge that are interchangeable for general curricular purposes and kinds that are not.[18]

While the logical ordering of knowledge offers a useful pedagogical framework upon which to structure a curriculum, it does not encom-

[14] *Ibid.*, p. 226.
[15] *Ibid.*, p. 228.
[16] *Ibid.*, p. 228.
[17] Philip H. Phenix, "The Architectonics of Knowledge," *Education and the Structure of Knowledge*, ed. Stanley Elam (Chicago: Rand McNally & Co., 1964), p. 45.
[18] *Ibid.*, p. 61.

pass all of the considerations. In deciding upon a curriculum, one is in fact stating a philosophy of education. We must, therefore, take into account the problems of stating the objectives of the educational program, for this is where curriculum planning actually begins.

STATING THE OBJECTIVES

If the purpose of stating the objectives were merely to publish something attractive and inspiring to include in the college catalogue, the task would not be too difficult. But to state educational objectives on which a curriculum can be based is entirely another matter.

The statement of objectives for the liberal arts college in the nineteenth century, when the purpose of the college was primarily to prepare ministers, lawyers, and doctors, was perhaps simpler than it is today. Yet, as Russell Thomas points out, even then the educational reformers of the nineteenth century had at least four important theories that differed in emphases and principles concerning the function of the college and its place in the educational system.[19] Francis Wayland, president of Brown University, published in 1842 *Thoughts on the Present Collegiate System in the United States*,[20] in which he advocated the concept of public service as being one of the major goals to which a college must devote itself. At the same time he proposed that there be higher admissions requirements, a reduction in the number of subjects studied, and more intensive work in those that remained, or an increase in the length of the college program to five or six years if a reduction in the number of subjects required should not prove feasible.[21]

Taking his model from the *Gymnasium*, Henry P. Tappan, president of the University of Michigan, conceived of the undergraduate college within the context of the entire university system and saw its aim:

. . . to make apparent the difference between a mere professional and technical education, and that large and generous culture which brings out the whole man, and which commits him to active life with the capacity of estimating from the highest points of view all the knowledges and agencies which enter into the wellbeing and progress of society. That is not really the most practical education which leads men soonest and most directly to practice, but that which fits them best for practice.[22]

President Charles William Eliot, in his inaugural address at Harvard in 1869, defended the elective system:

In education, the individual traits of different minds have not been suffi-

---

[19] Thomas, *The Search for a Common Learning: General Education 1800–1960* (New York: McGraw-Hill Book Co., 1962), chap. 2.
[20] Boston: Gould, Kendall & Lincoln, 1842.
[21] Thomas, *The Search for a Common Learning*, p. 21.
[22] Tappan, *University Education* (New York: G. P. Putnam's Sons, 1851).

ciently attended to. Through all the period of boyhood the school studies should be representative; all the main fields of knowledge should be entered upon. But the young man of nineteen or twenty ought to know what he likes best and is most fit for. If his previous training has been sufficiently wide, he will know by that time whether he is most apt at language or philosophy or natural science or mathematics.[23]

Paul Ansell Chadbourne, president of the University of Wisconsin, conceived of a college as an autonomous unit. As such its task is the broad cultural education of its students, and liberal education is thus an end in itself. While he was in favor of excellent technical and professional education, he sharply distinguished their roles.[24]

In reviewing just four theories of liberal education of the nineteenth century, it is clear that elements of the general objectives have not changed substantially. It is evident that these four educators, with magnificent foresight, anticipated the development of American education, and the questions they dealt with are the same as the problems today: To what extent should colleges prepare their students for public service and the practical problems of life; how much freedom should there be in the curriculum; is liberal arts education an end in itself? The similarity of current practices and objectives to earlier writings should not discourage the curriculum reformer. It does indicate, however, that statements of general philosophy and objectives are not sufficiently accurate tools for the work of curriculum reform. For while the general objectives have deviated only in theme and variation, the curriculum itself has been modified over the years in response to changing needs in the society as well as developments in the fields of knowledge. What is called for is a second step in the statement of objectives, one that can be more specific and, it is to be hoped, measurable.

One of the difficult problems for a faculty curriculum committee, even before it attempts to formulate objectives, is to find a vocabulary that promotes common understanding and precise meanings of educational objectives. Benjamin S. Bloom has attempted to classify educational goals in A Taxonomy of Educational Objectives.[25] By educational objectives Bloom means "explicit formulations of the ways in which students are expected to be changed by the educative process. That is, the ways in which they will change in their thinking, their feelings and their actions." Thus in Bloom's Taxonomy, the cognitive domain is broken down into the following categories: knowledge, knowledge of specifics, knowledge of terminology, knowledge of spe-

[23] Eliot, "Inaugural Address as President of Harvard College," Educational Reform: Essays and Addresses (New York: Century Co., 1898), p. 12.

[24] Thomas, The Search for a Common Learning, p. 33.

[25] Bloom and D. R. Krathwohl, A Taxonomy of Educational Objectives: The Classification of Educational Goals, Handbook I: Cognitive Domain (New York: Longmans, Green & Co., 1956).

cific facts, knowledge of ways and means of dealing with specifics, knowledge of convention, knowledge of trends and sequences, knowledge of classifications and categories, knowledge of criteria, knowledge of methodology, knowledge of the universals and abstractions in a field, knowledge of principles and generalizations, and knowledge of theories and structures. Intellectual abilities and skills are divided into: comprehension; translation; interpretation; extrapolation; application; analysis; analysis of elements; analyses of relationships; analysis of organizational principles; synthesis; production of a unique communication; production of a plan or proposed set of operations; derivation of a set of abstract relations; evaluation; judgments deriving from internal evidence; and judgments deriving from external criteria.

Ralph W. Tyler proposes that the considerations which enter into the selection of educational objectives include: (1) data on students to be taught; (2) an assessment of the conditions and problems of contemporary life; and (3) a deliberation of specialists in each subject-matter field to suggest what contributions their field can make.[26]

Tyler suggests that these three steps would result in more objectives than any institution can encompass. There is no doubt that the first is internal for each college, but what about the second and third? Should these assessments and deliberations be the responsibility of members of the faculty or of experts from off the campus? There is great value in having these assessments arrived at by the faculty itself. In formulating the educational objectives, the faculty is making a conscious choice of what it believes its students can and should learn and of what it believes to be personal and societal needs. In making a final selection and priority of the objectives, the faculty makes use of the structure of learning and the structure of knowledge. It arranges the curriculum for the maximum intellectual growth of the students, and it selects those disciplines which would make the greatest contribution to the growth of the student. In short, the faculty is forced to adopt the types and order of experiences required of students in order to produce behavioral changes. In the process of arriving at these conclusions, it becomes evident that no single course or discipline holds all the answers to educational objectives. Furthermore, educational objectives which do not fit neatly into the structure of knowledge—social maturity, physical and mental well-being, values, and the like—must nevertheless be considerations in the curriculum plan. But the knowledge structure approach, even if it does not encompass the entire panorama of educational objectives, does at least force the curriculum planner to raise the right questions.

[26] Tyler, *Achievement Testing and Curriculum Construction* (Chicago: University of Chicago Press, n.d.).

IMPLICATIONS OF KNOWLEDGE STRUCTURE
FOR CURRICULUM PLANNING

The most important implication of the logical ordering of knowledge is that the traditional classifications of disciplines need to be re-examined and re-formulated into broad subject-matter areas. Most colleges, for instance, have as their basic device for providing the student with a liberal education some scheme of distribution requirements that requires the student to take a number of courses in the areas of the sciences, the social sciences, and the humanities. The requirements are more often than not a matter of rule of thumb rather than of rational analysis. Insight into the structure of knowledge and the disciplines suggests that the traditional classifications of the subject areas are faulty. Phenix suggests in his conception of nine generic classes of knowledge that there are "kinds of knowledge that are interchangeable for general curricular purposes and kinds that are not." [27] He submits, for example, that

. . . a student may study either physics or anthropology in order to gain some sense of the empirical mode of understanding. He could not similarly interchange physics and mathematics or physics and history. Nor are existential psychology and experimental psychology interchangeable, since one is synnoetic and the other empirical. By studying all of the generic classes, the student is assured a complete and balanced education.[28]

This implies, in addition, a reconsideration of the perennial issue of depth and breadth in the liberal arts curriculum. Breadth is not the attempt to encapsulate all of human thought by means of survey courses touching on all the concerns of humanity; it is an awareness of the methods of inquiring into such problems.

The Berkeley Report of the Select Committee on Education said:

Clearly it is nonsensical to aim at introducing undergraduates to all major areas of knowledge. The effect of the attempt could be only the kind of superficiality and dilettantism that we condemn in the old-fashioned introductory survey course. The rationale behind the present Berkeley curriculum is to introduce students to different types of knowledge and different methods of acquiring knowledge.[29]

The Berkeley Report recommended that:

The College of Letters and Science should reconsider the breadth requirements in terms of "inner" and "outer" breadth related to the programs of the various majors or groups of majors rather than in terms of the three traditional areas of knowledge.[30]

---

[27] Phenix, "The Architectonics of Knowledge," p. 61.

[28] *Ibid.*, p. 61. Phenix defines "synnoetic" as "meanings in which a person has direct insight into other beings (or oneself) as concrete wholes existing in relation," in *Realms of Meaning* (New York: McGraw-Hill Book Co., 1964), p. 193.

[29] *Education at Berkeley: Report of the Select Committee on Education* (Berkeley: Academic Senate, University of California, March 1966), p. 153.

[30] *Ibid.*, p. 155.

In calling for a new approach to the problem of breadth to prevent narrow specialization, the committee defined "outer breadth" as

disciplines that are outside the major of the student but related to it in subject matter, methods and types of aptitude needed . . . inner breadth would include those subjects that, while outside the major, offer related or background material and methods for it, and provide a broadening and deepening effect on the major itself.[31]

As "inner" and "outer" breadth become defined in operational rules for inclusion or exclusion of subjects, a position on what the structure of knowledge is, at least for Berkeley, will become evident.

The structure of knowledge approach means that elementary or introductory courses would have to be scrutinized to see if they fit logically within the knowledge structure or structure of learning so that they do not become terminal, starting from nowhere and ending nowhere. Introductory courses must be a basis for the development of further inquiry and knowledge. Advanced courses are not judged to be advanced simply because they are intrinsically more difficult, but because they fall into the proper framework for a more sophisticated or mature conceptual analysis of the discipline and a more abstract mode of inquiry.

The structure of knowledge as a pedagogical framework also has implications for interdisciplinary studies. It is from the structural point of view that courses can truly be interdisciplinary and not simply surveys. This is not to say that general education core courses which give a background of the history of civilization and the problems of man are no longer necessary, but it does raise questions about the object of these courses and the logical sequence in which they should be taught. The types of general education courses, whether they be content-oriented, intellectually oriented or student-oriented, might also be re-examined from the view of the structure of knowledge.

If one believes that there are generic classes of knowledge which provide patterns of inquiry, then the curriculum cannot be a cafeteria of random subject matter. The curriculum arranges for the association of the student with materials and teachers, and this with a degree of continuity, sequence, and integration. Pedagogical devices such as independent study and free election of courses which enhance individual development do not necessarily conflict with the logical ordering of knowledge and of courses. Formulating the pedagogical framework for higher education is not an either-or proposition but a question of more or less. There is and must be sufficient freedom within an interpretation of the knowledge structure to allow for the use of pedagogical

[31] *Ibid.*, p. 154.

devices that will enhance individual development and other educational objectives.

CONCLUSIONS

It could be argued that not until each of the disciplines has developed a notion of the paradigm can the structure of knowledge be used as the basis for formulating the pedagogical framework of curriculum reform. But to argue so would ignore the obligation of the American college to seek its proper function between the high school and the graduate school; it also overlooks the necessity of teaching concepts rather than facts so that college graduates do not become hopelessly out of date intellectually after graduation.

To the difficult question of how much knowledge shall be required learning, a knowledge structure can suggest parameters for generic patterns of inquiry that offer insights into overlap of course requirements, problems of the ordering of the curriculum, and incompleteness of the curriculum. Questions about how best to organize knowledge for learning are similarly illuminated by the logical ordering of the disciplines.

There does not exist yet—perhaps there never will—an ordering of disciplines that unifies all human knowledge. Even if such an order did exist, it would not include all of the many societal and individual concerns which are considered to be legitimate and essential elements of educational objectives of the liberal arts college.

Approaching curricular reform and formulating the pedagogical framework according to a structure of knowledges stresses the modes of inquiry. The structure of knowledge serves as a heuristic blueprint that puts the issues of curriculum reform on neutral ground and engages the participants in a common enterprise. Whatever the discipline, it is, after all, an inquiry into truth.

Epilogue

COLLEGE TEACHING

THEN AND NOW

Dexter Perkins

N OBODY ASKED ME what I had written when I took my first job in 1914, and nobody badgered me to write a book after I got the job. The implication of that lack of concern about scholarly production is, I think, one of the basic differences between college teaching then and now.

Looking back on more than fifty years of classroom teaching, I can give only an impressionistic and personal view of the changes in the teaching profession. Perhaps the differences come out most clearly as one compares my career with that of the young teacher today. My first book was published thirteen years after I had started my teaching career. Frankly, I had not even taken graduate courses in several of the first history subjects I taught. I taught undergraduates throughout my career, and remained at one institution—the University of Rochester—for forty years.

I never thought of writing as a means of advancement. When I wrote, I did so because I wanted to and not because my position would be improved by publication. But let me not depreciate writing; after all, I must admit I have written seventeen books and am at work on three more. What is disturbing to me is that the published word is important today not so much because it is written as because it gives the author and his institution greater visibility. Whether this emphasis results from changes in our technology and our culture, or from a demand for teachers that has generated an unhealthy competition for what is called "production" (as compared with being "efficient" in the classroom), today the written word is given an exaggerated importance over the spoken word. I am old-fashioned enough to believe that some values to be communicated in the classroom are not easily communicated by the written word. One is a zeal for knowledge, another is perspective, and still another is an appreciation of other outlooks and points of view. When you have written a book, no matter how good it is, the ideas in it are frozen. When you talk, you continue to think. A class

405

full of students is a stimulus to thought as well as a recipient of learning, a constant challenge to do better. We learn from example in this world, and a teacher is an example of a man thinking.

I have asked several people lately whether they were influenced by books or by men. The answer has invariably been "by men." If those engaged in college teaching would recognize that their responsibility is not alone to advance knowledge, but to stimulate and inspire, they could more fully discharge their obligations to society.

One of the rationales for the emphasis on publishing is that a book can be evaluated whereas classroom teaching cannot. There is some truth to that, but it is largely a myth that the evaluation of books is any less subjective than the evaluation of classroom teaching. The judgment of a book depends in part on the disposition of the reviewer. It depends on one specialist's view of another. It rarely addresses itself to the large significance of the work. Authors are too often judged by quantity, rather than by quality. As to the judgment of teaching, there are plenty of ways to judge a young teacher. One of these is by visiting his classes. If done with consideration, no difficulty need result. Registrations have something to do with the matter; so, too, does the judgment of the more discerning and intelligent undergraduates—or graduate students.

It is strange that even now, what with all the research and empirical data collected on human behavior, the basic elements of instruction are hardly ever spoken of. When I was a young man, no attempt was made to guide me in the techniques of teaching, no one ever heard me lecture, no one knew my potential along these lines before I was hired. With regard to training doctoral students to teach, I would say that the situation has not changed at all. We didn't pay much attention to it then, and unfortunately we don't pay any attention to it now. Perhaps we cannot make every student a great teacher, but we can, at least, give the prospective teacher some techniques. We can make him feel that he has an opportunity to make a significant impact on young human beings. We can teach him to speak clearly, to talk (not read), to organize his material, and to establish rapport with his class. The essence of teaching is zeal for communication and concern for young people.

The academic profession has changed. Its prestige has grown enormously in my lifetime. When I was young, we were considered to be impractical academicians. At the beginning of my career, the people who went into academic life were primarily interested in classroom teaching, and there was much less emphasis on research. With societal and economic changes, the status of the profession has gained tremendously, and with this gain has come a recognition of the value of the profession in terms of financial rewards. In that sense, the profession has become more worldly than it was when I was a young man. The opportunities for a career in the profession are much greater. I don't mean that fifty years ago we went into teaching with a spirit of self-sacrifice, but today a more commercial spirit is evident in the profession, and it seems to me that one example of it is the way in which we diminish teaching loads. We really are a powerful union.

The administrative authorities have less and less to say about faculty appointments. The forms are still observed, but, practically speaking, a department often becomes an oligarchy. I believe college administrators should insist on an external view of a candidate for appointment, and not blindly accept departmental recommendations. I believe they should make certain they are getting effective teaching, and demand both teaching and scholarly gifts of the candidates for promotion.

I believe that the greatest challenge confronting scholars today is the challenge of the classroom. To meet it, we shall have to give to teaching a higher place in our scale of values than we do now. We shall have to select our students more definitely with this end in view; we shall have to give them an opportunity to exercise their capacities for teaching; we shall have to reward them adequately for their performance. And—it goes without saying—we shall ourselves have to be the best teachers that we know how to be, the most humane, the most sympathetic, the most dedicated.

AMERICAN COUNCIL ON EDUCATION

LOGAN WILSON, *President*

The American Council on Education, founded in 1918, is a *council* of educational organizations and institutions. Its purpose is to advance education and educational methods through comprehensive voluntary and cooperative action on the part of American educational associations, organizations, and institutions.